PONCEBADON
LEDIGOS
HALFWAY
SAHAGUN
LEON
ASTORGA
PONFERRADA
O CEBREIRO
SARRIA
100 KM
SANTIAGO DE COMPOSTE
DENIS
BUEN CAMINO
caresse
K152.5
OSSANTOS
GUT WEG
BUEN CAMINO
BON CHEMIN
GOOD ROAD
XACOBEO
GALICIA
9KM
BARAIMO
CRUZ DE
FERO
VETERANO
WW

The Way of STARS and STONES

The Way of
STARS
and STONES
Thoughts on a Pilgrimage
WILNA WILKINSON

JACANA

First published by Jacana Media (Pty) Ltd in 2009

10 Orange Street
Sunnyside
Auckland Park 2092
South Africa
(+27 11) 628-3200
www.jacana.co.za

© Wilna Wilkinson, 2009
twoxscotch@gmail.com

All rights reserved.

ISBN 978-1-77009-749-0

Cover design by banana republic
Text design and layout by Jacana Media
Photographs by Wilna Wilkinson
Set in Bembo
Printed by CTP Book Printers
Job No. 001030

See a complete list of Jacana titles at www.jacana.co.za

For Terrie

There is no insurmountable solitude. All paths lead to the same point: to the communication of who we are. And we must travel across rugged and lonely terrain, through isolation and silence, to reach the magic zone, the enchanted place where we can dance our awkward dance and sing our sorrowful song.
– Pablo Neruda, Nobel Literature Prize acceptance speech, 13 December 1971

All proceeds of this edition will be
donated to cancer research.

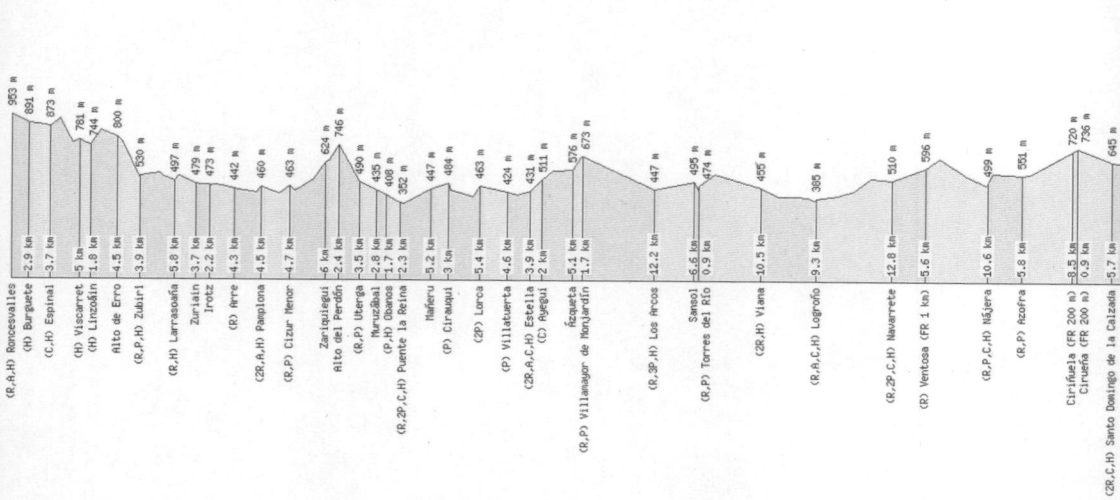

Location	Elevation	Distance
(R,A,H) Roncesvalles	953 m	
(H) Burguete	891 m	-2.9 km
(C,H) Espinal	873 m	-3.7 km
(H) Viscarret	781 m	-5 km
(H) Lincoáin	744 m	-1.8 km
Alto de Erro	800 m	-4.5 km
(R,P,H) Zubiri	530 m	-3.9 km
(R,H) Larrasoaña	497 m	-5.8 km
Zuriain	479 m	-3.7 km
Irotz	473 m	-2.2 km
(R) Arre	442 m	-4.3 km
(C2R,A,H) Pamplona	460 m	-4.5 km
(R,P) Cizur Menor	463 m	-4.7 km
Zariquiegui	624 m	-6 km
Alto del Perdón	746 m	-2.4 km
(R,P) Uterga	490 m	-3.5 km
Muruzábal	435 m	-2.8 km
(P,H) Obanos	408 m	-1.7 km
(R,2P,C,H) Puente la Reina	352 m	-2.3 km
Mañeru	447 m	-5.2 km
(P) Cirauqui	494 m	-3 km
(2P) Lorca	463 m	-5.4 km
(P) Villatuerta	424 m	-4.6 km
(C2R,A,C,H) Estella	431 m	-3.9 km
(C) Ayegui	511 m	-2 km
Azqueta	576 m	-5.1 km
(R,P) Villamayor de Monjardín	673 m	-1.7 km
(R,3P,H) Los Arcos	447 m	-12.2 km
Sansol	495 m	-6.6 km
(R,P) Torres del Río	474 m	-0.9 km
(2R,H) Viana	455 m	-10.5 km
(R,A,C,H) Logroño	385 m	-9.3 km
(R,2P,C,H) Navarrete	510 m	-12.8 km
(R) Ventosa (FR 1 km)	596 m	-5.6 km
(R,P,C,H) Nájera	499 m	-10.6 km
(R,P) Azofra	551 m	-5.8 km
Cirueña (FR 200 m)	720 m	-8.5 km
Ciruela (FR 200 m)	736 m	-0.9 km
(2R,C,H) Santo Domingo de la Calzada	645 m	-5.7 km

Contents

Prologue: Reaching the destination is not always the aim.................. xi

1 Cellulite is not enough reason to walk 800 kilometres 1
2 No journey can start unless you move away from where you are... 16
3 Only take photographs of the mountains you have already crossed 36
4 On solitude, silence, companions and friends......................... 55
5 The signs you see along your way don't necessarily point in the
   direction you want to take 62
6 Make friends with your shadow, because you can never leave
   home without it..79
7 About wolves, witches and hurricanes; in other words, on being
   prepared for the unexpected..96
8 The Devil must be grabbed by his tail: that is what tales are
   there for... 120
9 Courage is not the absence of fear – courage is the ability to
   enter unknown territory despite it 145
10 A lifetime searching for perfection is not a wasted life 166

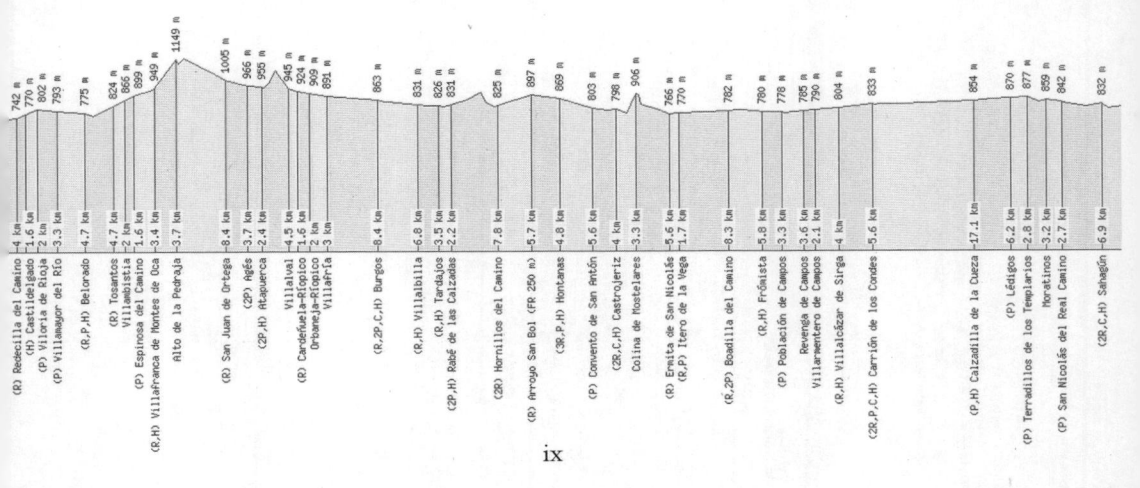

11 When life puts stones in your way, pick them up and build
    a bridge 178

12 Somewhere somebody knows your name......................... 187

13 What goes around, comes around… 204

14 Not every person you meet is a fellow-traveller, and not all
    fellow-travellers are fellow-pilgrims 227

15 Recognise your angels, for sometimes they may come past you
    but once (and remember, not all angels have wings)......... 236

16 The Camino changes people and the people change the Camino 245

17 Dream, believe, and dare to do 260

    Epilogue 276

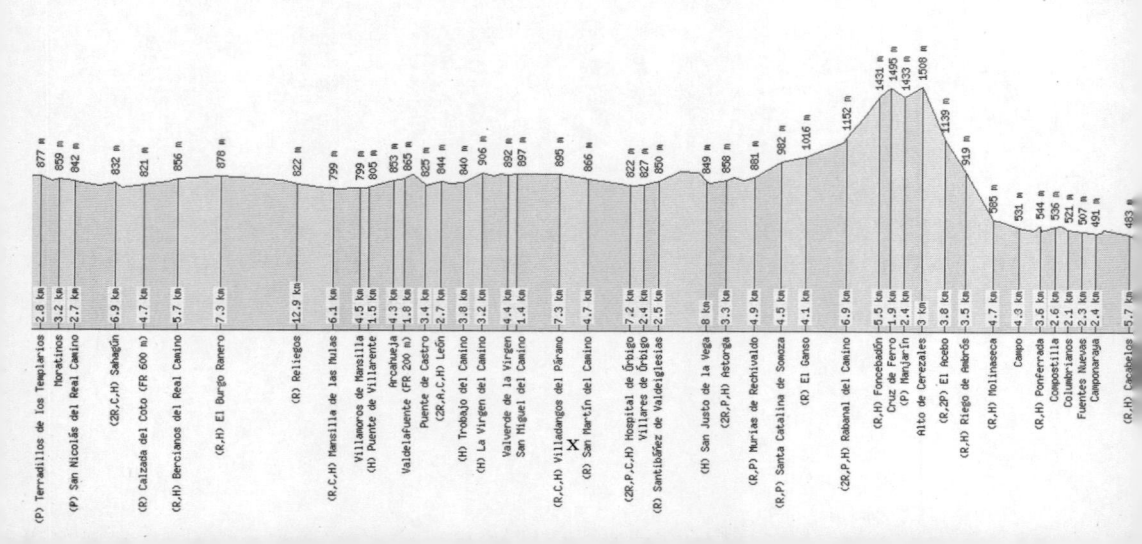

Prologue
Reaching the destination is not always the aim

A l'aurore, armés d'une ardente patience, nous entrerons aux splendides Villes.
(In the dawn, armed with a burning patience, we shall enter the splendid Cities.)

– Arthur Rimbaud

I stand, completely alone, a solitary figure in the giant square in front of the cathedral and watch with bated breath as the first golden rays of the sun tentatively touch one spire, then the next, and finally bathe the entire ornate skyline of the cathedral in a gilded glow. Refractions of light burst out, shooting off from the highest points like Renaissance halo crowns around the heads of the sanctified. It is magnificent – a glorious moment – the dawn of the fortieth day of my pilgrimage and I have reached my destination, the cathedral of Santiago de Compostela. For that moment the now-excruciating pain in my feet is forgotten. I am oblivious to the weight of the pack on my back and the tendrils of icy wind off the snow-capped mountains in the north dancing around my ears. I savour every second, drinking in the moment and trying to etch every tiny detail of this powerful feeling into my brain, my memory, my being. It is not a religious moment for me, nor a particularly spiritual one. I know this because I did experience some such moments during the long walk over the last 40 days. This moment is rather about a sense of achievement, a sense of having done something that is bigger than me. It is a sense of having overcome huge obstacles, difficult challenges, having found resources within myself that I never knew were there. It has truly been a life-changing experience.

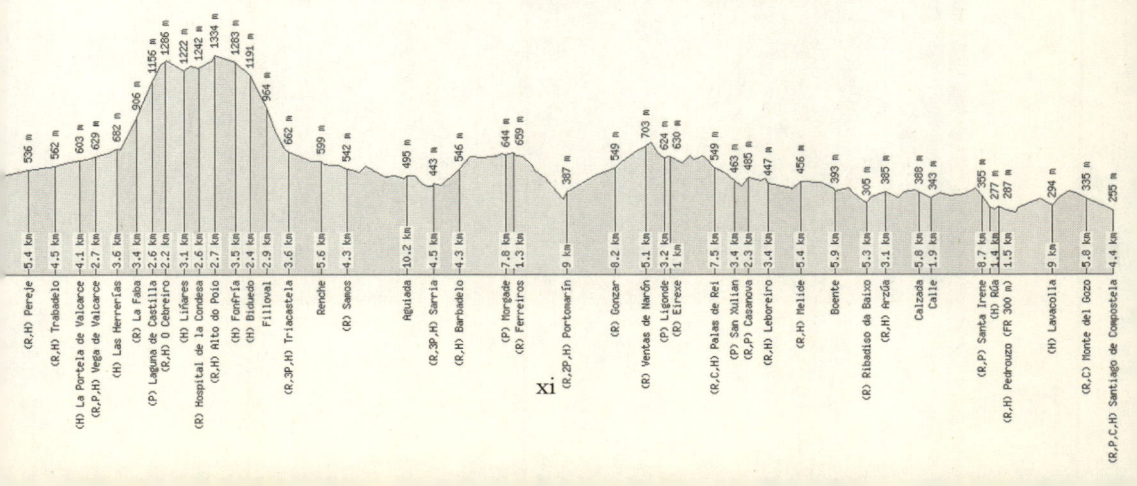

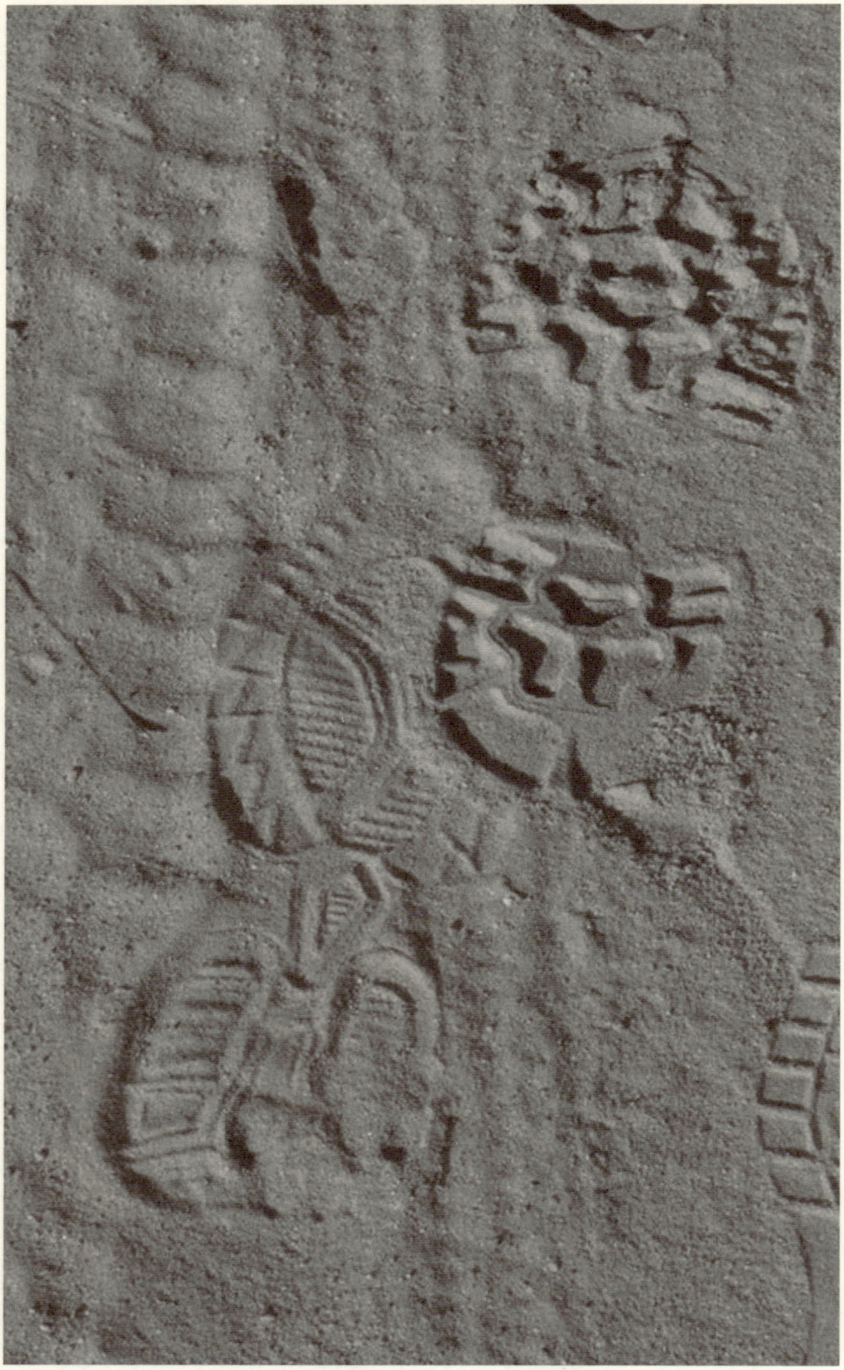

1
Cellulite is not enough reason to walk 800 kilometres

There are people who put their dreams in a little box and say, 'Yes, I've got dreams, of course I've got dreams'. Then they put the box away and bring it out once in a while to look in it, and yep, they're still there.
– Erma Bombeck

Can there be anything more exhilarating than stepping out of your front door, hearing that click of the lock behind you, and embarking on a journey into the unknown? What I experience every time I set off into what is new territory for me is a feeling of rebirth. To travel is to be reborn. Stepping out of your front door and starting a new journey is like being a child emerging from the womb.

The morning of the big day had finally arrived. Although a pilgrimage traditionally starts from your own home, your own front door, I couldn't do this because of time constraints and my friends and fellow-expats John and Jill had insisted on taking me to the local train station. At least I was going to begin from the 'official' starting point of the Camino Francés, St-Jean-Pied-de-Port.

All too soon John and Jill were there. They brought with them two bright-red, super-light, collapsible aluminium walking sticks. I'd had this silly notion that a pilgrim's stick would come to me, but though I was waiting with an open mind and open arms, my stick had not yet found me. I also knew that if ever I *was* going to need a stick, it would be when crossing the Pyrenees right at the start of the journey. Though the twin aluminium sticks did not really fit the image of the pilgrim walking with his crooked wooden staff, they came with so much love that, without hesitation, I named them John and Jill and tucked them into their own little catches on my new backpack. They looked like they felt at home immediately.

The next couple of hours passed in a whirl – getting on the train in Bergerac, travelling through the beautiful Dordogne and Gironde vineyards, and arriving at the station in Bordeaux. Seeing the train in which I was going to travel to St-Jean-Pied-de-Port took my breath away. It was not the usual clean and tidy blue train of the French SNCF, nor one you would have imagined catching on the first leg of a spiritual pilgrimage. In fact, it was more suited to taking a group of raucous punks to a heavy metal rock festival. I could well have believed that I was hallucinating. For there on Platform 1 stood a work of art. The train was only six coaches long but every square centimetre was covered in the brightest, most colourful graffiti I had ever seen: blues and reds, yellows and greens, purples and oranges, swirls and whirls, letters and geometric shapes. It was beautiful, it was wacky and it was all mine – for there was not a single other person boarding the train. It was like something in a dream. At fourteen minutes past one on Saturday, 9 February that wondrously psychedelic train pulled out of Bordeaux and, at nineteen minutes past four, I saw the mountains looming large behind the town of St-Jean-Pied-de-Port – St John at the Foot of the Pass – as I stepped off the train, into the icy cold air.

There was a spring in my step and joy in my heart as I walked into the town. Quite by chance I found a delightful little *refugio* up against the hill of the town, run by Janine, a woman 'of a certain age', as the French say. According to a yellowed newspaper cutting on her wall, she was known in these parts as the 'mother of the Camino', no doubt because so many people started in St-Jean-Pied-de-Port, spent their first night in this particular refuge and she was their first encounter with the pilgrimage. She was what the politically correct call 'vertically challenged', and what nature had given or not given her was further challenged by some serious effects of osteoporosis and shrinkage. Her face was lived-in, the lines deep grooves that showed a map of a hard and long life's journey here at the foot of the magnificent Pyrenees, but when I walked into her house I was struck by how smartly turned out she was. She either took pride in her appearance, which was rather endearing, or had dressed for a special guest. As I was the guest that night, I took it as a compliment.

However, there was not much else about her that could be called endearing. My impression was rather that she was as tough as nails. I quickly discovered that Janine was a font of information, and she was forceful with it; she was in charge. She showed me to my room behind the kitchen, told me to put my backpack down and to join her in the living room, with the seven euros that was the tariff for the night. I did what she told me to do. When I came back and gave her the money, she pressed five euros into my hand and instructed me to walk down the hill, go to a certain shop and buy a lettuce, two eggs and a small round of Camembert cheese for my supper. At first I protested that I was not really hungry and said not to worry, but for my sins I got an ear bashing about eating to keep my strength up for the journey ahead and was ordered to do as I was told. Again I obeyed. I went all the way down the hill, found the grocery shop she wanted me to go to (having passed several others on the way), bought the items she had requested and trudged back up the hill.

'Let me see what you got there.' Prodding the cheese to test its ripeness, she gave a hint of a smile to indicate that I had chosen the cheese well, took the eggs and the lettuce from me, counted the change and returned it to her purse. 'Now go out, turn left and walk further up the hill. You will see stairs going off to the right. You take those and walk up to the castle at the top, and from the ramparts there you will have an excellent view of the Pyrenees. Hurry now and you will see the sunset. Tomorrow morning you will get up early and you will walk over the mountains. I will now prepare your dinner.'

I dared to answer back. 'No Janine, my plan is to stay in St-Jean tomorrow to look around. I've never been here, so I would like to see something of the town.'

I also planned to start writing my journal, putting down my thoughts about the big adventure I was about to embark on. I wanted to drink in the atmosphere and, most importantly, I needed to prepare myself mentally for the journey.

'Nonsense, girl! Now that you have gone down the hill to buy the cheese, and once you have seen the view from the ramparts, you have seen everything there is to see in this town. You will not waste a day in St-Jean…'

'But I only want to start walking on Monday. That is the eleventh of February and that is the day I want to start my pilgrimage!' I persisted.

Janine was fast losing any semblance of patience with me. 'That is ridiculous!'

I was starting to find her domineering attitude quite rude and stood my ground. It was one thing doing her errands for her – after all she was an 'older' lady and the cobblestone street down the hill was long and steep – but this was *my* Camino and *my* decision, and who was she to dictate to me?

'Janine, I want to start on the eleventh because that is the day Nelson Mandela was released and ended his long walk to freedom. He is a very important person in my life and I want my long walk to start on the same day.'

Janine looked at me as if I'd just told her that her house had burned down. Whether she was aghast at my cheek in answering back or at my reason for wanting to start walking a day later, I didn't know, but for a moment she was speechless.

'You will go look at the sunset *now* and you will start walking *tomorrow*. Tomorrow the weather will be good on the mountain but on Monday it will rain, and you are walking alone and it is dangerous on the mountain and I will not let you walk on your own in the rain. You will get lost and I will be responsible.' Without taking a breath, she spluttered out the orders. It was clear that no more argument would be entertained. I felt like a 10-year-old being scolded, and, as before, I ended up doing exactly as I was told.

I went outside, turned left, found the stairs and the road going up the ramparts, and saw the sunset over the majestic Pyrenees. There seemed to be many bush fires on the mountains and the red haze hanging over the mountain range made for an extraordinarily colourful sunset that evening. There was a stillness on the hilltop, and only the very faint sounds of the town getting ready for the night could be heard. It was a good feeling standing there, alone, surveying the scene below, where people were doing what they'd done since the beginning of time. And above me, the towering and majestic mountains, swathed in a gauze of reds, oranges and greys, looking so regal, solid and invincible. As I stood there looking at the sky I felt the first tinge of fear. I was about to embark on something as dramatic and spectacular as this sunset. Was I ready for it? Was I adequately prepared? Did I have the courage to start the journey and the stamina to complete it? More importantly, did I have the strength of motivation and resolve to see me through the journey? The question everyone asks, I had to ask myself again: 'Why are you walking the Camino?'

I definitely wasn't looking for a religious experience. My spiritual quest was to experience a level of commitment to something so great, so important, that any fear, inhibition or shame faded in significance. I wanted to pledge myself to something that would take me out of myself and place me on a level far beyond my ken. I wanted to be transported to a spiritual plane where the pettiness and detail of a mundane life had no import and where the true sense of life, love, friendship and courage would become clear.

In my frequent travels across the globe, I have always envied the faithful their blind resolve in the face of a staring world – be it the believers who, in airports, stop off in a side room to kneel down towards Mecca; or the orthodox Jew, with his prayer shawl draped over his shoulders, standing by the porthole of the plane door, rocking his silent prayer to his God; or the New Ager standing naked in the field, arms outstretched, greeting the ever-reliable sun at dawn. In Japan I've looked with longing at the white-clad funny-hatted men and women who walk the route of the 88 Buddhist temples of Shikoku. Even in Memphis, in the United States, it was not with scorn or ridicule that I watched the long lines of people who patiently and silently inched their way forward to the open doors of Elvis Presley's home, Graceland; I watched with something approaching awe and admiration. And then, of course, I have been deeply moved by the thousands of pilgrims who cycle, walk or ride on horseback on their way to Santiago de Compostela in Spain.

Now, subconsciously, I sensed that this altered state of being I was yearning for was exactly what I'd seen in the faces of pilgrims at the airport, in the lines at Graceland – and on the Way of St James.

I did not need drugs, or alcohol, or an evangelist preacher to take me to that level. What I did need was total commitment – something I realised even before I started to research the requirements and demands of such a pilgrimage. This was not something I could do on a whim. It wouldn't count that I had often taken on exciting challenges and demanding adventures on no more than a sudden impulse, nor that I'd always achieved what I set out to do, sometimes courtesy of pure good fortune. But, without total commitment even I could quite possibly fail. This time, this challenge was to demand more than ever before.

Walking the Camino is not something you do to lose weight or reduce cellulite. I admit that if this benefit had featured on the 13th-century menu of promises I'd found on the internet, I would have been sorely tempted. To my chagrin, when I told people of my intention, more than half of them scanned me up and down and reminded me of this added advantage.

Many were convinced that I wanted to do it to prove something to myself. This was not the case, just as it was most certainly not something that I believed you could do simply because some time in your adventurous or idealistic youth, you'd written a list of '50 things I want to do before I turn 50' and 'Walking the Camino' happened to be there, below 'no. 35: Learn to play the cello' and above 'no. 41: Swim with dolphins'.

So, does that answer the question of why I wanted to walk the pilgrimage? No, it does not. I believe it begins to answer the question of what I was hoping to find on the pilgrimage, but the question of why remains unanswered. However – (I have to confess my story is full of 'howevers' because life is simply too filled with delicious complexities and fascinating diversity *not* to have 'howevers' dotted about) – I may not have been able then, or perhaps even now, to answer the question why I wanted to walk this pilgrimage, but I could answer the other question I was asked almost as often: Why now? Why all of a sudden now, in February 2008, when it was something I'd been wanting to do for so many years?

To answer this question, I have to backtrack to the night of 10 May 2006. It was about three o'clock in the morning when my mobile phone started vibrating across the bedside table like an angry de-winged bee. I remember being wide awake immediately, hearing in the phone's buzz the urgency of the message it had to transmit. Somehow, I knew it wasn't one of my children that was in trouble and needing me; I knew it was Terrie, my closest friend, sending me a text message from another time zone, another part of the world, Australia. And I was right. Her name flashed on the tiny screen, and in that moment my heart stopped. It was with a feeling of dread that I opened the message:

Colonoscopy shows possible bowel cancer. Going into surgery immediately.
Please keep your fingers crossed for me, my friend.

Not many of us have been spared a similar message at one or other time in our lives. I thought it might be a matter of perception, as I get older, that cancer seems to have become so prevalent that almost everyone has had to give that message to, or has received it, from at least one person near and dear to them. But statistics confirm that it's not just a perception: one in every three people has been touched by the dreaded scourge. It truly has become a disease that not only sneaks in at the back door, but then moves in and comes to stay – an unwanted long-term guest in our homes and in our lives. Yet its familiarity does not make us impervious to a direct personal assault. When someone close to you becomes the next victim of cancer, the shock is violent and leaves you reeling.

What probably made Terrie's message even more shocking was its complete unexpectedness. Terrie has always been the role model for what a woman past her fifties can look like when she takes care of herself. Apart from looking better in her favourite colour, aqua, than anyone else alive, she is tall and striking, trim and super-fit, confident and elegant, witty and sharp; and she's equally at home chairing an international board meeting, presenting a workshop to an audience of 800, or roughing it on a 500-kilometre bicycle ride with friends.

Terrie has always had a healthy lifestyle, the kind that most of us know we should strive for but seldom attain. So when she had started to experience pain in her lower back about a year before, no one – and most certainly not Terrie herself – suspected that it could be a result of cancer. She was impatient with the constant dull ache and consulted one doctor after another – traditional and homeopathic, specialist and general – to try to find the cause and ultimately the solution. But it was only after more than a year, when she happened to mention her situation to a colleague at a board meeting, that he expressed his surprise that a colonoscopy had never been recommended and suggested that she have one without delay. Terrie did so, and a few hours later, on that fateful night in May 2006, my mobile phone started its buzzing-bee dance across my bedside table.

Throughout my years of motherhood I have usually known when one of my children is in trouble or in pain; even if they're on the other side of the globe. I feel what they feel and I believe that, when they allow themselves to, they sense each other's and my emotions as well. In fact, when he was a toddler, I realised that my youngest son Pierre and I could even 'hear' each other's thoughts at times. When he was about five years old and suffering from debilitating migraines, one specialist we consulted picked up on this and, forgetting why we were there, excitedly started making plans to use us as guinea pigs for her research into ESP. Needless to say, we never went back. I believe anyone can do what we do if they allow themselves to be perceptive to those around them. Unfortunately most of us had any extra-sensory ability drummed out of us the moment we started formal schooling and if there are any of those abilities left in us, we tend to suppress them.

But those feelings of 'knowing' applied to my children – my own flesh and blood. It was different when it came to someone else, it seemed. When I heard, with no warning and no preparation, that my best friend had advanced bowel cancer, my first thought was to place myself in her shoes and try to 'feel' her reaction, right at that moment. I realised only too quickly that this was impossible. Although we say we understand how people feel when they suffer a loss, perhaps even because we have suffered a similar loss in the past, we can never truly empathise with them, because *their* emotions and *their* reactions are born out of *their* specific frame of reference. We can never feel another's pain or put ourselves in another's position and experience what they experience. I could never feel what Terrie felt when she was given her life sentence. Because, as well as I know and understand Terrie, I was not at her birth; I didn't share her growing up, her dreams, her loves, her triumphs, her disappointments, her passions or her fears. As much as I have shared with Terrie, my knowledge of her is but a drop in the ocean of her life.

When I read the text message on the screen, I rapidly passed through the classic Kübler-Ross cycle of shock or grief. In a flash, I passed from denial to anger to bargaining to depression and finally, to acceptance. On some level, I must have known I had to find my feet again quickly so I could focus, not on my own shock, but on being there to support my friend. Then, like a punch in the solar plexus, I was left breathless with a feeling of utter, total helplessness. There was no mercy in that moment, no anaesthetising feelings of depersonalisation, no reprieve from reality; just an utter helplessness. Nothing, nothing I could do would make it better for Terrie. Nothing in my power or my ability could make it go away. It was a first for me; a first time in my life when there was no plan to be made, no solution to be found, no compromise to be implemented, no innate talent to be sourced and used to change the situation. I was 57 years of age and I had met my nemesis. I had no possible way of changing those words on the screen of my mobile phone.

I remember getting out of bed and, in a stunned daze, walking out of my room and going downstairs to the kitchen. I don't remember going through the motions of boiling water or heating milk or spooning instant coffee into a mug, but I must have, for my next memory is of sitting outside on the terrace with a hot mug of milky coffee, looking up at the fading stars. I remember trying to come to grips with this feeling of helplessness, but being even helpless about that. Surely there had to be *something* I could do to make me feel as if I was helping to make it better for Terrie. What did others do in similar situations? With all the thousands of books on self-help and self-actualisation and coping with stress, coping with loss, coping with death, coping, there had to be an answer.

Perhaps if, like Hercules, I went off on a quest and performed some huge challenge, it would help to stop me from feeling so helpless and useless. But that was exactly the problem I was facing: whatever might make a difference to *my* feeling of helplessness would not change the fact that I was still helpless to make a difference to Terrie's situation. If I'd been closer, I could at least have supported her by going with her to the doctors and taking notes, driving her to treatments, answering her phone, bringing food and doing her shopping. But where I was, I could do none of this. And nothing I could say or do could lessen the sadness, the pain, the anger, the fear she must be feeling. Nothing I could do could give her relief, or take away the illness, not for a day or an hour or a moment. Nothing within my power could help her carry her burden. I knew that no matter how positive Terrie was, there were going to be times when her courage must lag, her strength must fade, when she must rage in anger and frustration, must cry a silent tear for the fate that had befallen her. And there was nothing I could do to change this. She had to bear it alone. And this realisation, I discovered, was a different kind of assault from cancer.

Sitting there in the cold pre-dawn air, I realised that this must be how every other person feels who has just received the news that a loved one is terminally ill. If I could discover how to deal with that feeling of utter helplessness and uselessness, I'd be in a better position to understand what I could do to help Terrie. Rather than *presuming* that she should be practising positive thinking or visualisation or any of the sure-fire panaceas prescribed by the 'experts', I first had to get my own house in order and then find out from her what she needed me to do to help.

Hours later, as the first sun-rays burst through the barrier of the horizon, I understood why friends of blind people sometimes spend long periods wearing a blindfold, or why friends of those undergoing chemotherapy sometimes shave their heads. They must feel helpless and useless as well, and therefore must believe that by doing these things they can come close to stepping into the shoes of the sufferer. It's their way of sharing the burden as much as they can, of showing solidarity, and trying to understand what the condition demands from the human spirit.

For years I had wanted to do the pilgrimage of Santiago de Compostela, but I needed a push and a shove to do it. Probably what had kept me back was the subconscious knowledge that I might not be able to do it. For years I'd presented workshops, lectures and coaching to people all over the world on subjects such as 'The power of the mind', 'Positive thinking', 'If you can dream it, you can do it'. I was first and foremost a positive thinker. Almost sickeningly Pollyanna-esque, I'd spent all my working life showing people how they could change their lives by being positive and by always looking for the positive side. From feedback I knew that I'd managed to help people change their lives, had inspired people to greater things. I had helped people discover their innate potential and talents.

However, it wasn't at the end of that night that it dawned on me how to cope with that feeling of helplessness in the face of my friend's illness; it didn't even come to me over the next 18 months, while Terrie was going through the extreme ups and downs of surgery, chemo- and radiotherapy, the good news, the bad news, the elation and the depths of despair… What did come to me during that difficult time was an increasingly powerless feeling born from the indisputable fact that my own tenets had never really been put to the test. I may have taught people how to overcome just about everything with the power of positive thinking, but my own belief in that idea had never really been tested. I knew enough to know how much effort, energy and, above all, strength of mind and spirit it would take for Terrie to fight her battle with cancer. I knew she would need positive thinking like never before. But I knew as well that I had no right to keep reminding her of this. Only by taking on the seemingly impossible myself, and believing that I could actually achieve it, could I practise the belief *with* her and at her side. Without expressing it in so many words, I realised that walking the pilgrimage would be taking on a challenge similar to the one Terrie faced – something supremely demanding and challenging, requiring you to force yourself to continue against all odds. She was my inspiration and would be my encouragement. You can jump off a bridge to be airborne but you need wind beneath your wings to fly; Terrie would be the wind beneath my wings on this huge challenge I set myself, but then, once I discovered I could fly, I might in turn be able to carry her on my back from time to time and help ease her journey.

As I stood there on the ramparts, on the eve of my own pilgrimage, gazing up at the majestic Pyrenees and had these thoughts chasing around my mind, little did I know just how many similarities there would be between Terrie's battle against cancer and the challenges on my pilgrimage. Little did I know how apt this pilgrimage would be as a vehicle for proving my own beliefs. Little did I know that there was a reason why this was one of the punishments of the Inquisition – as well as one of the most rewarding life-changing experiences.

And then I smiled again at my own thoughts. If I could survive the first challenge of returning to the *refugio* and facing Janine, then surely I would also be able to find the answers to all these questions. I turned round and made my way down the hill.

Back at the *refugio*, Janine had prepared a delicious meal for me. On the table was a large bowl of noodles with a tomato and onion sauce that looked as good as it smelled. But first, before being allowed to sit down and eat, I had another errand to run for Janine.

'Here, take this money. I need you to go back down the street to the same shop and buy two more eggs and a nice piece of Tomme. Get a good hard cheese. And make sure they give you one with a thick skin. I have a strong feeling that another pilgrim will arrive tonight and then you must talk to him. He will help you.' It was getting late and I knew the last train must have arrived in St-Jean hours before, but she was adamant that another pilgrim was going to come and, as it was my first time and I was walking alone, she thought it important that I meet up with a fellow pilgrim. By this stage I knew not to argue with her.

Later – after I'd gone down the hill yet a third time and returned with yet two more eggs, and had enjoyed the delicious meal – as I was washing the dishes (on her instruction), I was not surprised to hear a knock at the door and to see a young, blond, good-looking man enter from the dark and ask Janine if she had room for the night.

'Of course I have room for you. But first you will pay me and then you will sit down here at the table and talk to Wilna. She is walking alone for the first time and I think maybe you will look after her.' Without saying anything the young man took money out of his pocket, gave it to Janine and went to sit down at the table, smiling up at me.

'I see you have met Janine. She is the boss here. So you had better come talk, otherwise she will make life very hard for us, for sure.' He reached over the table and offered his hand to me. 'My name is Thorsten and I come from Cologne in Germany. This is the first time you make the Camino?'

Out of the corner of my eye I saw the expression on Janine's face as she turned away to go and lock the door and switch off the lights in the entrance. There was a wicked little smile playing around the corners of her mouth.

'You seem to know Janine already?'

'Yes, I stayed here last year when I walked the Camino. But don't worry too much about her. She is really very good and cares a lot about the pilgrims.'

'Well, I am sorry about this. I had wanted to go to my room early and write in my journal, but she wouldn't allow it.'

Thorsten just laughed. 'It is okay. I don't mind, for sure. It is always nice to meet the people who start at the same time as you.' And then, as if he had read my mind, he added, 'And don't worry about Janine saying I must look after you. If you are here alone, it means you probably want to walk alone. Is that right? So I walk alone too. I will not attach myself to you.'

It was a relief. At that stage I had absolutely no idea what the pilgrimage etiquette was and how to handle it if someone attached themselves to you. I realised that you wouldn't want to be rude or alienate those you met on the way. But I also knew that most people take things personally, and if you told someone you had just met that he or she was not welcome to walk with you, it would probably be regarded as an insult. Thorsten's simple, straightforward attitude was refreshing, especially coming from someone so young.

'So tell me what it's like. I went up to the ramparts today and saw the mountains – Janine made me! They are huge and they seem to go on forever. And there isn't just *one* to cross. It looks like you get over one, then there is another, and another. I'm so worried I won't even be able to get over the mountains, let alone all the way to Santiago de Compostela.'

I must have sounded like a runaway train. 'Whoa!' Thorsten threw up his hands, his eyes sparkling. 'You go so fast and you won't make it, for sure! Slow down.'

I laughed with him. 'You must realise I'm a middle-aged woman who, until recently, had never walked further than ten kilometres in one go. I wear high heels and I drive a car.'

'So, did you train for the walk?'

'No. Apart from walking about ten kilometres most mornings during the December holidays with my family – oh, and I assure you that was not normal for me; we were on a mission to become fitter and healthier

– and walking about twenty kilometres a few times these last few weeks just to see if I could actually do it, I have never done any training. I knew I should have, but I just didn't seem to have the time. I think running up and down this hill tonight going to buy eggs for Janine was more exercise than anything I've done in preparation!'

'That doesn't matter, you know,' Thorsten said with a suddenly serious face, giving his words immediate authority and credibility. 'The Camino is not in your body. It is not the physical fitness or strength. The Camino is in your head. It is about – how do you say? – the mental strength. Of course, if you think you can do it, you will do it. And for sure I will walk into Santiago with you, you will see.'

I smiled at Thorsten's frequent use of 'for sure' and 'of course'. It was almost as if, by adding these two filler phrases in just about every sentence, he was peppering his own mind with affirmation and positive-speak. Yet, my first reaction to his comment was, 'Yeah. I tell people that all the time, but is it true?' – but I did not say these words out loud. What I did say was, 'I believe that too. But I've never really had to prove it. Most things come to me quite easily, but this I'm not so sure about. This is something far more demanding than I've ever taken on. I'm sure my head is okay, but will my body be fine too?'

'The first thing you must do is of course you must stop to say those things. Don't even think them. You sow the tiny seed in your brain and the plant will grow. You only say, "Of course I can do it. Of course I will do it".'

With that he stood up from the table, pulled his woollen cap back over his curly blond mop and said he was going outside for a cigarette before going to bed. 'I think I will stop to smoke on this Camino – but not yet. And I think Janine will be very happy now we are friends, for sure. And tomorrow morning we will eat breakfast and I will make sure you take the right way to start your Camino. Good night. You must sleep now.'

And that is how Thorsten, my first Camino angel, crossed my Camino path.

I wished him good night, went to my room, brushed my teeth, undressed and, for the very first time in my life, wriggled into a sleeping bag. It was a good feeling. My fears had subsided and only anticipation and excitement remained to tease the fringes of my mind as I switched off the light and zipped the bag right up to my chin against the chill of the mountain air. For a fleeting moment I wondered about the eggs. Why had Janine made me run down the hill and back three times to buy two eggs on each trip? Whether that was my last thought, or whether it was of a beautiful young fellow pilgrim who reminded me of my children, I cannot remember, but I know I went to sleep with a big smile on my face – and dreamed about that magical night when I told my family about my decision to walk the Camino de Santiago – and it was good.

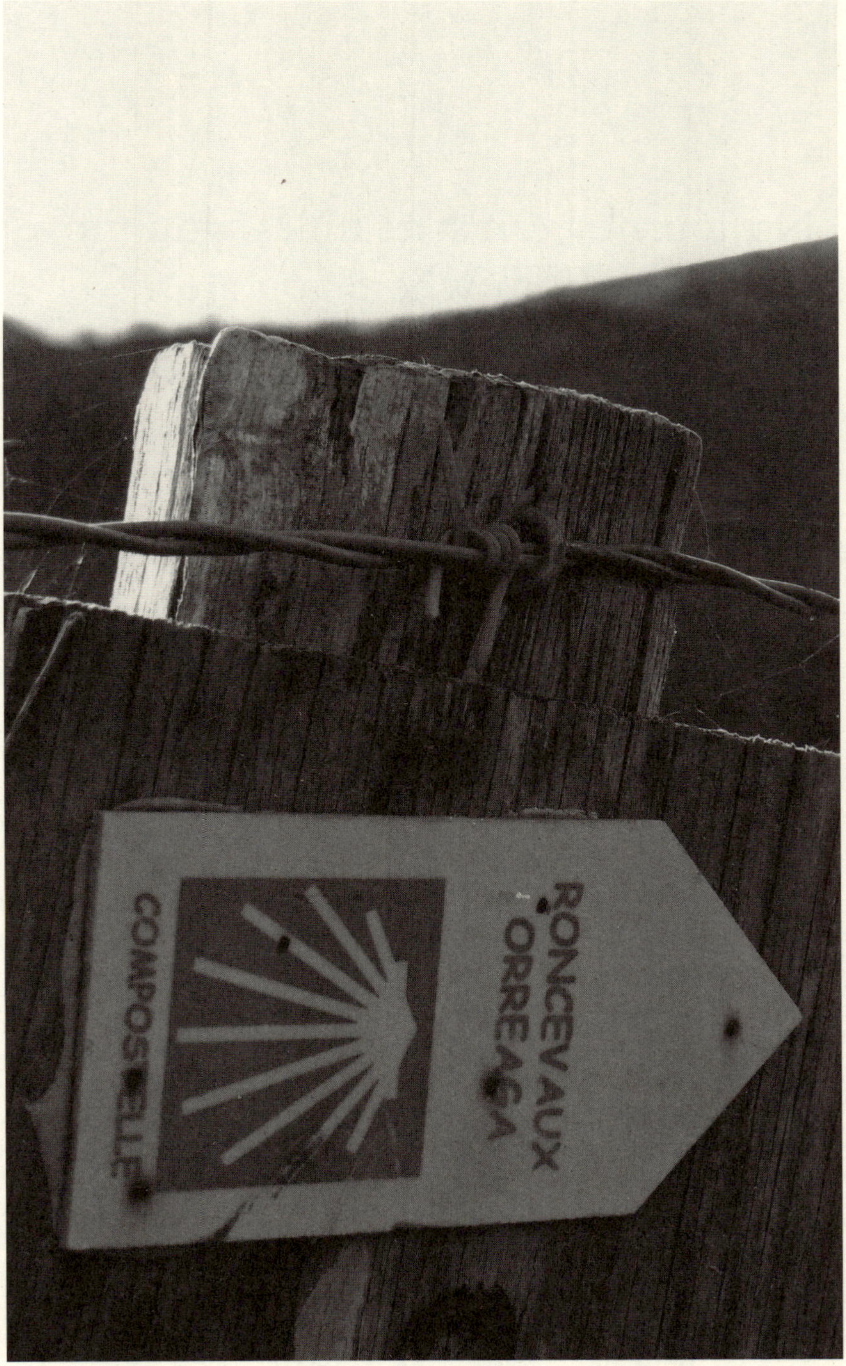
RONCEVAUX
ORREAGA

2

No journey can start unless you move away from where you are…

For the weather to change, the wind must blow.
— Tony Frost

'There's just one thing I want you to tell me,' Pierre said quietly, breaking that brief moment of silence as everyone sat stunned by the news that I intended to set out on the 800-kilometre walk that is the Camino de Santiago. '*Why* do you want to go on a pilgrimage?'

I had waited a long time for this – the perfect moment in a perfect holiday, among the people with whom I feel whole, complete and content – to break the news and say the words out loud for the first time: 'On the eleventh of February I'm going to start walking the Road under the Stars – the Camino de Santiago.'

It was late at night, towards the end of our annual gathering as a family – the time when we all come together from our different corners of the globe where we live and work. My husband, Terence, had arrived from London; our eldest son Marc and his wife Sacha, from Adelaide; Nici from Sydney where she had just finished her second year of medicine; and Pierre, our youngest, from Mexico where he'd spent the last year doing research on coral. I had journeyed from my little piece of paradise, on the edge of the Dordogne River in France, where I run a guest chateau.

We are a close-knit family and being apart is hard for everyone, so for a few precious weeks every year we get together somewhere in the world – 'in the same post code', as Pierre once remarked. We come together to catch up and to replenish the love, energy and sense of belonging that we rely on to get us through yet another year of being scattered around the world.

This time we'd gathered in South Africa, in the beautiful bush of Mpumalanga at a former game lodge that had been turned into accommodation for senior staff of the mining company Terence runs. We had the ultimate luxury of having the place entirely to ourselves, one tented hut each. Every night we would build a huge fire in the centre of the *boma* – a fenced-in enclosure in the bush – and we'd sit around it talking, telling stories, recounting experiences, swapping news of absent friends and family, and sharing thoughts, ideas and dreams.

I looked up at the sky, where the fire-fairies were trying to reach the brightest stars in the black velvety African night sky, wondering whether the stars of *la voje lade*, the 'Milky Way'– as the Way of St James or the Camino de Santiago de Compostela is also known – would be anywhere near as bright as these stars that have guided me since I was a little girl growing up on the southern tip of Africa.

Pierre waited. He did not repeat the question, sensing that I'd heard him but needed time to formulate a reply. But my gazing at the constellations of the southern hemisphere was not so much a play for time as a search for inspiration for the answer to his question.

'There was another pilgrim, Paulo Coelho,' I said slowly, 'who said that before the new chapter can begin, the old chapter must be closed. Change from being who you were to being who you are.' I looked across at Terence, who just smiled. He'd come to expect the unexpected from me and was always going to be the least surprised about my decision. But the children were another matter.

'What? *Another* new chapter then?' laughed Marc, the responsible oldest, quickly followed by the ever-pragmatic Nici: 'You've already done that, mom, – that change from who-you-were-to-who-you-are-now-thing, – when you packed up your old life and moved to France.'

'Yeah,' chipped in Sacha. 'That's right – and we pretty much like that new who-you-are-now!'

Although I welcomed the banter, and the light-hearted reaction was a sweet relief, there was an almost electric atmosphere around the fire, the sparks flying between us reflecting the sparks of the burning and crackling leadwood and sweet-smelling acacia in the fire. Everyone loves it when one of the gang starts a new project, be it Terence building a new mine, Marc and Sacha finding their first home, Nici starting a new module in her medicine studies or Pierre discovering another exotic place in his own pilgrimage through life. By sharing the enthusiasm, we gain much joy from each new venture.

When Marc, Nici and Pierre set off on a journey from London to Cape Town a few years ago, travelling overland for seven months through every African country, Terence and I lived every moment with them, following their every step via e-mail messages and rare phone calls. Soon though we could not contain ourselves any longer and, on the spur of the moment, we flew to Accra in Ghana to spend Christmas with them in Big Fat Milly's Backyard – a surreal travellers' campsite on the edge of a remote beach somewhere on the bulge of Africa. Some months later, when Nici was struggling to recover from a near-death meeting with typhoid and malaria, I once again followed my instinct and joined her for three days in Nairobi, Kenya. We went to the camping shop and spent a whole morning trying out the brightly coloured tents by lying inside them and continuing our non-stop catch-up of the last few months apart – until the irritated shop assistant threatened to throw us out unless we came out and showed ourselves, and the colour of our money. We giggled like schoolgirls as we bought a 'new aura' for Nici – a turquoise and florescent-pink tent. Then it was back to the historic Stanley Hotel where we spent the rest of the day painting each other's toenails bright blue in memory of that special shared moment.

'Yes, it's true, it's a new chapter.' I said, smiling at my offspring's almost exasperated tone. 'Why am I doing this pilgrimage? Why am I going to walk 800 kilometres on the Road under the Stars? They're not simple questions to answer.'

My children have never seen their mother as one to act and think like other mothers, and I have to wonder how many times in their lives they've come up with an acceptable explanation to their friends for one of my often slightly off-the-wall actions or outspoken comments. The reason I'd waited for the right moment to break the news to the family was not that I was worried about my sanity in making this decision (although, heaven knows I've wondered about it since) or that I had any doubts that this was something I had to do. It was because I know my family so well that I expected a thousand questions – about my fitness (or lack of it), my safety, my health and state of mind. The fact that I had given them their wings by inculcating in them a love of travel, adventure, discovery, and of pushing themselves to their own limits – and therefore had to let them fly when they went where their hearts took them – was fine by them, as long as it was *they* who wanted to take flight. But when their cool (but middle-aged), wacky (but middle-aged) mother wanted to spread her wings, the three of them were going to make sure every feather was in place and accounted for. I had wanted to be prepared with the answers to every one of their questions so I could allay their fears and assure them that I had not completely gone off the rails. However, the one question I could not answer then, and still cannot answer now, was the only question Pierre asked: 'Why do you want to go on a pilgrimage?'

I was an unlikely candidate to take on the challenge. Although well educated and fortunate to be moderately talented in a variety of disciplines as well as having had some success internationally as a motivational speaker, speech writer, trainer and coach in communication and presentation skills, none of this qualified me to set out on an 800-kilometre walk – about 790 kilometres further than any of the walks I'd previously done.

To those who do not know me well, I would seem more at home in a fine restaurant than heating a tin of something edible over a primus stove in a pilgrims' hostel kitchen; more likely to book into a lovely hotel room with crisp white sheets and a large bathroom with hot water and fluffy towels than unrolling my sleeping bag on a flea-ridden foam mattress on a rickety bunk bed in a pilgrims' dormitory alongside 30 strangers with smelly feet and loud snores.

While my decision raised eyebrows, my choice of timing puzzled people even more. I planned to set out, not in spring, with flowers in the fields and the soft April sun at my back, but in the depth of winter. My pilgrimage would be made in February, the coldest month in the Pyrenees and northern Spain; a time when the snow still lies thick on the ground and the frost and ice play deadly games with ankles and slippery shoe soles. Simply put, I'd always preferred winter to summer. I often remark that I should never have been born in Africa, because it is the cooler summers and cold winters in Europe that give me more energy and zest for life. Extreme heat leaves me listless and tired, and there was no way I would have been able to walk in the scorching heat of the Spanish summer.

Yet one more question mark over my timing was the lack of companionship. I planned to walk alone – it would never have entered my mind to do otherwise. This was something I felt the need to do, and I had to do it my way. My instinct told me that bringing another person into the picture could only result in conflict. As I live right on the edge of the French *Chemin* (Way), I was familiar with the sight of single walkers or groups of people purposefully treading their way along the road of St Jacques, as the Camino is better known in France. So, knowing that I would not be walking completely alone gave me courage and encouragement. The majority of the tens of thousands of pilgrims walk during summer, when the season brings not only the promise of long, dry, warm days, but a guarantee of company along the way. There seems to be an acceptance that it is better to walk with a partner, a friend or in a group. Yet, almost all those I spoke to or heard speak about their Camino experience *after* they'd done it warned against this.

'Depending on your motivation for walking the Camino, the choice of a walking partner could be crucial,' one speaker pointed out. 'The logical tendency of pilgrims is to walk with a partner, a spouse, a lover, a close friend or even with a group of friends. But be aware that this will change your Camino experience, and might very possibly change your relationship with those people as well.'

As I'd always leaned more towards being a loner than a member of a group, I puzzled at the need to have this pointed out. Of course it would change the experience. Of course it would change the relationship. Of course it is impossible to walk a pilgrimage with someone else. A pilgrimage is not a social event or a time to catch up on a friendship or a relationship. A pilgrimage is a deeply personal experience that can only be done alone.

I was aware of and respected people's religious motivation for walking the Camino. However, I knew it was not a religious experience I was craving, but a spiritual one.

And the question was still *why*? The Devil's advocates argued: 'It's not even as if this is in line with your usual choice of challenges – something unique, something different, something where you'd be a pioneer or groundbreaker. You've always taken the road less travelled, exploring unknown territory. Thousands walk this road every year and it's not even unknown territory; it's probably the best-known pilgrimage of all time.' To this particular argument I did have a rebuttal. For me it would be unknown territory. For me it would be a challenge like no other I'd ever undertaken. In my life it would be something unique, something different, something where I would be a pioneer and groundbreaker.

The Camino, or specifically the Camino Francés, the so-called French Way, leads from the Pyrenees across northern Spain to Santiago de

Compostela and is the best known and best travelled of the pilgrim roads to Santiago. Three of the main routes through France – from Paris, Vézelay and Le Puy-en-Velay – feed into it on the French side of the Pyrenees while the fourth, from Arles, joins it three to four days later, where it officially starts in Puente la Reina. From there it winds its way through the northern part of Spain, from east to west, over several steep mountain ranges, across the flat arid plains of the *Meseta*, through two major passes, La Cruz de Ferro and O Cebreiro, before finally descending into the lush green farmland of Galicia. The stony pathway is only a shoulder's breadth in some places, wide and open in others; one day it cuts through dense forests and the next through open fields where the horizons stretch forever. Sometimes, as if to remind pilgrims that they are still part of a world inhabited by other humans, it runs alongside busy freeways or becomes one with rough farm roads or main streets that run through the centre of a village or town.

Once an ancient pagan pilgrims' route, the Camino was adopted by the Celts as a holy route and later conveniently used by the Romans as an important trade route. Its religious significance allegedly began with medieval believers from all over Europe making pilgrimages to visit the tomb of the beheaded apostle Saint James (Sant Iago), who is said to have spread the gospel in Spain. The story goes that, when he died at the hands of King Herod in 44AD, his body was cast off on a stone boat, that the boat landed on the shores of Galicia and that his followers buried his remains on the site of what is now the city of Santiago de Compostela. Naturally, this legend has its detractors and, although carbon dating could solve the mystery of the true origin of the bones, the Vatican has consistently refused to allow it. The mystery of the true religious significance of the Camino is not something that could be solved as easily, with or without approval from the Vatican. People believe because they choose to believe and the Camino provides a beautiful backdrop against which to practise that belief.

According to yet another legend, it was only in 950AD when the Bishop of Le Puy went to Santiago as a 'Christian' pilgrim, that the Church officially claimed the route as a pilgrimage. It soon became the 'in thing' for Christians to do and in no time rivalled the popularity of pilgrimages to Jerusalem and Rome. Dante wrote that 'those who travel to Jerusalem may be called "palm-bringers", those who visit Rome are "Rome-goers", but the title of "pilgrim" belongs only to those who journey to Santiago'.

Later still it was regarded as among the lightest sentences given by the Inquisition – and that should have told me something about the severity of the walk before I began. This sort of 'penitential tariff' was definitely not the attraction for a 'so-not-a-martyr' like me. Nor were the pilgrimage's 'fringe benefits to Christians', according to which every mile of the Camino reduces your time in Purgatory. I do not believe in this halfway station for sinners, but for those who do, the menu of benefits must look tempting. A 13th-century document lists some of them as follows:

1. For making the Pilgrimage to Compostela: a remission of one third of your sins.
2. If you should die on the road, you obtain total remission of your sins.
3. If you participate in the religious processions in Santiago de Compostela, you get 40 days off.
4. If the procession is led by a mitred bishop, you get 200 days off.
5. If the procession is that of July 24, a holy day: a whopping 600 days.
6. If you attend a mass where a cardinal or an archbishop officiates, you spend 200 days less in limbo.

The list continues in this vein until, finally, the ultimate promise is made to the pilgrim: 'Walking the Camino naked assures you special dispensation from the Pope.' (I laughed out loud when I saw this last 'promise', wondering if the current Pope knew of this. And 'special dispensation'? Wouldn't *you* like to know what that meant, before setting off stark naked on an 800-kilometre pilgrimage through a conservatively Catholic country?)

However, I was not intending to walk naked, though that would have simplified my preparations. Did I say 'preparations'? Allowing myself only seven weeks to get my equipment – and myself – ready for such a demanding undertaking was certainly not what most people would call good preparation. If the wind must blow for the weather to change, then it was more like a whirlwind that tore through my life during those seven weeks prior to my arrival that day in St-Jean-Pied-de-Port.

My blog entry for 27 January 2008 reads:
… and the train ticket to Saint Jean-Pied-de-Port, my starting block, is

booked, bought and paid for. It is done.

The die is cast. A big red cross marks the spot on 9 February 2008 on my calendar.

Last night, on the internet, I bought my train ticket to Saint-Jean-Pied-de-Port. It was quite a dramatic little moment in this, the build-up to the pilgrimage to which I am now completely committed.

So it was interesting for me to find that my fingers actually hovered over the keys before committing to the letters that spelled out the date and time and place of departure and desired destination. I first did it all in my usual rushed, impulsive and haphazard way – clicking on *Next>* and continuing on to page two and then page three to fill in the payment details. Then, suddenly, as a stillness, a calmness descended around me, I slowed down and reflected. The mood changed. I felt the gravitas of the moment. I was about to click on the point of no return.

Even though I have been walking every day for the last five weeks, even though I have been reading and doing intensive research into the subject – the likes of which I have not done for any project for a very long time – even though I have spent days looking for and buying everything I need for the walk, and even spent a whole day packing, unpacking, packing and weighing my rucksack, even though my route is planned and my calendar blocked out for the next two months, clicking on the last *Next>* on the last page of the process in buying a single, one-way, 31.30 train ticket from Bergerac to Saint-Jean-Pied–de-Port caused me a full moment of hesitation. It was almost as if the train ticket was the final proof of commitment, the final point of no return – and *that* for a second-class, two-stop-and-change train ticket, and one that is changeable and refundable to boot!

It is done. I leave on Saturday, 9 February 2008 at 11.29 am from Bergerac and arrive in Saint-Jean-Pied-de-Port at 4.20 in the afternoon.

From the moment I decided to walk the Camino to the day I set off, barely seven weeks passed. It was most definitely not much time to prepare for such a huge challenge. Considering that I'd always been one to act on impulse, it was probably par for the course for me and seven weeks was not a short time at all. So, when friends asked me about the lack of preparation, I found the question a little puzzling. However, when they asked, 'Aren't you a little scared of what is lying ahead?' I had to admit – only to myself – that I was grateful I hadn't given myself more time to get ready. I had not allowed time for the occasional tinge of fear to niggle in the base of my stomach or to tug at the fringes of my mind. There was no idle time to sit and wonder. I did not want a single negative thought to have the opportunity to creep into my consciousness, or to find out that I was tackling something that just might prove too big for me.

I kept myself very busy. The hours, days and weeks were spent researching facts about the Camino on the internet. However, I stayed away from the plethora of books that have been written on the subject, as I was loath to read someone else's experiences, see it through their eyes or build my expectations on their perceptions. I wanted my canvas to be blank, the experience to be mine alone and not coloured by another's brushstrokes. This was quite difficult because almost daily there was a knock on the door and yet another friend would be standing on the step with one or two or more books about the Camino.

'Have you read Shirley MacLaine's *The Camino: A journey of the spirit*? I remembered I had it on my shelf and it's brilliant. You must read it!'

'I'm sure you must already have read Coelho's book on the Camino, *The Pilgrimage*, but just in case you haven't, I'd like to give it to you as a gift to inspire you.'

'A friend of mine walked the Camino and wrote about her experiences. I'm sure you'll find it very useful.'

Soon a little pile of books on the side of my desk started to take on a life of its own, growing and growing. Tempted as I was to devour them all in one sitting, digesting the mine of information that could no doubt be useful, inspirational, life-saving, encouraging and many other things, I resisted. Apart from an occasional glance at a paragraph here and a phrase there, they remained unopened. It soon became apparent that a fair percentage of the people who'd walked the pilgrimage had written a book about it, but just how many came as a surprise. It seemed there were hundreds of books in every size, format, style, genre and language. Later, while walking the Camino, I discovered that almost everyone I met had a favourite book that they'd read and studied before embarking on the pilgrimage. Apart from the German-speaking pilgrims, many of whom were on the pilgrimage as a result of the run-away bestseller *Ich bin dann mal weg* (I'm off for a bit, then) by the German comedian Hape Kerkeling, no two people quoted the same book as their source of inspiration or information. (It did appear, though, as if everyone had read Coelho's book).

It was therefore mostly on the internet and not in the library or from my growing pile of recommended reading that I researched the logistics of walking a pilgrimage – where you sleep, how far you walk in a day and how long it takes, where you eat, what clothes you need and the kind of people you're likely to come across. This is obviously essential information. For someone like me, reading lists of what was required and preparing shopping lists of what had to be bought were alien activities. My idea of preparation is to pack my passport, my toothbrush and a change of underwear, go to the train station, look on the departures board for a destination that I do not know, buy a ticket and board a train. But, for someone who'd never carried a backpack on her back, who had never owned a sleeping bag or a dedicated pair of walking shoes, preparing for an 800-kilometre walk was in itself a new discovery and an exciting adventure.

If there were hundreds of books written on the subject, there were thousands of websites, blogs, forums, chat rooms, entries for groups, clubs and associations on the internet. Anyone who's ever done research on the web will know that it's a self-propagating exercise; one click leads to ten others and each of those leads to ten more, ad infinitum. It was in this way that I accidentally stumbled upon the confraternities of the pilgrimage: those of St James (United Kingdom), St Jacques (France), St Jakob (Netherlands and Germany) and Sant Iago (Spain). It was like discovering a wonderfully intriguing remnant from the Middle Ages that had mysteriously made its way into the Modern Age and then miraculously found itself in the Age of Technology. It didn't take me long to conjure up an image of an old monk sitting in the dark, wood-panelled library of the monastery, his dusty cassock hanging heavy from his bulky frame, one hand on his lap, perhaps holding his rosary, while the other rested lightly on the mouse, his round face eerily lit by the blue light from the computer screen. This was a clever monk and definitely someone who had walked the pilgrimage himself – every step of the way, in every season, under every condition – because all the confraternity sites were most helpful with their information. No frilly descriptions to enthral, no fancy photographs to distract, no mention of bus schedules along the way or taxi telephone numbers or backpack forwarding services to corrupt the true pilgrim's heart; just straightforward, detailed, comprehensive and useful information. My 'medieval monk' later turned out to be any one of the many members of these confraternities – 'normal' people like you and me, who had most certainly walked the pilgrimage and who wanted to put something back after their wonderful experience. This new knowledge did not alter the conjured image in my mind, and to this day I see the monk at his computer, and I smile.

Just when I thought I had it all sorted out, done all the planning I intended to do and bought my train ticket, I received three long-distance phone calls. The first was from my eldest son, Marc.

No 'Hello, how are you, how are you feeling?' but straight into the reason for his call from Australia. 'Have you organised your insurance?' he asked. And so, once again it was my children who became my ultimate guides on what to organise and how to be well prepared for the adventure.

Even though they'd never walked this kind of distance, their wealth of practical experience accumulated while travelling overland through Africa, combined with their knowledge of me, made them the best equipped to give me advice. They knew I wouldn't be bothered with certain things and conveniently forget others, such as the medical insurance. Marc was also the one who checked to make sure that there would be reception for my mobile phone, and that I had all the necessary numbers easily accessible on my phone, including my ICE number: In Case of Emergency.

Pierre, my youngest, was the second one to call. 'Mom, the more I read about this Camino, the more worried I am about you walking alone.'

'Pierre, it's going to be fine. I can look after myself. After all, it's a pilgrimage so the people on the way will all be concentrating on surviving, not on causing problems for anyone.' I said. 'And anyway, I won't have anything on me worth taking.'

'Oh, mom, you're so naive!' This, coming from my youngest child, had to make me smile. 'From what I see on the Google Earth pictures, you'll be walking far away from roads and people and places. If there are hardly any people walking the Camino at this time of year, then there'll be long periods when you are completely alone. How easy is that for someone to attack you!'

I was delighted that he had taken the interest to look at the route so beautifully and clearly photographed from a satellite, but Pierre's comments about walking at a time of year when there is hardly anyone on the Way stirred a niggling concern in me. It was my considered wish to walk alone, rather than join a group or walk with a friend. During my hours of reading Camino-related entries on the internet, I had come across several references to the dangers of being a lone pilgrim. This was not only because an accident and possible injury could occur, but also because the time it might take for someone to realise you were missing, hurt or lost could well be the crucial difference between possible rescue and probable death. An added danger was of attacks on walkers. There were many areas on the Camino where unsuspecting pilgrims, happily on their way to redemption, had to walk through dense forests, where there was no habitation for tens of kilometres at a stretch and where bandits could well be lying in wait. I gathered that the odds were more in favour of getting lost, breaking a limb, falling down a mountain, dying of hypothermia or a heart attack, or being run over by a car, than of being attacked. Yet, deaths on the Camino do occur with alarming frequency. Perhaps this is not surprising when you consider just how many tens of thousands of pilgrims there are on the route every year. And in my case, it would have been particularly unsurprising given that I was approaching the whole experience with a little less than the respect and preparation it merited.

'Anyway,' continued Pierre, 'remember everything I taught you about self-defence. Better still, remember what you did that day you pushed those two bad guys right down the length of the passage and out the back door of our house. You already know that when you're walking like this, you *think* you won't have much energy to spare to do anything if someone attacks you. But you also know that fear and panic can work miracles. People are always surprised how much energy and strength a panic situation can give them. Your adrenalin is pumping, your senses are heightened. Remember the tricks I showed you. *Believe* you can do it, and you can. Use your fingers to find the lethal spots. And be careful!'

The black belt karateka of the family, who could throw a man twice his own size over his shoulder and disarm an attacker in the wink of an eye, was ostensibly giving his mother a little crash course in self defence, but what he was *really* doing was boosting my confidence in my own inherent strength, and the reminder did not go amiss. Armed with this knowledge and with the pepper spray he'd bought for me earlier, I felt much more confident about my safety. Later, on the pilgrimage, when I did need to defend myself, it was that confidence more than my self-defence skills that got me through a very sticky situation.

The last call was from Nici. This was a mere six days before I was due to leave and Nici was calling from a major camping shop in Sydney, Australia, to tell me that she'd found my backpack, but needed to know which colour I preferred.

Back in South Africa during our family get-together, she had accompanied me to the local camping shop and revealed her talent for knowing exactly what you needed to look for in that Aladdin's cave of pilgrim treasures.

'No, not that sleeping bag, mom. It's far too big and heavy!' I was looking at one of the biggest, bulkiest sleeping bags that weighed almost two kilograms and was suitable for Arctic conditions of down to -15°C.

Giving me no opportunity to debate the issue, she took the big bag out of my hands, hung it back on the rail and replaced it with her choice. 'Take this one: it's small and light and warm enough for zero degrees. It won't get colder than that indoors. And if you need something warmer, here's a space blanket, which you need anyway. Now for clothing…' and, with her idea of what would be needed, off she went to where the widest range of outdoor clothing I ever knew existed was on display. I was still comparing the many different jackets and parkas, windproof or waterproof, with or without hood, zip or Velcro, synthetic fill or down, when Nici called me to see what she had collected in her basket for me.

If at that time I had with me the list of items prescribed by the Confraternity of St James, I would have been able to cross off almost everything on it:

1 fleece base layer top
1 fleece jacket, zip-up and high-cut collar
2 pairs of thermal tights
2 thermal long-sleeved vests
2 pairs of thick pure wool moisture-wicking socks (allowing moisture out to keep the skin dry – so very important for the prevention of blisters)
2 pairs of thin wool socks
1 pair of silk gloves
1 pair of fur-lined sheepskin gloves
1 pair of earplugs

'There you go,' she proudly handed me the basket. 'Everything you need.' I took the basket from her, surprised at how light it felt. In it was everything I needed in terms of clothing and not even half the weight of the beautiful pale-pink, padded, fur-lined, hooded multi-weather jacket I was holding in the other hand.

'Oh mother dear, just as well I came with you today. Put that jacket back. You won't be needing it on this trip – unless you think you'll be meeting the King of Spain for drinks along the way. All you have to do now is try on these trousers. Look – they're great – lots of pockets for all sorts of things. In this one you can put your guidebook, and your phone can go in that one, and if it gets hot, you can unzip the bottoms and – voila! – you have a pair of long shorts.'

I was amazed at how simple she made it all seem. 'Nici, the pilgrimage is going to take at least fifty days. How am I possibly going to get by on these few pieces of clothing for all that time?'

'Mom,' she sighed, 'everything you take with you, you have to carry on your back. Your backpack can't be more than ten per cent of your weight, and what are you, 68, 69 kilograms? So that means you shouldn't have more than seven kilograms max on your back. And remember, you still have to add to that the little bits and pieces, odds and ends, and each one of those will add to the weight.'

She was right, of course. I still had to pack a rain poncho, an extra pair of shoes for the evenings, a small LED torch, Compeed plasters (for blisters), NOK anti-chafing cream for my feet, safety pins, a notebook, a couple of empty Jiffy bags, a toothbrush, bar of soap, a needle and thread (for blisters), and the three essentials my father had taught me never to go anywhere without: a Swiss Army knife, a piece of string and a handkerchief. Apart from the poncho and the knife, none of these weighed much on their own, but put them all together and they seemed to conspire to become a hefty weight. And then there was the camel pack for a litre and a half of water, which fitted into the backpack and lay snugly against the length of my back. One-and-a-half litres meant one-and-a-half kilos – a big part of the mere seven kilos I was allowing myself.

'Well, I suppose it could be done – washing underwear every night – if there's hot water and if there's somewhere to dry them…'

'Of course it can be done. Trust me. You'll be just fine. And look what I found for you. You'll love it!' With great excitement she presented me with the final item for my journey – a small, round, ball-like bag, no bigger than the palm of my hand. 'Open it! Have a look,' she bubbled. I pulled the top open and, like a magician pulling an endless string of handkerchiefs from his closed fist, I started drawing out a soft, light fabric from the small bag. It kept on coming, more and more of it, until finally I stood with a large rectangle in my hands, the size of an extra-large beach towel. 'Ta-ta-dummmmm!' came the drum roll. 'Your towel!' Nici proudly announced.

A 'Sea-to-Summit pocket towel – Large' I read on the label, superabsorbent and quick drying. And it fitted into a bag the size of my fist.

So, when Nici's call came from the backpackers' shop in Sydney a few weeks later, I already had all the items to take with me on the pilgrimage neatly laid out on my big dining-room table back in my home in France. Though each item on its own weighed absolutely nothing, I had no illusions about what was going to happen once I packed them all into the backpack.

Backpack? What backpack? It was one week before I was about to set off, and I still had no backpack. Two good friends, Sven and Charlotte, both veteran hikers and experienced in the mysteries of the paraphernalia of camping and rugged outdoor sports had insisted that I borrow Sven's backpack. Albeit large, it was a light pack and comfortable on my back. Empty, that was. But I was not happy about using someone else's backpack and, yet again, Nici came to my rescue.

'The Australian BlackWolf is the best, mom, otherwise the Caribee. You'll love them. Lots of little pockets and separate sections which make it very easy to store everything where you can find it and also to keep the pack well balanced. I'll send you the internet link so you can look at the different packs and choose one you like.'

A few weeks earlier, Nici's offer to get me a good backpack once she was back in Australia had sounded very attractive, but with only six days left before I was due to leave, this was cutting it very fine – even by my last-minute way of doing things – and did not leave us much time to choose, buy a backpack and get it to me in France, all the way from Australia.

'You go ahead and choose one for me, Nix,' I finally capitulated after staring at the internet site. 'Time is running short and if we don't get the bag by the end of the day there, I don't think it'll get here in time. Parcels usually take six or seven days between Sydney and France.'

An hour later Nici called again. 'Mom, I'm standing here in the shop and I have your bag. You can have either the dark and light charcoal or the orange and charcoal. Which is it?'

I laughed. This conversation could only take place between a mother and daughter; and not *any* mother and daughter at that. There we were, racing against time to procure me a backpack, *the* most essential item for a pilgrim. And yet, six days before I was due to start walking, I had everything I needed, everything *except* the pack in which to put it all. The pack was being bought for me in Australia and I was in France…

and still we were tossing up between dark and light charcoal or orange and charcoal. 'What kind of orange?' I had to know. There was orange *and* there was orange.

'Burnt orange, mom. It looks really cool with the charcoal. It'll make up for the sombre colours of your clothes. Put a little colour into the cold winter days. Good enough to wear in case you meet the King of Spain.'

'In that case, go ahead and buy it, Nici. And get them to send it by FedEx. If it goes today it will be here by Wednesday at the latest. Then at least we'll be sure that I'll have it a few days before I leave and I'll have time to practise packing it and feel what it's like carrying it on my back.'

Up to this point of my preparations, everything had gone smoothly. To an outsider there may have been a semblance of haphazardness or happenchance. I could possibly have been found guilty of being too trusting in my fellow-man to do what was expected from them, but all my life I had believed that delegating meant not only sharing out tasks or giving certain jobs to the experts, but it also meant giving those people sole responsibility for those tasks. Goethe's saying 'If you treat a person as he is, he will continue as he is, but if you treat him as he is capable of becoming, he will become what he is capable of becoming,' had served me well through the years, and when someone made me a promise, I never questioned or doubted that promise. So, with six days to go and a promise from FedEx of 'next flight, fastest international delivery within hours, door-to-door customs-cleared service', and having paid a king's ransom for the promised service, both Nici and I slept peacefully, trusting that the backpack would arrive with time to spare.

It was when I woke up before dawn on Wednesday morning, three days before my departure, that I felt the first tinge of concern. Almost at the exact moment that that little tinge squirmed in the pit of my stomach, the phone rang.

'Mom!' Nici's voice was filled with panic and unshed tears. 'I missed my classes today because I spent all afternoon at the FedEx offices. I called them this morning to confirm that you would be receiving the parcel today and they told me the parcel is still sitting here in Sydney. It hasn't been sent yet! The woman in the office says it's because one of the forms wasn't completed, but it turned out that it was a form I was never given. The reality is that your backpack is still in Sydney and there is no way you'll have it in time. I am so so so sorry, mom!'

What a disaster. By the end of Wednesday afternoon, I'd spoken to at least a dozen people. Some told me the parcel had left, others told me the parcel had not left. Some assured me that I'd have it by Friday, others assured me that it would not arrive in France until the following week.

I have often been called stubborn; of course I would prefer to have the words steadfast, persistent, tenacious, resolute – even dogged – used. Stubborn is not a word I like. But, if stubbornness is what is needed to get something done, then stubborn I shall be.

My only recourse was to let the powers that be know of the transgression and allow them the opportunity to make it right. I wrote to the president of the company at its headquarters in the US. I simply and clearly explained the situation and the consequences: publication of the entire issue. Ten minutes – exactly ten minutes after sending off the e-mail – I received a reply. Another five minutes later I 'met' via a phone call to Paris, the lovely Laura, the first understanding voice in this nightmare. And, at seven o'clock on Saturday morning, the day of my departure, there was a knock at my front door and the parcel with my new burnt orange and charcoal backpack was placed in my hands. At last I was equipped to start my pilgrimage.

When I opened my eyes on the morning of the 10th of February, I was as ready to start as I would ever be. While getting dressed, I thought about the previous night and it suddenly dawned on me that, in a very subtle way, I had been made to learn what would probably be some of the most important Camino lessons. I had learned not to be a stubborn know-all but to listen to people who had more experience than me. I had learned that people on the Camino might walk alone, stay alone and keep to themselves, but that it was pure joy to connect to someone who was a fellow pilgrim. I had learned that there was mutual respect among pilgrims – for their privacy, for their reasons for doing the Camino, for their own individual way of walking the pilgrimage. And I had already learned that it felt good to know there was someone else out there walking and that I would never be alone on this 800-kilometre walk.

I woke up feeling grateful to Janine for having insisted that I did not stay a whole day in St-Jean-Pied-de-Port. I had thought her 'tough as nails' the previous night, but it became obvious to me – and it was something that was confirmed to me time and time again in the following weeks –

that if *hospitaleros* (hosts) cared for the pilgrims, which most of them really did, they had to be tough. If just a small percentage of the thousands of pilgrims who pass through their *refugios* decided to spend an extra day, or get up late in the morning, or ignore the strict rules of the *refugios*, they would have endless problems. More importantly, few pilgrims would continue past the first 'soft' *hospitalero*'s place. It was all too easy – when you woke up in the morning and every muscle in your body ached and every bone in your body felt bruised or broken, and you were running a temperature and felt like you were starting a bad cold and you had done your washing too late the night before and it was still damp, for any of a million possible reasons – to find an excuse for not getting up and setting off on the road. And if the *hospitalero* was not as tough as nails and you thought you could wheedle your way into staying at the *refugio* for the day, almost no one would ever continue on the pilgrimage. That is the nature of man, and though you should never underestimate the courage and strength of people, you should also never underestimate their instinctive sense of survival, which very much includes doing nothing rather than venturing into the difficult, the demanding and the dangerous.

I got dressed, filled my camel bag with water, and packed my backpack, making sure it was well balanced. In the front room Thorsten was already having a mug of coffee and some bread and jam when I joined him at the table. Neither of us spoke and, not for the last time, I marvelled at the unspoken understanding between pilgrims: there were times when you needed to talk and there were times when silence was golden. On that morning, the first morning of my Camino, I was infinitely grateful for the silence.

As we got up and made ready to leave, Janine came in with a parcel for each of us. 'I have packed some food for you. You will need your strength to cross the mountains. It is very cold today and it is a long way and there is nothing on the way and nowhere to get food.'

I was about to argue with her again because the guidebook had said there was a *refugio* on the way. As if she was reading my mind, Janine continued.

'There is one *refugio* but it is closed. So I have put in three hard-boiled eggs for each of you. There is also an apple and a piece of the Tomme cheese. You must divide the bread you did not eat for breakfast. Thorsten must have more. He is a growing boy. That will be good food for the way. Now you must go. You will walk well and you will be in Roncesvalles tonight.'

With that, she almost pushed us out the door. I turned around to say goodbye and thank her again, this wizened old lady, the 'mother of the Camino', but the door was already closed. Thorsten put his backpack down against the wall and lazily got out a cigarette as if he had all the time in the world. I spent a couple of minutes adjusting my pack on my back and putting on my two pairs of gloves – first the thin silk gloves and then the fur-lined pair Terrie had given me, taking my time, reluctant to start walking. Our breath made little clouds in front of our faces, clouding the expressions, but then I was not looking to see what Thorsten was thinking. I was too busy trying to get my nervousness under control and settle the turbulence in my stomach.

I had not misjudged Thorsten's innate wisdom the night before. The way we met was almost as if it had been predestined – a strange thing for me to have thought as I didn't believe in predestination at all – but then, as I was going to find out over the next few weeks, strange things happen on the Camino. He knew exactly what I was going through, he'd been there once, and he broke the tension wonderfully. 'Now you know why you had to go and buy the eggs,' he laughed, adding a lungful of smoke to the hot vapour cloud around his head. 'We are very lucky, for sure. You will not find another *hospitalero* who will make food for you to take. Janine is a very special person.'

I took a deep breath and looked across at the massive mountains standing like an insurmountable wall in the distance. They were as beautiful that morning as they had been the night before – not because of the bush fires and the smoke against the sunset, but because of the first rays of a bright sun rising behind us in a crystal-clear blue sky. It was the most perfect day.

'It is better you only look at mountains when you are already on the other side' – his parting words of wisdom. He crushed his cigarette against the wall and walked over to a bin to throw away the stub. 'You will be okay. And I will see you in Roncesvalles tonight. *Buen Camino, peregrina.*'

The sweetest words! Good journey, good way, *bon chemin, hamba kahle, bon voyage* – all those greetings I knew and have used over the span of my life – but this was the first time someone had said to me '*Buen Camino!*' It was the first of many, many times over the next forty days 'for sure', and it was wonderful!

'*Buen Camino* to you too! See you tonight,' and with that I set off down the hill, over the bridge, up the other side... and there, on a fence post, was the first Camino sign I saw: a linear scallop shell in bright yellow on a bright blue background. I was on my way.

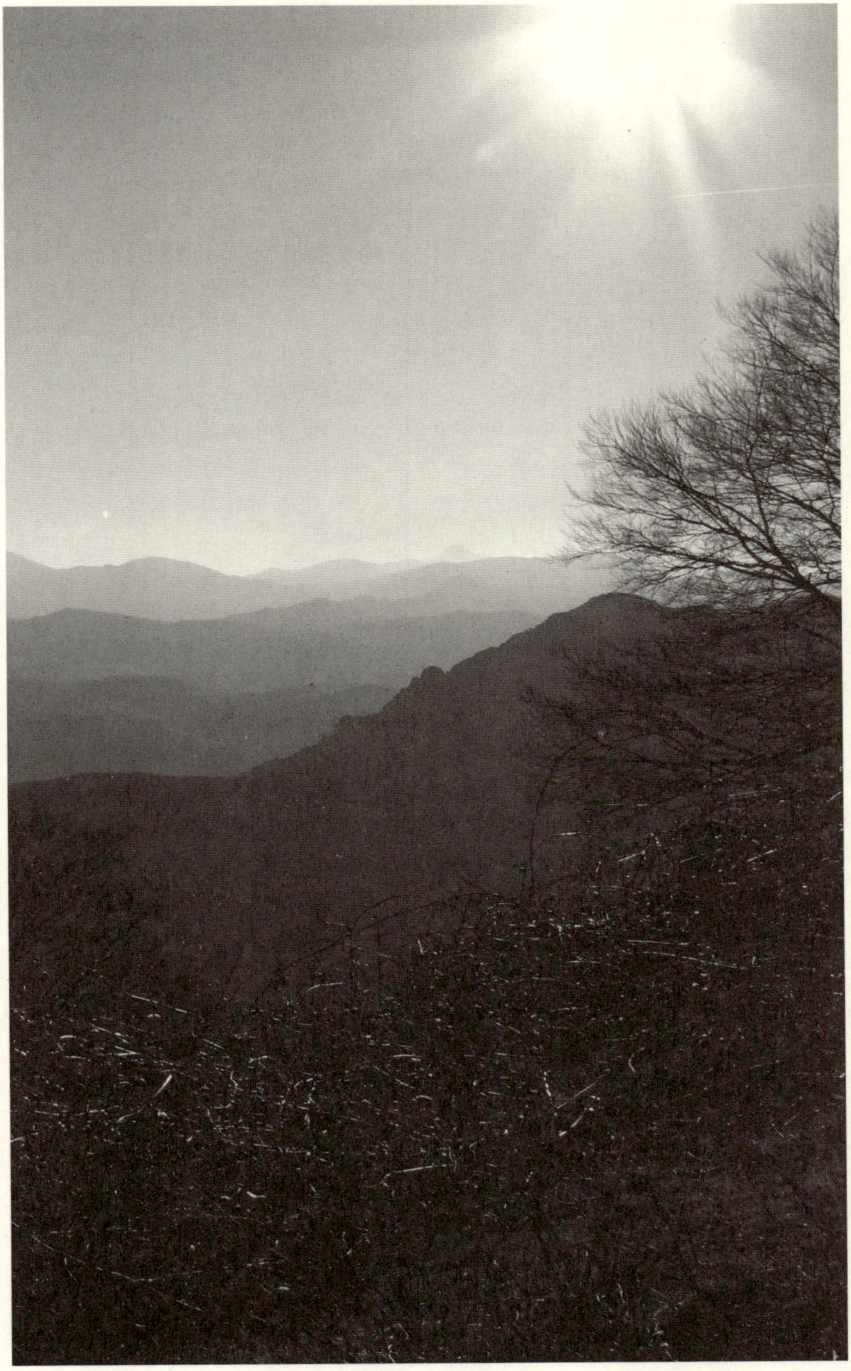

3

Only take photographs of the mountains you have already crossed

You begin to attach much more importance to the things around you because your survival depends upon them. You begin to be more accessible to others because they may be able to help you in difficult situations.

– Paolo Coelho, *The Pilgrimage*

If, on that first day, I had said the twenty-eight-kilometre walk across the Pyrenees was the most difficult thing I'd ever done, I would have to add two things. The first, that it was the understatement of the century, and the second, that it was indeed the most difficult thing I'd ever done – up to that particular day. Later I would find out that there was far harder to come, though that would have seemed impossible then. And, if I thought that I had learned important Camino and life lessons the night before, I was to find out that there were many more to be learned almost every step of the way.

As with so many things on the Camino, I discovered that you often have little or no control over what happens. It's not so much that you relinquish control as that circumstances, places and the people who cross your path sometimes cause your original plans to change. Things happen – and it's fine. Other people make decisions that affect yours and the world doesn't come to an end because of it. For the first time in my life I discovered that there are times when what I'd thought was very important lost its importance altogether. I learned to let go, to go with the flow and to accept whatever came my way. Is this what some call Zen? Previously, I would have called it folly. We are who we choose to be, we experience what we choose to experience. For me, going with the flow was a completely new mode. Significantly, I discovered that I didn't have to sacrifice anything in the process, least of all who I am.

When you start the pilgrimage in St-Jean-Pied-de-Port, the first of the three mountain ranges you need to cross along the Camino is the Pyrenees. It is a daunting prospect for any hiker, an intimidating challenge for an inexperienced tenderfoot like me. In a way, though, if this pilgrimage had been a 'designed' route, having a major mountain range as the first stage of the walk could not have been better planned. Standing at the foot of the mountains is scary. It is frighteningly overwhelming. Yet, somehow, as you climb the very first little hill, which has a gradient of 65° (though for no more than about 100 metres), you just know that whatever lies ahead, once you've conquered this first tiny step of the Camino, you will be able to conquer it all. I felt good and I felt positive.

About twenty minutes after I'd started, having reached the top of that first hill, and already beginning to feel the burn in my lungs and the strain on my legs, Thorsten came sauntering past.

'I reckon if I could get up this hill, I can get over the entire mountain easily,' I beamed.

Thorsten stopped, rubbed his chin, looked towards the sky, smiled and said nothing. Yet it was a response that said it all. That little smile told me that the hill I had just 'conquered' was not just a small foothill, it was a baby wannabe-hillock compared with the 1 000-metre climb over twenty-seven kilometres that lay ahead.

'You will do good, for sure,' was all he said with a debonair salute before setting off again. I watched him go. He walked at a steady, even pace, making the steep climb look as flat as a table, and I could almost hear the song in his head that was setting the rhythm of his step.

'*Buen Camino!*' I called after him, and resumed my own walk, feeling ready for what lay ahead.

Yes! I *will* 'do good', I told myself. If Hannibal's forty elephants, 80 000 foot soldiers and 10 000 cavalrymen could cross these mountains, so can I. If the Gallic chieftains and the Romans, the Celts and the Franks, the Visigoths and the Arabs could all cross these mountains, of course so can I. And, if the Forest of Flowering Spears – those 53 000 intrepid maidens who volunteered for Charlemagne's army (what a man he must have been to inspire them) to replace his warriors who had been wiped out by the Basques – could not only get to the top of these mountains, but then still fight a valiant battle, is there any possible reason why I should not get to the other side by the end of the day?

I took a deep breath, turned around one last time to see where I'd come from, and started the long climb over the Pyrenees. I was walking in the footsteps of all those who'd gone before.

It was tough, extremely tough. It was not the going that was so hard – the first ten kilometres or so were on the relatively smooth surface of a tarred road – but the relentless steepness of the path proved challenging. Because local farmers also used the road, driving cars, trucks or tractors, it was built in zigzags with sharp hairpin bends every 50 metres or so. A few times I looked up and saw the continuation of the road not far above my head, but any temptation to take a short cut would have been like trying to climb up a six-metre wall. I stuck to the road. When I did look up, craning my neck to see where the road was folding back and forth upon itself, I would catch a glimpse of Thorsten, no more than two kilometres in distance ahead of me, but already more than an hour in time. Whenever I saw him, he would stop and wave at me, both his arms wide open like angel wings. He must have known that as a novice I would look up the mountain, despite his advice not to, and those waves of his were like an injection of courage and energy straight into my system.

Then, once when I looked up again as far as I could see, he was gone. I realised that he must have reached the crest and I would not see him again. For a brief moment I felt a tinge of fear: I was now on my own, alone on the side of a very big mountain that I had to cross. I turned around again, and gasped. For there, not in front of me but far, far down below me, I could just make out the glint of the early morning winter sun on the tops of the buildings in St-Jean-Pied-de-Port. Was that where I'd started only a couple of hours before? Was it possible that I had actually climbed so high and come this far? I was overwhelmed by a sense of achievement. I wanted to whoop with joy. I wanted to shout at the top of my voice. I felt exhilarated. I felt on top of the world. I *was* on top of the world!

The lingering smoky haze of the bush fires was now hanging lazily over the valleys below, an occasional wisp escaping on an upward draft of air. Here and there a bush fire was still burning, sending smoke signals in an indecipherable code. In the far-off distance I could hear the occasional human voice calling or the sonorous sound of a church bell.

I noticed movement far below me. Could it be true? There, a long way down and barely discernible, was a pair of eagles circling, floating on the thermals curling up the flanks of the mountain. I was standing higher than the domain of eagles, and I had reached this spot on foot.

From that moment on, the pilgrimage was always going to take me twice as long as it did for anyone else. I had discovered the all-time adrenalin rush, the ultimate high, and I was well and truly hooked. That feeling of achieving something you'd never thought yourself capable of, of standing on the side of a mountain and looking down at the distance you have come, of seeing majestic eagles soaring below, is like soaring there with them. From that moment on, for the rest of the 800 kilometres, I continued to stop often to turn around, look at where I'd been and how far I had come.

In later days, fellow-pilgrims talked about dreading the mountains that lay ahead on the Camino. But I looked forward to them, perhaps because I only looked at them once they were behind me. I looked forward to that magical moment when, once I'd started the climb up a mountainside, I could turn around and try to spot my point of departure a few hours before. And I looked forward most of all to reaching the crest of a mountain when I could look back, not at where I'd started that morning, for that point would long since have disappeared in the folds of foothills and behind the smaller mountain tops, but at the previous highest peak where I'd stood a day or even two days before. That feeling was truly magical. It transformed my exhaustion into energy, my physical pain into euphoria, my mental turbulence into a Zen-like calm; for, believe me, exhaustion and pain and turbulence there were in abundance.

When I finally reached the spot on the Pyrenees where I had last seen Thorsten disappear, a shock awaited me. My immediate reaction was to recall the words of the song we sang as children:

The goat went over the mountain, what do you think he saw? He saw another mountain, he saw another mo-u-n-t-ai-i-i-n, and what do you think he did? The goat went over the mountain, the goat went...

It was one of those irritating songs that repeated itself over and over, without end – or until such time as either a parent would threaten us with instant incarceration if we didn't stop singing, or our voices trailed off in boredom.

What I had thought was the crest of the mountain was simply the first crest of a whole range. The road did indeed dip down into a slightly lower valley, but then proceeded again right up against the other side, to the very top of the next mountain. I suddenly realised why 'Pyrenees' is in the plural. It is not only one mountain, as in 'up one side, over the summit and down the other side.' It's a range of mountains, which means there is row upon row upon row of mountains. I knew how that goat felt that went over the mountain…

It was also the first time that I experienced the power the body can exert over the mind, if you give it half a chance. I could see why Thorsten had warned me against looking up while climbing the mountain. You can be as positive as the top end of a battery, but looking up at a very high mountain from the foot can be extremely discouraging. It's not hard at all to start hearing a tiny voice on your shoulder telling you that it is very high, it is very far, it is going to be very hard, and it takes no more than a few whining words from that little voice for your body to take note and respond with a will of its own. It goes on strike and digs in its heels. You can tell it whatever you wish, try giving it a pep-talk, psyche it up, challenge it, dare it, scold it, but it seems to say, 'No, I am going nowhere. There is no energy left to get you up there.' The same would happen when I planned to do a certain distance in a day and stop at a certain village and *refugio*. If, as was common during those winter months, I reached the village and found the *refugio* doors closed and locked, my body, as exhausted as it was, suddenly became alert and rebellious. It crossed its arms and straightened its back, stuck out its chin and started throwing little tantrums, long before my brain had even realised that we were going to have to continue another unplanned twelve kilometres to the next village and the next open *refugio*.

It never ceases to amaze me, this separateness of the human body, which kicks into survival mode. The power of the mind I was already familiar with, but here, on the first crest of the Pyrenees, I discovered the power of the human body. And it was probably then that I learned that sometimes it's best to cede control just a little bit and allow the body to dictate the terms. In a situation of survival, it is instinct, rather than reason, that merits an audience and demands respect.

As if on cue, I came across my first small wooden cross with a name and a date engraved on it. A casualty of the Camino, a pilgrim soul claimed by the mighty mountains, to spend eternity soaring with the eagles. My thought was: What a wonderful way to go. And I continued on my way.

More or less at this point, I did not need the sparseness of the vegetation and, soon afterwards the lack of trees, to tell me that I'd reached a height

I was not accustomed to. The landscape was now completely bare and windswept, looking lonely and abandoned. I realised it was not just because of unfitness that I was short of breath. There was a definite reduction in oxygen – not so much as to cause breathing difficulties for someone with strong lungs, but enough to make it increasingly challenging to inhale sufficient air. The other change was the wind. All of a sudden there was no longer a strong icy breeze against the side of my frozen cheek, but a gust growing in strength with each step and coming from straight ahead, hitting me in the chest and pushing against my legs, demanding that I double my energy to keep moving. I looked up at the sky and said a silent 'thank you' to Janine for insisting that I walk today and not wait until tomorrow, when the forecast was for storms and rain. At least it was dry and sunny, albeit with a weak wintry sun sitting low in the blue sky.

It must have been about one o'clock when I stopped, took off my backpack and leaned against the embankment to remove the little parcel that Janine had given me that morning. There, lying on its wrapping of waxed paper, was a feast fit for a king. A wedge of creamy Camembert cheese, a chunk of Tomme, a handful of raisins, fat and moist and juicy, a large shiny green apple, and three hard-boiled eggs.

I dived into the food, eating ravenously, making sure not a crumb was wasted. The cheese – with the two slices of bread I'd taken from the breakfast table – was the first to disappear. Then, slowing down, and with infinite care, I peeled the first of the eggs and savoured every bite. I had the second and then the third egg as well, and again I said a silent 'thank you' to Janine, laughing out loud as I thought back to the previous evening when she'd made me traipse up and down the streets of St-Jean-Pied-de-Port to do 'her' errands.

The egg shells were carefully wrapped in the wax paper and tucked into my backpack, the apple went into my jacket pocket and the backpack settled comfortably on my back, now remarkably lighter than before. I took the little bronze Tibetan bell that Nici had given me for encouragement out of the backpack and pinned it on the side, thinking I would probably need the happy tinkle for company and encouragement over the next stretch. Lastly I had a deep draught of my water, and was about to continue up the mountain when I heard a female voice and a metallic *tac-tac, tac-tac, tac-tac*. I peered down the path behind me and there, far below, I saw two figures. One was dressed in bright red, the other, a smaller person, in bright blue. It was the bright red figure with the two sticks that had made the sound on the tarred road. They were both carrying huge rucksacks, the tops towering high over their heads, and I assumed they must be a couple, a man and a woman, on a mountain hike. I could not imagine that pilgrims would carry such large packs.

The steep incline started to ease off slightly and, other than the strong cold wind that tried to wrestle me to the ground, the going became slightly easier. It looked like I'd reached the summit, but I refused to entertain the thought. I was not going to give my body any reason to throw another tantrum in case it wasn't the actual summit and there were more to come. I kept going.

Suddenly something said to me that I was not going in the right direction. Though I'd continued along the tarred pathway, I seemed to be walking south-east rather than south-west. The strong wind was now assaulting me from the right rather than from the front and, more importantly, my shadow was accompanying me on my side instead of following me. I looked around, realising I hadn't seen a sign for a long time, but as I was not yet as attuned to the signs as I was later to become, it hadn't bothered me. I pulled the guidebook out of my trouser pocket. On the map, I saw that the pathway veered off to the right at the stone cross. Stone cross? It took me a few moments before I remembered that I'd passed a cross. But what I'd seen had looked like a memorial, almost like a tombstone, rather than a pilgrims' cross. It had been surrounded by a little fence covered with ribbons and bits of fabric that fluttered in the wind, giving it a festive air. There had definitely not been any red and white horizontal stripes – the French GR trail signs – or a scallop shell or any other noticeable indication that there was a path leading off to the rocks on the crest in the distance. And the cross was now almost an hour's walk behind me.

I turned around, trying hard not to feel dejected. All at once I became aware of several things. For the first time I became aware of the fact that despite the freezing cold temperature, my body was drenched in perspiration. I also realised that I had been drinking a lot of water, taking a few sips regularly along the way – again, not so much to quench a thirst as to satisfy some need my body was manifesting. My pack had become a lot lighter, and I wondered how much water I had left. And I became aware of the dropping temperature and the fading light. It wasn't getting dark yet, but the light was dimming, almost as if there was a cloud that had moved across the face of the sun. And that was when I realised that there were indeed clouds appearing in the sky. Their shadows were racing past me, one after the other, and behind me there was a rapid gathering and closing of ranks in the skies. They were starting to look very menacing. 'Enough of this melodrama,' I admonished myself. 'You've lost an hour. You have to make it up. It won't take long. It is downhill all the way to the cross.'

I set off at quite a pace, finding it awkward walking on the steep downward slope, and feeling muscles in my legs that I hadn't used before creaking into action, unwilling, complaining. Then, coming round the next bend, I saw the red person *tac-tac, tac-tac, tac-tac*-ing towards me and, about twenty metres behind, the blue person walking slowly and with difficulty. The moment they saw me, they stopped. The blue person found the nearest rock and sat down, looking utterly dispirited.

'You are walking back?' her companion asked. Coming closer, I could now see that she was a woman of slight build, probably in her forties, but hard to place as she had a woollen cap pulled low over her eyes and wore dark glasses.

'This is the wrong road,' I replied. 'We should have turned right ages ago, at that cross we passed.'

'The cross with all the pretty ribbons? But there was no path there. And there was no sign either.'

'I am afraid it seems that that was where we were supposed to turn off anyway,' I said.

'This is a catastrophe!' She glanced back at the blue person, still sitting slumped on the rock. 'My sister is finished. She says she can't go on.'

I looked back to where her sister was sitting. It didn't take an expert to see that she was indeed finished. She had that look about her that I had barely warded off only ten minutes before, when I discovered that I'd walked at least three or more kilometres in the wrong direction. Her body was not throwing a tantrum; it had simply thrown in the towel.

'She has to get up and keep walking,' I said, making my way back to where she was sitting.

'The problem is that we did not bring enough water and we have no food. We thought the *refugio* at Orisson was open, and that we would eat lunch there, but it was shut.'

I had a fleeting tinge of guilt when I remembered the sumptuous meal I had enjoyed. 'And water? How can you have no water?'

'Well, our bottles are empty because we also thought we would find fountains on the way. Oh, sorry. My name is Brigitte and this is my sister

Lisl.' She was distraught, and I could well understand why. To be caught out with no water halfway up the mountain was dangerous. After Orisson, at the seven-kilometre mark, there was absolutely no *refugio* of any kind until you reached Roncesvalles on the other side of the range and at the end of the twenty-seven-kilometre stretch. In addition to having to contend with all these taxing conditions – exhaustion, cramp, blisters (this is where most pilgrims had their first experience with that ubiquitous pilgrim's pal), reduced oxygen, the cold, the wet and the blustering wind – hypothermia and dehydration were to be avoided at all cost. Looking at the state that Lisl was in, it was not too hard to see that her body had simply given up, and the chances were good that the reason was dehydration and lack of fuel.

I bent down and offered Lisl my water pipe. She hardly looked up, but grabbed the pipe and started sucking strongly on it, pulling me down with it so that I stood bent almost double, my face close to hers. I watched the life-saving water course through the plastic pipe, from my backpack into Lisl's mouth. I stood by helplessly as she drank her fill, until only bubbles passed through the pipe. Now all my precious water was gone as well.

'Oh, I'm so sorry. I did not want to drink it all.' She looked at me for the first time. Almost immediately there was life in her face again, animation in her body, gratitude in her eyes.

'That's okay. I'm just so pleased that I could help. Here,' I took the beautiful big green apple out of my pocket, 'take this. If you two haven't eaten since breakfast, you must be starving and there's no way you can continue without having eaten something.'

Both Brigitte and Lisl looked at me with such relief that I wondered what would have happened to them if all three of us had not missed the turn-off and met in this forsaken spot on top of the mountain. The thought was too scary to contemplate.

'We heard your bell,' Brigitte said. 'All the way we could hear your bell.'

'Oh, that is my daughter, Nici,' I laughed. 'It is her voice that says, "Come on mom, you can do it! You can do it! You can do it!" She urges me on all the way.'

They both laughed. 'We will remember that. When we want to stop and not go on, we will remember your little bell, Nici saying, "You can do it!"'

'I shall see you tonight in Roncesvalles?' I asked.

'Yes, tonight in Roncesvalles,' they beamed together, 'and thank you, thank you, thank you again.'

'*Buen Camino!*' I called over my shoulder, satisfied that the water, the apple and the thought of Nici, the bell, would get them over the mountain. When I finally reached the turn-off at the cross, it took me a little while to find the pathway, but then I set off into the wilderness. No more tarred roads, no more signs of people or animals or even birds; just the sad sough of the wind over the rocks and crags and the tinkle of the little bell pinned to my backpack, urging me on: 'Come on Mom, you can do it! You can do it! You can do it!'

The next few hours were much more demanding than anything that went before. The footpath was often hardly visible and the signs were few and far between. It seemed that the path was formed by nothing more than the footprints of countless pilgrims. It did not seem to be tended where it cut through copses of pine trees, over stones and rocks. As soon as I came over what I thought was the last summit of the mountain, I just smiled, for I saw that there was yet another, higher mountain looming ahead. This time I was not surprised or caught off guard. I was ready for it. What did catch me unawares, though, was that suddenly everything was covered in white. It was difficult to see where to go as the snow had turned to rock-hard, treacherously slippery ice. There were no tracks to confirm the route and mostly it was a guessing game as to whether I was still on track. What made it even harder was that I was now walking in deep shadow, as the sun had already dipped behind the mountain peaks. And it was cold, oh so bitterly cold.

I was slipping and sliding all over the show and was worried that I would fall and break a wrist or an arm. Having fallen some years before, I knew how easily it could happen. I took the two sticks, 'John' and 'Jill', off my backpack, extended them to a comfortable length and started using them to keep my balance on the slippery ice.

Soon the extra exertion started making me very thirsty. My throat was on fire, my chest felt as if there were burning coals smouldering in it, my legs screamed to be given a rest. And I had no water left. But there was the snow. I started picking up handfuls and stuffing it into my mouth. It was heaven. I ignored the fact that my gloves were getting drenched and that the cold was seeping in. It did not take much time before my fingers were completely frozen and painfully numb and I had difficulty keeping a grip on the sticks. Every now and then the sun flashed over the horizon behind the trees and lit up the ice, a million diamonds coruscating in the rays piercing through the black branches.

At one stage, just when I had a moment of doubt about my ability to stay the course, I heard a sound behind me. I stopped, leaning hard on my sticks and struggling to find my balance, and looked around. A tall man was walking towards me with long assertive strides, his face practically hidden by a woollen cap pulled low over his forehead, his eyes fixed on the ground in front of him. His concentration was fierce, his body taut, every step a deliberate action. He looked as if he was crashing through an invisible barrier, every muscle strained against the fatigue and exertion trying to hold him back. He had to walk right by me, and I stood ready with a smile and a 'thank you' for coming at exactly the right moment to give a much-needed boost to my own struggle against that barrier. But he brushed right past me, his concentration on the slippery ice not allowing him to look up even fleetingly. In fact, I don't think he even noticed me standing there. I watched him determinedly forging ahead, and sent a quiet '*Buen Camino*' after him as he disappeared over the next rise.

It was only months later, after I returned home and read what I'd written in my journal that night, that I recalled the incident:

Journal entry:
The hardest day in my life. *Nothing* has ever been this demanding, not only physically, but mentally as well. On that stretch through the snow and over the ice, before the last steep climb to the summit (yes, I eventually did reach that elusive summit!), I seriously wanted to wrap myself in my space blanket and crawl under a bush, shut my eyes and shut out reality. I just wanted to stop the world and get off. I wanted to go to sleep and wake up and find that it was all a dream. I started bombarding myself with questions. Why was I there? Why was I doing this? What had possessed me to start in St-Jean-Pied-de-Port? Why had I not just started in Roncesvalles? Was I mad? And then another pilgrim came storming past me. I never saw him before and never saw him again. One moment he was there and the next moment he was gone. A strong reminder that to survive I had to keep going. To stop was to die. No one was going to come fetch me and take me to warmth and safety. No one could walk for me. No one could continue to put my one foot in front of the other – only I could do that. And to do that, it served no purpose to remind me of the man with one leg who had completed the Camino several times, or the woman in a

wheelchair who had done this only a few months ago. I did not need an example of someone who had done it with much more difficulty than I. I, and I alone, had to dig deep to find strength and resources within *me* – resources that I never even knew existed. I was amazed at my own strength. And then I thought of Terrie and her battle against cancer. Is this what she experiences every day? Is this *anything* compared with her own daily mental struggle? My awe and amazement shifted to my friend and I felt renewed admiration for her. But it took a stranger – who never even spoke a word to me, who never even looked at me – to make me realise that inherent strength and resolve within me. Thank you, pilgrim, whoever you are! (– but how I wish now you would make a small detour and go walk past my friend, Terrie, today…)

Since my return, I have often been asked the question, 'Didn't you ever want to give up?' Each time I reply, 'No, there was no way I could even allow that thought in my head, for if I thought it, my body would have collapsed and refused to continue. So I did not ever think that I would give up.'

But, recalling that first day, that first mountain crossing, and reading what I had written in my journal that night, I realised that later I so successfully pushed any negative thoughts out of my mind that I even managed to forget that they had once existed. It was a little like childbirth – you only remember the pleasure and the joy, and it's impossible afterwards to recall the pain. Again I realised that if I had not experienced the hardship and feeling of defeat – *and overcome it* – on that first day, I might never have completed the pilgrimage, for later there were many times when the challenges were far greater, far more demanding, and the temptation to wrap myself in my space blanket far more appealing. But reaching that final summit of the Pyrenees on day one assured me that there were resources deep within that were mine for the taking if only I cared to dig for them.

The next few hours passed in silence and solitude. The path started climbing a much steeper course, and the only sounds were my heart beating – a deafening noise in my ears – and the scrunching of my boots on the snow. From time to time I stopped to scoop up some snow for the thirst and need for water, each time feeling guilty that I was not following Pierre's strict instructions: 'Never drink cold water, and when you're on top of a mountain and you want to eat snow, put the snow in your camel bag and let it melt and warm up against your body before you drink it.

When you're exerting yourself and your system is warmed up, ice-cold water can be very bad for you.' But there was no way I wanted to stop long enough to take off my backpack, get out my camel bag and struggle to push snow into the small opening. I decided to take my chances.

When I did stop and turn around, my own single file of tracks in the hard crust of the snow surprised me. I felt so alone on top of this mountain, but the tracks made it look as if there was someone right behind me. I wondered what had happened to the tracks of the man who'd passed me earlier and, for that matter, to Thorsten's tracks. Where were they? Had I gone off the path again? But I pushed the doubts away. There was only this one possible way to go. Despite the lack of signs or directions, I was quite sure I was not lost.

The last crest, the highest summit, was a glorious moment. By the time I reached it, I felt as if there was fire pumping through my veins, hot embers in my lungs, acid poured over my muscles. Every part of me was burning. As if to confirm the feeling, my hot breath formed a cloud around me in the icy air. I looked down and imagined I saw steam rising from my body. My backpack seemed to weigh a hundred kilos and my feet felt like lead.

And yet, the moment I took the final step that placed me on Col de Lepoeder, the highest point where, from the dizzy height of 1 410 metres, I could look down the other side of the range and see Spain stretched out in front of me, all pain was momentarily forgotten. The ordeal was something of the past. In front of me was a sprawling plain that seemed to go on for days. I could see other mountain ranges on the horizon, and, as if choreographed, the sun hovered low over them, highlighting their beauty. Almost immediately the villages and houses that dotted the plain started flickering as people switched on their lights and lit their fires. The menacing clouds that had accumulated earlier on the other side of the peaks were now nowhere to be seen and only soft wisps of stratus clouds streaked the sky. Below me I could make out the rooftops of the big monastery of Roncesvalles. As I looked at my watch, the church bells started chiming – a joyous intricate pattern – the deep tenor reverberating off the rock face of the mountain, the treble rippling down the valley: the perfect welcome to a first-time pilgrim who had just reached the top of her first mountain.

The last five or so kilometres to the monastery were straight down, or so it seemed. At times it almost felt as if I was shooting down on a wire-slide. I had to put on the brakes so as not to break into a run. But it was also a section that made a profound impression on me, for dotted all along the pathway were small, compact stone-built bunkers or hideouts that must have dated back to the Spanish Civil War or, possibly even earlier to the *Falange* fascist movement, then the second World War. Did the Basque separatists perhaps use them too? Something ominous and menacing held me back from entering one of them, but from the outside they looked like a smallish dugout, reinforced with stone walls and a stone door frame. All that remained of what must once have been life-saving- or death-dealing shelters, were now nothing more than sinister black holes leading to the unknown space inside – dark, one-eyed Cyclopses hiding in the undergrowth, crouching with their backs against the steep incline, ready to pounce on anyone who dared to come up the winding pathway.

Later, all along the Camino, I came across more remnants of wars that had been fought in these mountains of northern Spain – the stark reminders of the violence and desperation of people fighting for what they believed in. It was interesting to be making a pilgrimage – a journey that would hopefully lead to spiritual enlightenment and better understanding of yourself and of the world we live in – through a landscape that bore testimony to so many wars and so much violence. Perhaps, though, it was fitting on this journey of self-discovery, for the pilgrim to be reminded of the countless people who believed so strongly in an ideal or a god or a way of life, that they would lay down their lives for their belief. A thought-provoking concept…

I have always abhorred apathetic people and their subsequent lives of mediocrity. Not aspiring to improve or enrich or enhance, when excellence is within reach for every one of us, must surely be *the* most mortal of sins. Apathy and mediocrity kill the human spirit; it kills the soul. Yet, it is frightening how many people, in trying to rise above mediocrity, do not pursue excellence, but adopt fanaticism instead. Going from the one extreme to the other is far easier than finding the balanced, rational, moderate middle way. I admitted before how I've stood in awe of, and envied, those who believe so strongly that they can discard inhibitions and embrace their beliefs, their faith or their ideals. This is particularly true in a society where anyone who speaks out for their beliefs – be they ideological, religious or lifestyle – are immediately labelled and shot down as fundamentalists, racists, bigots, neo-something-or-other, fanatics, and yes, terrorists. But there's a very fine line between faithful and fundamentalist, between fundamentalist and fanatic. There is also a fine line between awe and horror. Be it religious persuasion or political conviction, when a commitment becomes an obsession – when a strong belief becomes blind fanaticism, when principles become prejudices, when a freedom fighter becomes a terrorist – it is not admiration that you feel, but horror and fear. And the consequence is more often than not a war, when the worst in man is brought out and then made acceptable in the name of the cause. Perhaps everyone who has given orders to torture, to shoot, or bomb or destroy should be made to walk the Camino barefoot and empty handed…

But the sun was setting, it had been a long and eventful day, rich with new experiences and fraught with confrontational challenges, and I needed to get to my first *refugio* on the Camino, so I left the history of those conflicts, brave spirits and unfortunate souls behind and set off again to make my own history.

It was about six o'clock that evening, already dusk, when I arrived in Roncesvalles, the 'Valley of Thorns'. As the main and 'official' starting point of the Camino in Spain, this was where the Confraternity of St James had their offices. It was very impressive. There was a large, imposing 11th-century Augustinian monastery complex with a chapel in the centre, administrative offices as well as dormitories for pilgrims. As with many of the *refugios* along the Way, it had originally been a hospital for pilgrims. This one at Roncesvalles, being on the 'other' side of the mountain, and precariously stuck halfway down the side of the western mountain face, was built on the graves of pilgrims who had not been as successful as I in crossing the mountain. According to legend, it was open to 'all, sick and well, not only Catholics but also pagans, Jews, heretics and vagabonds'. I was happy in the assurance that there was a place for me too. Not certain where to go and what to do, I walked in at the main entrance and made a beeline for the first open door. Behind a huge oak desk sat a stern-looking priest, sorting through a pile of papers.

'*Bienvenida*,' he said in a serious tone, with no smile, no warmth to underline the words. For a moment I felt quite awkward. This was the first time I'd met a Spanish-speaking person on the Camino and my complete lack of knowledge of the language suddenly made me feel at a distinct disadvantage. I knew that you should learn a basic minimum of Spanish as not many people on the Camino spoke anything else. Not only does that make sense, but it has always been my custom to learn at least a few necessary words before embarking on a journey to a foreign country. I don't have a particular gift for languages, but learning the thank-yous, pleases, good mornings, good afternoons and goodbyes in any language is not too difficult for anyone. And yet the short time I'd had available before starting the Camino somehow flew by so fast that, I'm ashamed to say, I had not even learned so much as two words more than my previously acquired Spanish vocabulary. Later I found that my knowledge of French went a long way to bridge the language gap, although sometimes even that was not enough to make myself understood, and on more than one occasion I said a silent *muchas gracias* to the authors of the Camino guidebooks for including a few basic terms in Spanish.

'Good evening,' I replied in French. 'I am starting the Camino and wish to register here with you. I hope I'm not too late. Could you tell me where to go?'

'You have come to the right place. This is where you register. Please take off your backpack outside and come back with your passport and nine euros,' the man replied in fluent French.

Still he did not smile or make me feel *bienvenida* or welcome at all. I was slightly bemused. Was this the Camino spirit? Or was it just bad luck that the priest on duty happened to have come to the end of a long, bad day? I relieved myself of my backpack and went back inside.

'Sit down,' he said, without looking up from his paperwork. 'You must be tired.' Some more shuffling. 'I will be with you in a minute.' He took his time stapling a bunch of papers together and tossing them on to a high pile next to his blotting pad.

'*Alors! Vous êtes française? Laissez-moi voir votre passeport s'il vous plait.*' And suddenly all his attention was focused on me, his eyes lit up and a smile chased the scowl from his face.

He took my passport and opened it. 'Ah, you are English!' he exclaimed, this time in perfect English.

'Um, well actually no. I am a resident of France but I was born in South Africa and I have a British passport. I have dual citizenship...' For a moment the look on his face was very confused.

'Not important,' he said. 'South African, English, French — you are now on the Camino and you are a pilgrim. Welcome to Spain and to the Camino de Santiago de Compostela!'

He started writing my details on the yellowed pages of a thick register. I craned my neck to see how many other pilgrims had arrived before me. (It did not take me long to learn to read the register book upside-down to see exactly who had arrived before me or had gone through the *refugio* the day before.)

'Only two other pilgrims,' he murmured without looking up. 'You are the third one tonight and probably the last. It is too dark now to be walking in the mountains. It is very different from the summer. Then we get several hundred pilgrims every day.'

I wondered who the two pilgrims were. Was it Thorsten – and who else? And what about Brigitte and Lisl?

'I met two women on the mountain earlier today. Have you seen them?'

'No, not yet. But perhaps they are not staying here. There is a little hotel in the village.' I wondered again what the Camino etiquette was. What do you do when you know there is someone on the path and you're not sure of their safety? I liked to think that if the roles were reversed, they would have worried about me too.

'Don't worry,' he read my thoughts. 'I will check to make sure they have arrived safely.' My fears were allayed and, many times in the following weeks, I realised how much assurance those words had given me. Someone on the Camino was always on the lookout for you. You were never completely alone.

'Is this a religious or spiritual pilgrimage for you, or a non-religious pilgrimage?' I had been asked countless times why I was walking the pilgrimage, but no one had ever specifically posed the question. Interesting, I thought, particularly as this was not just a long walk, but a *pilgrimage* ... Perhaps it was also a question that should be asked again at the end. After only one demanding day, I already had the feeling that the experience would change many people's initial motivation.

'Spiritual,' I said, and he wrote it in the book. Name, place of birth, nationality, birthday, gender, place where I had started my pilgrimage, and reason for doing it. All my details noted in the Camino register.

Next he took a small concertina-folded document from the top drawer of his desk. On the front was the line drawing of a pilgrim's staff with a gourd for water and the scallop shell, the *coquille St Jacques*, attached at the top, and on the back, a map of the route of the Camino.

'These are your *credenciales*, the pilgrim's passport,' he explained as he unfolded the metre-long document. There were at least 50 little blocks in a grid in the passport. All the details about me that had gone into the register were now being filled in on the flyleaf of the passport.

'You must keep this in a safe, dry place and look after it, and every night when you stop at a *refugio*, you will be asked for it. You can only stay in the *refugios* if you have *credenciales*. Then the host of the *refugio* will stamp it for you and he will write down your details. If you don't stay in a Camino *refugio* but in a private one or a hostel or a *posada*, they will also be able to put the *sella*, the stamp, in it for you. There are places like the churches you walk past where they also give stamps. When you get to Santiago de Compostela, you take it to the Camino office next to the cathedral and they will give you your *compostela*, your certificate.' With a flourish he stamped the first little square, dated it and handed the pilgrim's passport over to me. I felt a lurch of excitement.

'*Buen Camino, peregrina!*' Suddenly I felt different; I *was* different – a different person from the one who had come into the room only thirty minutes before. I was officially a pilgrim.

The Roncesvalles priest (I never learned his name) then emerged from behind the large oak desk and told me to follow him. After carefully locking the office door behind him, he led me across the now-dark courtyard to the other side of the building, through a large double door, down a cold corridor and to the entrance of a big room filled with row upon row of steel bunk beds.

'Choose one of the beds.' Pointing to two beds with backpacks already lying on them, he added, 'You will see, like here, when pilgrims arrive at the *refugio*, they claim their beds with their backpacks. These packs belong to the two boys that are already here. Over there is the bathroom where there is plenty of hot water. There are no cooking facilities, so you must eat in the little restaurant next door. They have a good pilgrims' menu for eight euros. The food is very good, but you must order your food before seven o'clock, otherwise you will not get food. You'd better hurry. It is almost time. At nine o'clock there's a mass in the chapel for pilgrims.'

I was still digesting all this information when I realised that he'd left the room. I heard him walking down the stone corridor and then the big double doors slamming behind him. I looked around. Two backpacks were already there. Who did they belong to? If one was Thorsten's, whose was the other? The prospect of sharing my 'bedroom' with two strangers was a new experience for me. In my 57 years, I had never, ever slept in a dormitory before, or with total strangers. Bed number four, right in the corner, under the window, that was mine. I leant my backpack neatly against the bed, hung my sticks on the corner of the bunk above mine, took a photograph and went out to look for the restaurant.

And that was the night that Akira, my second Camino angel, crossed my Camino path.

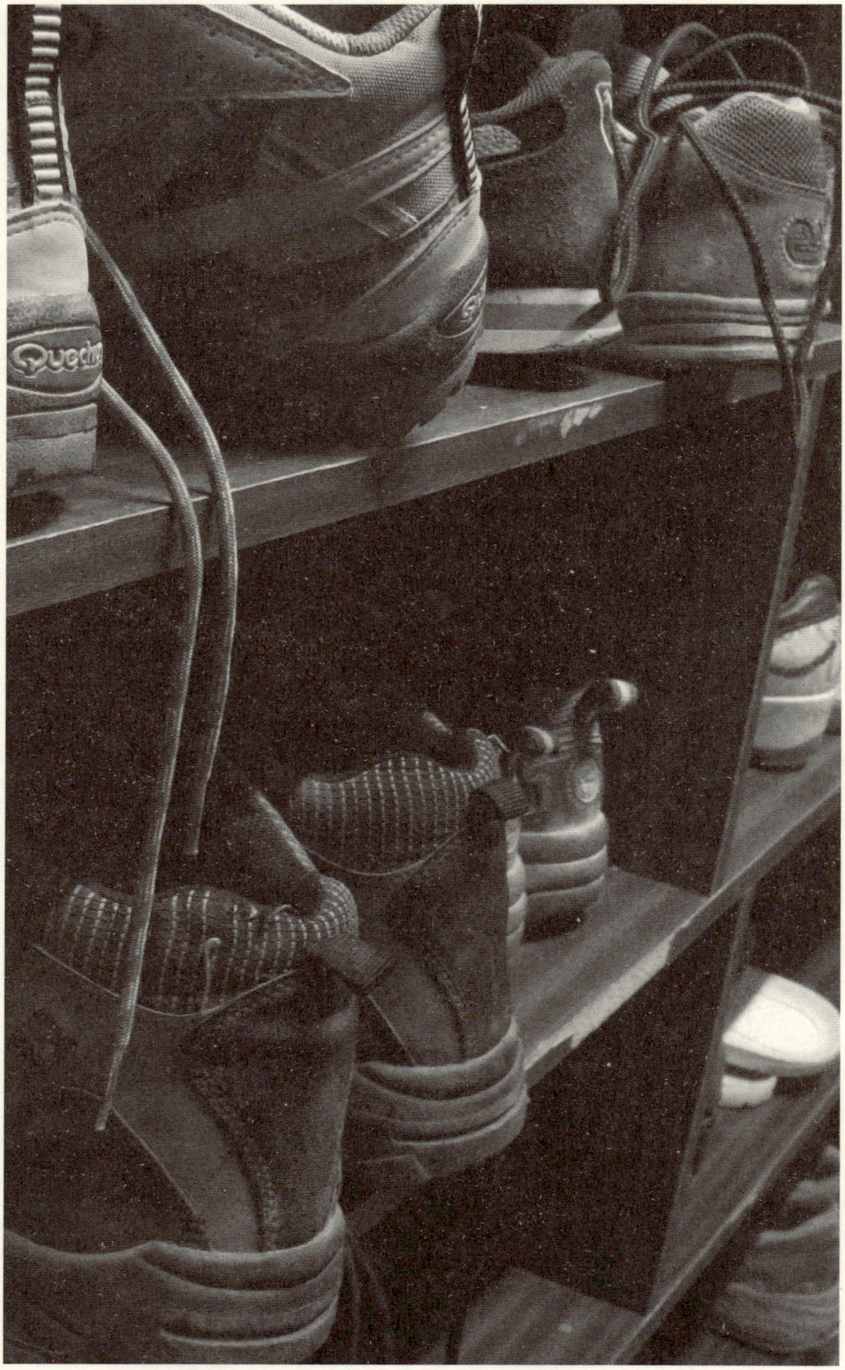

4

On solitude, silence, companions and friends

Experience shows that the spirit is nothing but awareness. Whoever has greater awareness has greater spirit… When the spirit becomes greater and passes beyond all bounds, the spirits of all things become obedient to it.

– Rumi

When I walked into the warm, smoky little restaurant, it took me a moment to take in the noise and the large number of people. It seemed so utterly incongruent with what I'd experienced that entire day – the silence, the solitude, the serenity of that overpowering but empty landscape.

'There she is! Wilna, here! Come, your beer is waiting.' What a welcome! I saw the smile and the open arms first. I was expected – as if it was the most natural thing in the world for me to walk in where 'my' beer was already waiting, to be among old friends, where I belonged. At a table in the corner, Thorsten was sitting with a young Japanese man; three big frosted pint glasses of beer in front of them. Judging by the other empty glasses on the table, I guessed they'd had a substantial head-start on me.

I walked over to them and felt as if I was coming home. 'This is Akira. Akira, this is Wilna, she has just walked over the Pyrenees today.'

'Ah-soh!' Akira's eyes stretched wide open, his eyebrows shooting up, the exclamation sincere and very complimentary. My smile was hooked behind my ears.

'Yes, I did it, didn't I? Whoo, Thorsten, that was fantastic! And now I really *am* ready for anything that comes my way.'

'I fly to Pamplona and I come here with the train today,' Akira responded to my question. 'I have only three weeks, so I can't start in

St-Jean. But that is *my* Camino'. What Akira's very broken English lacked was more than made up for by his animated face and gestures. And his expression 'That is *my* Camino' was something we were to hear often over the following weeks. What others would possibly have called fate, karma, destiny, luck or misfortune, Akira called '*his* Camino', as if the Camino was his particular cross he'd been made to carry, or a particular pleasure he had been awarded. It was an acceptance of whatever came his way that was not only admirable, but enviable as well.

I immediately took to Akira and found in him a kindred spirit. He was a tall, trim man, whom I judged to be in his mid-twenties. It was only a couple of weeks later that I realised he was much older, but still, when he told me he was 38, I found it hard to believe. His face, at first glance, looked younger. Possibly it had something to do with his profession as a musical actor; and the fact that his build was lithe and athletic, his face always highly animated and that he moved like a dancer – light and with an energy that was electric. Probably the youthful image may also have had something to do with his endearing use of English. A language can so easily create an illusion of an almost childlike naivety, as the speaker struggles to express his thoughts in a language he has not mastered. The ultimate luxury is having the vocabulary with which to express yourself; not being able to find the words you need, or knowing the grammatical framework in which to place them, brings you down to the level of a child. No matter how intelligent or knowledgeable you are, if you don't have the means with which to express that intelligence or knowledge you'll always be at a disadvantage.

I might have misjudged his age for any of these reasons, but it very soon became abundantly clear that this young man had an intellect and wisdom far superior to the average. Despite his limited English, he was witty, funny, sharp and fascinatingly interesting. I had not spent half an hour in his company when I already wished I'd met and known this man all my life.

Through the years, I've had the extreme good fortune of visiting Japan on many occasions, accompanying my husband on his business commitments as well as in my own capacity as a trainer and speaker. From the moment my feet first touched Japanese soil, it was love at first sight. I loved everything about the country and the people. I loved the Japanese system of honour, Japanese traditions, their attitude towards religion; I loved Japanese food, culture, the arts, the theatre; I loved their tenacity and their striving for excellence in everything they do. Although I have mixed feelings about the notion of reincarnation, one thing I am certain about is that if I had a previous life, it was lived in Japan. Consequently, on this pilgrimage – which already felt like a rebirth for me – there was something poetic in my meeting a Japanese kindred spirit on that first night, over a first beer and a first pilgrim's meal in the 'Valley of the Thorns'.

Long before my beer glass was empty, Akira and I were chatting like old friends who hadn't seen each other in a long time. Thorsten stayed quiet and smiling for most of the time, while Akira and I were behaving a bit like children, not able to contain our excitement about the three of us meeting and the anticipation of the journey ahead. As Thorsten had walked the Camino before, and this was our first time, we knew that his experience would be invaluable to us and we had a million questions to ask him.

'You will experience many things on the Camino that you are not expecting or anticipating. Be ready for when that happens, because of course sometimes it is a little bit frightening.' It was interesting that Thorsten did not sound like a young obnoxious know-all, but rather like someone who definitely knew what he was speaking about. In the weeks ahead, Akira and I often remarked to each other how remarkably wise this lovely young man was for his twenty-four years, with an insight into people – and an understanding of what makes them tick – that neither of us had seen in people twice his age. We never doubted his words, and we wanted to know more.

'No, you will find the pleasures and the surprises yourselves. Maybe they will be different from the ones I have experienced. Maybe sometimes they will be the same. But I promise you, there will be many times that you will laugh and many times you will cry, but for sure you will have many very wonderful experiences.'

Three weeks later, after one particularly long day on the *Meseta*, the mostly flat and featureless tableland of the central part of the route between Burgos and León, I found myself in Calzadilla de la Cueza. Although this was one of the smallest hamlets that I stayed in, there was internet access, albeit very basic. I had a strong suspicion that there was a little boy behind the wall, blowing on coals to keep them going and provide the steam which generated the power to work this very archaic piece of equipment. Except, that is, one never saw little boys or little girls. In fact, there seemed to be no children in this country. If there were, I had no idea where they were.

What's more, I had no idea where the people were. For three weeks I'd walked through one village after the next that looked like an abandoned set on a Universal Studios plot, ghost towns all of them. It was very eerie. Far off on the horizon I could see big trucks on the highways and occasionally I heard a train somewhere in the distance. But I rarely saw people along the Way. I had read about the depopulation of the countryside and was aware of the problems this posed, not only to the future of the Camino, but also to the region's economy. Still, it was a strange, other-worldly experience to see a vast landscape devoid of human life. Only in the big places such as Burgos were there lots of people, lots of traffic, smells and noise as well, and then it was hard to stay calm and keep my composure. I realised how easy it is to forget what it's like to live in a world full of people.

That night, in Calzadilla de la Cueza, a village with a name longer than its main street, I sat alone in front of the monitor, tucked away in a dark back corner of the room, trying to get to grips with a keyboard with only blank keys – the letters having been completely worn away by the fingertips of thousands of pilgrims who had preceded me. As I looked down in exasperation at this tired and worn keyboard, I suddenly had a wave of recognition wash over me. I felt the presence of all those pilgrims who'd sat where I was sitting; who had tried to have their fingers remember which keys represented the letters they needed to write a message home to loved ones – to tell them they were still safe on their pilgrimage. I could almost hear them cursing under their breath when they typed and the wrong letters came up, turning their messages into gobbledegook. I could almost feel their breath on my back as they paced the floor waiting for me to finish so they could have their turn. I could almost see their smiles as the screen lit up and they found messages in their inbox from someone back home telling them that they were missed. In that moment of solitude, I felt utterly and wholly part of this confraternity of the Camino. At the same time, I was aware that this feeling had slowly been creeping up on me for a long time. In fact, it was a feeling that had started to manifest itself on that very first night in Roncesvalles when I shared a beer with Thorsten and Akira and we spoke late into the night – about why we were on the Camino, about our fears and hopes and expectations.

It was over that first meal from the pilgrim's menu, bought for the princely sum of eight euros – a delicious and nourishing broad bean and potato soup, a huge plate of tender veal stew and a large glass of ice-cold, frothy beer – that we quickly recognised in each other fellow-pilgrims.

Perhaps it was that the three of us were starting our pilgrimage from the same place and at the same time. There was definitely something special about the bond formed between we strangers who had embarked on a journey together. Or perhaps it was that we'd been brought together by a common purpose. As individuals, we were different in every way – age, background, culture and language – yet we sensed subconsciously that where one lacked, another might be able to compensate. Each individual's assets and characteristics complemented those of the others – a type of a synergy where the combined whole of our little band was far, far greater than the sum of the individuals.

In his book on the Camino, Coelho speaks of being more accessible to others around you on the journey because instinctively you know that they may be able to help you in difficult situations. The Camino was in many ways a survival course: you had to dig deep to find the resources within yourself in order to get through each day. It was astonishing to find resources you'd never been aware of, but it was also frightening when a needed resource was simply not there, no matter how deep you dug. And it was then that you came to appreciate the other pilgrims around you. Everyone has talent. Sometimes we only discover that talent late in life, but the talent is there for the finding. And the Camino was the perfect place for the 'big reveal' of those hidden talents. If I could find resources within myself that I'd never known I had, so could every other pilgrim. And it was the pooling of those resources that created the bond among pilgrims. Not only did each have the wondrous pleasure of discovering their own latent potential, but each also had the unrivalled pleasure of being with other people who had a need for their particular talent.

Later I learned that for many pilgrims this was the one special aspect of their Camino – the remarkable goodwill, generosity and voluntary interdependence among pilgrims. I frequently heard pilgrims talk about this wonderful phenomenon of the Camino. It could be something that a fellow-pilgrim had offered in the form of advice or spiritual guidance, clothing or toiletries, water or food. Often the biggest source of surprise was the fact that the generosity came from someone who 'wasn't even a Christian'. There seems to be an unspoken assumption that someone who walks the pilgrimage has to have some degree of religious motivation, and the expectation is that, to show kindness, their religion must be Christian. Whenever this subject came up in conversation, I was astounded at people's preconceived ideas about other religions, because almost every time an act of random kindness surprised a pilgrim, it came from a non-Christian. My only surprise was that those who offered assistance seldom realised that what they were really offering was not necessarily something tangible or material, but something of themselves. They were releasing a small piece of their own spirit into the universe, and the universe was the richer for it.

I have always believed that 'what goes around, comes around'. My smile, my positive attitude, my helpfulness, my generosity of time and energy almost unfailingly generate a similar response from people around me – friends and strangers alike. The payback may not happen immediately, and perhaps it will come from someone completely different, but people's actions and behaviour towards you are often a reflection of what you transmit. And yet many pilgrims seemed to find this to be the most amazing thing about their pilgrimage, because they'd obviously not come across this side of the human spirit very often before. How incredibly sad that people should be surprised at the random kindness of others; but how incredibly wonderful that they make this discovery on the Camino. For this seemed to be the way of the Camino – bringing the spirit of people together from all ends of the planet, all walks of life, all faiths and creeds, but with a single goal, to walk 'the Way under the Stars'.

Whatever it was that acted as the glue binding us together, my little 'Camino family' was formed that night: Thorsten, a 24-year-old university student from Cologne; Akira, a 38-year-old gay musical theatre actor from Japan; and me, a 57-year-old Eurocentric African woman from France. And even on that first night we knew the bond between us was stronger than most people experience among their blood relatives.

'You two are my Camino family,' Akira said many times during the following three weeks. 'You are my Camino mother and Thorsten is my Camino father.' That Akira was years older than Thorsten, whom he called his 'father', and was possibly not quite young enough to my 'son' was neither here nor there. For once, age was not the issue, and for me this was wonderfully refreshing. The three of us – without having to say anything about it – felt that a close bond had been forged that night, and for all of us the bond was to prove very important over the next few weeks.

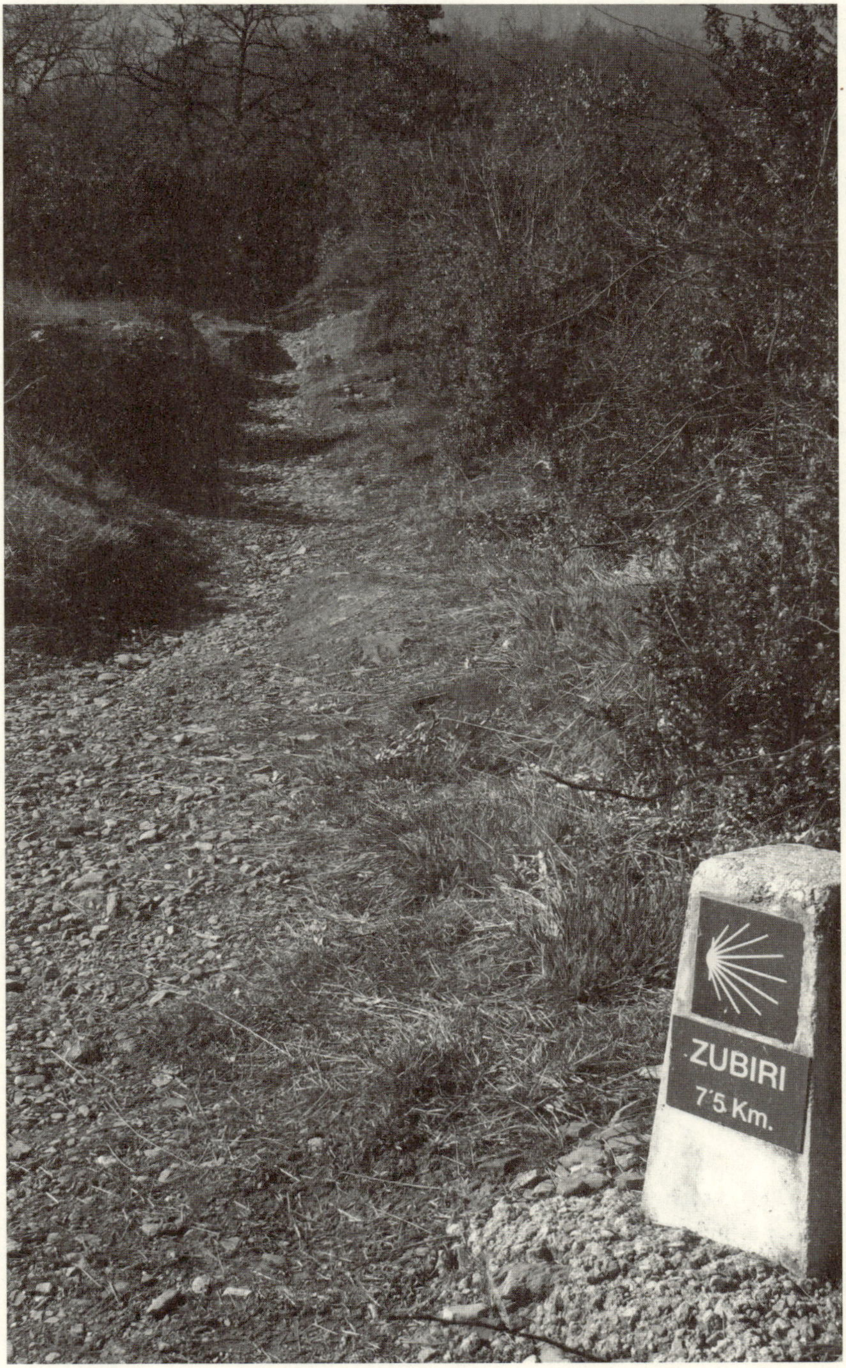
ZUBIRI
7'5 Km.

5

The signs you see along your way don't necessarily point in the direction you want to take

Life is one big road with lots of signs. So when you are riding through the ruts, don't complicate your mind... Don't bury your thoughts, put your vision to reality.

— Bob Marley

Journal entry:
There was something ironic about following a pathway where there were signs at just about every 50-metre interval to show you the way, but where there was not a single sign to warn the pilgrim of any danger.

It took a walk along an ancient pilgrims' path for me to realise the importance of signs. As I wrote in my journal: there was something extremely comforting in knowing that every ten or twenty minutes there would be a sign to show the way. And once I learned how to recognise them, realised their importance and how convenient they were, it wasn't difficult to start recognising all the 'other' signs and understanding the roles they play in our lives and survival — all those signs that become our means of navigating our pilgrimage through life.

There are numerous signs on today's Camino; and to every pilgrim, they're a lifeline. Before I began the pilgrimage, I'd promised myself that I would never get to the stage where I talked to myself. It was very tempting, walking alone as I did, to start having conversations with myself, but somehow, somewhere (probably in my childhood) I was persuaded that it was the first sign of losing your marbles. So I continued conversations with myself, but only in my head, and the few times I did speak out loud to an empty space was when I needed direction.

'A sign please! I need a sign!' I would call out whenever I realised that I'd been walking for twenty or thirty minutes without seeing a sign. This didn't happen too often, but every now and then – when I doubted for a moment that I was still on the right path, or when I reached a crossroads or a fork in the road and didn't see a sign – I broke my promise to myself. It was quite uncanny (and I could easily have come to the conclusion that there really were magical things that happened on the Camino); every time I called out loud for a sign, one 'appeared'; a shell on a stone pillar or a fence post or on the corner of a building, or a little bright yellow arrow painted on a tree trunk, a rock, a stone wall or on any possible flat surface.

The yellow arrows are more numerous than the shells, probably because they simply require a brush and enamel paint. Kilometre after kilometre I wondered about who was responsible for all the little arrows. Someone had to have walked the entire way with a tin of paint and a brush, looking for any surface where an arrow could be painted, in spots where they, the painters, felt the need for direction. How heavy was that tin of paint? Did they have a ladder to get to the higher spots? What did they do when the paint was finished? Where were these arrow-painters? You never saw them, yet some of the arrows looked as if they'd been painted only days before. There must have been many of them; it wasn't just a single arrow-painter, because sometimes you could see that the arrow-painter was a perfectionist, the outlines and angles of the arrows being meticulously executed; at other times the arrow-painter was sloppy, the arrow smudged and streaks of too-wet paint running down the side of the wall. There were times when the arrow was camouflaged by the exact same colour bright yellow lichen that grew everywhere – on tree branches and rocks and stone walls – and it was a little like playing 'Where's Wally' to find the arrows.

'I think the arrow-painters are little trolls that only come out at night,' a fellow-pilgrim remarked one night when the subject came up for the umpteenth time. It really was a riddle we all wanted to solve.

'Don't be silly.' (Humour does not travel well across the boundaries of language and culture and often misses its mark by miles.) 'It must be the people from the different municipalities who are responsible for keeping the pathways clear and clean.'

Apparently every village and town through which the Camino passes has at least one employee who takes care of the pathways within a certain radius of that community. This in itself must be a mammoth task and these people are heroes in the eyes of pilgrims. This 800-kilometre footpath, through forests, over fields, across plains, up and down mountains and alongside rivers, is always kept immaculate. Debris is cleared, stones are laid where rainy weather would create slippery mud, scrub and undergrowth are clipped and cut back and trees and pretty plants are planted, watered and tended along stretches where no natural flora grows.

'I saw one of those workers the other day. He was cutting back the bushes on the side of the pathway, and I asked him if he was also the man who painted the yellow arrows. He said no, he wasn't. And when I asked him who the arrow-painters were, he just smiled and shrugged his shoulders.'

'Ha! You see! It's definitely little trolls that come out from under the rocks!' We all laughed, but then fell silent, each wondering about gnomes and buckets of paint and little yellow arrows. We never did decide that night who painted the yellow arrows, but we were infinitely grateful to whomever it was, for without those little arrows, there would be many a pilgrim wandering in the wilderness, lost to this world.

It was only about two thirds of the way, in the stunningly picturesque village of O Cebreiro, that I discovered the history behind the yellow arrows. There, at the summit of the last big (and really tough) mountain a pilgrim has to climb, at 1 300 metres, was a memorial to this wonderful man who had the idea of painting the arrows. The village, with its single, cobblestone street, has no more than about twenty houses, some of them the original *pallozas* – oval-shaped stone and thatch dwellings that are typically Galician and date back to Celtic times. There is also a little church that holds one of the most important relics of the entire pilgrims' route; two vials containing the bread and wine that had turned to flesh and blood when the miracle occurred early in the 16th century. The pilgrims' hospital was built in the 11th century, and still stands, beautifully preserved. In contrast, the pilgrims' refuge is now one of the most modern on the Camino, and without a doubt, the refuge with the best view. It was while discovering all these treasures of O Cebreiro that I came across the bronze bust and the legend of the very first arrow-painter, Don Elias Valiña Sampedro. After reading about his contribution to the Camino, I decided this man was most definitely no little troll!

Again, as with most of the history, the myths and the legends of the Camino, the story of this great man differs among sources. What everyone agrees on though, is that he was a Doctor of Law, an expert on Compostelan studies and the parish priest at O Cebreiro, all at a very young age. Don Elias was passionate about the Camino de Santiago de Compostela. From the time when he came to O Cebreiro, he dedicated his life to the pilgrimage. Not only did he help to restore the village to its current World Heritage status, but he also wrote the criteria for the pilgrims' refuges and helped restore and revitalise the ancient Jacobean pilgrim routes. He drew the first comprehensive set of maps of the route and then produced the first simple but detailed guide book, small and light enough to fit into a pilgrim's pocket and inclusive of a complete list of all the religious sites and relics along the way.

And then of course, it was Don Elias who initiated the way-marking of the entire length of the Camino Frances. In the early eighties, he went to the Galician highway authority and begged them for their surplus yellow road-sign paint. Then, all the way from the Pyrenees to the Cathedral in Santiago de Compostela, he painted bright yellow arrows on every surface he could find – walls, gates, trees, rocks and roads.

Definitely another Camino angel. Or was that Sant Iago himself disguised as a humble parish priest?

Anyway, I say ¡*Muchas gracias, Don Elias! ¡Usted es el amigo verdadero de un peregrino!*

As much as the yellow arrows are indispensable, the sign we generally associate with the Camino is the scallop shell, the other symbol that soon becomes your friend on the long walk. It comes in many shapes and sizes, sometimes painted, sometimes carved, sometimes cast in bronze and laid into the cement or tar of the roads. How can you ever describe that feeling of elation and joy when, at the end of a long arduous day, you trudge through the noisy, crowded and busy streets of one of the big cities, looking for the refuge and you stand at a traffic light, look down, and there you see a beautiful bronze shell nestling against your feet, nudging you to go in the right direction? Or when you walk through a dark, silent forest, on a pathway of fallen leaves, alone with your thoughts, and as you look up you see a stone pillar with a carving of the scallop shell on its side, pointing you in the right direction? How can you ever explain the sensation of your spirit being lifted when you see the shell above the refuge door and you know that you have arrived – in a warm, safe and welcoming place where you can rest your weary bones, be with friends and be re-energised. There's something quite magical about that shell – whether it's presented in its natural shape or in a modern stylised form, it is just as much the symbol of the Camino today as it has been for more than a millennium.

I am aware of the wondrous fact that animals, such as the magnificent Namibian elephants, can walk hundreds of kilometers through the Namib Desert in search of water, and that they do so using some innate sense of direction; and that homing pigeons can fly across oceans and find their own particular coop on the rooftop of a Manhattan skyscraper. I'm sure that aeons ago our forefathers must also have had an instinctive sense of direction that took them to warmer climes or more abundant food and water. How sad it is then that we've allowed that useful talent to be swept away by waves of easy living, gadget lures and technological decoys. It is said that the total length of the Way lies directly on a ley line, where the energy force of the earth and the cosmos come together with the greatest strength. Perhaps it is exactly that force that gives all creatures an instinctive sense of direction. Celtic druids held such places sacred, and you can imagine that finding a ley line 800 kilometres long must have been the greatest discovery of their time. The fact that the end of this line was where the life-giving sun dipped into the sea at the end of each day explains why they used this route as a pilgrimage for thousands of years. But sometimes I did wonder how the pilgrims in ancient times coped. Other than the Milky Way at night (and I've yet to be convinced that it can give more than a general direction) and the sun during the day, at your back in the morning and on your face in the afternoon, I don't know of any other indicators they would have had for direction. Anyone who's ever walked cross-country without modern tools such as a GPS, or even an old fashioned compass, will tell you that going in the general direction of west is one thing, but going along a specific route where there are water stops, rest stops and places to sleep overnight is a completely different matter. And add to that the fact that you're walking on average nine or ten hours a day, every day, for thirty or forty days, you will want more than the sun in the sky or the stars by night to guide you. There were of course the carved stones along the way as well. The first pilgrims on this route came even before the Celts, but they left little of themselves behind. When those clever Celtic tribes started walking towards the sun, they left signs for us everywhere and the Celtic rose (or sun motif) with which they marked the way, is still to be seen – albeit mostly incorporated into more recent Christian symbols.

Walking always with the sun close to you, either behind you in the mornings warming your back, or overhead at midday, or in front of you, leading you through the afternoon, was a remarkably comforting and reassuring feeling. Seeing the familiar Celtic sun carvings on the stone crosses or ancient fountains along the way made me feel as if I was in the presence of the thousands of pilgrims who'd come that same way before me; pilgrims who must have had exactly the same feeling as I did. The Celtic sun was arguably the strongest universal symbol of protection known to man and it is therefore no surprise that the motif, sometimes further developed into a spiral, epitomised eternal life. Growth, warmth, protection, giver of life... No wonder the original pagan pilgrims walked this way across Europe and the width of the Iberian Peninsula to get to the end of the earth, to Finisterre, where the sun dipped into the sea.

How clever then of the Church to incorporate that Celtic sun into their own designs. It was fascinating to see just how many pagan symbols appeared in stone carvings all along the way. The Pilgrims' Cross, which can be found at regular intervals on the entire Camino, is a good example. On the Camino, the pilgrim cross has two sides. Coming from the East – from Rome or Jerusalem, or your own back door on the European continent, you see a carving in the stone of the Christ crucified. Coming from the west, after having completed your pilgrimage, the carving is either of the Madonna and Child or of the Celtic rose or sun. As the pilgrimage was a kind of life insurance for Christians against the threat of eternal damnation, it made sense; going towards redemption, you were reminded of Christ dying on the cross for you, and coming back you had the new promise of life after death – depicted by the Christian or pagan symbol of rebirth and eternal life.

Walking during the winter months – the countryside only just starting to emerge from its long sleep, still tucked under its grey blanket with lots of snow, hoary frost and thickly iced-over streams in its deepest folds, a woolly layer of mist softening its contours – the sun was a welcome sight at any time. To feel its warmth on your back in the mornings or on your face in the afternoons was wonderful. But the most encouraging thing about the sun – which had, no doubt, deified it through the passage of time – was the sure fact that it would appear in the east every morning. Its consistency, its reliability, its power was what would have made it the one constant in a pilgrim's journey. No matter how dull the morning, there was – and always will be – light at the end of a long, dark night.

Later, apart from adopting and adapting the pagan symbols, the Church also added its own symbols, and to this day, the scallop shell is the recognised sign showing pilgrims the direction they need to take.

Why the scallop shell? Remember the legend of how Saint James's remains reached the shores of Galicia, in a crew-less boat? The story continues that a wedding was taking place as the ship approached land and the horse on which the bridegroom was mounted took fright, plunging them both into the sea. Miraculously, they emerged, covered in shells. The scallop shell also had practical associations with the Camino – it was the perfect size for scooping water or to function as a bowl. And, because it is native to the shores of Galicia, it served as proof that a pilgrim had reached what was then thought to be 'the end of the world'. One of the Confraternities of Santiago websites elaborates on the metaphor of the scallop shell:

> The grooves in the shell, which come together at a single point, represent the various routes pilgrims travelled, eventually arriving at a single destination, the tomb of Saint James in Santiago de Compostela. The scallop shell is also a metaphor for the pilgrim. As the waves of the ocean washed scallop shells up on the shores of Galicia, God's hand also guided the pilgrims to Santiago.

Reading these stories about the origins of the ubiquitous scallop shell sign, I couldn't help wondering again at our need to attach symbolism and meaning to everything in our lives. Is this just another way of finding a sign in all that surrounds us, in all that happens to us? Is this ultimately our way of looking for direction in our lives?

The 19th century French philosopher and poet, Charles Baudelaire, said: 'The whole visible universe is but a storehouse of images and signs to which the imagination will give a relative place and value; it is a sort of pasture which the imagination must digest and transform.'

I marvel at people's ability to find a sign in just about everything, or their penchant for using their imagination to give a meaning, a relative place and value, to everything in their lives. It never ceases to amaze me that people can let the *Bible* fall open, look down, pick up on one single random verse and than rely on their selective interpretation of that verse to provide an answer to a crucially important question in their life. Realistically this is no different from tossing a coin and finding the answer in the *I Ching*. The answer is no more than the relative place and value your imagination gives to it. We all do it to some degree, but this phenomenon is probably no more prevalent anywhere than on a pilgrims' route, such as the Camino. Somehow, I could relate to it in this context, and to the people who felt the need for signs in their lives to give them direction and show them the way.

There were so few people on the Camino with me during those cold winter months that I knew there was no way for me to gauge the average profile of a Camino pilgrim. During summer, when tens of thousands of people walked the Way, it would be far easier to establish a notion of nationalities, gender, age, religion and other aspects of origin. But, judging from the handful of people that did cross my path, I found the demographic of the Camino that I'd read about to be well represented: there were at least three men for every woman; most pilgrims were between twenty and thirty years of age, with probably about one in ten older than fifty; most came from the European continent and most were on foot. Of my fellow walkers, at least eighty per cent were between twenty-four and twenty-eight years old. Most of them came from Germany and Scandinavia, with a smattering from other European countries, from Australia, China and Japan. But after reaching Sarria, everything changed. Sarria was the magic hundred kilometres-to-Santiago mark, where hundreds of (mostly Spanish) people started an abbreviated pilgrimage in order to arrive on Easter Sunday. Anyone who has walked the last hundred kilometres of the Camino, or cycled the last 200, and who has had their *credenciales* stamped along the way (at least twice a day), receives one of the two official pilgrims' certificates. Pilgrims who walk the Way with religious or spiritual motivation receive a beautifully designed, Latin inscribed *compostela*. Anyone who completes the pilgrimage with any other motivation is recognised and honoured as well, but with a plainer-looking certificate.

The few fellow-pilgrims on the Camino with me were there for different reasons, but there was one thing they had in common – they were hoping to find *some* answer on the Way – be it to do with their spirituality, their future, their choices in life, or their relationships. Reading their signs, it was clear that, particularly those in their twenties, were affected by the crazy, mixed-up world we live in. Their search for clarity was often what motivated them to subject themselves, spiritually and physically, to the ordeal of an 800-hundred kilometre pilgrimage. These lovely young people came with a huge amount of baggage dragging them down. Some came with a wall of preconceived ideas surrounding them — a wall so high and thick that it was sometimes almost impossible to find a chink somewhere and start breaking through, not to get in, but to allow them some light by which they could start breaking down the wall from the inside. There were those who came with brains washed so clean of traditional and meaningful values and principles, and jammed so full of brand names, media jargon and slogans that sometimes all you could see when looking into their blinkered eyes was a large billboard or a flickering plasma screen. This was the generation that had grown up with too few direction signs and too many warning signs; the generation whose lives had become so cluttered with warning signs that familiarity had bred contempt and these signs had now become almost invisible to them. But all had a need to find their unique place on this planet of ours.

As a teenager, Pierre had made a sign to hang over his bed that read: 'Do not get out of bed unless you are willing to learn the lesson of the day — even if it is a tough and painful one. Otherwise, kindly remove yourself from the human gene pool.' He believed that was the only warning sign there should be. Unfortunately though, he is not the world's official sign writer. When you think about it, we live in a world where we are warned against every possible danger — real or imagined, possible or probable, relevant or totally random. It seems to be the ultimate advantage of living in a first world country with a sophisticated western civilisation. From the moment we wake up in the morning to the moment we switch off the bedside light, the warning signs are there: Keep out of reach of children. Keep away from eyes. Wash hands carefully after use. Do not breathe in the fumes. Do not place near heat. Do not open near a flame. Do not use when pregnant. May be hazardous to health. Beware of dog. Parental control advised. Not for children over twelve. Not for children under twelve. Use at own risk. May be subject to terms and conditions. Could be harmful to health. May contain lactose, nuts, wheat, gluten, protein...

It was probably not surprising that, from the first day I started walking the pilgrimage, I was struck by the fact that there was an abundance of direction signs, but a complete lack of warning signs. It was clear that Health and Safety had never heard of the Way of St James, or they would have been in there a long time ago putting up signs on every lamp post, every tree, every fence post, every rock along the 800-kilometre pathway. They would have warned the weak hearted, the faint hearted, the frail and the feeble against the many dangers and demands of the pilgrimage. For, be warned – severe dangers and exacting demands there are aplenty!

Every time I walked up one side of a mountain and every time I descended the other side I wondered how people coped who came from a background where everyone was warned against every possible danger and never had to use any natural instinct or sense of survival and therefore became ill equipped for the real world. How on earth did they manage to stay alive?

There were no barriers anywhere and no warning that there were no barriers, even though the sheer drop directly on the edge of the path was often hundreds of metres, ending in a gorge far below, where there was no human access. There were no signs to warn that on the next stretch of twenty-six kilometres there was no fountain, no tap, no stream, no source of water at all, and if you walked during summer when the temperatures often rose to the upper forties, the lack of water could mean sure death. There were no warnings of uneven ground and slippery mud, of dangerous road crossings, of poisonous plants or contaminated water, of unstable rocks at river crossings, of snakes or spiders or of human predators. And there were no warnings against possible shifts of tectonic plates – even if those were only going to occur in your own personal landscape.

I was soon to have a more expert opinion on the lack of warning signs on the Camino, from the wonderfully named Michelangelo. 'If you had all those warnings on this pilgrimage, you'd have to close it to the public. It is far too dangerous.' Michelangelo was one of those *hospitaleros* or refuge keepers that you could write an entire book about. A long, frizzy beard – 'free-spirited' was the phrase that came to mind – and equally long and free-spirited hair that surrounded a shiny bald pate and dominated his small frame. His colourful mohair cardigan, which was probably a regular size for a regular-sized man, hung down to his knees and added to the gnome-like impression he gave. To round off the caricature, he sported a pair of small, round John Lennon glasses on the end of his nose; the lenses as thick and distorting as two highly polished pebbles. He presided over a beautiful refuge in a picturesque village named San Xulian, where I had dashed through an inviting open door to escape from the cold and drenching rain.

'Added to the dangers, there are also the dangers of the pilgrim being tired or preoccupied with his thoughts and not concentrating on where he steps or what he does.'

'Yes! Like being occupied with taking photographs! Going up Alto del Perdon, I was trying to get a photograph from right under one of the windmills against the blue sky. I kept inching my way back further and further to get a perfect angle, when I became aware of being watched. There, no more than two metres away was a wild pony on the narrow pathway – or at least, I think he was wild because he was just there, on his own, on the side of the mountain. The pony saw me looking at him, stared at me for a minute or so, and then turned away and disappeared around the next bend in the path. That was when I looked down and realised that I was standing right on the outer rim of the pathway and that there was nothing, but nothing, behind me. If I'd stepped one more centimetre back I would have fallen straight down the side of that mountain.'

'So! You met Sant Iago, then! He is the reason we don't put warning signs on the Camino.' Michelangelo was buttering a chunk of freshly baked bread and adding thick slices of home cured ham. He pulled a paper napkin out of a basket standing on the beautifully polished oak counter of the bar, placed it on a decoratively cracked and chipped saucer, put the tasty looking sandwich on top and pushed it across to me. I glanced at him, waiting for a telltale smile to show that he was speaking in jest, but he looked up at me and in all seriousness asked, 'Is that the only time you have seen Sant Iago?'

If this conversation had taken place anywhere other than on the Camino, I would probably have been tut-tutting and sniggering, but there were too many signs on the Camino that were loud and clear in this context, even if they could never be explained or justified anywhere else. In fact, it didn't even enter my mind to comment about the fact that the pony had appeared from nowhere and had disappeared again into nowhere. The only place any animal would have been able to walk on the side of that mountain was on the pilgrims' pathway. Anywhere else would have been too steep for even a mountain goat. Yet one moment the pony was there and the next moment he was gone, and I never saw him again.

But, as many pilgrims often mused when something surreal or illogical or just plain strange happened: 'This is the Camino...' There I was, sitting at the bar counter in the entrance of a charming little refuge, my sticks and backpack leaning against the legs of the stool and a number of backpacks with name tags in a pile at the door where the taxi had dropped them for walkers who were arriving that night. While eating a deliciously fresh and succulent ham sandwich and drinking steaming hot chocolate from a large earthenware mug, I was having a conversation with a charming, if somewhat hairy gnome named Michelangelo about saints that appear to pilgrims in the shape of wild ponies – and it all seemed quite normal.

'I never realised how much easier life is when there are signs to follow,' I continued, wiping the crumbs from my chin. 'It's only now that I realise our lives are full of signs keeping us on the right road – only we hardly notice them because of all the warning signs that clutter the roadside.'

'It is good that you realise that. But you know, even the good signs on the Camino – the shells and the arrows – mean that sometimes the pilgrims don't see any other important signs. That is the way of our world.'

I looked around me, at the walls that were covered from ceiling to floor and from corner to corner with photographs, postcards, mementoes, all sorts of colourful and interesting things. It was one of those rooms where you could spend days looking and still find something you hadn't seen before.

'When I look at your collection of memorabilia, I see signs of someone who probably also believes the saying, "If you are under twenty-five and not a communist, you have no heart; if you are over twenty-five and still a communist, you have no head".'

'Ah! George Bernard Shaw! And you have seen the signs on my wall! Bravo!' The two of us moved closer to one wall where, in a prominent place in the middle of the crowded wall, was a collection of signed photographs and hand-written letters – all featuring Che Guevara.

'If you look there, that man standing next to Che, that is my father's brother. That picture there shows the small group of intimate comrades of Che. They were together for a long time… There is another photograph of the two of them. They were good friends. And the letters… I think every day I must put them in a special place or maybe frame them…'

Michelangelo (it *really* was his name) smiled wistfully and I could almost see the many ghosts and memories swirling round his head as he thought back to the stories his uncle had told him.

'So was that him too? He looks very handsome!' I pointed to a dapper looking man in full military regalia.

'No. He looks like his brother, no? But that is my father. He fought in the Spanish army in Morocco.'

There were pictures from all over the world. 'And this? It is you!'

'Yes – in the Gobi desert. When I go away from here once a year, I go practise my hobby. I am a bit of a caveman.' He continued to tell me about all the places where he had climbed mountains and explored caves – Gobi, Jordan, Morocco, Mount Ararat… a far cry from a small twenty-bed *refugio* in the middle of a pilgrimage route in northern Spain.

'You are full of surprises! And on top of it all you like beautiful music. That is Donizetti playing, isn't it?'

'Yes. My daughter is a classical guitarist and is playing in that piece you are hearing. Her name is Minerva Gomez. Perhaps you have heard of her?' I had to admit I had not, but made a note to find that CD, for the music was sublime.

'Another sign on the Camino that shows you that people are not always what they seem at first glance?' I laughed at the way he had so cleverly brought the conversation right back to the subject of signs – obviously a topic close to his heart as well.

'You know, there are not many people on the Camino at the moment, but I have met only three so far who are walking the pilgrimage for religious reasons. One is a young woman who was raised behind the Iron Curtain and is now hoping to find the signs that will lead her to God. So she is in fact looking for God on the Camino. I suppose that has been the motivation for millions of people through the centuries.'

'Definitely. That used to be the main reason why people walked the Camino – to find a sign of God.'

'Well, I suppose that's understandable. But it worries me that they're looking for a preconceived idea of what that sign should be – and they're missing all the true and clear signs that are all around them.'

I thought about Brigitte, who had told me she was hoping to find God on the Camino and have Him reveal Himself to her so that she could be baptised in Santiago at the end of her pilgrimage. However, she had a fixed idea of what God looked like, and how He should appear to someone who was seeking Him. What Brigitte could not see and did not realise was that God was already in her. She'd brought her sister, who'd had a major personal upheaval in her life a few days before Brigitte was due to leave. Lisl didn't want to come and I'm quite sure someone would have told Brigitte she was mad to take her unwilling sister with her. But, as important as this pilgrimage was to Brigitte, she still didn't listen to warnings and insisted her sister should join her. Lisl gave the impression of being a difficult travelling companion; she was a hard-smoking, hard-drinking woman, and seemed to be focused on a path of self-destruction. But Brigitte nurtured her through each day and eventually, by the time they reached Santiago de Compostela, managed to change Lisl's bitter outlook on life completely.

God did not appear to Brigitte; or so she thought. She did not find what she was hoping to find. There was no bearded face in the clouds in the sky, no sudden beam of light that fell at her feet, no epiphany in the mist. But, anyone standing on the side of the Way watching her, would have been able to tell her that God *had* appeared to her. Anyone looking at her photographs of the Camino would have recognised that the way Brigitte saw the world was with the eyes of a person with a deep faith, someone who believed in something far greater than herself. She was the most generous, unselfish and caring person. Of all the pilgrims I met who were walking the Camino for their religion or their faith, no one's inner light shone brighter than Brigitte's.

'Always the problem with preconceptions, and none more so than in religion... But if only they would look, the signs are all there and that is for every person, whatever your religion, whoever your god.' It was so true what Michelangelo was saying. I'd had several conversations with people on the Camino who had never experienced anything other than the tiredness, the sore feet, the everyday survival, and sometimes, but not always, the incredible beauty of the Way. When you spoke of the signs of the Camino, they agreed that the yellow arrows were indispensable. But when you asked them about the many other 'signs', most of them looked at you blankly, or in that way that fellow travellers looked at pilgrims when they started talking about spiritual things.

Every now and then one would ask, 'What signs are you talking about? Not that mumbo-jumbo nonsense of some saint appearing to the pilgrims?'

'No – that apart,' and I would try very hard not roll my eyes in exasperation at the kind of people who seem to have lost all contact with their environment as well as with themselves. 'There are so many other signs.' The subject usually had me as excited as only a convert to a new idea could be. A typical conversation around an old refectory table in a refuge kitchen invariably provided opportunity for me to develop my thoughts on the subject.

'The signs are all around you. Think about it. There are the messages in one form or another that pilgrims leave for each other. I wonder every time I see such a message, like when someone wrote in the damp soil with a stick or scratched with a stone onto another stone. Or when someone broke a branch and left it hanging from a tree, or even a slip of paper sticking out from under a little pile of stones or tucked in a crack next to a fountain. Each time I see a message like that I wonder whether that was also the way the pilgrims of ancient times communicated with each other. They say the Camino was the main communication highway of Europe during its heyday in the 11th and 12th centuries when more than a million people walked it in a year. They didn't have internet or mobile phones to send messages to each other on the Camino, so they must have had other ways to send each other signals.'

'Yes, but those aren't "signs". Those are just messages.'

'Well, if a message telling you that this fountain is the last water you can get for the rest of the day, or that a friend is waiting for you at the next refuge – if that message is not a sign, then what is? It is something that tells you something; that prepares you for something you need to know. Just like the yellow arrow tells you which direction to take.'

'Mmm... I suppose you're right. I hadn't looked at it like that.'

'But there are lots of other signs... There are the signs of the *refugios*. They must be the most welcome sign to any pilgrim at the end of the day, especially if there's the added sign on the door saying '*Operto*'. And yes – there are also the signs that nature gives you, like the clouds building up ahead of you in the west telling you to get out your poncho because it's going to rain. If you don't see that sign, you'll get soaking wet in a sudden downpour because there's never enough time to get your backpack off your back, open it and get out your poncho. And walking in wet clothes in this cold is not funny!'

By this time, others would join in as they started warming to the subject, adding something about a sign we'd all been noticing: 'Or what about the wonderful signs of spring? The further we go now, the more blossoms and flowers there are and the new green leaves on the trees! It is a good sign of the promise of warmer days ahead!'

'Oh yes! Did you guys see those pink trees against the stone wall in that village just outside Ponferrada today? I think it's some kind of quince tree...'

'And the bright yellow acacias against those dark black storm clouds this afternoon?'

'I saw them – they were spectacular! But those aren't signs...'

'And then there are the signs your body gives you: telling you it needs food or water or a rest, or that your shoes are not tied correctly, and you'll get blisters – those are signs!'

'Tell me about it! My body never stops talking to me and giving me the signs! Now I know that my backpack is not balanced when my knees start aching or my shoulders start hurting. It's true, there are lots of signs, you just have to be aware of them and understand them!'

It did not take much to get everyone enthusing about the subject. 'Jokes aside, if you think about it, life is full of signs for us, but we've become almost immune to seeing them. We follow advertising, fashion and fads blindly, and we're so keen to fit in and be part of the crowd that we often miss the signs that have been in place for generations. Signs that are there to show us the correct and honourable way to go through life.'

'Oh come on!' There was always the one in a group. 'Not another Camino lecture!'

In my experience, people who'd chosen to take the road most travelled preferred not to talk about those things that they'd left behind at the crossroads. Being confronted with that fact was not something anyone wanted, but not to face up to it when you were walking the Camino would have been difficult. We live in a world where everything is dictated to us, with no subtleties and no real need for difficult personal choice. And that dictation rarely comes in a positive way – such as little yellow arrows. More often than not it comes in a negative way – via a multitude of warning signs.

People who stand out in a crowd are often the ones who follow the signs of their own making. People, like the explorer Sir Ranulph Fiennes, who are not scared to be the first to chart a course across unknown territory, are the ones who find the safest route up the cliff face; the ones who knock in the first pegs, test the strength of the pitons, discover the safe resting places. Most of us are the *seconds* – the climbers who come after, the ninety-nine point nine per cent who simply follow the footsteps and the signs left behind by the Ranulph Fienneses of this world. Marching to the rhythm of your own drum is of course nothing new, but those people are scarce in this world where conformity is vital for social survival.

And I was not the only one to wonder how I was going to cope once I returned to the 'real' world and the yellow arrows were no longer there…

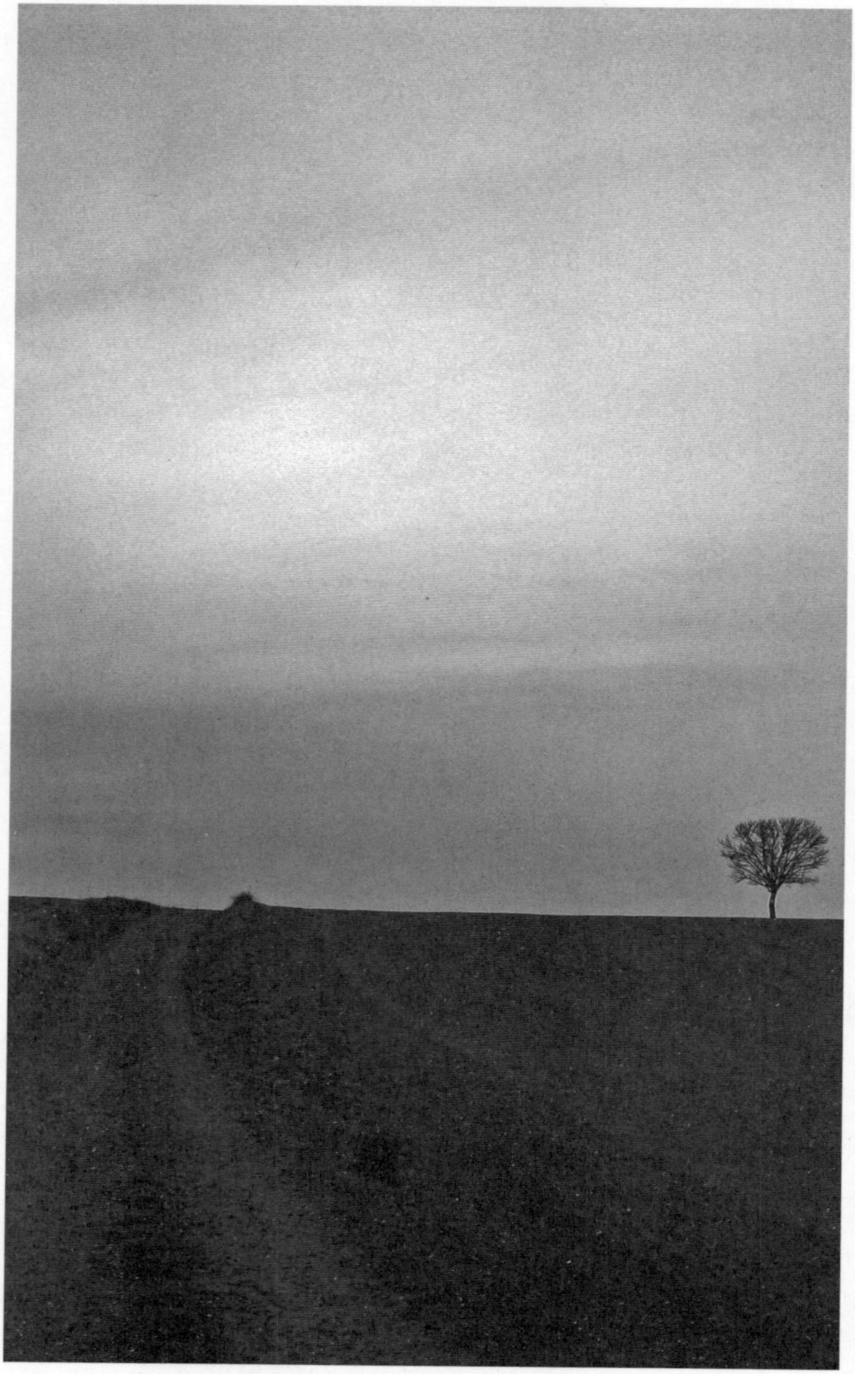

6

Make friends with your shadow, because you can never leave home without it

My barn having burned to the ground, I can now see the moon.
— Leo Buscaglia

On the last day of every term in high school, our Latin teacher told us a story. She had a gift for story telling, and her description of people and places, battles and victories, deception and intrigue made them come alive in front of our eyes. It was only much later that I realised how each of these stories had contained a distinct and useful message that was to stand me in good stead on many occasions during my life. But it was one story in particular that I remembered while walking the Camino.

On the day they signed up as soldiers, all Roman centurions were issued with a bronze shield, which was theirs and theirs alone and, for a common soldier, the only thing he ever owned. Although the shield was heavy to carry, especially on long, difficult marches across the length and breadth of the Roman Empire, this shield served many purposes and a soldier would have been lost without it. When the sun beat down on their heads on the vast arid plains of Iberia, they used it to provide shade and protect themselves from sunstroke. When the wind, the rain, the sleet and the snow pelted down on them in the northern corners of Gaul, they could hold it up as a barrier against the harsh elements. When they were in battle, the shield could stop hot tar or boiling oil from raining down on them as they stormed the gates or climbed the ramparts of an enemy fortress. Out on an open battlefield, they could join their comrades in a tortoise formation, creating a carapace of shields around and over them to stop a flight of a thousand arrows from finding its target and killing them. When they reached a stream, they could scoop up the clear, cool water and drink their fill. And at night, when they finally came to a halt and set up camp, they could lay their weary heads on their shields and go to sleep and dream of the fields of Elysium. And on every Roman soldier's shield, etched into the heavy metal, was an inscription that read: *Hoc quoque transibit*, which means 'this too shall pass'. Consequently, whether the soldier had seen his best friend killed at his side, whether he had a painful injury or his battalion had suffered a crushing defeat that day; or perhaps won a glorious victory, the very last thing each soldier saw before he laid his head down on his shield and went to sleep was the assurance: this too shall pass.

Many times during the years after my children were born, I thought of my Latin teacher's story of the Roman centurion's shield. Every mother should be issued with such a shield to keep on the wall above her bed. When your teenager rages against the injustices of life or floats in an ethereal cloud of first love, when the hormones rage and the young bodies seem to be nothing but an awkward bag of bones hanging loosely on the hinges of the elbows and knees, when you look at them and know that only a mother could love what you see, when your heart bursts with joy or aches with sorrow as you watch your little ones grow into beautiful adulthood… almost daily a parent should be reminded that 'this too shall pass.'

So, what do *you* believe you should never leave home without? An inscribed Roman soldier's shield? Or, as my father taught me: a penknife, a man's handkerchief and a piece of string? Of course the serious answer could be life-saving insulin for a diabetic, or blood-thinning pills for a coronary emergency. That's not the kind of thing most of us feel vulnerable without, but everyone has *some*thing without which they *think* they'll find it difficult to survive.

One of the all-time favourite questions radio and television interviewers ask of the bright, the rich and the famous is, 'If you were stranded on an island and you could choose three items to have with you to survive, what would they be?'

Another favourite question is, 'What is the one single thing you will never leave home without?'

The premise is that the answer will tell us more about the celebrities than they would otherwise willingly have made known. Revealing what you cannot leave home without is the same as revealing your secret weakness, obsession or dream. And the world thrives on hot gossip about celebrities, especially any titbits that show them to be as human as the rest of us. But, when it comes down to survival, this can be a very important question to think about – either for your journey through life, or when you have to pack a backpack that weighs no more than ten per cent of your body weight and which you'll be carrying with you on an 800-kilometre pilgrimage. In both cases, your response is crucial.

For most of us the item we feel we cannot leave home without reflects a habit that's a 'left-over' from childhood – when our security was a worn and frayed old baby blanket that we dragged behind us, or our beloved teddy bear, with his single button eye, his dog-chewed ear and his stuffing spilling out from under his arm, but without which we could not fall asleep. Often the 'blankie' or the teddy was replaced in adulthood with a gadget that was easily explained – a lipstick 'to look well-groomed at all times' or a portable phone 'to be contactable should my office need me'. But, at the end of the day, this item fulfils the same basic human need that the 'blankie' or the teddy did in your childhood.

For others the item is more like a mild obsession. This could be because of a superstition that dictates you can't leave home without your lucky charm, be it a rabbit's foot attached to a key ring, a special handkerchief or a shirt in a lucky colour. You always keep this item with you because you're convinced that you'll be inviting bad luck if you don't. This lucky charm is expected to do what the 'blankie' and the teddy did – make you feel safe and secure. No matter how level-headed we are, how pragmatic or rational, most of us have something that makes us feel more whole and more confident. Anyone who's ever acted as an invigilator for an exam will probably be able to make a list of the bizarre, the weird and the wonderful items that are taken out of pockets and put on desk corners to watch over the owners.

During the years when my own children were at school and university I would always send them off in the morning armed with two things. I'd prepared for them our own special exam-fortifying-energiser raw egg, milk, sugar and vanilla milkshake (exactly as my mother had done every single time I'd gone off to write an exam, run a race or perform a piano recital), and I slipped into their hands a small cowry shell – shiny and rich in browns, blacks and creams – beautifully perfect and fitting exactly into the palm of their closed hand. There it could nestle coolly for the duration of the exam, as a reminder of their confidence, knowledge and serenity. If I had not continued a custom that had been passed down through generations, would they have found something else to take with them? I'm willing to bet they would have. It seems to be human nature, no matter where you come from.

There's definitely much more that can be deducted from a person's choice of 'what they would never leave home without'... and how I wished I'd had those analysing capabilities on the Camino. For all pilgrims come with baggage.

Although the heaviest and most cumbersome baggage pilgrims carry is usually not the contents of the backpacks on their backs, those could be quite revealing as well – and definitely great fun to analyse. Every now and then, when pilgrims arrived early enough at a refuge, straight after the doors opened at around four-thirty in the afternoon, they would unpack, sort out and re-pack their backpacks. At times like these it was astounding to see what some of the pilgrims carried with them. There were, for instance, those who carried what seemed like an entire pharmacy in their packs. Laid on the bed would be cures and palliatives, herbs and spices, plasters, creams and balms, bandages and tape – enough to keep a mobile clinic in a war-torn battleground going for a week. These pilgrims were usually handy to have around, for no matter what your ache or pain, they'd have a sure-fire solution for it. But even after dozens of glimpses into the contents of fellow-pilgrims' backpacks, I never ceased to be amazed. I suppose others wondered about me as well – not so much about the contents of my bag, as the lack thereof. I carried so little that I often found myself at the centre of attention, pilgrims wanting to know how I managed with so little. Even my one 'luxury', a flamboyantly colourful scarf which served as warmth for my neck and face in the early icy mornings, as something dry to sit on when resting or as tablecloth for my simple meals alongside the path, changed from being a source of mirth to being a source of envy when I discovered that if I wrapped it around my backpack and knotted it in front of my waist and so carried my backpack like an African baby, the weight of my pack almost dissipated into nothing at all.

One afternoon, a little earlier than my usual time to stop, I'd escaped from the punishing cold rain into the welcome warmth of a *refugio*, had had my shower, washed my clothes and was lying on my bed, snug in my sleeping bag and writing in my journal. I saw a big, strong man limp into the dormitory and slump down on the edge of a bunk bed right by the door, clearly not able to walk one step further. Lines of pain were etched deep into his weather-beaten face and he seemed to be shaking and in the grip of a fever. I was about to make my presence known, but, even though we were the only two people in the room, something held me back. His whole demeanour cried out 'agony – torture!' When he bent down to untie his bootlaces, I felt I had to avert my eyes, for there were tears running down his cheeks. I did not feel I could add to his suffering by letting him know he was being watched. I felt like a voyeur intruding on a very intimate moment between a man and his pain. So I played possum, lying dead still with my eyes closed.

A few minutes later, however, my eyes flew open. There were strange noises coming from his corner. Swearing, cursing, cries of pain, gasps and sobs. And then, a new sound… At first I didn't know what it was and, even when I saw what was happening, I could not believe my eyes. He'd taken off his boots and then his socks and, when I saw his feet – two big lumps of blood blisters – I could understand the swearing and cursing. But what he proceeded to do was beyond belief. With a small mechanical drill – like one you'd use in the making of jewellery perhaps, he was drilling little holes into each of his toenails.

'What are you doing?' I exclaimed. I simply couldn't contain myself. The poor man got such a fright when I cried out that the little drill slipped and drew blood from his toe. 'Oh! I'm so sorry! I didn't mean to startle you, but I've just seen what you were doing and it looks… Well, it looks…' I could not find a word to describe this macabre behaviour.

'Gross?' he smiled weakly, wiping the blood from his toe. 'I am sorry too – I've been so consumed with this pain that I didn't realise there was someone else in the dorm.' The tears were still glistening in silver slug trails down his cheeks, but he resumed his drilling. I could not bear to watch. 'I'm drilling holes in my toenails to relieve the pressure from the blisters under the nails,' came the voice. 'If I don't do this, the nails will lift after a little while and I'll lose them all.'

I had seen bad blisters. I had seen people's feet where the entire sole was one large blood blister. I had even seen toenails lifting because of blisters underneath them and people then sticking in needles under the nails to relieve the pressure. But I'd never seen anyone – and never thought I would see anyone – voluntarily drilling holes into their toenails. But, the incredible thing was that at that moment, as I stood there wishing I was still lying with my head pulled in under the sleeping bag and trying to pretend that this medieval torture chamber scene didn't really exist, I couldn't decide which was the more surreal: a man drilling holes into his nails, or a pilgrim who carries a drill in his backpack! I knew that I would not be asking him what else he had in his pack.

Less surprising but no less revealing were the little stuffed toys impishly peeping out of side pockets. Scraps of an antique silk kimono tied to a shoulder strap; an enamel coffee mug dangling from a belt; a small plastic bag of flour with which to make a white sauce base for delicious meals; a book on architecture; a few sheets of paper, a handful of envelopes and a strip of stamps – to write letters (those people still exist). A small stash of dope; a pillow case; a dictionary; luminescent pink bed socks; a framed photograph; a box of washing powder; an alarm clock, the alarm a crowing rooster...and yes: a little bronze Tibetan bell whose delicate tinkle reminded a pilgrim of her beautiful daughter. Each item a little peep into the life and personality of its owner. What added to the unexpectedness was that the people who carried the strangest things were invariably also the people who had *not* brought the most essential and practical things with them which every pilgrim needs – such as ear plugs for a peaceful night's sleep in a dormitory full of snorers, or NOK cream or Vaseline to cover your feet every morning so you don't get blisters. It was also surprising that those items that were thought to be indispensable for the pilgrimage experience sometimes did the exact opposite: they prevented the pilgrims from experiencing something rare and unique.

A good example of how the 'indispensable survival item' could become a hindrance was the ubiquitous iPod. Several pilgrims would have left everything behind if they had to, but their iPods were a permanent fixture – plugged in, regardless, as if they were attached to an umbilical cord. Hour after hour, day after day, they walked from one magnificent landscape to the next breathtaking scene – and everything they saw, they saw through a haze of hip-hop sounds, reggae rhythms or heavy-metal decibels. I could, to a degree, understand their need for the constant noise beating on their ear drums; in many ways the iPod was the company they craved, their replacement for their childhood teddy, or their way of 'breathing out' the pain.

But the Camino is not only about the face of nature – the beautiful scenery, majestic mountain ranges, mysterious forests or medieval hill-top towns. The Camino is also about the voice of nature.

Between San Bol, with its colourful murals and tattered Tibetan flags providing splashes of colour in the otherwise-bleak landscape, and the picturesque village of Hontanas was a gradual series of steep rises. At the top of the highest hill, the ground levelled out onto a large plateau. There was a blanket of low-lying mist that day, but having reached this high plateau, I found myself above the mist in bright sunshine, under an azure sky. I felt as if I'd been lifted up on top of the world. I could see for a few hundred metres in every direction, but beyond the rim of this plateau everything was obscured by the thick mist. The terrain was completely flat and round – it was like standing in the middle of a large disc floating on top of the clouds, and should you walk to the edge, you'd disappear into a void. There were no trees and nothing other than stony tilled fields that did not look as if anything would ever grow in them. The only raised relief-feature was the slightly higher sides of the pathway where the stones had been pushed up over many years by countless ploughs. I stopped, wanting to take in the feeling of standing in the middle of this vast flat space, completely alone. And then I heard it: the chorus of a thousand birds. I looked around but there was no movement, no living creature to be seen anywhere. I thought the birds must be very small and must be somewhere on the tilled soil, but as hard as I peered at the fields, I saw nothing – only stones. Yet the sound was as if I were standing inside a giant aviary. It was melodious birdsong, and it was exquisite.

I walked a little further to where there was an opening in the stony embankment of the pathway onto the field. This was a good place to stop and rest a little, perhaps even fall asleep for twenty minutes with this beautiful concerto playing around me. As I started to take off my backpack, I suddenly noticed that I was not alone. There, already lying with their backs against their packs, their faces turned up to the welcome sunshine, was 'my little Camino family' – Thorsten and Akira. I had not seen either of them for a few days, but somehow it made perfect sense for the three of us to meet here. As if it were the most natural thing in the world for me to arrive right at that moment, and, as if they'd been waiting for me all along, they both languidly turned their eyes towards me and smiled.

'It is very beautiful, don't you think?' Thorsten asked. 'We don't know where the birds are. But they sing for us, for sure.'

I had no need to say anything. I simply put my backpack down and lay down against it, closed my eyes, and drifted off into the sweet sound of nature's music, my two boys close by.

Later, when I spoke about the birdsong in those fields, it struck me how few pilgrims had heard it. And the saddest thing was that everyone who'd missed it was plugged into an iPod.

But, as the days wore on and the backpacks felt heavier and heavier, as the kilometres piled up and the knees and the hips and the feet felt the burden more, pilgrims gradually became aware of the extra weight they were lugging along with them. Like a snake shedding its skin, people started shedding their baggage. That which was previously thought to be indispensable showed itself first as completely unnecessary, and then as an irritating burden. From about one third of the way into the Camino, whenever they arrived in a slightly bigger, populated town, many a pilgrim headed straight for the post office to mail their little parcel of unnecessary and unwanted possessions – addressed to themselves at Poste Restante, Santiago de Compostela. The intention was, at the end of their pilgrimage, to pick it up and take it back home, but I often wondered how many of those parcels were never picked up. How much of that baggage that was shed along the way was left unclaimed long after the pilgrims had returned home? I spent many an evening sitting on my bunk bed rifling through the contents of my backpack, looking for something I could send to myself in Santiago. But every time, I found myself shaking my head in astonishment at just how little I'd brought with me. There really was nothing superfluous in my pack, nothing that I could remove and so lighten my load; even the handle of my toothbrush had already been broken off to lessen the weight! And for someone who regularly had to pay for overweight luggage on aircraft, this was truly a wondrous discovery to make! If there was one thing everyone learned on the Camino, then it was that you don't need much in the form of worldly possessions to get you through life. Not much at all.

Yes, it definitely was interesting and fun to guess pilgrims' secrets from what had replaced their childhood security blanket, but sadly, the most burdensome, the heaviest, the most redundant baggage that many pilgrims had brought with them were the things that could not be parcelled up and sent to a Poste Restante mailbox.

Lack of confidence, false pride, futile regret, prejudice… and more prejudice, preconceived ideas about any- and everything under the sun, feelings of being lost, feelings of confusion about the world we live in, fear of being alone, fear of commitment, frustration with mediocrity – these were all elements of the baggage I saw fellow-pilgrims carry with them. And the irony was that, more often than not, the pilgrim's back was bent so low under the burden of their baggage that, had the answers to all their questions jumped onto their path and stood right in front of them, waving a flag to get their attention, they would not have recognised those answers.

In all fairness it has to be added that it took a lot of courage and determination to find the answers, for it invariably meant having to search within yourself, a painful exercise at the best of times, and those answers you found were not always the ones you'd hoped to find. While walking the Camino, I found that every now and then I'd get an answer to a question I never knew I had. Sometimes it takes being in an environment or a situation that is so alien to you, so new, so different, to highlight the question marks in your life. It was as I was pondering on the sentimental baggage in my own life that I suddenly realised where I'd gone off course during the almost ten years that I'd lived in Britain.

In the years after I moved from my land of birth in Africa to the northern hemisphere, I often lamented the fact that I'd lost my sense of direction. Being a child of Africa, I believed, gave me an inborn sense of place, of where I was and where I belonged on the planet. With the ever-present sun always exactly where it should be, my life played itself out in the centre of the compass rose. Anywhere, at anytime, I knew not only where north, east, south and west were, but I could also tell the time of day by looking at my shadow. As a child it was a good feeling to have that surety, that 'knowing' where you were at all times. No matter what happened around you, no matter how many crossroads you arrived at or forks in the road appeared before you, the sun came up in the east every morning, travelled in a true path straight overhead, blazing a perfect line across the blue dome of the vast African sky, and gently melted in a glowing red mass onto the western horizon at the end of the day.

'Well, isn't that what it does in England as well?' people asked, perplexed, whenever I raised the problem of having lost my sense of direction when I moved to Britain.

'The fact that it gets light every day doesn't necessarily mean that you see the sun. You know it's there, but you don't see it. And when you do, it stays somewhere just above the horizon for most of the day, almost as if it's too shy to raise its head above the parapet; just like people who're scared of the Tall Poppy Syndrome. Scared that if it shows itself above the tops of the highest trees it'll get shot down. And, what's more, you live without a shadow here. How can you ever have a sense of direction or a sense of where you are, or of *what* you are, if you have no shadow?'

Perhaps the loss of my sense of physical direction had nothing to do with my loss of every other sense of direction during my years in Britain. Perhaps the feeling of being an alien – albeit a legal alien – in my newly adopted country had nothing to do with the fact that I no longer cast a shadow. But somehow, I did not think that was true.

'Accept this as your new country,' I had told my children. 'Accept that this is where we are now and where we'll stay, because otherwise you'll always feel like you're simply passing through. You won't make friends, because your sense of survival and your fear of painful farewells will prevent you from making long-term commitments. You'll be so busy longing for what you've left behind that you won't realise what wonderful opportunities are right here within your reach.'

However, in the enthusiasm to integrate completely into our new country, we not only tried to prevent our memories from lingering on what we had left behind, but we neglected to realise that is was exactly those that gave us substance; that gave us a shadow. For fear of yearning for the past and far-away family and friends, we left our most precious possessions unpacked, unopened in the boxes in the attic. We stopped telling stories about them to each other; we stopped reminiscing over the yellowing pages of photo albums, we no longer opened the stained recipe books, or reminded each other of what so-and-so said at such-and-such time. We stopped speaking the names of our ancestors – those who had left us such a proud legacy.

In my keenness for us all to adjust and adapt and integrate, we kept quiet about our past and listened instead to the stories our new neighbours told us of theirs; a past that belonged to other people and that would never become our own, just as we were never going to become part of theirs. No matter how well we integrated into their lifestyles and their activities, their passions and their causes, we were from a different world and would always be. We were never, and never would be, considered to be part of their history.

I had lost direction and all sense of direction. By shedding the wrong baggage, I had made an ill-fated judgement. Leaving my foundation, my roots along the wayside, I had also left my guidelines, my role-models – I had left behind an integral part of what is me. Not only could I not find my way again, I could not show my children the way either. I was pitifully stumbling in the dark. I had become a being without substance; a being without a shadow.

One of the unspoken rules of the Camino is that you never ask another pilgrim to carry anything for you. The weight on your back was your choice. If it became redundant, or too heavy (backpacks are renowned for their daily spontaneous weight gain) and you could not mail it to yourself, you would rather leave behind something very sentimental or precious than expect someone else to carry it for you. The same rule applied when it came to problems, hang-ups, doubts and worries. While walking during the day, if you walked with someone else, the understanding was that, unless asked, you never raised your problems. In the evenings in the refuges, when pilgrims got together after a long day and talked late into the night, it was in the odd remark or during a more serious discussion or the telling of an interesting experience that you could find nuggets of wisdom to help solve your problems. But, because everyone has some burden to carry, Camino protocol dictates that you never add to another's load. Unfortunately, not everyone was aware of the protocol.

'I don't know how you can walk on your own,' was often the remark of the younger fellow-pilgrims who'd caught up with me on the path and who had not simply left me with a '*Buen Camino*' over their shoulder, as was the usual custom of passing pilgrims, but slowed down to chat for a little while. Mostly we would then part company again; they would go ahead and I would fall back a little to be on my own. On rare occasions though, it wasn't possible to shake off the company and I would just have to accept that, on that particular occasion, it was to be 'my Camino' to be companionable. But I never encouraged anyone to stay to talk. For me, the warm camaraderie of the evenings in the *refugios* was the time to share stories and thoughts and dreams. There you had a choice of whether you wanted to stay at the kitchen table or in front of the log fire to talk, or sit on the side to read, or write your journal. The younger people were the ones who seemed unable to cope with solitude and the few who'd started on their own usually quickly found other pilgrims with whom to walk the rest of the way.

Karina, a lovely German girl in her mid-twenties who had interrupted her university studies to 'find herself' on the Camino, caught up with me one day. I'd heard her long before I saw her. She had a beautiful alto voice and, when she was on her own, used to sing choral music at full tilt, the sweet sounds echoing over the vast landscape, the soprano and mezzo-soprano voices seemingly to come from nature itself. The moment she reached me, she stayed at my side and soon explained to me why she could not walk alone.

'I'm sorry, I see you are alone. How can you walk alone? I can never walk alone. I must walk with someone. I have so many problems to sort out. I don't know what I must do with my life. I'm not happy at home. I have a boyfriend but I think now he is not the man I want to spend the rest of my life with. How do I tell him that? He thinks we will be married one day. I don't like my university course but it is so hard to change now. I hope to find all the answers on the Camino. I have to. I cannot go back to my old life.' It all spilled out so fast that from the moment she'd joined me to the point where I knew her whole life history, I'd never had a chance to say 'hello', let alone 'yes, I walk alone and I prefer to walk alone' – and we hadn't even covered twenty metres of the way. I almost stumbled. It was as if she'd taken all the baggage she was carrying, hurled it onto my shoulders and said, 'There! You take it now and carry my problems for me.'

That day I understood just how cruel it was to have high expectations of something and then have them dashed. So many books, websites and articles that have been written about the Camino make mention of how you find answers to questions and solutions to problems on the Camino. I have made that statement myself. But, those publications then give the impression that it is the Camino – the pilgrimage – that is the great panacea for all the problems of the world. And that is not true. Yes, the answers and the solutions are there for the finding, but it is not the Camino that holds them. The Camino simply provides the ideal environment and the many opportunities for the pilgrim to find those answers and solutions within his or her own heart and soul and mind. Walking hour after hour and day after day across a landscape that is so vast and so beautiful, being in touch with nature and the elements, feeling the energy that comes from the earth, feeling that closeness with your creator, having the time – oh the luxury – the ultimate luxury of endless time to meditate, to think, to pray, to enjoy the solitude and the silence! All this is the backdrop against which you can place every question you have, and those are the perfect conditions in which the answers will come to you.

How could I tell Karina that her answers were probably never going to be found on the Camino, unless she looked to herself for them. She'd read the books – all the well-known and talked-about Camino books, and from them she'd gleaned that the answers were obtainable from her fellow-pilgrims. She did not understand that talking to anyone who would listen and spilling out her life story to strangers was going to result in solutions that may have worked for those individuals, but may be completely wrong for her. Everyone has a different background, a different culture, a different set of rules. If I'd told Karina my suggestions, she would have got different suggestions from the next and the next and the next person she spoke to, and every day her head would be filled with more conflicting bits of advice and more and more confusion. For a while, I felt guilty that I hadn't sat Karina down and given her counselling, but then I quickly realised how utterly silly that guilt was. I was not a youth counsellor, nor a career guide, nor her mother or her friend. Those were the people, back home where she came from, that she needed to go to for answers – not every stranger she met on the Camino. Later, when I met other pilgrims who'd encountered Karina along the way, I was again reminded of her sad plight, and that of so many young people who walk the Camino. And again I felt regret that I could not give her what she wanted, that I had not carried her load for just a little of the way. By that time she'd taken to drinking or smoking too much dope every night; sleeping with whichever boy was willing; and had started to accumulate far more baggage than she had when she set off on her Camino.

But it was not only the young people who were the victims of false expectations or who seemed to feel that they were carrying the weight of the world on their shoulders. Exactly what the burden was that pilgrims bore was also not always as transparent as it was with Karina.

The pretty, blonde Gabi who kept more or less the same pace as our little group and joined us from time to time, walked with me for a while one day.

'The thing that really makes me sad on the Camino,' she said, 'is the fact that we meet people one day and then never see them again. And unless you walk with someone for a long time, you never get to know them at all. I so wish we had more time to get to know people better because I think so many people on the Camino are very special and would make wonderful friends.'

I remembered how, when I was twenty-something like Gabi, I had regretted the same thing when I travelled all over Europe. I'd met the most amazing people; in train compartments, on steps of museums, outside the American Express offices where we collected mail and money and travelling companions, sharing a beach for the night or a table on a sidewalk… But then, after the all-too-brief encounters we never saw each other again and we never kept in touch. In those days there was no internet and convenient e-mails, but I was never sure that that was the reason we didn't maintain contact. Chance encounters are often so interesting and enriching exactly because they are so brief. You have the pleasure of skimming off only the cream that has risen to the top and don't face the risk of finding that, a little deeper, there's nothing of value. People who know they're unlikely to meet you again are also more open and uninhibited, and you have the benefit of seeing the most exciting and interesting side of them. Like a holiday romance, it's often better to remember the good moments and leave it at that. And yet, the encounters on the Camino seemed to be different; like-minded people, kindred spirits, soul brothers and sisters are attracted to each other by the common purpose of walking the Way of Stars and Stones.

'Have you spoken to Golda yet?' Gabi wanted to know. 'She is fascinating! She's travelled all over the world and lived and worked just about everywhere.'

I had indeed spoken to Golda. When I saw her for the first time, I thought she must have walked straight out of a Rossetti painting, and then I remembered where I'd seen her before; she *was* Millais's *Sophie Gray*, that hypnotic image of the young girl at the onset of maturity, sexual awakening and power. Golda was, I guessed, about twenty years older than the fourteen-year old Sophie, but her marble-like face, haloed by a wild abundant mass of flamboyantly russet curls, and her large, dark eyes so alive with mirth and mischief mixed with deep thought and unanswerable questions, made her the classic pre-Raphaelite beauty. Golda was also one of those pilgrims who was in a transition in her life and came to the Camino in search of answers. She'd been all over the planet. She had lived and worked in just about every major city and every country in the world. Golda knew what she wanted to do; she wanted to help people. Her entire life was about alleviating the burdens being carried by the underprivileged and the victims of the world. And yet, my impression was that each one of those places and every one of those jobs was no different to this, the pilgrimage in Spain – just one more place where she was hoping to find out who she's really supposed to help and where her destiny lies. The fact that she made a lasting impression on everyone she met, and that the younger pilgrims on the Camino found her inspiring and probably had their own questions answered by her mere presence, was something she was completely unaware of. There are people who spend their lives searching – not because they can never find the answers, but because when the answers do present themselves, they're still so busy searching *out there* that they never recognise the answers *right here*.

One evening, in a small, very noisy, very smoky little bar, Golda and I decided to splash out and share a large plate of *empanada*, an all-time favourite of pilgrims with a bit of money to spare. It's a selection of fresh and mouthwatering open sandwiches and little squares of a pie which consists of layers of an oily saffron-coloured pastry – like phyllo dough, filled with an imaginative variety of different kinds of meat and fish and onion. I also introduced her to the decadent pleasure of Bailey's Irish Cream-on-ice – to wash down the food, oil the grey cells, banish the cold and soothe the aches and pain. Hours later we were both a little closer to recognising some answers… but then the evening was over, the old men had packed away their playing cards for another night, the owner was polishing the zinc counter and his wife had started to sweep the floor. We had to leave. The two of us may have solved a few of the problems of the western world that night, but we also nearly managed to get completely lost on the way back to the refuge. Even though the little village had only one short street and about ten houses, the refuge door was closed – and its door looked exactly like every other door on the street. We were more than slightly *beschwipst* and giggling too much to remember anything. But, just then, the world did seem like such a lovely place in which to get lost…

An evening in a tapas bar and a few glasses of creamy Irish nectar did not always do the trick though. Sometimes, my impression was that the heavier the burden and the longer a pilgrim had carried it the less likely it was that they'd show it to anyone else. It was almost as if some people had lived so long with their troubles that they became possessive of them. They jealously guarded them and carried them with pride, as if it was *their* cross that *they* had been chosen to bear.

The idea of martyrdom itself, no matter for which religion or ideology, often becomes a selfish behaviour or action; it's not about what you can do for your beliefs or your ideals, but what your sacrifice for them can do for you. Martyrdom brings fame – the fifteen minutes everyone dreams of. It puts your name on the front pages, it places you in the centre of the spotlight. What other merit is there in being a martyr for your beliefs? Who else gains or benefits from it? Does it strengthen others' faith or deepen their belief? If it is to set an example, what is that example in aid of? And if there is merit, how many times do you have to cross the earth to obtain absolution? Just how many wrongs must you have committed to have to keep seeking penitence for the rest of your life?

Or was there a different reason altogether for some pilgrims *not* to let go of their burden, *not* to stop walking the pilgrimage, *never* to reach any one destination?

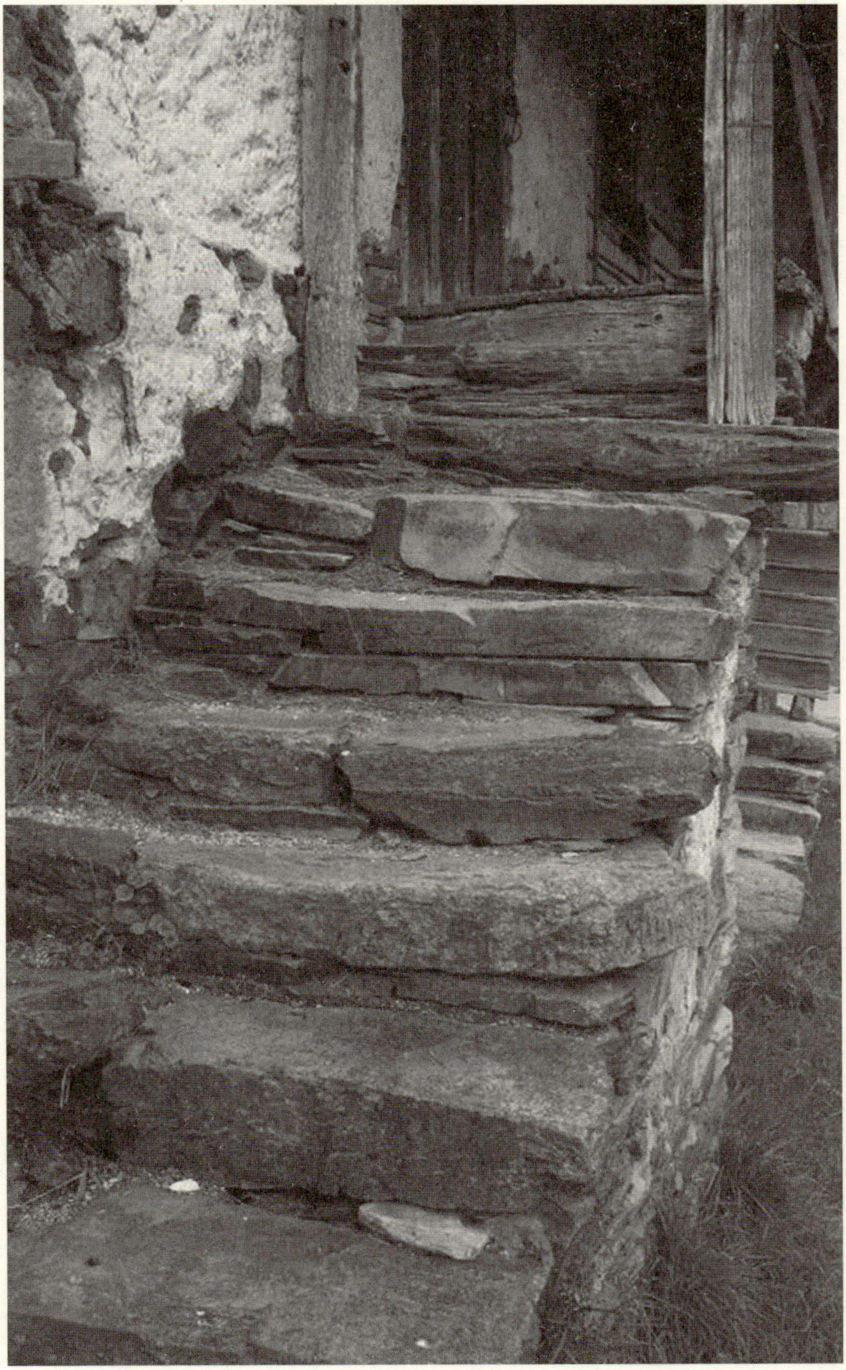

7

About wolves, witches and hurricanes; in other words, on being prepared for the unexpected

One step at a time is good walking
— Chinese proverb

Journal entry:
(Day 29) One of the most difficult days so far, but also one of the most beautiful.

I limped into the *refugio* on the outskirts of Molinaseca, exhausted, drenched to the bone, frozen to the marrow – and not a little grumpy that I had to walk right through the length of the town and yet another kilometre on the other side to get to the refuge. Nevertheless, the grumpiness soon evaporated as I undid my elaborately makeshift rain gear of plastic rubbish bags and bits of string and shed my heavy muddy boots at the front door. I was pleasantly surprised, and infinitely grateful, that the refuge looked quite new, clean and welcomingly warm.

Felipe, the *hospitalero*, was a big man with a magnificent black moustache underlined by a wide, friendly smile. He helped release me from my backpack and waited patiently as I went through the ritual of taking off two pairs of (wet) gloves, digging in under my (wet) fleece top to get to my (wet) hip pack, unzipping it – careful not to catch anything in the teeth of the zip – unwrapping the layers of plastic around my papers and finally producing my precious *credenciales*, or pilgrims' passport.

Reading my information, he noticed that I'd spent the previous night in Rabanal del Camino, and remarked, 'Ah! You must be congratulated!' Like most of the hosts of the refuges on the Camino, Felipe spoke only Spanish but by this stage of my pilgrimage I'd become quite adept at fooling myself that I understood most of what the Spaniards said to me and that I was replying in a French that most of them seemed to grasp.

I laughed. I had immediately assumed he'd seen my age on the passport and, after twenty-nine days, I was still enough of a novice to be surprised at the fact that I was still there, still on the pilgrimage, and still walking. Any or all compliments – about my age, my stamina, my courage – whatever people wanted to compliment me on, were welcomed with alacrity and pure joy. But, apparently it was not the fact that I was walking the pilgrimage – at my age – that he was congratulating me on. This particular compliment, it transpired, was for the fact that I had just survived one of the worst hurricanes that had ever hit northern Spain.

'You must have had a very hard time today.' Felipe was speaking slowly, in deference to my lack of Spanish, I imagined, and there was a lot of gesticulating and raising of his thick black eye brows to emphasise each word. His whole body became animated as he informed me that the eye of the hurricane had passed over Monte Irago, in the León mountain range, at around noon, earlier that day, at the same place and the same time as I was crossing the mountain.

'Yes!' I agreed. 'It was extremely hard and there were moments when I really feared for my life. But I just assumed it must be normal for this time of year. I never thought it might be an actual hurricane!'

As usual, I had been walking alone and only once seen another man who passed me – but he did so very quickly, as if blown on by the wind, and apart from the '*Buen Camino!*' I caught flying past; there was no communication between us. I had a few worrying moments though. At times the wind was so strong that, as I rounded a particularly sharp bend in the pathway along the side of the mountain, it lifted me off my feet and unceremoniously dumped me a good few centimetres further along where I fell against the rough gorse and slippery side of the pathway. I'd found it surprising that with such a strong wind there could also be such dense mist. Then I realised that it probably wasn't mist but a thick cloud through which I was walking. I knew that the strongest winds are found in the heart of a cumulus bravo and so it should not have been surprising that a few times it nearly lifted me right off the mountain.

'I was thinking it was just as well that I couldn't see further than a step or two ahead of me,' I continued, warming to the telling of the adventure I'd lived through without even realising its seriousness at the time. 'Every now and then there was a slight lifting of the mist and I could catch a glimpse of the sheer drop to the side of the pathway. I thought that if I fell down there, no one would ever find me in a million years. Perhaps all that would have remained of me would be a little cross with my name and the date to mark the spot where it was believed I must have disappeared.'

There were many such small memorials for pilgrims who'd died on the way. Some were elaborate stone or metal memorials with bronze plaques or engravings giving the details of the departed beloved. Others were simple wooden crosses with a carved name and date. Most of these had moved passing pilgrims to place a stone in front, and often this resulted in a beautiful little cairn at the foot of the memorial, each small stone a homage to a fellow pilgrim. Hardly a day went by without me seeing at least one of these, and on this particular day the memorial I passed – a humorous upside-down sculpture of a bicycle – was for a German named Heinrich Krause. It surprised me that these crosses or memorials were not always where you'd expect them to be. You would think the places where pilgrims died would be on the side of a steep mountain or in a dense forest or on a stretch of pathway that was treacherously stony or steep or slippery, but several of these spots were on flat, relatively easy bits of the way. Sometimes it was a place where there were beautiful shady trees or where a river or stream gently bubbled over colourful pebbles, and I would wonder how the pilgrim had died. Did he decide to sit down for a little rest in this lovely place, take out his water bottle and have a long, deep drink of cool, refreshing water while looking back at the pathway from where he'd just come? Then perhaps he leaned back against an ancient tree, looked up at the shiny leaves dancing in the sunlight, smiled – and passed away? But I imagine it couldn't always have been that gentle and peaceful.

Apparently, many deaths resulted from heart attacks, which was quite understandable if you considered that most pilgrims walked during summer when the temperature seldom fell below 40°C. Others died of hypothermia during the winter months, or even during autumn or spring when unexpected cold fronts come raging through the mountains. Only months before I started walking the Camino, a woman roughly my age had died of cold and exposure.

In one place, just outside Estella, there was a memorial right on the edge of a busy road, on a hill and on a bend. It was one of those dangerous places where pilgrims had to cross the main road to get back onto the footpath leading down the hill into the town. The memorial was for Mary Catherine Kimpton, *Peregrina Canadiense*. It was easy to guess that she'd come to this dangerous crossing at the end of a long day's walk. She would have been tired, her legs feeling heavy and sluggish, her reactions not quite as quick as needed and when she crossed the road a car had hit and killed her. The last line on the memorial touched me deeply: *Pueda ella caminar siempre sobre los campos de oro* – and I said silently, 'Yes Mary – may you always walk in golden fields'.

'It is sometimes very difficult to find the people who are missing, especially when people walk alone, like yourself.' Felipe's words were far from reassuring. 'And when the weather is bad like today, we cannot look for them until it clears up. Sometimes it's too late then. But you are safe and that is good.'

He finished writing my details in the refuge register – name, age, country of origin and point of departure on the Camino – then stamped my passport and handed it back to me. Before putting it away safely, I looked at the stamp. It was always an interesting little moment, seeing the stamp of the *refugio*. Each refuge had its own stamp, each one different and often reflecting some particular aspect of that refuge. A little like opening the windows of an advent calendar before Christmas, I thought each night as I waited for the *hospitalero* to stamp my passport. Every now and then you'd see a group of pilgrims sitting in a circle around the table in a refuge kitchen or in a warm cosy bar, sharing a bottle of wine or a couple of beers and comparing the stamps in their passports. One pilgrim I met, not even halfway along the Camino, already had three passports stapled together, forming a concertina-like document three metres long. He collected pilgrim stamps like a little boy collects super-hero cards, and stopped in each and every village, at every church, at every refuge, in every bar along the way to get his passport stamped. Here, in Molinaseca, the stamp of the Albergue de Santa Marina was a big circle around a pilgrim's cross. The cross was firmly planted on a route map of the Camino Frances, and what I loved most about it was the burst of stars on the one side of the cross – a reminder that this was after all *la voje lade*, the way under the stars.

'I will now take you to the dormitory. It is upstairs and there are hot showers downstairs. You must take off your wet clothes. There are enough heaters here where you can hang them to dry. And when you have taken a shower, you must come and soak your feet – I will get the ice water, vinegar and salt ready for you. Then I will rub your feet. I can see they are hurting, no?' The man was a saint, no doubt about it!

Later, after the luxury of a long hot shower, I changed into my one and only extra set of clean, dry clothes. Felipe was already in the dormitory hard at work massaging and doing shaman-like things to the painful knee of one of four Latvians who'd arrived while I was in the shower.

I had met the Latvians that afternoon in El Acebo, the first village after the hurricane and halfway down the mountain. I'd hoped to be able to stop for a short rest out of the wind and sleet. I was in desperate need of a bit of warmth and a large mug of steamy hot chocolate, so was elated when I saw a smoky *bar* – not a restaurant or a bar as we know it, but something in between, and one of the most welcoming sights on the way for any pilgrim. The Latvians were four good-looking young men. Two turned out to be father and son (though I thought they looked more like brothers), and two friends. They all had shoulder-length hair, beautiful faces and the bodies of dock-workers – or personal trainers, depending on your frame of reference. None of them spoke a word of anything other than Latvian, which made for very interesting, albeit laborious, communication with them. I later wondered whether this was the reason they walked faster than anyone else I'd met on the Camino. They were completely ensconced in a world of their own – a comfortable, warm and friendly little world. Obviously great friends, there was a lovely relationship among them and they seemed perfectly content to spend hours walking together, sometimes in silence, sometimes in vociferous conversation, never needing to stop and talk to anyone else on the way. Otherwise, the reason for their walking so fast was a much simpler one. Every night, as they did there in Molinaseca, they arrived at a reasonable time at the refuge, claimed their beds, changed, washed clothes and then went out to find a place where they could eat and drink until late into the night. I wasn't sure what they did in places where there was no bar, no place to eat, and not even a shop to buy provisions. My gestures and sign language could not adequately convey that question so I could get a comprehensible answer, but I had to assume that the nights when they did have somewhere to eat and drink, they more than made up for the places without. I knew that, because there was one thing I'd learned early on the Camino and which was confirmed on this night: drunk exhausted men snore much more and much louder than sober exhausted men – be they from Latvia, Lichfield or Launceston.

Felipe was right about the heaters. There were at least ten of them around the large room and I soon had my wet clothes draped over one, left to dry overnight. Like the rest of the refuge, the dormitory was airy and light and clean and one of the few places where there were normal single beds rather than bunk beds. Another welcome sight was the mattress covers, which looked fresh and laundered. There were windows on three sides of the room and I claimed a bed near a window that looked out in the direction of the Monte Irago, the mountain I'd crossed that day.

While waiting for Felipe to finish with the Latvian's knee, I unpacked my backpack to make sure that no water had seeped through during the storm. Thankfully everything was dry, so I took the opportunity to repack the few items in my bag, leaving my sleeping bag out for the night. But Felipe stopped me.

'Ah, wait! While you have everything out, let me show all of you how you *should* pack your backpack.' He gathered everyone around my bed; the Latvians, two Spanish pilgrims who'd just arrived, Paco and Tonio, Annie – a young South African woman, and her pilgrim friend she'd met on the way, Christl, a graphic artist from Germany. My backpack, with all its contents, was the centre of attraction. Felipe began. Everyone in his audience had already walked at least several hundred kilometres and my guess was that few of them were paying much attention to Felipe's lecture, as they no doubt thought they'd mastered the art of packing. Rather, I suspected their interest was out of some burning curiosity to see what a fellow pilgrim had stashed away in what was one of the smallest backpacks on the Camino. Whichever it was, I was grateful that the meagre belongings in my bag included nothing that could possibly embarrass anyone – or was that just because, at my age, I simply did not get embarrassed any more about anything?

Felipe was completely unaware of the possibility that I might suffer embarrassment at having all my personal effects strewn out in front of total strangers and being used in a demonstration of back-packing techniques. He started to show us how the placement and balance of the backpack could make all the difference to the injuries that you incur – or not – while walking an 800-kilometre pilgrimage. Pulling the Latvian, on whose knee he'd been working, closer to use him as a model, Felipe showed us why pilgrims often have problems with their knees.

'Most of you put your sleeping bag at the bottom of the backpack and then stuff as much as you can, as tightly as you can, around it. The result is that the biggest weight is at the bottom. You then carry the backpack low on your back, so the weight is pressing on these tendons on the side of your hips.' He turned the Latvian around and indicated a line stretching from the back of the hip, going around and down the thigh and ending in the knee. 'These tendons form the connecting points to the skeleton of these muscles and it is the same muscle that is connected to the top, at the hip, as at the bottom, to the knee. If you press down on these tendons…' he pressed down on the back of the Latvian's hip, eliciting a yelp of pain and causing the man to hop on one leg, clutching an obviously very painful knee. '…you see? If you press down on those tendons in the hip, you have a painful knee!' Felipe ended with a flourish and a big smile, satisfied that he'd given such a vivid demonstration that would definitely be taken on board by all of us. There was no doubt in any of our minds how the imbalance of weight of the backpack on the hip could cause pain in the knees. After all, a huge tough man had almost been brought to tears right there in front of our eyes. I was sure that from then on all of us always took particular care that our backpacks had equal weight on both sides and that the heavy stuff was packed in the middle of the bag, halfway down our backs.

After this little lesson I wasn't so sure I still wanted a foot massage – a prospect that had seemed so inviting only thirty minutes before. However, having witnessed Felipe's obvious knowledge of all things pilgrim, I sat back on the bed and allowed him to take my feet into his large warm hands. It was wonderful. Without exerting overmuch pressure, simply by cupping one foot at a time in both his big hands, I could feel the healing taking place inside my feet. It felt as if my feet were being infused with Felipe's warmth and energy while the pain was drawn out at the same time.

'Your hands remind me of my father's healing hands,' I said. 'He used to put his hands on my head when I was little and within minutes a blinding headache would just fade away.' Felipe just smiled and continued to do his magic with my aching feet. I didn't really want to spoil the moment by talking and could easily have lain back and fallen asleep, but my inquisitive mind was like an impatient child at the door and made me ask my usual questions of the *hospitalero*.

'I know for you to be a *hospitalero* of a registered *refugio* you must have walked the Camino, so the question is: How many times did you walk it, Felipe?'

Finding a particularly painful spot on my foot and gently massaging it until the pain eased away, Felipe replied, 'Eleven times.'

Paco, the dashing young Spanish architect lying on the bed next to mine, looked up from where he was studying the next day's route in his Camino map book and asked the obvious question, 'Why eleven times?'

Felipe laughed. 'I lost myself the first time I walked the Camino and now I keep on walking the Camino in the hope of finding myself again!'

It was when he started talking about the refuge and about the people who'd stayed there that everyone began to gather round, interested in hearing more from a man with so much Camino experience. Even the Latvians came closer, as if being near would make it easier to understand what Felipe was saying. It was more common meeting fellow-pilgrims who were walking the Camino for the second, third, or fourth time, than someone like me doing it for the first time. I'd stopped being surprised when I heard how many times people walked the Camino. But *eleven* times – that was a lot of kilometres! What's more, Felipe had started in Le Puy or Vézelay most of those times, both places almost 2 000 kilometres from Santiago de Compostela. No wonder he knew what caused pain in the knees and how to massage aching feet.

'When this refuge opened, it was the queen of Spain who came for the official opening – and the king accompanied her. There are photographs downstairs of me with them,' he told us with pride. What a great moment that must have been for him. 'And in the year 2000, the current pope, Benedict, stayed here on his Camino. You can have a look – their names are all in the register.'

'Have any other famous people, like celebrities who've walked the Camino, stayed here?' asked Annie.

'Yes, a few of them… But not many of them stay in refuges, you know. They prefer the *hostals* or a *posada de país* where they can have the luxuries you don't get in the *refugios*. They like to write their books and talk about the *refugios*, but you can ask all the *hospitaleros* and they will all tell you they have not seen these people who say they stayed with them.'

'Did you meet ---?' Christl asked excitedly, mentioning the name of probably the most famous of Camino pilgrims.

'Bah!' Felipe spat. 'Don't talk to me about him! They say he has just recently walked the Camino again. But I ask all my friends in the *refugios*, "Did you see him?" and they all say "No! He just came to Spain to a few of the big cities along the way for a press conference and then went home again. And he most certainly did not see the inside of a *refugio*!'"

It was a terrible indictment of all those 'famous' people. But then, when you're a pilgrim on the Camino, you quickly learn that it is 'each to his own'. Each individual has his or her own way of walking a pilgrimage. Each person does it for their own reasons and has their own motivation, and each one gains something different from the experience. If people wanted to sleep in comfort between crisp clean sheets, rather than in a sleeping bag on a foam rubber mattress on a bunk bed in a dormitory with a dozen other snoring pilgrims, let them. If they'd rather send their backpacks ahead of themselves in a vehicle and have it waiting for them at the next town, so be it. There were pilgrims who spoke out strongly against those who were 'not true pilgrims', who took the easy – or easier – way. But who was to judge? And yet, when it was a 'famous' person who walked the Camino and used his or her experience as a big publicity opportunity, even the most phlegmatic and tolerant among us could get a little irritated and disapproving. And when that very well-known person walked only parts of the Camino and got on a bus, or worse still had a driver and car that transported him over the difficult parts, walked with no backpack, had someone wait for him along the way with food and drink, and then went home and wrote a book about the hardships, the pain, the discomfort and the agony of pilgrimage, the pilgrim's heart rebelled.

Yet, did it really matter? Was it any skin off my back if someone else capitalised on the experience they'd had, albeit embroidered and enhanced with some good research? If those accounts influenced people to walk their own Camino, then good on them. Probably that story, which might have been somewhat romanticised, but had been ostensibly 'lived' by someone so well known and so much in the public eye, would be far more attractive and motivational than a true account of a mere mortal who'd done it the hard way. Ultimately, everyone still had to find out for themselves how to survive and how to find the courage to continue each day.

What I did find objectionable, however, was that several pilgrims whom I'd met were walking the Camino as a result of reading some famous person's account of it and subsequently did not find what they were led to believe they would. They were expecting to encounter 'life lessons'; to experience religious enlightenment and spiritual revelations... And all too often the enlightenment and the revelations never came. I did hear a couple of pilgrims remark, 'If so-and-so could do it, then so can I!' and they'd push on regardless of the pain and the exhaustion. That would be the good outcome, because the end result would be a person stronger for his experience, richer for having found resources within himself that he might never have known about otherwise. But more often I spoke to people who were utterly disillusioned with the reality. Their 'hero' had written this amazing book about the Camino and their experiences, but the reality was very different, and this not only disappointed them but also made them feel disheartened and angry. They felt betrayed. They felt as if they'd been cheated by a person they, and the public, adored and admired.

But what right has anyone to blame another for disappointing them? We must take responsibility for our own actions, because our actions are the consequences of our choices. And perhaps that was why, before embarking on this pilgrimage, it was so important to know: 'Why do *you* want to walk the Camino?'

When I'd set off that morning from Rabanal, I had no idea that I was going to fight my way across a mountain in the grip of a hurricane, gale force winds and cutting ice-rain. What I was expecting to find somewhere along the way was a couple of wolves, a bandit or two, at least one witch – and most certainly the last living Templar. I also set off that morning in great anticipation, knowing this was to be the stretch where I was going to see the Cruz de Ferro, one of the highlights of the Camino – because that is what the guidebooks had led me to expect.

I had slept the night before in Rabanal after quite an eventful evening. Rabanal was the last stop before the steep and arduous crossing of the Montes de León range and Monte Irago – 'also dangerous on account of the wolves, bandits and witches', according to my pocket guidebook. An interesting place, with its well kept stone buildings and carved wooden doors and the San Salvador monastery, founded by Benedictine monks as recently as 2001, and affiliated to the Bavarian arch abbey of St. Ottilien. I was thrilled to learn from Isabella, the *hospitalero* of the *Albergue el Pilar* and one of only three female *hospitaleros* that I came across, that there were to be prayers (Offices) sung – in Latin and in the Gregorian tradition – at seven o'clock that evening in the village chapel. What a glorious experience that was, one I would not have missed for anything in the world! There were only two monks that sang, but the richness of their voices and their adeptness in Gregorian chant gave their 'performance' a superbly professional quality, the likes of which I thought you'd only hear on a professional recording. The thought that there, in a remote village on the side of a mountain somewhere in northern Spain, could be two German monks who sang their prayers in this ancient way, to a small audience of bedraggled and exhausted pilgrims, was wonderful – and the experience left me enriched and renewed. Afterwards we all walked back to the *refugio*, smiling and happy and feeling very fortunate and privileged.

We were welcomed with a roaring log fire and a delicious meal that Isabella had cooked for the dozen or so pilgrims who'd stopped there for the night. We all sat around a long refectory table and enjoyed the soup, the thick slices of home-cured ham and the tortillas – Spanish omelettes made with potatoes and onions. It was one of those magical evenings and, although communication was limited as there were probably as many languages spoken at that table as there were pilgrims, it did not lessen the continuous conversations; the conviviality and laughter. I had a Spaniard named Santiago sitting next to me – an exceptionally large man with a grisly grey beard to match. It turned out that he was sixty-nine years of age and was walking the Camino for the ninth time. His wife, a lovely woman half his size, was walking with him on this occasion. At the end of the table sat four friends, all in their late fifties to early sixties, who shared their story with us.

'Every year, for many years now, the four of us go on a holiday together, and every year we tell our wives that we're going on the Camino, but every year we go somewhere else.'

'Yes, it is true!' the second truant husband laughed. 'Last year we went to Cuba. That was very good. And another time we went to Hawaii, but most of the time we don't go that far.'

'And your wives never suspected? They never found out, or asked questions?' asked Santiago, perplexed – and slightly in awe – that four men could get away with such a scam for such a long time.

'No. Our wives always believed us, and they never suspected that our "pilgrimages" were to holiday resorts and beer canteens. But this time we decided to stay in Spain and *really* walk the Camino. And we're loving it so much that now we regret that we've never done it before.' And then he added, chuckling, 'But we suspect this time, for the first time, they are wondering if we are where we say we are...'

We all stayed silent for a few moments, digesting this information, none of us quite sure what to make of these four 'confidence tricksters'.

Next, one of the four petite and gentle women at the other end of the table spoke. 'We also travel together, but our "boss at home" knows exactly where we are. Only, she does not know what we're doing.' I say these women were petite and gentle, because that is how I saw them. They almost seemed incongruous with this environment – as if they were from a different place and a different time to the rest of us. The fact that they sat at the opposite side of the table from the four errant husbands somehow underlined their incongruity in this particular group. Then my first impression was clarified.

'We are nuns, you see. Our Convent is in the south-west of France and we were given leave to walk the pilgrimage, but we have to confess, we too are guilty of deceiving those who trust us.'

'Surely not!' Isabelle interjected. You haven't misbehaved in any way that I've seen,' she added, smiling.

'Ah! But we have,' the sister persisted. 'We are not wearing our habits.' This was true. None of them looked like traditional nuns. They were dressed in hikers' trousers and fleece jackets, like the rest of us. 'We are supposed to wear our full habit, which includes the veil, but it is so uncomfortable that we decided to get ourselves these clothes and walk in mufti. When we go to mass in the churches on the way we change into our habits.' The sister blushed a little as she made this confession, but no one around that table showed anything other than admiration for their candour – and initiative.

'Well, *that* should help us with our defence if our wives should ever find out about our little charade,' said one of the truant husbands, breaking the slight tension brought on by all these frank confessions. 'We'll just tell them we walked with four nuns!' Isabelle was quick to pass the jug of wine around and make sure that everyone had had enough to eat.

Across from me at the table was Klaus, a charming German from Munich. Klaus had a different story. He told us he'd walked the Camino many years before with his partner at the time. On several occasions she'd begged him to let them take the bus for the particularly hard sections. He hadn't wanted to, but eventually could no longer resist her tears and had given in – and had regretted the decision ever since. Years later, he'd attended the university in Santiago de Compostela and had eventually married a Spanish girl, so the Camino had continued to have significance in his life. He finally decided to walk the entire Camino again, because he'd never felt that he had actually done it that first time. However, work commitments did not allow him to complete it all in one go, so he was only walking from Astorga, the place where he'd taken the bus for a few kilometres to please his girlfriend all those years before.

I had come across Klaus earlier that day and he'd walked with me for a short while, during which time he taught me how to use my sticks effectively. By this stage of the pilgrimage my feet had become agonisingly painful and I had started using both my sticks in an attempt to take some of the weight off each step. This was doing more harm than good – it gave no relief to my feet and the additional muscles I was using in my arms and back were becoming strained and painful as well.

'Originally man walked on all fours,' Klaus told me. 'With Alpine walking it is like adding on the two extra limbs again so it is like walking on all fours. It causes your body to be much better balanced and it keeps your feet much flatter on the ground, instead of leaning too much on the outside – or the inside – of the foot.'

He demonstrated how to hold the sticks with my arms bent at just the right angle and, going down on his knees in front of me, he adjusted the length of the sticks to exactly the right height for me. The difference was remarkable. I couldn't believe how much easier and more natural it felt when I held the sticks correctly and used them in the correct 'Alpine' way. I was infinitely grateful to Klaus for his advice and always regretted never seeing him again after Rabanal to thank him again – and again. It was only later that I realised that if he had not corrected my walk, I would probably not have been able to finish the Camino. Although my feet continued to be extremely painful, using the sticks gave some small measure of relief. More importantly, it stopped me from damaging other muscles. Klaus was an experienced walker and very tall, which meant he covered many more kilometres in a day than I did, so when he passed me the following morning and disappeared into the mist, that was the last I saw of him.

And so – apart from the hurricane, did I find the wolves, the bandits, the witches and the Templar on the Way that day?

I did indeed see many wolves, but not the kind you'd expect to find from reading the guidebooks. Apparently there was a good number of Iberian wolves still around, particularly in this region of the north-western quarter of Spain – that is to say in Galicia, Asturias, part of Cantabria and specifically in Castilla-León, the area I was walking through just then. According to Juan Carlos Blanco, a Spanish government scientist and one of the founding members of the Brown Bear Foundation, this wilderness region still provided a refuge for large predators such as the Brown Bear and the wolf. At last count in 1988, there were about 2 000 wolves in Spain – and it was considered to be a growing population. This was mainly due to the fact that in the previous twenty or thirty years there'd been a migration of people from the country to the towns and large parts of the countryside had been left devoid of people. I could vouch for that after having walked, often for days on end, without seeing a single living soul in any of the villages that the Camino passes through. Empty fields lying fallow, endless stretches of rough foot paths through the mountain ranges, closed shutters, locked doors, a few dead leaves scurrying along the cobblestone streets, dry fountains – and total silence – was all that greeted the weary pilgrim as he or she walked through this hauntingly beautiful but desolate landscape.

However, every now and then, here and there, you'd come across the welcome sight of an active farm or cluster of humanity, where, always present, would be the 'wolves'; wolves that had been banished into slavery; heavily chained Alsatians (German Shepherds), the ubiquitous dog of rural Spain. I was aware that these dogs were the direct descendents; you could even say the brothers of the real McCoy – the Iberian Wolf. What a sad lot for the once proud predators of Europe. The Spanish, generally a very religious lot from whom one would have expected compassion and empathy towards other living creatures, did not seem to care much for their animals, if at all.

I found it heart-breaking to see how the people along the Camino treated their dogs. It also made me very, very angry. On more than one occasion I went up to a farmhouse door, knocked until I had a response, and then got into a heated discussion with a farmer or his wife about this issue. Sometimes small puppies had heavy chains around their necks, so heavy that they could not lift their heads, let alone get up – I suppose with the intent that the dog would one day grow into his chains. I saw long-haired German Shepherds chained in filthy farmyards with their fur so caked with mud and cow dung that they had difficulty in moving. I heard the weak whimpering of dogs behind locked barn doors on farms that looked as if they'd been deserted for a long time. On more than one occasion I saw a dog, in chains and in a cage in the middle of a field – in the middle of nowhere. What he was supposed to guard was a riddle. Why there would be a cage built for him, miles away from the nearest house or habitation, I could not guess. And why a dog in a small cage had to be chained as well, remained a puzzle to me.

Once I'd walked into Galicia – the last province on the pilgrimage and in which Santiago de Compostela is situated, conditions seemed to improve a little. Here there were fewer chains and I saw dogs running free, happily doing their guarding duty or herding goats and sheep. A message to my family and friends included another mention:

E-mail 18 March 2008
I have many dog stories – I have mentioned how cruel the Spaniards are with locking their dogs in barns or in cages and always with thick heavy chains around their necks – and that I am writing a letter to the King of Spain to tell him to do something about this. Well, the last couple of weeks most of the dogs I saw have been running free and/or working, doing what they love doing, looking after either sheep or herds of cattle.

In fact, there were many magical moments. This morning I watched a big old scruffy whitish dog watching over his little herd of sheep. Only six sheep and two lambs, the one of about two weeks and the other no more than a few days. They were trying to find something to eat on a small patch of scruffy grass squeezed in between the edge of the road and a wire fence, next to a parking lot of a restaurant. Why they were there, I do not know, but it was where the dog with his charges had been left – perhaps the shepherd was having his lunch in the restaurant? The road alongside was not too busy but where cars came past at a tremendous speed. The dog stood almost in the road, looking towards possible oncoming traffic, and every time he saw a car coming over the hill he would shove the sheep with his nose back from the edge, keeping them pinned against the fence. And the smallest lamb he would practically push under its mother every time. Then, when the car had passed, he would back track, all the time watching the road and leaving the sheep alone to graze again, until the next car came – it was quite amazing to watch.

So, when I approached a little farming village and heard a dog wail very woefully, my hackles were up and bristling. I walked through the village until I found where the crying came from. In front of a closed barn door was a female dog – her full teats swinging heavy between her legs, trying to scratch the door open. Under the door, through a little gap, was the head of a tiny puppy — no more than a few weeks old — trying desperately to get through but unable to. And it was this puppy that was crying so heartbreakingly. I could also hear that there were more puppies inside — all in a state about being separated from their mother.

I called ¡Hola! as loud as I could — which put the poor mother in a predicament as she had to protect the gate but also wanted to be with her puppies — but I told her to stay calm — help is at hand.

I kept on shouting until eventually an old farmer came from another building across the way. I told him in every language I know — which does not include his, namely Spanish — that the mother should be with her babies. He just smiled and said yes, it is the mother and she has babies. After this heated and frustrating conversation had been going on about ten minutes, the owner of the dog finally came out of the house. I shouted at him to immediately let the puppies out or the mother in. He and his mate just chuckled and made a few, no doubt rude comments, and he gingerly stepped across to the barn and opened the door. The mother immediately rushed inside and three little pups greeted her with much relief and joy. After a few more reprimands — which included my intention to write to their king about this, I continued on my walk.

So — sore feet and aching muscles or not — you will be pleased to hear that I still have enough energy to fight a few battles...

One of the guidebooks I read had an entire section on Spanish dogs. It advised walkers to have a stick handy, 'for a number of reasons, including keeping a dog at bay'. It went on to tell you not to make eye contact, not to turn your back on a dog until at a safe distance, and even to buy a high-pitched alarm to scare off packs of dogs.

The thought of these warnings had me smiling on several occasions — in fact, on many occasions, for there were far more dogs on the Camino than people. I would conjure up this scenario in my mind every time I saw a dog ahead of me: *Walk slowly towards the dog, eyes firmly fixed to the ground, stick held high like a warrior spear. When in line with the dog — eyes still firmly fixed to the ground, spear still at the ready — slowly rotate in order to avoid turning your back to the dog. Now walk backwards for several metres.*

If the dog was not chained, which was unlikely, and he saw this strange behaviour, he was far more likely to immediately become suspicious and consequently aggressive. A stick at the ready would have made even the most placid dog wary and hostile and, a human with a stick, but with his eyes downcast, projected such a mixed message – *I am armed, beware, but lo! I am submissive and you are in charge!* – that the poor animal would have attacked even if just to assure itself that, even if no one else was, he is still sane and in control of himself.

Apart from on the *Meseta*, a pilgrim was likely to see or hear a dog every few hundred metres at least. So imagine during summer, when, on any given day several hundred humans came past a dog's territory, all brandishing their sticks and walking backwards with their eyes fixed to the ground, what a weird sight this would be. Perhaps it was no wonder the poor dogs had to be chained and kept in cages?

And the witches? Once again, most guidebooks warn that there probably are witches in these mountains. A typical entry in the guidebooks reads: '…of course they do not really exist – but do take care just in case you do come across a witch.' Perhaps witches – or *meigas* – are again just another figment of a slightly deranged pilgrim's imagination? People see what they want to see. They see what they expect to see. I most certainly did not really want or expect to see a witch, and I know that if I told you about my experience in Foncebadón, someone is bound to bring out the thermometer or take my temperature. And perhaps they would be right to do so. No one else saw him, he did not show himself to any of the other pilgrims that walked up the side of the mountain that day, he definitely did not offer a new rain poncho or a bowl of cornflakes to anyone else I know of. I was the only one who saw him come out of the crumbling old house on the main street through Foncebadón, the only one to whom he spoke, the only one who was invited to come inside and dry out in front of his fire. But then again, possibly the others expected the witch to be a woman, to be wearing black and a large pointy hat, to have a broom standing against her door frame or to have a black cat sitting on her step. Possibly they never expected a witch to be a tall, thin man with ice-blue eyes, a shaved head and wearing a strange checked waistcoat with little bells dangling from the tails at the back…

The reality is that we do all experience things in different ways. You only had to compare your photographs with a fellow-pilgrim's at the end of a day's walk to have this confirmed. It was astounding how you both could have walked exactly the same pathway, through the same landscape and past the same villages, both have taken fifty photographs throughout the day, but end up not having two photographs of the same thing. In fact, more often than not you wouldn't even be able to recognise that you'd been in the same country.

'Where did you see *that*?'

'Wow! That's beautiful! I never saw that! Did you walk a different route?'

'You must have an incredible zoom lens on your camera! I never saw those birds/cows/horses/people!'

Often people saw what their guidebooks told them to expect to see. If you had a different guidebook, you might miss a certain lovely monastery that was slightly off the pathway up against a hill, or an interesting old Roman bridge, or a particularly holy relic tucked away in the small church in the forest.

But then, guidebooks never mention to look out for the little Robin Red-breast that sits and waits for you every morning on the side of the pathway, ready to keep you company for a hundred, two hundred, three hundred metres, hopping along the embankment, looking over his shoulder to see if you're coming, singing his joyful trilling song to announce to the world that we are ready to enjoy everything it has to offer us. Guidebooks cannot warn you of the rabbit that might jump out in front of your feet on the long open stretch after Calzadilla de los Hermanillos, or the red bushy-tailed squirrel that will invite you to play hide-and-seek in the big old chestnut just after the turn-off to Puente de Villarente. Nowhere did I see it written that you should watch where you tread when you're close to pine forests in case you step on an eccentrically dressed progressive caterpillar, resplendent in his spiky red and black and gold party clothes on his way to join his gang where they are dining out on (read: destroying) yet another Spanish pine tree. No one tells you to watch out for the little shiny black beetles or the comical centipedes or the colourful grasshoppers underfoot, or for the fox chasing butterflies over the fields outside Castrojeriz, and not a single guidebook let slip the secret of the chickens that nest under the bright yellow gorse, in the middle of nowhere, halfway between El Burgo Ranero and Reliegos, and the deliciously fat, brown egg that is on offer for a passing pilgrim.

Perhaps it is just as well, or else we would be so busy looking to experience every sight and event that the authors of the guidebooks had described, and completely miss the magic moment when the farmer and his wife, their ancient granny, the two dogs and the neighbour all gently and excitedly help the cow into the barn for her to give birth to a gorgeous shiny little calf. You might never hear the click songs of the storks in Puente de la Reina or on the tops of church spires all along the way, or meet the wonderful old man with his little dog in Burgos, who, despite his obviously advanced Alzheimers, is the best guide to this fascinating city of *El Cid*-fame that you could ever wish for. If you were off on a mission to find 'the little house where a very eccentric old woman lived', who a couple of authors had found colourful enough to describe in their guidebooks, or to enjoy a specific meal that another famous author had had while on his own Camino, you would probably never experience the pleasure of watching the intense concentration, the excitement, nor feel the suspense building up as the cards are slapped down on bright red or yellow Formica table tops where the old men of the district come together every night to play their card games in the warm, noisy, smoke-filled bars. You may finish your Camino and never have seen the sun falling on the elaborately ornate gilded carving of the altarpiece in the Le Corbusier-esque church outside León, or have felt the thrill when you were wished a '*Buen Camino*' for the first time. And depending on the author of your particular guidebook, when you get to Santiago de Compostela and you experience the drama and pomp and tradition of the church processions at Easter, and you feel the vibrations of those iron crosses stamped in unison on the cold flagstones, sense the dampened sound of the shuffle of bare feet under the weight they carry, witness the energy and brute force that tremble through the cold night air as the sinisterly masked men carry their precious relics through the shimmering wet streets, the rain trickling down their backs, little rivulets meeting up with the rivulets of sweat and blood, you might either be filled with revulsion or overwhelmed with awe.

However, probably because pilgrims like to believe that they are 'part of' the whole myth of the Camino, (while not always realising that it is *they* who cultivate and grow the Camino urban legends that become the Camino myth), most guidebooks play along. A good example of this is how every pilgrim seems to know about 'the last Templar' who runs the *refugio* in Manjarín, at the top of the León mountain range, because almost every guidebook has a different story to tell about Tomás, an eccentric, middle-aged bearded man who claims to be the last remaining Knight Templar on the Camino. Apparently he left a 'normal' middle-class life, a wife and two daughters in Madrid some twenty or thirty years ago to come and live here in Manjarín to help the pilgrims on the Camino. The typical introduction to Tomás in the guidebooks reads: 'Tomás devotes his life year round, in an almost medieval manner, to caring for pilgrims in this high, desolate spot where bad weather (fog, rain, wind, snow) is almost the norm… mattresses for 20, basic WC, outdoor kitchen. Gregorian chant provided.' Consequently many pilgrims stop and stay, in order to meet the man and tell their own stories about him. His refuge is definitely a perfect Kodak moment. Originally a stone building, probably built at the time when the Dark Ages melded into the Middle Ages, and added to over the centuries in timber and more stone and other bits and pieces, it greets you in all its untidy splendour as you walk over a little rise in the road on the last crest of the range. Your first view of it is the display of carved fingerposts, each one painted in a different colour, each one indicating the distance from this spot to a place of 'significance' (– the 'significance' not necessarily very obvious):

Santiago 222km
Roma 2 475km
Machu Pichu 9 453km
Jerusalem 5 000km
Finisterre 295km
Trondheim 5 000km
Gatova 712km
Galiza 70km

The blue fingerpost to Munich was hanging precariously at an angle, only one crooked nail preserving it from total oblivion, so I couldn't see how far I would have had to walk, should I, for some inexplicable reason, have wished to go to this Bavarian city. On the timber gable of the roof another carved sign announced:

Bienvenido Peregrinos
Sellado de Credenciales

When I walked a little further onto the property in search of some sort of front door where I could ring a bell or knock, several cats of various sizes and colours scampered off into what looked like a large carpenter's workroom, a thick carpet of wood shavings on the floor and the smell of freshly sawn timber filling the air with a sweet aroma. There was a dilapidated old garden chair slouched against a woodpile, a large satellite dish to one side, elaborately wired up to an old rusty Land Rover, bundles of rags pushed into gaps among the stones, several television antennae attached to random bits of wood or tree stumps, some of them adorned with scraps of fabric, hessian and rope, an ancient looking black Alsatian sleeping in the corner, not even bothering to open more than one eye as I greeted it, a big flag flapping in the breeze, the red Spanish mark of the Templars, the Templar 'T', emblazoned on a white background, wind chimes and an assortment of bells hanging from the trellis overhead.

'*¡Hola!*' I called, but there was no reply other than the cats' inquisitive looks and the sleeping dog's soft snore. No one seemed to be home. I was sorry that I'd missed this legendary Camino character. And I was not impressed with the state of the place. 'Hovel' was the word that came to mind. I remembered learning at school about the Knights Templar being the medieval order of monastic militants who became the repository for much of Europe's banking treasure during the early Middle Ages, who went on to fight the bloody Crusades and who were, most importantly for the pilgrims, the official protectors of the Camino until the 14th century. I would have loved chatting to Tomás about the history of the Templars on the Camino and about his particular claim to fame, but there was no sight or sound of the man. I waited around a little longer, but was uncomfortable in the filth and chaos of the place and then I quickly dismissed a sudden funny suspicion that he might have sensed that I was a sceptic and had therefore disappeared. Yet, later, when a group of us chatted about experiences we had crossing the mountains that day, and the inevitable subject of Tomás, The Last Templar, came up, everyone who'd passed through Manjarín not long before or not long after me talked about their meeting with the man. When I heard this I had to wonder whether my suspicion had been right after all.

'What an interesting character!' David commented. 'How authentic he is, is debatable, but it was fascinating meeting him.'

'I wouldn't have liked to stay there overnight, though,' Marilyn continued.

'Apparently you just put your sleeping bag on one of the benches built around the fire in the middle of the floor,' she went on to explain, 'but the toilet is outside and very, very basic, and there is no electricity or running water in the place!'

Annie shuddered. 'The man gave me the creeps,' she said quietly.

'You did leave rather quickly!' David looked across at Annie with a puzzled expression. 'One moment you were there and the next moment you were gone! We thought you might have gone outside to look at his interesting electrical generator, which he runs to work his computer and internet system. It is quite an engineering feat!'

Annie shuddered again, as if someone had just walked over her grave. 'No, I just had to get out of there. There was something strange about him. Something very strange and sinister. I couldn't stand to be in the same space as him. I just had to leave. It wasn't before I got far away from that place that I started to feel a little better.'

Of all the pilgrims on the Way, Annie was probably the least likely to be influenced by the paranormal and her reaction to Tomás was a surprise to me. But then, the man has established himself as one of the main 'features' of the Camino, so perhaps there has to be something rather special and extraordinary about him. Such is the way of the Camino after all…

Some weeks after Molinaseca and the crossing of Monte Irago, the area renowned for its bandits, wolves and witches – and Tomás The Last Templar, Annie, Christl and I found ourselves in a small dormitory in Ruitelán, at the foot of the mountains leading up to O Cebreiro. I had just enjoyed a scrumptious meal of pumpkin soup, freshly baked bread, a huge omelette and salad, all prepared for me by Carlos, one half of a gay couple who ran the beautiful little refuge, when Annie and Christl arrived through the brightly painted blue door. Carlos and his partner also offered massages to pilgrims, but we'd arrived too late and missed out on this rare treat, so the three of us sat on our bunks and caught up with Camino news.

'So, did you ever get to see a witch?' Christl asked.

I laughed. 'You know what the books say: "They don't *really* exist but be on the lookout for them – you never know when you might bump into one!" For a moment I considered sharing with them my experience with the witch of Foncebadón, but before I'd made up my mind one way or the other, I noticed Annie's expression.

She was looking down at her foot as she pushed her shoe this way and that over the floor in front of her. 'I believe I saw a witch,' she mumbled.

'Annie, *you* are the one who thinks all this church stuff and Camino legends and stories and things are a load of rubbish! I can't *believe* you're saying that!' Christl's blue eyes were as big as saucers.

'Well, I *don't* believe all this nonsense, and all that stuff *is* a load of nonsense. I am so not into all this spiritual stuff. The Camino is just a long hard walk, and not even a very difficult long walk at that. I mean, there are other trails that are far, far more demanding and challenging – like the Otter Trail in the Cape. This is nothing compared to that! These people talking about how hard it is, they would never last a day on the Otter Trail. I can't even see the sense of this whole Camino thing.'

Annie was a merino sheep farmer from the Free State Province in South Africa, one of the harshest occupations in one of the harshest environments, and something that was definitely not for the fainthearted. But Annie was tough and anything but fainthearted. So, for her to admit to having seen a witch would have been hard to believe for anyone who'd met her.

'But that man Tomás, that guy who claimed to be the last Templar or whatever, he was not altogether from this world. I still have nightmares just thinking about him. I walked into his refuge that day and suddenly felt like there was something crawling all over my soul. It was scary. I don't know – perhaps he wasn't a witch, but how else do you explain it?'

Indeed, how else do you explain it? And yes, such is the way of the Camino, after all…

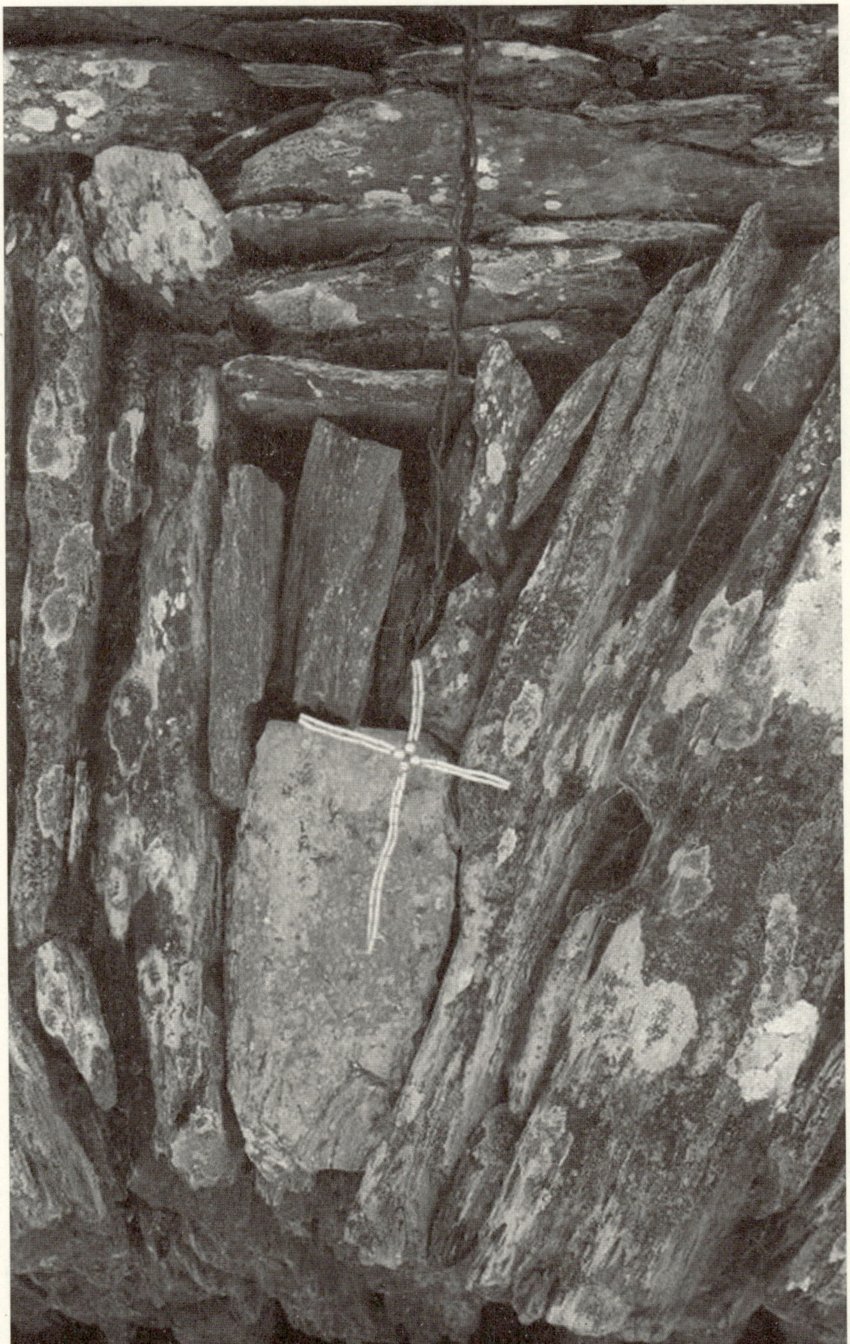

8
The Devil must be grabbed by his tail: that is what tales are there for...

月日は百代の過客にして行かふ年も又旅人也。人生そのもの旅也。

The passing days and months are eternal travellers in time. The years that come and go are travellers too. Life itself is a journey.

– Matsuo Basho, Japanese haiku poet

Akira and I had, without talking about it, started walking side-by-side for the last few days of his Camino. He had only three weeks in Spain and had decided right from the start not to try to finish the whole pilgrimage and reach Santiago within the limited time, but just to walk to where his time allowed him. No doubt if anyone could have walked the entire distance from Roncesvalles in twenty-one days, Akira could. He was super fit and in superb condition. As a dancer and actor he looked after his body extremely well. He always liked to take the top bed of the bunk beds in the refuges and every night and every morning he'd do at least half an hour – but sometimes well over an hour's worth – of exercises, stretching and bending and contorting his body into shapes I'd never seen before. If he ever had a problem with hips or knees or feet, he most certainly never told anyone about it.

'Do you remember that first night we met Kamil?' Akira was busy stuffing balls of newspaper he'd managed to find somewhere into our wet boots, which we had drying in front of the radiator to prevent them from shrinking. I had my feet in a bright pink plastic tub filled with ice cubes, cups of vinegar and coarse sea salt, and was enjoying the relief this magical formula was giving me.

'I think that night he will never make it! But now maybe he is in front of us. He is so good!'

'Yes, he would definitely be in front of us because otherwise we would have seen him today. If you consider how far we walked today it's incredible that we never bumped into anyone!' We had done a marathon forty-seven and a half kilometres that day – almost double the 'normal' distance for the average walker.

'But Kamil! He is soooo amazing, for sure!' If 'amazing' had been my favourite word, Akira had completely taken ownership of it, as he had of Thorsten's 'for sure', and usually it was preceded by a long drawn out 'soooo'. But in this particular instance, his way of describing Kamil was definitely the truest description.

Way back in Puente la Reina, Thorsten, Akira and I had arrived at the refuge at almost the same time. They'd gone off to the church to look for someone to come and register us while I had a shower and washed my clothes. It didn't take me long, because the water was freezing cold and there was no heating in the dormitory, but when I came out, the priest from the church was already sitting behind the desk in the entrance, the passports spread out in front of him and explaining to Thorsten the significance of the *refugio*'s stamp. Thorsten was sitting in front of the desk, leaning forward in intense concentration, drinking in every word from the priest – who, responding to this young man who was obviously enjoying and appreciating the story, kept on and on with his history lesson.

Not understanding a word of the Spanish – except that he was talking about the stamp and the 'triangular' or Y-shaped cross depicted on it, I collected my passport and returned to the dormitory to go and read up in my guidebook what the story was about the strange looking crucifix. Akira had also had a shower and came back into the dormitory dancing around and jumping up and down trying to get warm. 'Listen to this Akira! Apparently this Y-shaped crucifix is one of only two – the other one is in Carrión de los Condes. It was a gift from pilgrims from the Rhineland back in the fifteenth century. We'll have to go and look at it either here or when we go through there...'

'I think maybe Thorsten will also come to tell the story. The *hospitalero* tells him about it.'

Just then Thorsten came into the dorm with the stamped passports and the good news that someone was coming to bring us some wood to burn in the fireplace in the common room.

'Ah! That will be wonderful! Imagine sitting in front of a fire tonight. Perhaps we can see if we can get some sausages to barbeque, or at least some marshmallows. By the way Thorsten – I didn't know you could understand Spanish?'

'No, I don't, for sure,' was the reply.

'But you were listening with such an intelligent look on your face and responding and nodding your head and even laughing at his jokes. And he was talking to you for half an hour!' Thorsten had told me that first night we met that he only knew a few essential Spanish words, but when I'd seen him that evening with the priest it most certainly looked as if he understood the whole long story.

'Yes, but I didn't understand what he said, for sure. I just put on my "school face".'

'Your school face? What's that?' Akira wanted to know.

Thorsten laughed. 'It isn't only you who can act, Akira-san! I put on my school face and the teacher thinks that of course I am concentrating and listening and understanding, but all the time I am thinking of other things.'

'So you can't tell us about the cross?' I asked.

'What cross?' Thorsten looked perplexed.

Akira and I just cracked up laughing. Thorsten was the one who'd sat for thirty minutes listening attentively to the animated lecture by the priest, while Akira and I had only walked past but had nevertheless managed, in those few moments, to pick up what the lecture was about.

'He was telling you about the "triangular" cross, Thorsten! It is the only one of two crosses that depicts Christ on a Y-shaped crucifix, with his arms stretched out above his shoulders so that the body was in a Y-shape as well. The other Y-shaped cross is in Carrión de los Condes…'

We laughed so much that we almost didn't hear the commotion in the entrance next door. The next moment, there, in the door, stood a sight so sorry that it wiped the smiles off our faces in a second, and crowding in behind him, were Brigitte and Lisl, the twin sisters, originally from a farm near Dresden in the then East Germany, and whom I had last seen on top of the Pyrenees mountains.

'We are so happy you're here!' Brigitte came in and dropped her big backpack onto a bed. 'We need help here with Kamil. He is not good. Come Kamil, come say hello to Thorsten and Akira and Wilna,' and with this she pulled Kamil into the room.

My first impression of Kamil was that he was a round man. Everything about him was round. There was not a hair on his head – and when I think back, I don't remember ever seeing any stubble on his head, so I can't tell whether it was shaved or naturally bald – but his head was round, shiny and red. And, at that moment when I saw Kamil for the first time, he was a round picture of misery. Everyone was galvanised into action. Thorsten pulled the backpack off Kamil's back, Akira made him sit down on a chair, I brought a cup of water, and Brigitte started telling us about how they'd found him.

It transpired that Kamil had started the pilgrimage earlier that day in Pamplona. Right from the first steps things went wrong for him. His backpack was one of the old designs that had an aluminium framework sewn into its structure and, during the flight from Berlin, the backpack must have been squashed out of shape. The aluminium struts were no longer a comfortable flat grid against his back, but a contorted mangle that gouged holes into Kamil's back wherever it made contact with his body. When he pulled up his shirt, it looked like the back of someone who'd been kicked and punched by an army of jackbooted hoodlums.

'I can't go on. I am going to take the bus in the morning and go back to Pamplona.' Kamil's eyes welled up.

'Don't be ridiculous. Of course you can go on. You will go on.' Brigitte started rubbing cream onto his bruised back. Kamil squirmed. 'Not too hard! It is very painful! I will not be able to carry my backpack and how do I do the Camino if I can't carry a backpack?'

'We will fix the backpack,' Thorsten stated from the corner where he'd already unpacked Kamil's pack and had started unravelling the seams in the fabric to pull the entire aluminium framework out.

'Don't do that!' wailed Kamil, his face now wet with tears, his body dejected. A bundle of misery. 'You are ruining my pack!'

'It is already ruined, Kamil. That is why your back looks like that. I am now fixing it for you. If I take the framework out it will be much better, for sure. You don't need the framework in the backpack.'

'Oh but my feet hurt too! Everything hurts!'

'Come Kamil. Stop complaining and go take a shower, then we'll look at your feet.'

Akira led Kamil off to the bathroom to have a shower. I returned to the kitchen to continue with my version of the *Menestra de Peregrin* that I'd started to prepare a little earlier. As Puente de la Reina was a biggish town, it had grocery shops where we could buy food, so the dinner that night promised to be a feast. I already had the chard and broad beans boiling in the big old saucepan I'd found in the cupboard – its battered round sides looking a bit like Kamil's back. I still had to add the tin of creamy white butter beans that I was using instead of the more traditional peas, a couple of slices of ham, as well as a few potatoes the boys had picked up in a field on the way into Puente de la Reina that afternoon. Akira came and joined me in the kitchen, wanting to know what he could do to help.

'Flowers for the table, please, Akira. Go see what you can find – even if just a few pretty leaves.'

Akira had loved my insistence on always 'laying the table' when we made meals in the refuges. Adding a small plastic cup or glass with a few wild flowers or pretty leaves on the *refugio* kitchen tables immediately made everyone sitting around the table for their evening meal feel a little more special and 'at home'. Having to rough it in the very basic refuge kitchens, the dormitories with their dozens of bunk beds and the bathrooms where even shower curtains were often lacking, did not mean that you had to forget about any form of refinement or luxury. A little bunch of flowers or greenery in the middle of a scrubbed wooden table worked magic on a group of dusty and footsore pilgrims.

Thorsten, in the meantime, had de-boned the offending backpack and, when Kamil came out of the shower, stood ready to present it to him. But there were to be more tears. Kamil's inner thighs were an angry inflamed-looking mess. Because his legs chafed against each other when he walked, and because he had not been wearing any tight-fitting underwear under his trousers, the day's chafing had resulted in almost all the skin being rubbed off completely. If we thought his back had to be painful and the blisters on his feet had to be cause for complaint, no one who saw his inner thighs needed convincing that he had more than enough reason to feel very, very sorry for himself. We all stood around his bed, horrified at the sight in front of us.

'I must go back tomorrow. It will be impossible for me to continue on the Camino!' he resumed his wailing.

'Kamil! Do you *want* to walk the Camino? Do you *want* to go to Santiago de Compostela?' I asked.

'Yes! Of course I do. But I cannot continue with my sore back and my blisters and now these legs. I can't walk one more step. It is too painful!'

'Right, then. Stop complaining now and let's see what we need to do for you to get there. Have you anything that you can wear under your trousers so that your legs don't chafe. Did you bring thermal underwear?'

It turned out he had not. But what he did have was a pair of woollen pyjamas with pants that were tight fitting. 'These are perfect. Pure wool! Nothing is better for something like this! From tomorrow you wear these under your trousers. That way you won't even know when your legs chafe together. Brigitte will give you more of her cream to put on the raw skin and she will also show you how to treat your blisters. I will give you some of my NOK cream to rub on your feet and tomorrow you can stop at a pharmacy before leaving the town and buy your own. Thorsten has fixed your backpack so it won't hurt your back anymore. And dinner is ready and on the table. Let's go eat and you will feel better. A lot better!'

A short while later we had a big blazing fire going in the fire place, a bottle of wine had been opened, Akira had provided the flowers for the table and the six of us slid into the long benches on either side of the old refectory table; Thorsten and Akira, Brigitte and Lisl, me – and Kamil, the newest member of the little Camino pilgrims' group that found itself on the Way that third week of February, 2008. We sat around that table on that night in Puente de la Reina and talked late into the night. We learned from Kamil that he was a recently qualified doctor of medicine from Berlin. After he'd nearly died of some strange illness as a new-born baby, his father had refused to accept that there was no hope for him and had rushed him across the city to try to find someone who could save him. He eventually was saved and, at the time, his father vowed that his son's life had been saved for a purpose. Named after the patron saint of nurses and nurses' associations, St. Camillus de Lellis, Kamil, right there, from a few days old, was already pre-ordained to be the first in his family to go and study at university and to have a life that was to be dedicated to the healing and care of others.

Recently I read the introduction to a beautiful Lonely Planet publication called *One People: Many Journeys*. What Lonely Planet co-founder Maureen Wheeler wrote in the introduction could have been written for our little band around that table on that magical night:

> The boundaries we cross (when we travel) are not always physical – travel involves an internal journey as well as an external one, as we discover more about ourselves. When we travel we come up against the boundaries inside us: our prejudices, our limits, our willingness to understand and our ability to empathise. We are confronted by what we see and challenged to

respond. As travellers we experience what it is like to be on the outside, the 'different' one. To the people we meet we are exotic, we bring with us beliefs and attitudes from another place, and it is in the mutual exchange of our stories that our transformation begins.

At no time did these words ring more true than among those fellow-pilgrims on that night in Puente de la Reina.

Needless to say Kamil continued on the pilgrimage and finished it and when I arrived in Santiago de Compostela weeks later, he was there, ahead of everyone, and waiting to welcome the rest of us. By that time he'd slimmed down substantially and he looked handsome, fit and healthy, and his only tears were the tears of joy at being reunited with Brigitte, Lisl and me; Thorsten had had to return to Germany ten days before and Akira's three weeks were over and he'd already returned to 'real life' in Tokyo. Meeting up with Kamil again in Santiago was for me, personally, one of the highlights of Santiago.

On several occasions the thick, late-winter morning mist was the topic of conversation around the *refugio* kitchen table where pilgrims got together of an evening for a shared meal, warmth and conversation.

'It makes me very scared to walk in the dark. And when there is mist, it is so hard for me!'

Akira had grown up in Tokyo, a city that was probably more densely populated than any other, that was always busy, bustling and most certainly never dark. He made no secret of the fact that he was petrified of the dark and I could well imagine that this bare, empty landscape of the Camino must have been overwhelming for him – especially before sunrise and in thick mist.

Nevertheless, one morning, at a stage of the pilgrimage when I was at least half a day's walk ahead of him, he had woken up extra early and left the *refugio* a couple of hours before dawn to try to catch up with me. It meant that it was still pitch dark and, on that particular day, it was clear why heavy mist was often described as being as thick as pea soup.

'I was sooooooooo scared!' His oriental eyes stretched wide and round as he relived the moment.

'But I took out my little torch...' and he pulled out of his pocket the tiniest of tiny objects, dangling on the end of a key chain… 'Look! A friend in Japan give this to me for good luck gift and I think he was joking. But it is a torch!'

We took a closer look. The little object looked like no more than a small plastic ball attached to the end of the chain. It was no bigger than a pinkie nail. But Akira held it between his forefinger and thumb and squeezed, and there, even in broad daylight, a sharp clear beam of light shone out of this magical miniature torch.

'I had to walk zigzag all the way,' he continued, bending his tall lanky body over double to act out his words, his neck and nose stuck out at an unnatural angle; the almost invisible little torch in his extended hand in front of him, '…shining my magic torch to find the signs. I did not know which way I must go. So I run this way. Then I run that way, and I shine my magic light everywhere. I think maybe if somebody sees me, he is still laughing!' Then, a little quieter, 'The mist was like a wall around me. I did not like it very much… but I sing the song Thorsten teach me and I find the way. And I find you!'

Akira's broken English and wild caricature gestures made the vivid description hilarious and he had us laughing so much there were tears running down our cheeks. And when he started singing, in flawless German, the children's St. Martin Day song, *Laterne Laterne*, that Thorsten had taught him to help overcome his fear of darkness, we thought our sides would split with laughing.

'Ich geh mit meiner Laterne und meine Laterne mit mir … Laternenlicht erlösche nicht rabimmel, rabammel, rebumm bum bum' – the last words rumbling loud and deep and dramatic in his sonorous tenor voice.

As a highly acclaimed actor in musical theatre back in Tokyo, he was also an accomplished mimic, and his body language always more than compensated for his lack of English.

'I quite like walking in the mist. It makes you lose all sense of time and place,' Brigitte laughed, as she lit up yet another cigarette. 'It's a little like when you're smoking a joint – only the clouds aren't in your head, they're all around you!'

Nothing scared Brigitte, which was just as well, because she and Lisl were walking much faster than anyone else and they intended finishing the pilgrimage in thirty days. That often meant they had to get up and start walking in the dark in order to fit in the required number of kilometres before sunset.

'Ah – but it is usually in the mist that you see the saints of the pilgrimage.' Kamil was the only one among our little group in the *refugio* that night who was motivated by his strong Catholic faith. And, strangely enough, I later discovered that he was also probably the only one among us who'd never encountered, or was never aware of having encountered, a saint or an angel.

Akira and I looked at each other. Only the day before we had come across not a saint, but the Devil himself.

No! Don't laugh or feel my forehead for a temperature or roll your eyes! Did I not say 'Such is the way of the Camino'? Get yourself a mug of coffee or a cup of green tea, join our group, make yourself comfortable and listen as the story unfolds...

'Do you remember that long stretch alongside the road – between Fromista and Carrión de los Condes?'

Everyone nodded their heads. That particular stretch was memorable in that it was straighter and flatter than any other section, and as the guidebook warned, an 'unspectacular path parallel to the country road, and an almost endless section.' These infrequent manmade pathways along the roads were called '*senda de Peregrine*', and on this particular one someone, for some unknown reason, had built pairs of cement bollards, each pair standing side by side, one metre apart and roughly fifty metres from the next pair, for the entire length of the section. Perhaps this was to break the monotony, as this was a long stretch with nothing to concentrate on other than putting one foot in front of the other. Each bollard – and we had stopped counting when we got to the seventy-fifth pair – had the scallop shell of the Camino in relief on the side, so perhaps this may have been considered to be an excellent opportunity to remind the pilgrim what the Camino was supposed to be about; about saints and sinners, redemption and contemplation.

'We had stopped at the beautiful locks at Fromista...' Akira started and then, as usually happened during these conversations that were about something we'd all experienced, Lisl interrupted:

'Yes! We stopped there too – we liked that place!'

The 18th century Canal de Castilla stretched for two hundred and seven kilometres through this region and the pilgrims' path went alongside for a long way, until, just before Fromista, the pathway crossed over to the other side at the top gate of an elaborate lock system – a lock ladder of seven gates that overcame fourteen vertical metres. Quite an engineering feat;

and a wondrous source of fascination for someone who loved watching cascading water as much as I did. It soon turned out that Akira did as well and we spent almost two hours, either sitting or lying flat on our stomachs on the edge of the top weir, watching in awe as the tons and tons of cubic metres of water crashed down one lock, then the next, then the next. Except for the uppermost lock gates, the other gates had been removed, so the water tumbled unhindered down six manmade waterfalls. Eventually, after the last fall, it seemed suddenly to run out of power as it dropped down into the continuing canal. It was mesmerising. As this was no longer a functional lock system with traffic on the canal – the water now only used for irrigation – you would have thought the lock keeper had become redundant. Yet, there he was, spending his days clearing the never-ending stream of water lilies and other aquatic plants floating down the canal. With a long pitchfork he released the lily plants from the top gates as they arrived, and then pushed them to the side and down the overflow. The plants sped down with the water, only to get caught in a maelstrom in the first basin below the lock gates, competing with empty wine bottles, estate agents' broken *for sale* signs, an old boot – and an eclectic collection of debris, no doubt each item able to tell a gripping life story.

'But then we were late and there was no *refugio* open in Fromista, so we had to continue. And it was raining so much! I never see so much rain in all my life.' Akira must have been dead on his feet by this time. (This was the same day he'd left before dawn to catch up with me and so had already done twelve kilometres before finding me on the path just after sunrise.) The disappointment of not finding an open refuge in Fromista was crushing.

'Of course, the guidebooks – both Akira's and mine – said that there were supposed to be at least two refuges open, but neither of them was.'

Brigitte's eyes widened. 'We went through Fromista early in the day and looked for a place to have something to drink, but also found everything closed.'

'And the next refuge was only in Carrión de los Condes, another twenty kilometres, four hours away!' Brigitte and Lisl were both aghast at our bad luck.

More often than not the villages and refuges were not that far apart. But this was one of the exceptions, and to get to the end of an already long day's walk and find you had another twenty kilometres – or four hours to walk, was a tough call.

We had no choice but to continue once again, tired, sore, and in the pouring rain. But, as pilgrims do, we did just that. If we had foreseen the difficulty of finding a place to stop and stay, we would never have spent such a long time at the weir. And yet, the long rest next to the weir had helped, in the sense that it gave us the feeling that we were just starting on a new adventure. Or at least, we managed to fool ourselves that we were.

A good way to distract from the exhaustion and pain was to get an interesting conversation going – something I'd realised I was missing out on when walking alone – (not that my own company was not interesting). When I did, very occasionally, walk with someone for an hour or two, I loved the variety and novelty of the different subjects that came up for discussion among pilgrims. I could well imagine that this was something that had not changed over the centuries that pilgrims had been walking these pathways. I could also understand completely how this Camino, the Way under the Stars, had been a major route of communication centuries ago when there was no other means of long-distance communication between individuals; the Camino was a main artery for the cultural and intellectual lifeblood of Europe.

Jaffa Raza wrote in his guidebook, *The village to village guide*:

> The footpath created since the very beginning an extraordinary spiritual, cultural and economic vitality: it bred literature, music, art and history and, on its account, cities and villages were born…markets appeared, roads and bridges were planned and cathedrals and churches, that elevated the Romanesque art to a magnificence not reached by other styles, were built. … The Camino still passes through the same villages, crosses the same rivers, visits the same chapels as did the path taken when the numbers walking peaked in the eleventh and twelfth centuries – the time when over half a million people in a year are said to have made the pilgrimage from different parts of Europe.

What a networking opportunity! Imagine the people, from every walk of life, rich and poor, important and humble, educated and illiterate, all converging, as equals, on this 800-kilometre, one-metre-wide stony pathway under the Milky Way! Imagine the stories they must have told each other, how they must have learned about the other side of the world from each other. Imagine how they must have exchanged ideas and ideals, knowledge and know-how, theories, ideologies. The mind boggles at the sheer magnitude of this window of opportunity for communication, for cross-pollination of ideas, for exchange of knowledge and vision. Where in the world have we ever had a more effective conduit of person-to-person communication among people from every nationality in the world?

And the beauty of the Camino for me was that none of this had changed over time. Despite electronic communication opportunities, despite technology and every wonderful aspect of modern communication, that window of opportunity that existed in the eleventh and the twelfth centuries on the pilgrimage of Santiago de Compostela, had remained unchanged.

So, when Akira and I were turned away by the closed doors and shutters of the refuges in Fromista and we followed the yellow arrows in the direction of where the setting sun would have been, had it not been pouring with rain, I was not too worried; there were a million things I still wanted to learn from this lovely Japanese fellow-pilgrim and friend. Top of our conversation was our shared love of Japanese traditions.

'I was horrified when I learned that my son has a tattoo,' I confided. 'But when I heard what the tattoo meant – it is done in Japanese kanji – I have to admit I smiled secretly and felt very proud. It says: *Fudan Misao* (Always Honour). It does not condone writing indelibly across one's beautiful body, but it does show the commitment to a life philosophy that is commendable.'

'That is a good way to live,' Akira nodded, 'always with honour.' 'You are very lucky your son chooses to walk the way of bushido, the way of the samurai.' '*Gi*' in Japanese means 'honour' but also translates as 'duty'. It is not only the samurai or the warriors that have always, since the sun first rose over Japan, upheld the code of bushido, the way of honour and loyalty; it has been a way of life for all Japanese, and even today, in modern Japan, where many of the ancient traditions are being eroded by a demanding world of technology and economics and the need for global acceptance, that inherent sense of honour and loyalty remains. How sad then that that same sense of honour, which can elicit such noble behaviour, such courage and selflessness, can also drive people to such atrocious and inhumane behaviour as was witnessed in the prisoner-of-war camps during the Second World War. How sad that a philosophy that is so noble could also be the cause of actions that turn a wonderful person into an animal. Again: the fine line between passion and terrorism, between religion and fanaticism, between a sense of honour and loyalty and the blind pursuit of madness. We talked about the nature of man and how the most intolerant people can also be guilty of the most intolerable behaviour.

Inadvertently, as happens when two people on a pilgrimage get talking – and both love practising lateral thinking – the conversation flowed into our thoughts on reincarnation, on a life after death, Buddhism, Shintoism, and religious myths and legends.

'And it was just about then, at that point in the conversation, when we were talking about Sant Iago or Saint James and the weird and convenient way in which he had been adopted into the history books of Spain and the Camino, how he "appeared" to pilgrims on the way, that we saw *him*. Not the saint and not an angel, but that "other one" – the Devil himself.'

I was out of breath already and had only just arrived back at the crux of the story. I took a sip of the now-cold green tea, savouring the deliciously delicate aroma.

'*Lateral thinking* you call it?' Brigitte laughed. 'Never be in a hurry when you try to follow the story a *lateral thinker* is telling!'

'Well, the Devil is the main character of this tale, so it was always going to demand some extra time!

'Anyway. It was a few kilometres from Carrión de los Condes. We could already make out the church spire in the distance as well as some of the rooftops of buildings and the sight was glorious! At last, after forty-five plus kilometres, the longest either of us had ever walked in one single day: the promise of a bed and warmth and dry clothes and rest!'

At this point, Akira, who was dying to be telling the story but did not have the words with which to express himself, used the means that he did have available to him and started a colourfully vivid acting out of the story, exaggerating the actions and turning the entire narration into a one-man mime performance. I stepped up to the challenge and started putting a lot more drama into my voice.

'As you are all aware, there are bad spirits that lie in wait for us pilgrims, hoping to tempt us to stop or abandon our pilgrimage. Some people call them bad spirits, some call them the pagan spirits that have stayed and continue to linger on the Way. Some are even bold enough to call him by his name – The Devil.' Everyone was listening intently and nodding their heads. I paused and kept silent as I turned my thoughts inward for a moment, reflecting on the amazing phenomenon of the Camino. People do not often care to admit to having had an 'encounter' with an angel or a saint, let alone the Devil! And yet, there are so many anecdotes, myths and legends about the Devil appearing to pilgrims and trying to steer them off course or to get them to do some wicked things. Every time someone writes about the Camino, they include a few of these anecdotes, so, whether people will admit to having had such bizarre experiences or not, someone out there is adding to the folklore of the Camino all the time.

'Well, my friends, we saw him that night. Akira and I saw the Devil. In person. In the flesh.'

There was a hushed silence in the room. Not even one of them looked cynical or incredulous. Akira and I had a spellbound audience.

'It was, as I mentioned, pouring with rain. For hours we'd been walking in the rain, the pitta-patta sound of the heavy rain drops on our ponchos and backpack covers making hearing each other difficult but providing a wonderful background rhythm to the squelching of our boots in the mud and our sticks marking the pace on the never-ending *senda*. We continued to walk at a steady pace and to talk about a thousand interesting topics. In all that time no more than a couple of cars passed us in either direction and we both felt as if we were the only people left in the world.

'Then, from far, far away, we both saw this strange sight. Way off in the distance, there seemed to be a man standing in the middle of the tarred main road. Not in the pathway, but in the main road. He seemed not to move. Like a statue, he just stood there, with his back towards us, facing in the direction of the town, in the rain, holding an umbrella over his head. As if on cue, a car came from behind us and we held our breaths as the car sped towards the man, a large fan of water spraying out from its sides. Surely the man would have to move out of the way, or be run over and killed by the speeding car? But he never moved – he just stood there, motionless, holding his umbrella. The car didn't swerve when it came close to the man. And when it had passed, he was still standing in the exact same place. We looked at each other and I said, "It has to be a mirage, Akira! Too many kilometres in one day. We've been walking more than eleven hours and we must obviously be hallucinating."

'Akira shook his head. "He is the Devil," he said. "Oh come on Akira-san..." I started, but then fell silent. How else do you explain what we'd just seen?

'When we got a little closer, we saw that it was in fact a man and that he was real. How the driver had not seen him or the car flattened him when he drove "right over" him, we could not explain. Nor could we explain that the man was hardly wet. If the car had not driven straight over him, the spray of the car must have drenched him – and yet his raincoat had no more than a few wet splotches on it. He was very smartly dressed in black trousers and shiny black leather shoes, a white shirt and a black tie, and what looked like an expensive raincoat. His head was large and bald on top, with a fringe of longish hair curling over the back of his raincoat. As we came closer still, we could see a big nose. Thinking back, he really did look like a good model for a stone gargoyle. When we came parallel to him, without turning towards us but as if he'd sensed our presence, he started walking diagonally across the road to come close to the ditch that separated the road and the *senda*, and fell into an easy, natural step with us. After a short while, he suddenly jumped over the ditch and joined us on the muddy pathway. Somewhere in my mind I wanted to object to the intrusion, to the fact that the stones and mud would dirty his clothes, that his shoes were not suited to the pathway. But I looked down and saw that his shiny black leather shoes were still shiny and black. There was no mud on them. They didn't even look wet.

'Next to me, I could feel a shudder go through Akira. "We must stop, Wilna-san," he muttered urgently and under his breath. At the same moment he laid a hand on my arm and brought me to a stop. He then stepped in front of me and raised his arms out and above his shoulders, his pilgrim stick brandished aloft like a samurai sword, as if to protect me from this strange man…'

All those weeks later, as we sat there that night in the *refugio* kitchen among our fellow-pilgrims and recounted this story, I listened to my own words and still wondered at my memory of the event. It did seem so surreal. The words telling the story seemed strange in my mouth. I looked across at Akira who was still in full flight, miming the story as I told it. He'd been there too. He had seen what I'd seen, felt what I had felt. And at that time, his first instinct had been to want to protect me. I smiled across at him. My Camino angel, I thought.

'I was so scared!' he laughed. 'But I think I must protect you. I must be very mad to think I can do this. I think maybe it is my bushido…'

'Your sense of loyalty and honour did you and your ancestors proud, my friend,' I laughed. 'Especially if you consider who our adversary was!'

'Ad – ver –?' Akira quizzed. 'Ah so! The Devil you mean!'

'Yes, the Devil. We both realised at the same time that there was something very unreal about this "man". And we both sensed the evil at the exact same moment. People talk about a sulphur smell when in the presence of the Devil. Neither of us smelt sulphur, but what we sensed was far worse. It was pure evil.'

'So what happened next?' Lisl, normally so quiet, was sitting forward, on the edge of the chair, her face serious. 'Go on. Continue the story!'

'The man slowed down and came to a halt as well,' I took my thoughts back to that strange day on the *senda*.

'"You have walked a very long way today," he said. "You started in Itero de la Vega," he said to me, and then turned to Akira, still standing there like an avenging angel, "and you started in the dark in Castrojeriz this morning."'

'Huh? Is that where you had started? How did he know?' Everyone listening to the story was incredulous that this stranger could possibly have known where both Akira and I had started our walk that morning. And Akira and I had not even started from the same place that day. There is communication between refuges, but who would go to this kind of trouble to find out who had started where – and why?

'Akira just told the man: "*Basta*! *Vada via*!"' We all laughed. Akira knew very little English, but he'd picked up an assortment of words and phrases from the lyrics of the musicals in which he performed. And, as many of these productions were operettas, he knew more Italian words and phrases than any or all of us together. He spoke not a word of Spanish, but just as I had found that my French went a long way to making myself understood, so he found his knowledge of Italian did the same for him.

However, whether the man did not understand Akira's Italian, or whether he was impervious to being told to go away, he continued alongside us. With gestures accompanying his speech, we understood his Spanish to mean: "There is no refuge open in Carrión." We were about one kilometre away, and in a hurry to get there. From our guidebook we knew that there was a refuge in Carrión that did not have a *hospitalero* on duty during winter, but for which we could get a key from the bar on the square.

'"*Vada via*!" Akira persevered, trying to shoo the man along ahead.

'"You will not get accommodation in the village. There are no beds. You will sleep in my house. You must give me money and I will give you a bed." Rubbing his fingers together and demanding payment was the same in any language. "That is nonsense," I said. We know there is a refuge in the village and that we can get the key from the bar." He gave a little smile that sent a shiver through my veins. "There is no refuge. There is no key. You will stay in my house."

'There was no mistaking what this man was after. It was not our money; it was our souls. But, it was not that he was telling us a lie, or trying to get money out of us or trying to steal our souls that made Akira and myself wary of this man; there was no kindness in him. There was no feeling of hospitality or helpfulness coming from him. He never touched us. He did not even look at us. He simply continued to walk at the same speed as us, to look straight ahead. His shoes continued to stay dry and shiny despite the wet and the puddles and the mud. There was no colour in his face. There was no expression either. But, there was only this feeling of something crawling up our spines, a chill in the atmosphere, a heavy cold stone coming to sit in the pits of our stomachs.

'"*Grazie ma nessun grazie!*" Akira said softly. Then, much louder, "*Gracias ma no gracias!*" And building into a crescendo, his voice echoed over the flat landscape, loud and clear "*Gracias – ma – no – gracias!*"

'The man threw one quick angry and cold glance in our direction, stepped over the ditch and returned to the hard surface of the road. He picked up his pace and walked ahead. Akira continued to walk in front of me with his arms outstretched, a barrier between the Devil and me. Something made me take my camera out of its pouch and take a photograph of the man and of Akira, his arms stretched wide, his pilgrims' stick held high. Something made me want to prove to myself later that the man really did exist. The photograph says that he did – shiny shoes, umbrella and all. The photograph does not show the iciness in the atmosphere around him…

'When we finally arrived at the bar across the square about half an hour later, wet and tired and shaken by the experience, neither of us was really surprised to see the gargoyle man himself standing at the bar. He did not look around at us as we went up to the bar owner and asked for the refuge key. "No, the refuge is closed," the bar owner said firmly. "We know it has to be opened for us or that you should give us a key for it," we objected. "It is closed. You will not sleep in this town tonight. There is no room for you here. We don't want you here. Go away!" The next village was another ten kilometres and there was no way Akira or I could walk that distance. "Please, give us the key for the refuge," I asked again. "We don't want you here. You will not get a bed in this town tonight."

'Akira took me by my arm and turned me away. "Come Wilna-san, leave this people. We go."

'He quietly herded me out of the bar and started walking across the square to the information centre. "Perhaps they help us," he tried to sound positive.

'I think we knew the answer before we got it. As we walked into the small information centre attached to the church, there were three young people busy sorting brochures and pamphlets. They looked up as we stepped into the room. "Go away. We won't give you the key. We don't want you here. You will not have a bed in our town tonight."

'We did not even object. Akira and I knew that something had happened on that day that we would probably never be able to explain. We had crossed swords with the Devil and were not going to go unpunished.

'We went outside and stood in the rain…'

Suddenly I could understand why a pilgrim would lose their way or renounce their faith or do some such silly or irresponsible thing. It was not too hard to be tempted to do anything when you've walked almost twelve hours in the pouring rain and cold and mist and past that many closed refuge doors. Strip someone of all physical comforts for long enough, and the higher levels of the Maslow pyramid become a little less important. In fact, I lost the little respect I'd had for the Devil's cunning on that day; after all, it was not *that* difficult to make a person forfeit everything in return for relief from hardship.

'…But – Akira and I both had the samurai spirit, alive and well, within us. We looked at each other, nodded and started walking. As we got to the outskirts of the town, there was a lovely little stone building with a very welcome sign on the front: *Hostal*.

'"You like a long hot bath tonight, Wilna-san?" Akira smiled at me. "And would you enjoy resting your exhausted legs in front of a fire with a cold bottle of beer tonight, Akira-san?"

'We both laughed and walked in. The man behind the counter looked up from his computer screen and gave a huge grin. "Welcome! One room or two?" he asked. "One room with two beds, please. And a bathroom would make that perfect, thank you!" I said, feeling infinitely grateful.

'It was only much later, after I had blissfully soaked in a deep hot bath for an hour (the first and only time on the entire Camino!) and Akira had taped my feet again, we had done all our washing and hung it over the heater, Akira had stuffed our boots with newspaper to prevent them from drying hard and misshapen and shrunken, and we had enjoyed a delicious pilgrim's menu in front of a crackling fire, that we reviewed the events of the day. We had no doubt that we'd encountered the Devil. Strange and irrational as it may seem to anyone who heard the story, there was nothing that could negate the feeling we'd both had during our encounter with that strange apparition on the road.

'And that, my friends,' I concluded my story, 'that was the day Akira and I met the Devil!'

We all laughed, a little nervously, everyone relieved that the story ended well and that we'd survived to tell the tale. And we all, once again, counted our blessings for the knowledge that no matter how clever the evil forces were, the pilgrims would always be protected. Not one of those in that little band of pilgrims that night was into airy-fairy theories and beliefs. None of us took the stories of extra-terrestrials on the Camino seriously; not one among us necessarily believed in the authenticity of the relics that were kept in some of the churches. But, Akira and I both knew what we had seen, and believed the feelings we'd experienced on that day on the *senda*, and we all knew that the Devil's presence on the Camino was a little like the existence of the witches on Monte Irago; no one *really* believed in them, but everyone took some extra care, just in case they were there, or there-abouts.

Then, suddenly, I gulped and looked across at Akira. A flash of recognition mirrored between us. Without saying a word, we both suddenly realised something we'd never thought of: perhaps the man in the road was not the Devil at all. Perhaps he was just one of the Devil's workers – just another fallen angel. Perhaps we *had* succumbed to the Devil's temptation after all. Perhaps the Devil was the man who was sitting behind the computer in the *hostal* reception...

There was still a hushed silence in the group as everyone sat quietly reflecting on our story. Almost imperceptibly Akira shook his head. I nodded and smiled. I could only guess that his thoughts were the same as mine: whether we had grabbed the Devil by his tail that night, or whether the Devil and his helpers had grabbed the two of us by the nose and given us a good old shake while leading us down the path to perdition, the accommodation that night had been excellent, the hot bath had been worth a great deal more than we'd paid, and the story we had been left with to tell was a good one!

'What is that thing you have pinned to your jacket?'

About four or five of us were sitting on the wooden picnic tables and benches on top of the little mound behind the refuge in O Cebreiro. It was around six o'clock in the morning and one of those perfect days; the sky was a crystal dome above our heads and the magnificent mountain ranges we'd had to cross and climb to get here, were laid out like a velvet blanket at our feet. All of us were surprised to find we were not alone when we climbed up to the top of the hill in the almost-darkness and freezing pre-dawn cold, but again accepted it as one of those Camino phenomena; each one of us had woken up in the dark dormitory and felt the urge to get dressed and go outside to watch the sun rise. Nature has a funny way sometimes of waking you up and letting you know that this day is going to be a very special one – and to go out there and enjoy it!

The view from that 1 350-metre vantage point was breathtaking and we'd all been sitting quietly reflecting on the spectacular colours starting to blaze in the east as the sun came to greet us, when one of the boys noticed my pepper spray and (rudely) snapped us all out of our reverie by asking what it was.

'It's a pepper spray,' I replied. 'I suppose it seems a little incongruous in this idyllic landscape, doesn't it?'

'Is it for dogs?' Ernst looked at me sideways, raising one eyebrow in a question mark.

'Well yes – for the two-legged kind!' I quipped back. (Ernst told me much later that he had worried about me, a middle-aged woman walking alone – until I made that particular remark. After that he was confident that I would be able to handle myself, no matter what peril came my way.)

They all laughed, and the magical spell of the silent sunrise changed character; it became yet another special moment among fellow-pilgrims.

'Have you ever had to use it? I don't envy the poor two-legged dog that tries to make life difficult for you!'

'No I haven't used it, thank goodness. There was one time, right after Cezur Menor, when I walked past that little lake right after sunrise. I felt uncomfortable there and realised that if anyone was going to lie in wait for an unsuspecting pilgrim that would have been the perfect place – surrounded by the hills and with all those trees and bushes around. It was so remote. Not a good feeling at all.'

'Yes, I remember that spot. It did seem sinister, although I couldn't say why. But if anyone were going to attack a pilgrim, the dense forests would be a far better place. No one will ever find your body if something happened to you there!'

I shivered. Forests are where people have been attacked. And, as pilgrims don't carry anything of great value with them, except their lives, that is what they generally lose when attacked on the Way. Fortunately it does not happen often…

'But I must tell you – when I walk through any of these areas where shadows move and dry leaves rustle and bad feelings lurk behind the rocks or the trees, I stop and look down at my pepper spray – and smile. And I don't smile because the pepper spray gives me comfort; I smile at the ludicrous thought of having to use the spray.' I got up from the bench and stood in front of my little audience to better demonstrate what I was about to explain.

'Look. There I am, a woman alone on the pathway. A man jumps out from behind a bush where he has been waiting all his life for me, a gorgeous vulnerable woman, to come walking past.' Everyone was now leaning forward and enjoying the story.

'I see him coming, but I'm not worried because I have my pepper spray. One spurt of this spray will put him out of action for a long time – vomiting, foaming at the mouth, burning eyes, lungs on fire and mucous membranes that are wrecked for all time.'

Argh! Yuck! Oooh! Everyone could well envisage the scene – and it was not a pleasant one.

'But then I think to myself, I would have to say to the man: You have waited all your life for me, so wait a little longer – just give me a few moments. You see, I wear two pairs of gloves – a pair of silk gloves under the fur-lined gloves and I am walking with two sticks, one in each hand. I would first have to take off the two gloves from my right hand and put them in my pocket. Then I must take the stick from one arm and hang it over the other arm – I don't want to put anything down on the ground because it is difficult to bend over and pick things up when you have your backback on. Then I must open my hip bag, careful not to let my *credenciales* get bent or my passport fall out, and take out my glasses. I can't see without my glasses and I can't use the pepper spray without being able to see.'

By this time everyone was rolling with mirth. I acted out the scene and milked it for all it was worth. Holding up the pepper spray, I showed them why being able to see was rather crucial in the use of it. 'Look! There is a small safety catch on it that has to be lifted. Then the top has to be turned and then it must be held up like this. Only then do you push down to spray. But, if the nozzle is not pointing in the right direction, I would be spraying myself and not the attacker. And *that* would be a disaster!'

'And you think the man will listen to you and stop and wait for you to do all that?' Ernst had tears in his eyes from laughing.

'Well, probably not,' I admitted. 'So I decided I would just have to say to him: I think you are silly because I am a little past my prime, you know, but if you insist, have your way with me but please promise you will let me know when you are done and then be sure to help me up afterwards, because lying on your back on top of a backpack is just like an upturned tortoise – it is not easy to get back up again!'

The group had by now forgotten about the incredible sunrise in the distance and were thoroughly enjoying the pepper spray story.

I watched them all, fingering the now-famous pepper spray that my youngest son had bought me for protection, and which I carried pinned to my fleece. Now was probably not the moment to tell them about the experience I'd had only the day before, climbing the last stretch of the mountain between La Faba and O Cebreiro. This time it was not just a bad feeling that lurked, but a real man. He was a farm worker, judging from his muddy blue overalls, his dirty fingernails and the hoe he had over his shoulder. He was on a horse when he crashed through the bushes on the side of the pathway, having stormed up the side of the steep mountainside. I suspected he was as surprised to see me right there where he'd emerged as I was to see him. I hadn't heard him coming – probably due to the steepness of the mountainside or the direction of the strong wind or the beating of my own labouring heart in my ears – but all of a sudden, there he was, a farmer on a horse in front of me on the narrow pathway.

'Why are you walking alone?' he asked gruffly in Spanish. I replied in French; 'Good morning! I walk alone because I want to walk alone. Anyway, I have my *campana* – that is my daughter keeping me company.'

He did not quite grasp the idea that a little Tibetan temple bell could be my daughter keeping me company, but continued on about women who should not be alone – about them needing a man, needing love, needing to be protected. My understanding of Spanish had not improved too much, but what he was saying was an age-old macho-male litany and not difficult to translate. While he was ranting along, I removed my gloves, took out my camera and took a couple of photographs of him and his horse.

I was obviously not about to enter into a discussion, so he jumped off his horse and pushed up against me to prove his point. Whether it was the need for *love* or for *protection* he had in mind to demonstrate, I'm not sure, but in a flash he had his big burly arm around my neck and was pulling me towards him. It happened so suddenly that I was completely unprepared for it. My first reaction was to squeeze my hand in between our bodies and grab a hold of the pepper spray. As quickly, I realised that the pepper spray would be too late; I had to be far away enough from my attacker to use it or else the noxious spray would have the same effect on me as on him.

My thoughts were as clear and calm as if I'd been contemplating an interesting scene in nature. His eyes were watery and pleading. There were three thick black hairs and a grey one sprouting from a wart on his bulbous nose. His overall sleeve smelt like dry mud and cut straw – a pleasant farm smell, but there must have been some straw stuck in the fabric because I could feel it scratching the skin on my neck. He was still talking, still on the theme of *mujer-necesita-hombre-no sola-un amante-amor* – a husky, hungry voice, but I was no longer hearing what he was saying. All I was aware of was that his breath smelt like old tobacco and yellow teeth.

From deep down, Pierre's advice came back to me: *Remember the tricks I showed you. Believe you can do it, and you can. Use your fingers to find the lethal spots...* I released the tension in my body and let it go limp. For a nano-second a spark of surprise flashed in his glazed trance, but before he could act on my more vulnerable state, I used the extra space created between us to bring my right hand out and up – so fast he never saw it coming – and with my fingers in a claw, I went for those watery eyes. The tip of my index finger dug into the soft wrinkly flesh under the one eye and my fourth finger dug in under the other, and with all my emergency strength I pushed as hard as I could. The iron grip on my neck was released as he stumbled back, falling awkwardly against his horse, which was still standing patiently munching at the grass stubble on the side of the pathway, waiting for his master to return to sanity.

'Stupid old fool!' was the only thing I mumbled under my breath, not wanting to waste any more precious energy on his ridiculous behaviour, and I left him standing there next to his horse, stunned and unsure about exactly what had just happened.

This time, as I continued up that mountain, I did not believe that I'd met the Devil himself, but that he most definitely had been working his wily ways in this hapless farmer and would-be attacker. But this time I *did* feel I'd managed to outwit the Devil – not with pepper spray, but with an ingrained and probably inherently instinctive presence of mind. We are not without resources; we only have to believe that when we need them, we *will* find them within ourselves.

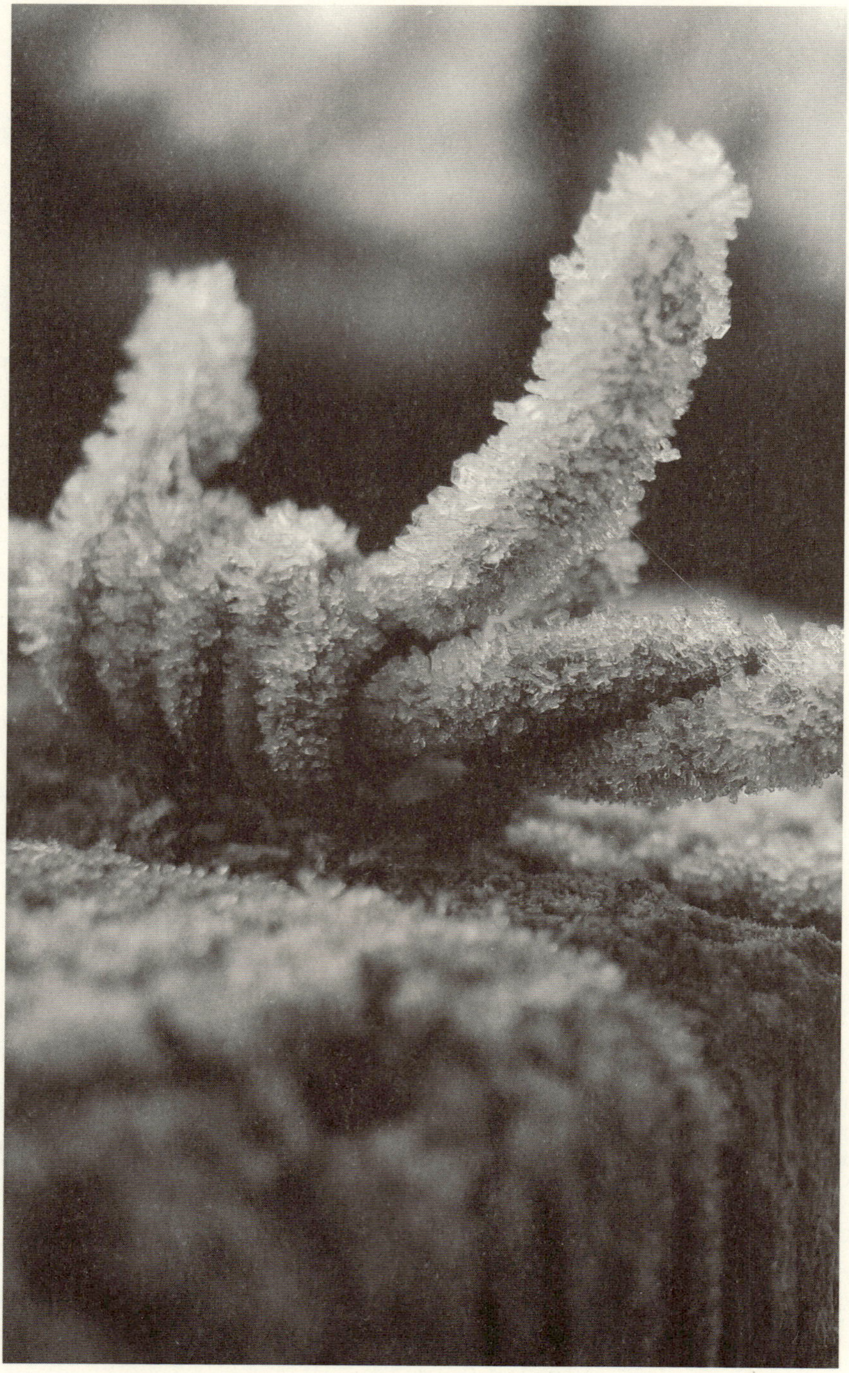

9

Courage is not the absence of fear – courage is the ability to enter unknown territory despite it

'It's all in your head,' Thorsten had told me that very first night in St-Jean-Pied-de-Port when I told him about my fears that I was unfit and ill-prepared for an 800-kilometre walk. I had known that – that it's all in the head; in fact, I had spent my working career coaching people into believing in the power of their own minds. There are countless case studies of the power of positive thinking, of visualising and turning dreams into reality, of making wishes come true by means of a relatively simple and positive thought process. 'Thoughts become things ... choose the good ones', says Mike Dooley, founder of Totally Unique Thoughts. 'If you can think it, you can do it' has become a slogan that slips off the tongues of even young children these days. It's lucrative as a topic of self-help books, and the bread, butter *and* strawberry jam of many motivational speakers.

But not only the 'feel-good, be-better' business has been exploiting the idea. On a much more serious level, scientists have been working for decades on the effects and the possible applications of that powerful human mind. Ruediger Fabian, of German Pain Aid, published a paper on how mind power can help people control pain and their perception of pain by changing their thinking habits.

'The brain has to decide what's important and what's not,' he said. Pain is a protective device of the body – it stops you from damaging yourself. But often pain is an emotional reaction rather than a physical one. A thinking adult can look at a bleeding graze on an arm and realise that it looks far worse than it is, and so cut off the impulse to feel the pain. It is a matter of how your brain evaluates the pain – and you can actively influence your brain in that evaluation. Consequently, the results of experiments show that people who want influence over their perception of pain should learn not to fear it, and should not see it as being worse than it really is.

Most of us experienced physical pain at some point on the Camino, mainly because of blisters, hips, knees or backs. Everyone had different solutions for the various ailments, but circumstances did not always allow for the most ideal treatments. Due to his profession, Akira knew the human body in its finest detail – especially the workings of the muscular and skeletal systems, and he was a gem to have nearby. With intricate cutting and complicated binding with strips of tape, he could 'create' new tendons for a knee or new muscles in a leg and so let the painful or damaged muscles rest. His massages were excellent too – albeit extremely painful – in particular when he found the source of the problem and kneaded out the knots and the lactic acid build-up in the muscles.

'Br-e-a-th-e out!' he would say. 'Br-e-a-th-e out. Take a d-e-e-p breath and breathe the pain o-u-t of your system.' We had lots of giggles about the way this ancient breathing technique and visualisation of the pain being pushed out of our bodies was given to us, but the end result was amazing. Anyone who has practised it, will know that it really does work, and every pilgrim who had come across Akira during the three weeks that he walked the Camino, would have a story to tell of how he or she had 'breathed out their pain.' (I have a lovely photograph of Akira with his face all scrunched up after eating a wedge of one of my lemons. 'B-r-e-a-th-e out, Akira-san!' I told him at the time. He did not think that was very funny, and so continued to believe that I had to be completely mad to eat lemons.)

But the breathing worked for me only up to a point. Early on, about ten days into the pilgrimage, I developed severe tendonitis in one leg. It was very, very painful, and no matter how much I repeated the Roman Centurion's shield inscription to myself that 'this too shall pass,' and no matter how hard I breathed, I was in agony. Anyone who knows me will confirm that my pain threshold is higher than most. But my shin throbbed and burned and felt as if there was a red-hot poker pushed into the marrow of my shin bone. I continued to limp badly, concentrating all the time on 'breathing out the pain', but with little success. Halfway through one afternoon of a particularly hard day, I arrived at the open door of a refuge in Redecilla del Camino. Never had I been so relieved to see an open refuge door! I walked in – only to be stopped by an unfriendly looking man who, judging by his clothing, was one of the plasterers.

'You can't come in. We are closed. We are getting ready for the Camino season.'

'But your door is open!' Generally refuge doors remained shut between half-past eight in the morning and four o' clock or half-past four in the afternoon. 'Please, I know it is too early, I can see you are painting and building, but I don't want to stay, I just want to rest my leg for a little while. If I can just sit down, out of the cold, and put my leg up, I promise not to get in anyone's way. I would be very grateful!'

I was ready to sell my body for the privilege of putting my leg up and getting relief from the burning throb. But the man did not budge, other than to shake his head, purse his lips, put his hand on my chest and push me backwards out the door. I tripped on the raised threshold of the big double doors and almost fell flat on my back on the pavement outside. The door slammed shut.

I sat there on the cold pavement, and I cried. A red-hot poker down my tibia, an unwarranted tongue-lashing from a stranger, a door slammed in my face... no amount of breathing in, breathing out or breathing otherwise was going to make this one better. I cried, and I cried, until I had no tears left. Then I did what pilgrims do; I wiped my face, blew my nose, picked myself up and followed the little yellow arrow.

About an hour later I walked up a hill and saw something like an illustration out of a children's book; a pale cream stone house with blue shutters, pretty pots with pretty flowers, shiny windowpanes and whale song music spilling out of the open doors. Best of all, there was a scallop shell in yellow and blue above the doors. I felt like Little Red Riding Hood. No! Hansel and Gretel. Was this the grandmother's cottage, or was it *the* gingerbread house? Whichever it was, there then had to be a big bad wolf or a nasty witch inside. But I didn't care. An hour before I was willing to sell my body for a bit of warmth and relief. Now I was willing to sell my soul. I limped right in.

The wolf and the witch were aged hippies, but they were warm, welcoming, wonderful aged hippies. They helped me out of my backpack and my shoes, sat me down on a bench at a rough wooden table and put a huge bowl of lentils in front of me. (Gretel immediately wondered whether she was being fattened up by the witch, but was too hungry to care.) This might be my last supper, I thought, so I might as well make the most of it. I looked around at the room. The rough stone walls were covered in an eclectic and colourful mix of art, wood carvings and woven wall hangings, some of them quite beautiful. South America, Africa, China were all represented – the tell-tale signs of the home of world travellers. There was a large wood burner in the corner where the most delicious heat was coming from. A few frayed but comfortable easy chairs stood around a low table on which an impressive array of glossy books was piled – the kind of books that don't come cheap, and would have looked more at home on a glass table in a Manhattan apartment. There were pretty white lace curtains at the windows, fresh wild flowers and bunches of grasses in pottery vases on the window sills. In one corner of the room was the kitchen area. A big old coal stove stood proudly against the wall, an earthenware pot on top – the one from which my lentils had come. On the bench were glasses and mugs and a little sign, adorned with flowers: 'Help yourself to water or herbal tea. Please wash up after yourself.' And on the wall next to the entrance was a larger-than-life poster portrait of Paolo Coelho, with the title 'The Patron of the Camino.' There was an all-pervasive smell in the air of something sweet...

The witch came and sat next to me, while the wolf went back to his easy chair, picked up an open book and carried on reading.

'Do you have problems with your knee?' she asked.

I put my spoon down and wiped my mouth. 'No, tendonitis,' I replied. 'These lentils are really delicious. Thank you so much for taking me in.'

'Ah, tendonitis is probably the most painful injury that pilgrims can get. Are you taking an anti-inflammatory?'

'Yes, I am, but so far it hasn't been too helpful. My worry is that I can feel the rest of my body is trying to compensate for my leg and that I'm causing more damage to other muscles now.'

'You probably are. And the cold doesn't really help either. It makes you tense up all your muscles. You really should try to concentrate on keeping the rest of your body in balance when you are walking. And breathe out. That helps for the pain.'

I burst out laughing. I told her about Akira. 'I am breathing out as hard as I can – Akira would be proud of me, but somehow it's not working this time. But, I am using both my sticks and that helps enormously to keep my body straight and balanced. Still, I can feel my feet starting to play up.' I did not add that I was a bit wary of breathing too deeply in their *refugio*. By that time I'd recognised that sweet smell in the air. It was without a doubt dope of an excellent quality.

'Finish your meal, then go lie down in the dormitory. You can stay for as long as you like.' She got up to join the wolf by the wood burner. (I was pleased to note that they weren't fanning the already glowing fire, in readiness for the cooking of their festively plumped pilgrim meal.)

I took another mouthful of the delicious lentils. 'I see Paolo Coelho over there. Did he stay here when he walked the Camino?' I still had to find a *refugio* where he *had* stayed. No *hospitalero* had ever laid eyes on this elusive 'patron', it seemed. But if these two had such a big photograph of him dominating their main room, it looked as if I may have finally found a place where Coelho had actually shared a dormitory with real pilgrims.

Wolf and Witch laughed. 'Oh no! It would have been the most wonderful honour, but he did not stay here with us. How we wish he had! But as you can see – we keep everything really nice and ready in case he comes knocking on our door one day!'

I wiped the breadcrumbs on the table into my empty bowl and took it to the sink to wash, smiling and keeping my opinion to myself. Let them live in hope. Why not? If that was what made their hippy hearts happy.

For the next hour I lay down in what was definitely the 'prettiest' dormitory on the Camino. It was airy and light and spotlessly clean. There were lovely naturally pale yellow pine bunk beds in the room, each resplendent with a cornflower-blue bed spread. Different sized dream catchers swayed from the rafters, catching the occasional sunbeam that pierced through the blanket of clouds outside, and the mesmerising New Age music wafted through the door. I did not intend to fall asleep, but smiled at my silly notion of the fairy tales that had ended violently when the wolf was shot and the witch was pushed into the oven. This wolf and witch were far too nice to have such a thing happen to them. I let the sweet smell of their hashish carry me off to dreamland – where only pain-free smiles, cuddly wolves and colourful witches holding bowls of steaming lentils, were waiting for me.

During the eighties and the nineties there was a wild craze among the more flamboyant motivational speakers on the international speaking circuit. They spent a day with their audience, convincing them that they could achieve anything – *if* they set their minds to it. Then, at the end of the day, when everyone was psyched up and in a state of an all-time daring-do, gung-ho bravado, they were taken outside and invited to walk across a carpet of red-hot glowing embers. I never personally participated in one of these sessions, but everyone I knew who'd done it never stopped raving about the amazing feeling of power that this experience produced.

'I can conquer the world after the fire-walk!' 'Having done the fire-walk, I now know I can do anything! Nothing can stop me now; if I can think it, I can do it! If I can dream it, I can make it happen!' And so sure were they of themselves and their own powers, that I never had a doubt that they were right. If they could dream it, they could make it happen.

And that is how walking the Camino made me feel. Just about every day I, too, had a fire-walk experience, each experience affirming the one I'd had before, each one strengthening my power and belief in myself. It made sense to want the experience to continue, no matter what. Except, my feet had become instruments of torture. I was walking on fire every step of the way – and in slow motion.

It is claimed, and I believe this to be true, that in extreme situations, the body itself provides the strongest painkillers. I had first-hand experience of how you can switch off your pain. It hadn't worked for me when I struggled with the tendonitis in my leg, but later, when both my feet became excruciatingly painful – with what I was only much later to learn were stress fractures – did I experience what it is that pushes marathon runners, weight lifters and other extreme sports athletes past the pain threshold.

The human brain releases endorphins and adrenalin – chemicals that are known as neurotransmitters. These neurotransmitters are the miracle workers that produce the 'runner's high' in trained athletes and make them insensitive to pain. The latest research shows that the release of these chemicals, which act as pain inhibitors, can in fact be triggered by anyone, simply by using the power of the mind. 'Anyone with initiative and an alert mind can do that,' say the experts. A pain impulse can be stopped before it gets to the brain, either by painkillers – or by releasing the necessary neurotransmitters through sheer lack of fear of the pain and conviction that it is possible.

It was about two thirds of the Way, when I reached Astorga, that I finally succumbed to the messages my body had been sending my brain. I suppose the moment had come that I simply no longer could claim to be someone 'with initiative and an alert mind.' The neurotransmitters had gone AWOL, those impulses from my feet could no longer be stopped; instead, they had put on their jackboots, donned their armour, flexed their muscles and were storming my defences with battering rams and super-missiles. And whether it was Sant Iago that came to my rescue or yet another one of those Camino angels, I will never know, but Astorga was where a gorgeous and charming osteopath was waiting to tend to my feet.

Astorga! Hobbling down the picturesque cobblestone streets, it did not take long to discover why this was a favourite stop for pilgrims on the Camino: it is the pilgrimage destination of all chocoholics! Wonderfully flamboyant window displays of brown, green, yellow, orange, pink, red and purple chocolate slabs filled with whole almonds had pilgrims salivating and drooling as they trudged along their way through the town. And not only is Astorga the centre of the Spanish chocolate industry, but it is also where the Camino Frances and the *Via de la Plata* from Seville, two important Camino routes, converge and so where a whole new group of pilgrims join the route. *Asturica Augusta*, as it was known in the first century, was the military base that controlled the Roman gold mines in the Toleno mountains and in the Medulas, where the Way takes you after Astorga. (These mines – zig-zag cuts made into the mountains – are still prominent in the area and well worth a moment of admiration, as are the forests of chestnut trees that the Romans planted to provide food for the thousands of slaves who worked their mines.) Today Astorga is one of the few larger places on the Camino, and a beautiful town with a long and illustrious history – as well as the most roundabout and convoluted signposting to enter it! Pilgrims beware! Follow your nose when you approach the town and you will cut off several unnecessary and uninteresting kilometres from your day's walk. The architect Antoni Gaudí was commissioned in 1886 to build the Episcopal Palace, next to the Santa Maria cathedral, and as it was never consecrated as a bishop's palace, it now houses an interesting museum of Camino history.

Upon entering Astorga, I had limped past the refuge at the entrance of the town, which was apparently run by the British Confraternity of Saint James, and continued deeper into the town to look for a private refuge where I could spend more than one night. By the time I'd reached Astorga, with less than a third of the way still to go, my feet had become so painful that each step of the way was pure agony. I knew that unless I got to see a medical person who could give advice and possibly make it better for me, there was a very real possibility that I would not be able to continue. As happens on the Camino, I chanced upon one of the most beautiful refuges that I'd stayed in. It was a private refuge, meaning that it cost nine euros per night as opposed to the lesser fees of the state- or church-run 'official' refuges, but it was worth ten times that price.

Walking into the entrance was like walking onto the pages of a slick interior design magazine. There was a large room with thick, rough, white-plastered walls, massive dark oak beams and a staircase of the same dark ancient wood leading up to the first floor and the dorms. The far wall was glass, revealing the sunny courtyard beyond, and providing the exquisite quality of light that permeated the whole interior. In the centre of the room was a big old iron wood burner that glowed red and filled the room with a welcoming warmth. And best of all, Gustav, the *hospitalero* of the refuge, was a tall, dashing Spaniard who looked like a character more suited to a film about passion, flamenco dancing, matadors and fighting bulls than the kind and gentle, erudite guardian of a pilgrims' refuge that he was.

When Gustav saw me limping into the refuge, he immediately came out from behind his desk to help me off with my backpack.

'*Alemán? Americano? Australiano?*' he questioned. 'I am sorry. I speak very little.'

'Do you speak French?' I asked.

'*Eh ben, si! Soyez la bienvenue!* Welcome to the *refugio*! Come, let us take your shoes off and put them on the shelf there.' He bent down and, despite my protestations, started untying my shoelaces. It was such a relief to just go with the flow that I simply rested my hand on his shoulder as he took off first the one shoe, then the other, and put them neatly on the shelf against the entrance wall.

'Now, sit down and give me your *credenciales* so that I can fill it in for you and stamp it.' He took me by my arm and helped me to a chair in front of the desk.

'Thank you, but first I have to know whether it will be possible for me to stay an extra day?' His solicitous attention and concern for my welfare was washing over me like a warm, soothing wave, but also eroding into the strong and invincible façade I'd been wearing for more than a week. I felt close to tears and must have looked a sad and sorry sight.

'You can stay as long as you need to be strong enough to continue. *Pas de problème.*'

Gustav spoke far better French than I did, but that last comment could have been in any language and it could not have brought more comfort.

Knowing that I was now committed to taking my first break was suddenly a huge relief. Stopping along the way was something I'd planned to do before I started. The idea was to stop every three or four days for at least one extra night in a place – not only to rest, but also to spend some time looking around, taking in the sights, visiting places of interest and just, in general, to enjoy the surroundings. I had factored those days into my schedule, planning to finish the pilgrimage in fifty days. However, once you get going, it's not all that simple to stop, for when you do, you break your momentum. And, it is not always 'easy' – to use a euphemism, to get up and start walking in the mornings. It takes determination, strength of will, and above all, a huge amount of discipline.

I maintained that it was important to watch out for the signs your body sends you – to listen to what your body tells you. A pilgrim's body demands respect. No will in the world can make a defunct body perform. Unless you look after your body and keep it in reasonable shape, there is no way even the most devout pilgrim can continue the pilgrimage. I had never liked the particular body my creator had chosen for me; some bits were bigger than I would have wished for and others were smaller; some bits were too long and others too short. A couple of the shortcomings could be camouflaged or hidden or changed, with patience and hard work; most of them I'd simply learned to live with over the years. My body had let me down in the past – such as the time when the ballet teacher suggested that an anorexic hippopotamus might be made to look cute in a Walt Disney production but that it was demanding more of her talents than she was willing to give. My body had embarrassed me – such as when the boys in my class in junior school suggested we use *me* as the diving board our swimming pool lacked. It had cautioned me not to play certain sports, it had kicked in its heels at being asked to do somersaults and cartwheels, it had demanded to stay covered except when in the pitch dark. Yet, when I embarked on this challenge of walking 800 kilometres, up and over mountains, in freezing temperatures, through hurricanes and tempestuous weather conditions, hour after hour, day after day, week after week, it had not let me down, it had not embarrassed me, it had not made any demands. I developed a serious respect for this body of mine. It was performing miracles for me. It was continuing long after most others would have thrown in the towel. It was withstanding whatever came its way and it was showing its willingness to persevere and continue no matter what – not without complaining, but continuing nevertheless. I was impressed with my body; she may not be beautiful, but she is tough, and that is what counts on the Camino. Around that time, when I had written in e-mails that I was suffering extreme pain in my feet, but was continuing nevertheless, a wise friend (Mike Dooley, from Totally Unique Thoughts, to be exact) sent me a message, a message which I decided was the perfect tribute to my hither-to unappreciated body, the body that had brought me so far:

> Don't disguise your tears, Wilna, don't hide your sadness, don't be afraid to find out who you really are. Because in those fleeting moments you'll summon such beauty and strength that, in no time at all, you'll fully grasp exactly why you're so gossiped about here in the unseen. And you'll understand, maybe for the first time ever, how grand you are, because you'll discover that vulnerable doesn't mean powerless, scared doesn't mean lacking in beauty, and uncertainty doesn't mean that you're lost.

Waking up each morning, when it is pitch dark, when it is freezing cold and, putting your arm outside the sleeping bag is like sticking it into a bucket full of ice, your body is stiff after the night's inactivity; every muscle complaining, joints tight and reluctant to loosen up. And if you've suffered any injuries, waking up in the morning is waking up those injuries as well, re-awakening the discomfort and the pain and the torture. So, once you've become accustomed to the routine of waking up and immediately, without thinking, getting up and getting dressed – and you've done it for a week, two weeks, three weeks – it becomes an automatic action: you wake up, you get up and you get dressed. You don't think about it; you just do it. And you learn very quickly that if you did stop to think about it, getting up and getting dressed and starting walking would be *the* hardest thing to do. Sometimes, particularly on the very cold days, even stopping along the way to rest for a few moments or have a bite to eat did not seem like too good an idea. If you allowed your muscles to cool down too much, the action of getting up, putting the backpack back on and starting walking again, could be a huge effort.

But here, in Astorga, for the first time in over a week of walking with incredible pain, I knew that even if I did stop for a couple of days, it was going to be all right; I *was* going to continue and I *was* going to finish the pilgrimage.

After completing the register and stamping my pilgrims' passport,

Gustav picked up my backpack and led me upstairs to show me the dorm. There were already a few other pilgrims busy tidying their backpacks, lying on their beds reading or writing, or sitting together chatting about all sorts of things. Theirs were all faces I hadn't seen before, which was in itself a very interesting experience.

Up to that stage of the Camino, there had been so few of us that I knew everyone who was within three or four days' walk from where I was. I knew them all by name, and knew something about each one of them, and a type of bond had formed among us; we were fellow-pilgrims in the truest sense of the word. Suddenly, here in Astorga, the scene changed; not only had a whole new set of characters entered left stage, but the two main characters of the play up to that point had gone. Since a day before I reached Astorga, my little Camino family was no more. Thorsten and Akira had both left the Camino. Thorsten had stayed behind in León four days before with a tooth abscess and we subsequently learned that he'd had to fly back to Germany for surgery. It must have been a devastating blow for him. And I had said goodbye to Akira that very morning. Act one was over, Astorga was to be the interval, and the second and final act was about to commence. The whole dynamic of the Camino had completely changed for me and Astorga seemed an opportune and appropriate place to stop for some maintenance and repairs.

I enjoyed a long hot shower and washed my hair with a little shampoo, pinched from a bottle someone had left behind. Normally my single bar of natural soap served well to wash me, my hair and my clothes, as well as clean my teeth, but smelling the wonderfully luxurious foam of a real shampoo on my hair was pure bliss, and when I came out of the bathroom, I felt like a million dollars.

'I took the liberty of using someone's shampoo,' I confessed when I walked back into the dormitory. I was so aware of the delicious smell that I was sure they would all have noticed and realised that I'd used shampoo that belonged to one of them.

'Oh! That's my shampoo that I must have left in the shower, but you are welcome to use it!' A pretty girl with beautiful long blonde hair smiled down from a top bunk at the end of the room. 'I am very naughty. I buy shampoo every time I see a shop that sells it, but then I leave the heavy bottle behind after I've washed my hair. I just cannot bear to wash my hair with soap, but shampoo is too heavy to carry!'

'Not naughty at all – just very generous to other pilgrims! Thank you. I can't remember when last I felt so good, and I find that when my hair has had a good shampoo, all of me feels a lot better too.' I hung my washing over the heater to dry and, leaving everyone discussing their ideas of the ultimate luxury on the Camino, I padded downstairs in a clean pair of socks to find out about seeing a doctor for my tortured feet.

Gustav had already organised everything for me. 'I've called my son to come with his car and I have made an appointment with a doctor at the physiotherapy centre. My son will be here after work at six o'clock to pick you up and take you.'

I was overwhelmed by his kindness. 'Thank you so much, Gustav, that's wonderful. I cannot tell you how grateful I am. I'm very worried about my feet. I don't know what's wrong with them, but it worries me that I might be doing permanent damage to them and that I'll regret it later.'

'It is a pleasure. I think maybe it was meant to be that you arrived in Astorga today, because we have the best osteopath in all of Spain right here. He is young, but he knows his business. He will make your feet better for you.'

I was thinking to myself – no, to be honest, I was *hoping* that all I needed was to rest my feet, when Gustav responded to the unspoken thought: 'And if the doctor says that you must rest before you can go on, you can stay here for as long as it is necessary!'

It was already five o'clock, so I went into the open plan kitchen area and boiled some water for a cup of tea. Just as I sat down with my cup in front of the wood-burning stove, another wave of pilgrims arrived.

'Stay here by the warmth, and put your feet up and relax. I will call you when my son arrives,' he told me in parting and over his shoulder, as he left to welcome and register the new pilgrims.

Among this new group was a young man from Japan named Sato, who had the 'longest' *credenciales* I'd ever seen. He had three passports stapled together as, it transpired, his main aim on the Camino was to collect as many *sellos* or stamps as possible. Then there was Andy, a tall, good looking twenty-something Australian with the loveliest smile, an equally pleasant German boy, Johannes, a German couple who were obviously very much in love and only had eyes for each other, a grey-haired elderly man, who later told me that he was honouring a pact he'd made with God. His daughter, who had been diagnosed with breast cancer eighteen months before, had recently been told that she was in remission, and his promise to God for curing her was that he would walk the Camino. These 'new' pilgrims had all flown into Astorga that afternoon to start their Camino from there, and were bright-eyed and bushy-tailed and excited at the prospect of starting their pilgrimages the next day. The last two to come in were David and Marilyn, a delightful Canadian couple I'd met about a week before. The day I met them was the day they 'resumed' the Camino, in the village where they'd had to stop their pilgrimage the previous year as result of David's broken ankle. Added to the pilgrims already upstairs, this was by far the most people I had ever seen on the Camino, let alone in one refuge.

At six o'clock sharp Gustav's son walked in the door and came over to where I was sitting. 'Come, I have the car ready outside.' He shook my hand. 'You will not have to walk far. I will take you to the doctor now.'

I followed him out to his car, which was parked almost in the entrance of the building, and for the first time in what felt like a lifetime, I got into a car. But, no sooner had we started driving, than we stopped again; the rooms were so close to the refuge that I had to smile at the elaborate arrangements that had been made to get me there. I'd walked over six hundred kilometres, but had to go in a car for the hundred metres to the doctor's rooms.

Nevertheless, I was grateful for Gustav's son's assistance, because he could come into the rooms with me and explain to the receptionist why I was there. The son offered to stay and wait to take me back to the refuge, but I insisted that he should go and that I would walk back. Later, when I hobbled painfully back to the refuge, I regretted being so stubborn; my feet had really come to the end of their tether.

Etched in large letters, on the frosted glass front window, was written:

Centro de fisioterapeuta
Tratameinto del dolor
Recuperacion functional
Masale terapeutico
Osteopatia

Physiotherapy centre. Treatment of pain. Functional recuperation. Muscle therapy. Osteopathy. I had come to the right place. Whatever these people could do for my feet could only be an improvement.

A few weeks before, I'd realised that, because of the tendonitis in my leg, I was favouring the painful leg and overcompensating with the other. I had started to walk a little 'funny'. One foot was turned in and the weight was being put on the outside of the sole, while the other foot was turned out and was bearing all the weight on the inside of the sole. If I tried to do this again to demonstrate I probably couldn't; it is a strange and most unnatural way to walk. At the time I'd tried to correct it because I realised that I was possibly doing damage to other joints and parts of my body. My knees were starting to feel the strain, as were my hips, and I was also discovering muscles in my back that I hadn't been aware of before. Added to this self-inflicted deformity, was the fact that the stones on the pathway made it impossible for your feet ever to be flat on the ground. The thick rubber soles of my boots protected my feet as much as it was possible for good boots to do, but even they could not distract from the fact that every time I put my foot on the ground, it landed on a stone and the foot was either turned in or turned out by it, or slipping forwards or sliding backwards. It was therefore not really surprising when I realised that a dull ache had been developing in my feet. I assumed that it must be bruising, combined with some muscle tension as a result of the contortions my feet had been required to perform. In my reading before starting the pilgrimage, I'd come across plenty of typical pilgrimage injuries. The most mention was made of blisters, then of knee and hip pain and some mention of shoulder and back problems. But what I was experiencing with my feet, I had seen no mention of anywhere.

The dull ache had become acute pain and had grown into a monster of excruciating agony. Every step of my pilgrimage had become not a day less in purgatory, but a moment in hell itself. At first I wondered how it was that I had not read about this pain in any of the literature about the Camino. Then I realised why; no words could describe it.

Later though, I did remember reading a little passage somewhere where the author tried to explain what it was that the feet had to endure on the Camino. Every time you put your foot on the ground, he wrote, you put the sum of your total weight plus the weight of anything you carry (in my case that added up to 76kg) on a concentrated three points under your feet – with force. This was exactly the same as if you were sitting with your legs stretched out in front of you, with someone standing at your feet who was hitting, with all his strength, the soles of your feet with a seventy-six kilogram sledgehammer. If he were doing this continuously, every second, for about nine to ten hours a day, and for thirty-six concurrent days, it would be a good reflection of what I was putting my feet through. No wonder then that I was finding myself sitting in the waiting room of an osteopath in Astorga. My only surprise was that there were not at least fifty other pilgrims there waiting with me.

Did I mention that the osteopath was gorgeous and charming? When he opened the door to his surgery, his smile enveloped me in warmth and a sense of total trust. He helped me up and led me into his surgery, up onto the bench, invited me to lie back, removed my socks and took my feet into his hands – and I just melted into his care. What bliss. It was a huge relief handing over my concerns about my feet. Ever since they'd started being so painful, I had no idea what had been happening to them, but common sense told me that it was not good. As much as I had a strict policy of never worrying in the future perfect, in other words never worrying about what *might* happen about something *if...* I had started conjuring up visions of myself, for the rest of my days, having to walk to my village market for my weekly shopping with the help of a walking frame (not the standard grey aluminium, but a gleaming bright red sports model, please). With every bit of pressure applied by the doctor examining my feet, or even the slightest touch in certain places, I had to grit my teeth and stop myself from involuntarily kicking out. That image in my head of the walking frame became even brighter and even redder than before.

There was total silence at the foot end of the bed. I opened one eye to see what was happening down there. The doctor's big smile had disappeared and had been replaced by a deep frown (but he was still gorgeous). He shook his head vigorously and sighed deeply.

'Can you see what the problem is?' I ventured.

Continuing to shake his head, he gently put my foot down. Another long silence. I waited for the verdict. 'Do you have to finish your pilgrimage now, or can you come back at another time to walk the last stage?' I raised myself onto my elbows to see him better and make sure I understood him correctly. He only spoke Spanish, and I suddenly realised that my lack of knowledge of the language could now prove very dangerous indeed.

'No! I *have* to finish now,' I said. 'I cannot *not* finish the Camino! I *have* to continue!' My French was not adequate to allow me to remonstrate strongly enough and I was vaguely aware that my subjunctives and conditionals and double negatives came out in a spluttering gibberish. I was now sitting straight up, my two swollen feet the stark, ugly, guilty reality between us.

He stayed completely calm. 'How long have you allowed yourself for the pilgrimage?' he asked, laying both hands gently over my feet to ensure they were kept still during this agitated state I was working myself into.

'Fifty days,' I replied. 'I had allowed myself fifty days, and today is day twenty-six,' I continued, trying very hard to regain my composure.

'That is good then,' his smile was re-appearing. 'You need only about ten days to reach Santiago de Compostela from here, so you have more than enough days spare to rest your feet. Give them five or six days and they *will* get better.' He held up his fingers to show me the numbers and he was speaking slowly, but I knew that I was only guessing at what he was trying to convey to me. His frown and his body language told me that the true meaning of his message had not translated in my mind yet.

'But what is wrong with my feet?' I wanted to know.

He looked at me in silence. In a surgery, the language barrier is a shiny stainless steel wall between doctor and patient. Another deep sigh. 'Wait,' he softly pushed his hand down on my shoulder to make me lie back again and disappeared somewhere behind me. I could hear him being busy, doing something, moving things around. A few minutes later his face was once again by my side. Without saying anything more, he again pulled up his stool and started ministering to me feet.

First, with a large wooden spatula, he applied to each foot a thick layer of what looked and smelled like a rich dark honey, covering them completely in the brown sticky goo. It was an interesting sensation and I wondered whether it was my imagination or whether the pain in my feet was already fading. I was back on my elbows to better see what was happening. 'Is that honey?' I asked. 'Buzzzzzz-zz-zz-zz,' my hand flying in circles above imaginary flowers. He smiled his gorgeous smile and nodded. 'Si, si! – *miel!*'

Mmmm… A layer of honey covering my feet? I looked across at the sign I'd read earlier. Yes – even back to front the words made sense. This *was* a professional surgery. The doctor *was* an osteopath and he *had* to know what he was doing…

Next he sprinkled a dark brown-black powder over my feet. It looked like black pepper. Or gunpowder. Or… 'Don't be ridiculous!' I told myself, stopping myself from going 'Boom-Boom?' to find out if it was indeed gunpowder and if next he intended to put a match to my feet and rid me of my pain for all time. I decided that my head must have been turned – either by too much pain, or by the relief of having my feet tended to, or perhaps by the osteopath himself – but once again I was just going to go with the flow, trust in the man and believe that whatever he was concocting, it was going to enable me to continue my pilgrimage.

Finally the doctor bandaged my feet, gently rolling layer upon layer of tight crepe around each foot, leaving my feet looking like two brand new mummies ready to be lain in their sarcophagi.

'There!' He looked satisfied with a job well done. 'Five days' he pointed to my feet and held up five fingers to make sure I understood. 'Five days of rest, feet up, no walking.' He repeated the gestures and words a few times, wanting to know that I would follow his instructions. I repeated them in French. 'Five days' rest, feet up, no walking.' He looked happy, and helped me as I swung my legs down and gingerly put my weight onto my feet. It felt strange. And looked even stranger. My socks stretched tightly over the two huge bandaged feet. The pain was still there, but now seemed to be dulled and distanced by the layers and layers of honey and gunpowder and bandages covering them. A very strange sensation indeed.

I paid the (gorgeous) osteopath five euros for the consultation and treatment – for which he insisted on writing out a receipt – 'to claim from your insurance' – and hobbled out the door, checking one last time that the sign on the window really did say what I knew it said. It did.

I felt so much better. Even though I still didn't know what was actually wrong with my feet, I felt better about them, about the future of my feet, about the prospect of walking into my old age without the help of a walking frame, be it the national health issue standard grey or the bright red sports model, and most importantly, about my finishing the Camino. In fact, I felt so good that I stopped on the way back to the refuge at a small supermarket and bought some delicious-looking salmon, a lettuce, two tomatoes, an onion and a bottle of Rioja, aptly named 'Peregrino.' I was ready to conquer the world, and the event was going to be celebrated in style!

Annie, the sheep farmer from South Africa, who didn't believe in 'all that mumbo-jumbo spiritual stuff' and who didn't even find the walk particularly challenging, was not alone on the Camino. There are probably more people on the Way like her than any other kind. You only have to read the countless blogs and internet discussions to see the scepticism and scorn of many of the travellers on the Camino. They find any discussion of the metaphysical or mention of anything spiritual or even remotely out of the ordinary, ridiculous and silly. They often walk the entire Camino wondering what people find so difficult. They hop on buses when the fancy grabs them, or they hold speed races to see who'll get to a destination first. And the common denominator among them is their irreverence for any deeper meaning attached to the Camino, as well as their lack of respect for, or understanding of, any pilgrim who does *not* snigger at the spiritual or religious aspect of the pilgrimage in the same way as they do.

When I'd walked more than halfway, I mentioned this in an e-mail to my family. Marc, my older son, wrote back:

'You have to remember that everyone is different. Everyone experiences things differently. Just as you cannot understand those people's mentality, they can't understand yours. It is a bit like us sitting here on the other side of the world and reading your e-mails. You talk about having walked ten hours today, about feeling immense pain every time you put a foot down on the ground. You talk about eating an entire tin of sardines, oil and all. You talk about getting drenched in the rain or about perspiring when the temperatures are below freezing. You write about saints and angels and signs and sleeping in bunk beds and about people who walk fourteen times from Jerusalem to Rome to Santiago, and back.

Think about it, mom. You are living an experience that is completely alien to the world that you come from – which is the world we live in. When I go off to work in the morning, I think of you walking. When I get home from work in the evening I think: She is still walking. That, in itself, is mind-boggling! It is not possible to visualise what you are doing because it is not possible to imagine what you are doing. It is even more impossible to understand why you are doing this – and continuing when you are obviously suffering. Unless you have done something yourself, you cannot put yourself into someone else's shoes. You remember when we came back from our trip through Africa? The same thing happened to us then. We couldn't really tell anyone about our experiences – about travelling on a truck through the desert where there are no roads, about going to Timbuktu, about staying off the roads in Chad and driving through the bush for days without water or food so that we wouldn't get involved in the war there, about slaughtering the goat so we could have some meat that wasn't totally rotten for a change – we couldn't tell anyone about it because the moment we did, their eyes would glaze over and we could see they weren't listening. It was not because they weren't interested. It was just because they had no understanding of what we were talking about. And the moment we stopped, they would immediately start talking about some interesting thing they had done — interesting to them, but again, not necessarily interesting to us. If people cannot relate to something, they don't understand it. So, when people ridicule something that is spiritually important to you, it means they have never had a similar spiritual experience and therefore they are the ones to feel sorry for, because it can only mean they live a life that goes no deeper than the surface.'

Marc's message gave me much food for thought. It was true what he said. I myself had spoken about not being able to imagine what someone like Terrie must be experiencing in her battle against cancer. It's difficult to relate to anything that you have not experienced yourself. But, this knowledge was not going to stop me from telling my story the way it was. The sceptics who were going to ridicule my spiritual experience — and the experience of the pilgrim who walked with a religious purpose, or the pilgrim who felt moved by the pagan Celtic energy of the Camino, or even the pilgrim who believed that there were aliens walking beside him, had as much right to their opinions as any other. The Camino is a pathway for any person who wishes to take it, and what you make of it and what you find on it is up to you, and you alone.

I knew what it felt like to reach the top of a mountain or to walk those extra ten kilometres, long after you thought you'd reached your physical, as well as your mental, limit. I knew that feeling you had every single time you achieved something that, only a month before, you would never, not in your wildest dreams, have thought possible. For me, that feeling was empowering beyond description.

Over the previous few days however, I'd come to the realisation that no matter how empowered I felt, no matter how many near-miracles a positive attitude could bring about, no matter how many feats my body could perform and how many times I had astounded myself, even I had limits. I had made light of the pain I'd been suffering with every single step I walked, but that afternoon, after I'd had my lovely hot shower, the scarred and mottled mirror in the refuge bathroom — the first mirror I'd looked at in weeks — told a different story. The face that looked back at me was of someone I barely recognised. I was aware that I'd lost some weight and that my body was more toned than it had ever been, but the person who looked back at me from that mirror was looking very tired, very haggard, very old. There were dark rings under her puffy eyes. And not only her eyes were puffed up; her entire face looked swollen. I would have expected to see a glowing skin, considering the days and days of fresh air, the healthy eating and all the exercise. But the skin I saw looked pale and grey-ishly pasty and not healthy at all. I had been worried about the future of my feet. The face in the mirror told me that the constant and severe pain had been affecting far more than just my feet.

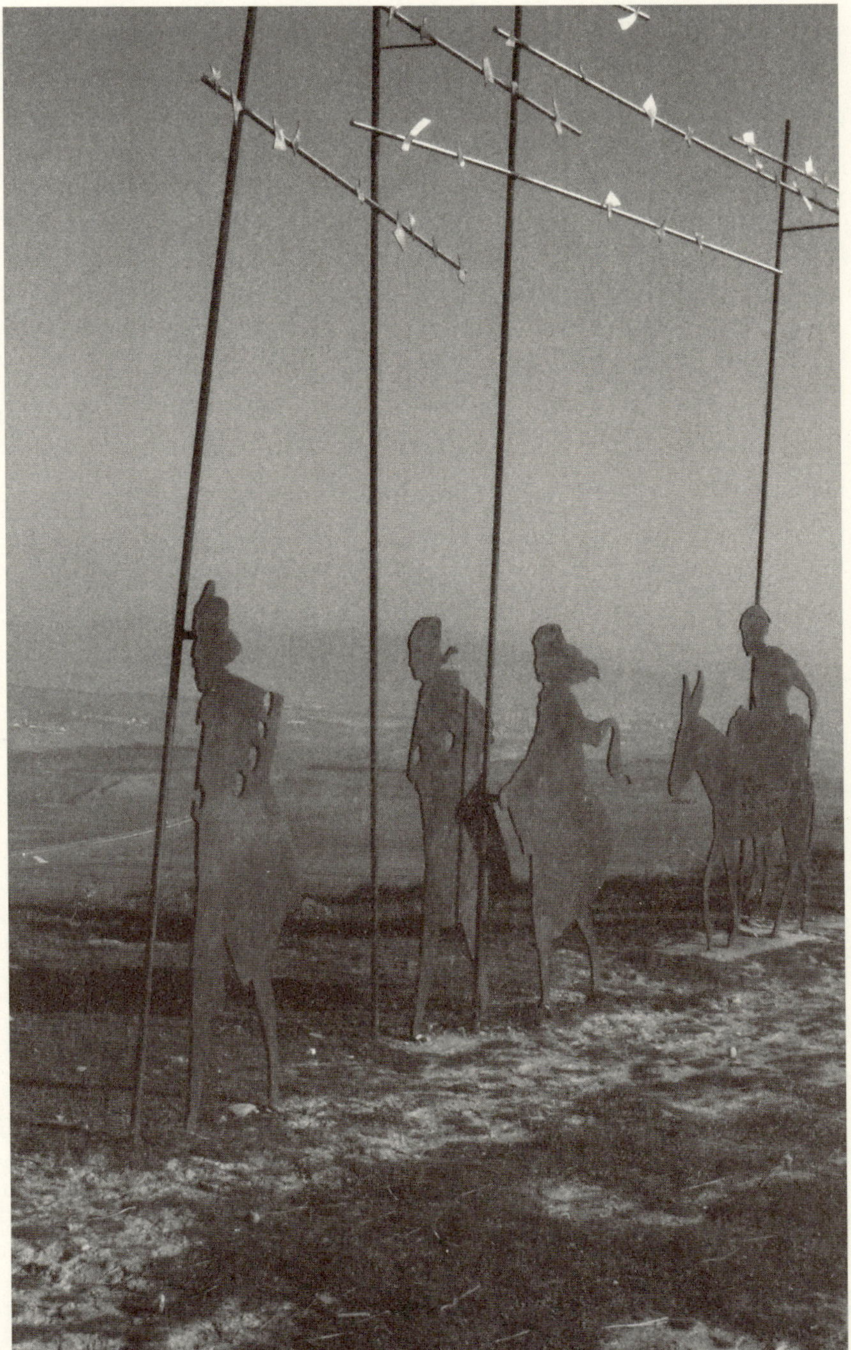

10

A lifetime searching for perfection is not a wasted life

– Pierre Wilkinson

I lost myself the first time I walked the Camino and now I keep on walking the Camino in the hope of finding myself again!

– Felipe

When I got back from the osteopath that night, I prepared my fresh green salad, sliced the dark red tomatoes, grilled my two beautiful pink slabs of salmon in some butter that I'd found in the fridge (generously left behind by an unknown pilgrim), while sipping a glass of the deliciously rich and smooth 'Peregrino' Rioja. As I stood there at the stove preparing this feast, I took stock of my situation. I still didn't know what was wrong with my feet, but I believed I'd been given the assurance that my feet would heal – eventually. I could therefore continue to walk and complete the pilgrimage to Santiago de Compostela, as soon as I'd given my feet a few days' rest, and if I was willing to walk in pain. However, the idea that had quietly been creeping up on my mind and had started to manifest itself over the previous days – the idea *not* to take a train back home after reaching Santiago, but to turn around and walk back home – *that* idea was no longer feasible. I would have loved to extend my journey. I would have loved to do what pilgrims of old had always done – to complete their pilgrimage and then return home the same way they'd come, and the only way they had – on foot. But it seemed that I was going to have to return the modern way – by train or by plane.

The first time I met a pilgrim who was 'walking backwards' was in the refuge in Belorado. I had passed only a few pilgrims who were walking 'the other way' and each time, I stopped, turned around and watched them heading off to the east. At that stage I still wondered what made someone walk all the way to Santiago de Compostela and then have the energy or the courage to turn around and retrace their steps. It was only later, as I came closer to Santiago, that I realised it was the most natural thing to do – not to *have* to, but to *want* to walk back home. I realised then that this was also the way to make the experience continue. Only, there were no little yellow arrows pointing the way for the returning pilgrim. But, having walked hundreds, sometimes more than a thousand kilometres following the little yellow arrows, and then suddenly having to walk without directions, and finding your way back home without getting hopelessly lost, must have been yet another incredibly empowering Camino experience.

Rene was a man probably in his late thirties, although it was difficult to tell his age from his face, which bore the deep grooves of hardship and sorrow. He had walked from his home in the Czech Republic all the way to Santiago de Compostela on the Northern Route along the coastline, down to Sevilla, across to Portugal, back up on the Portuguese Camino and, when I met him, he was on his way back home on the Camino Frances. He spoke a few words of Spanish, but no other language than his own and could therefore not really communicate with anyone. When I saw him the first time, he was sitting at the table in the kitchen, painstakingly trimming loose strands of unravelling wool on the fingers of his knitted gloves. In fact, there was not much left of the frayed gloves, and I wondered how he coped in the below-freezing temperatures of the early mornings with exposed fingers. I had noticed in the dorm that he had a very small backpack that could not have had room for even the basics, and his shoes, which were in the shoe rack in the entrance hall, were ordinary cheap-looking trainers, worn through on the toes and looking very much like they were ready for the scrap heap.

With gestures and pointing and laughter, we established each other's names and origins and that, yes, he would love to share a bowl of my precious Japanese green tea.

'It must be so hard to walk backwards,' I said, mimicking someone walking forward while constantly looking under his arm behind to see where the yellow arrows were and so make sure he was still on the right road. The arrows and the shell signs were always painted on the eastern side of walls or trees or rocks, to be visible for pilgrims walking westwards.

Pilgrims who walked back home therefore discovered what is so true about life itself; that looking at the same thing from a different angle gives you a completely different perspective. Turn the map upside-down, and the well-trodden path becomes an adventure into the unknown.

(I almost felt that it was a pity that someone had recently started a new sign for those returning home – a blue spiral that ends in an arrow. There were no more than a handful of these signs on the Camino, but somehow I thought they subtracted a little from the amazing achievement of finding your way home – like a homing pigeon, like a Namib elephant – like a Sir Ranulph Fiennes – without directions, purely on instinct…)

Rene laughed at my mime performance of the pilgrim walking backwards, and it was wonderful to see his whole face light up. For a moment that broad smile seemed to banish all the suffering on his craggy face. I so wanted to ask him what had motivated him to walk such a very long way, when he obviously had very little means, but by this time I'd learned enough Camino etiquette to know not to ask questions that may be intrusive. Yet, I also realised that if he did not have language with which to communicate and he'd been walking for almost four months, with another two months to go, there had to have been times when he must have felt incredibly lonely. Had he found what he had looked for on the Camino? More importantly, had he been able to unload the unpleasant, the unwanted, the unnecessary baggage from his life, somewhere along the way?

Later, when I told a friend about Rene having walked from the Czech Republic to Santiago and back, she made the comment: 'There has to be something mentally wrong with a person to want to do that. He must have some psychological problem. Or else he is running away from something – and that something is probably himself.'

A harsh assumption, I thought, and a somewhat prejudiced judgement of someone she didn't even know. However, we do tend to judge people within our own frame of reference. If you cannot envisage yourself feeling the need to walk thousands of kilometres with only yourself for company, then the first response is to judge the person who does have that need as having 'something mentally wrong or as having a psychological problem.' It comes back, time and time again, to the fear and the distrust we feel of those things we do not understand.

I can well imagine there are people who walk the Camino to get away from something in their lives, but if that's their aim, they're not likely to achieve it. Human nature does not allow us to simply step out the door and leave everything behind. What we have experienced, what we have learned, what we know, what we have lived, all become part of our very fibre and of who we are. Most things that have ever happened to us and that have touched our lives are not written on our slate in soft white chalk; they are scratched for all time into the slate with a graphite stylus. It is not that easy to wipe the slate clean. My friend said of Rene that he was probably walking the pilgrimage to get away from himself. But that is not possible. Just as you can't walk away from your shadow, you cannot ever walk away from yourself. When someone comes onto the Camino, they bring their background and their history with them. They therefore also bring their whole frame of reference. So, if they come hoping to find the answers as to how to bring about change in their lives or what to do with the rest of their lives, they first have to recognise the pieces of the *unnecessary* baggage that should be left along the way; the chips they carry on their shoulders, the accumulated guilt, the bad habits, the clutter – and then find the courage and the strength and the confidence to do so.

I never did find out from Rene what had made him set off on this long, long journey, but it must have been a very strong conviction to have taken him on such a hard road for such a long time, with no comforts, no money, no proper equipment – and not even with the means to communicate with other pilgrims. The lines on his face mapped out the hardship he'd endured; bore testimony to his suffering.

I will always remember Rene, and when I think of him, I still see him sitting at that table, carefully cutting the strands of wool that were dangling from his unravelling knitted gloves, and my heart goes out to him, to wherever he finds himself right now. I wonder whether he managed to save enough of his gloves to still serve some purpose, or whether they just continued to unravel until there was nothing left. I can only hope, for his sake, that he had at least been able to dump some of the heavy baggage of his life that had dragged him down; that he'd managed to shed the old skin that had caused him so much pain.

Rene was not able to have long discussions with other pilgrims because of a language barrier. This was the case with other pilgrims I came across as well, like the very young, very lovely Kim from North Korea who spoke not a word of English or Spanish but was always around other pilgrims and always smiling. It must have been terribly hard for such a young girl, so far away from home, to not be able to communicate at all – not to express herself and not even to understand anything anyone said to her. Her smiling complacency in the face of her impossible situation reminded me of something I read a long time ago – a comment made by the Nobel Laureate, Jean-Marie Le Clézio. He referred to his language as his *heimat*, his country; '...*c'était ma langue, c'est- à-dire la chair et le sang, les nerfs, la lymphe, le désir et la mémoire, la colère, l'amour...*' he writes. '... *ce que j'avais respiré...la langue française est mon seul pays, le seul lieu où j'habite.*' (My language is my flesh and my blood, my nerves and my lymph, desire and memory, anger and love... that which I breathe... the French language is my only country, the only place that I live.) Having spent the greater part of my life in a 'country' where hardly anyone speaks or understands my mother tongue, I relate well to Le Clézio's comment; for me, not being able to express and share my thoughts is as good as not having the thoughts at all.

There was also the young man, tall, attractive, a beautiful open smiling face, who walked in silence. No one knew his name or anything about him, and if he was approached by anyone, he would just shake his finger, point to his mouth and shake his head to indicate that he maintained silence. From time to time I saw him somewhere along the way, sitting under a tree or on a rock, writing in his journal. When I greeted him in passing, he would respond with a wide, warm smile and wave, but never utter a single word.

I often wondered to myself what it would be like to *not* engage in conversation with people along the way. I was walking alone, and there were many days when I didn't see a solitary soul from one refuge to the next. It was also my choice to walk in silence – but not in total silence. During these winter months, many of the small communities and villages that were still populated were closed up and shuttered, so there were not too many people around, other than the few dozen pilgrims on the Way. And, because I've always believed that it is not so much the different scenery or geography or architecture that make a country, but rather the *people* of that country, I did tend to talk to everyone I met, though they were few and far between. Consequently I ended up really enjoying any little conversation when the opportunity presented itself. Just a few words here, a greeting there, a request for information or a comment about the weather – nothing more than touching another soul across the barriers of culture, language, country, religion or age. Not speaking at all, by self-volition, surely had to have been an added hardship, a self-inflicted penitence that only the most committed could have endured. And the sad thing is that we'll never know what it was that motivated them to make that choice of silence, or what it was that they experienced, or gained from the experience. All I could do was wish them a heart-felt *Buen Camino* as we passed each other.

And then there were the mendicant pilgrims, those pilgrims who 'live' the Camino, who devote their entire lives to walking the pilgrimage. They would spend a couple of days at the entrance or the exit of the larger towns begging for a few handouts. Most of the refuges where I stayed allowed them to stay free of charge. Where there were the occasional grocery stores on the way, they would sometimes be able to pick up food parcels of supplies that were past their sell-by dates. I cannot speak for the large summer pilgrim masses, but among the rare winter pilgrims there seemed to be an understanding that these free food parcels were reserved for the mendicant pilgrims alone.

During my walk, I met three mendicant pilgrims, and I'm sure that anyone who has walked the Camino will recognise them, as over the many years they must have become well-known figures on the pilgrimage.

The first was Denis – or should I say Denis and Caresse, for the two of them, man and dog, were a unit and inseparable. I had noticed their 'tracks' a few times before I reached Astorga. I say 'their tracks', because they were ahead of me and I hadn't seen them in person, but, written on far too many sign boards, in subway passages – where, surprisingly, the only serious graffiti of the Camino could be seen – and sometimes on lamp posts, I saw the message '*Buen Camino, Denis et Caresse.*' It irritated me. Who was this couple that felt they had to immortalise themselves by writing their names on every surface that would take a marker pen, and wishing every pilgrim that followed them a '*Buen Camino*'? What arrogance to think that they could deface the Camino with their names! By the time I reached Astorga, I was ready to do battle with Denis and Caresse, whoever they were.

It was while I was preparing the salad and frying the salmon that night after I'd returned from the osteopath that they walked into the refuge, Denis and Caresse, man and dog.

Denis was a tall, muscular man, who looked as if he was carved out of a solid block of beautiful rosewood – a rich, gleaming reddish-brown – his shaved head and round face the perfect backdrop for his big smile and gentle gaze. Caresse was a kelpie with a black, white and tan coat that was always soft and shiny and groomed. She sported a cheeky red scarf knotted around her neck and her whole little body seemed wired with energy, always ready to get going again at the slightest indication from Denis. There was an amazing bond between the two and they seemed to be able to communicate without the need for sound or words. I had assumed they were a couple when I'd seen their names written everywhere, and yes, they were a couple, but with more harmony between them and better understanding than I had seen in any human couple for a very long time.

After Denis had been 'signed in' in the refuge register and settled Caresse outside in the courtyard with a blanket and a bowl of water, he came into the kitchen area where I was busy, and introduced himself. I offered him a glass of wine, which he accepted and then started to take his food out of a plastic bag; bread, cheese, a dry sausage – the staple food of a pilgrim.

'Wouldn't you rather share my meal with me? I asked. 'I am celebrating tonight and there is more than enough for two of us – or three of us! Does Caresse like fish?'

Denis's face beamed in response to my offer – or so I thought. It transpired that what pleased him even more than the prospect of a feast of fresh salad and grilled salmon, was the fact that I spoke French.

'Ah! What a pleasure!' he smiled. 'Not many people on the Camino speak French.'

'Where are you from?' I picked up from his accent that it was not from France and guessed he was probably from the Antilles or Martinique.

'Reunion,' he replied. 'I was born in Reunion and came to Europe to walk the Camino only a few years ago.'

It did not take long for the two of us to get a conversation going that was to last late into the night. We shared my celebratory feast, took some out to Caresse, who kept on licking her lips long after her bowl was licked completely clean, finished the bottle of wine and then talked some more. Denis was a well-read man and could chat about the 18th and 19th century philosophers as easily as the current literature in France. He was more up to date with world news and events than most pilgrims – who tend to cut themselves off from the outside world while walking, not necessarily out of choice but because they don't have access to current affairs. He knew about history, about global warming, about the French wine industry (he worked as a migrant labourer and grape picker during the summer to earn some money to continue walking the pilgrimage), about religions and art and astronomy and architecture. The most fascinating discussion we chanced upon was about his interest in and knowledge of medicinal plants. I had to explain what we were celebrating and when I recounted the adventure with the (gorgeous) osteopath and the honey and 'gunpowder' on my bandaged feet, Denis told me about the plants along the way which he collected and used to help fellow-pilgrims with their aches and pains and injuries. He explained how he'd been taught the skills as a child on the knee of his grandmother back in Reunion, and how he was astonished to discover that so many of the plants he had learned about and knew so well were similar or the same here, in the northern hemisphere, in the mountains of Spain.

Later, when I thought back on this conversation, I realised that right through the evening I had not once looked at him and wondered about his being a 'beggar', a 'vagrant', a 'homeless person', a 'tramp' or, as I'd heard several times people refer to mendicant pilgrims, a 'nutter'. In the true sense of all those words, he was all those things, but I remember him as a gentleman – polite, charming, interesting, well-spoken and a pleasure to know.

It was also Denis who was the first to mention 'stress fractures' to me, and the possibility that that was what was wrong with my feet – especially as I was already aware of having shown signs of osteoporosis. Much later, back in France, when I finally went to have my feet scanned and discovered that there were in fact three fractures in one foot and two in the other, and I realised the seriousness of their condition, I vividly recalled the evening I'd spent drinking wine and enjoying a celebratory feast with a lovely man and his dog. A surreal evening with a surreal man.

And I never did tell him that I was not impressed with his and Caresse's graffiti messages!

The second mendicant pilgrim that I came across, and I never knew his name, was walking the 'return pilgrimage' between Rome and Santiago de Compostela and was doing so for the fourteenth time. He was of an indeterminate age – his grey, unkempt beard and red, weather-beaten face a testimony of his thousands of kilometres and dozens of years of walking, rather than of his actual life span. He wore a bright yellow parka, soiled and stained from sleeping in the open, and a striped woollen cap pulled low on his head. In one hand he carried a pilgrims' staff with the traditional gourd for water or wine tied to the top, and in the other hand a plastic supermarket bag that contained all his worldly possessions. And his companion was a gorgeous little dog. She looked like a border collie cross, her russet-coloured fur soft and shiny, her eyes bright and her nose wet.

One day when I came across him, he was sitting on the side of the path, sharing his meal, a chunk of bread and a few slices of ham, with his dog. I was very curious to know what it was like to walk with a dog, but it was not easy to understand each other, or to make ourselves understood. He spoke a mumbling bread-crumbed Spanish as he was eating his meal, and I spoke a slow French, but my impression was that it was not so much the language barrier that was causing the obstacle, but rather that he was not keen to engage in any lengthy conversation. Having walked fourteen times – there and back, across an entire continent, alone and with only a little dog as company, must make you skittish about too much human intrusion. He had become a wandering hermit, a mobile recluse. I felt the reluctance and showed my understanding by not taking my weight off my sticks. I was not going to linger, and as much as I would have loved to know what made a man spend his life on the Camino, and sensed I should not ask, I did want to know about walking with a dog.

'Has the dog been with you long?' I started, wanting him to know that my questions would be about his companion and not about himself. It was a good opening gambit, for his face creased into a big proud smile as he looked down at the dog and caressed the back of her neck.

'This is the ninth time that she walks with me. Nine times to Rome and now the tenth time to Santiago. Before I walk alone, like you, but it is better with the dog. She is a good listener.'

I smiled. The answer to every pilgrim's prayers; a companion that does not speak but only listens!

'I hear what you are saying. I use my shadow as my listener. But my shadow doesn't look at me with such loving eyes!' The dog's adoring look at her fellow-pilgrim was a sight to behold. 'I can see that she looks very happy to be with you. You must provide her with very interesting and good conversation then!'

He laughed, ruffling the dog's ears in appreciation. If my shadow had looked that appreciatively at me, I would have ruffled its ears too.

'But what about her feet? Don't they get worn through – especially on the parts that are tarred or in concrete?' I knew all about painful feet!

'Ah! You must remember she doesn't have to stick to the path, and sometimes she shows me where the softer places are. But I put special cream on her paws and make sure there are no stones or thorns between the pads. We make her "little toilette" every evening.'

The man had one supermarket shopping bag with him, and yet he had special cream to put on his companion's paws to prevent them from becoming worn or injured. I was impressed. No, more than impressed. I was reassured of the inherent kindness of my fellow-man.

'Just one last question before I go…' I was beginning to get the hint that my demand on his solitude was already starting to exceed my ration.

'I would have thought you'd get the dog to help you carry something, even if it was just a small parcel with its own food?'

The man looked down at his dog and smiled. 'No. She would carry *me*, if I asked her. But I don't ask her. It is not her choice to walk the Camino. It is my choice. So I will never ask her to carry anything for me.'

It seemed the Camino rule of carrying your own burden applied to all pilgrims, not only the human kind.

Although there were several dogs on the Camino, I didn't see a pilgrim walking with a donkey. Yet the traditional association seems to persist because one of the questions I am frequently asked is, 'So, did you do the whole pilgrims thing – walk with the donkey, and all?' Back in the heyday of the Camino, in the 10th, 11th and 12th centuries, only royalty and nobility, the Knights Templar, and those who had money and standing, could afford horses, mules and donkeys. The 'normal' person had no such luxury and had to walk. Today, animal rights organisations point out the cruelty of riding a donkey over the Camino pathway, even though most pilgrims don't ride them – the donkey carries the pilgrim's pack and food to sustain it along the way. At the best of times it's hard going, not only for humans, but for animals as well. It really doesn't make sense to walk with an animal that size – I'm sure it's more of a burden than a burden-carrying companion. And I have the distinct impression that people who walk with donkeys do it for the effect; they do it because it 'looks cool.' Recently a friend suggested that the 'walking with a donkey-thing' was a subtle biblical reference to Jesus. If that is true, I believe it to be a modern, slightly clichéd interpretation – and again, one that is about image, rather than sentiment. Sweeping generalisations? Perhaps. But, if anyone can convince me that walking with a donkey is done for any other reason, I'm open to your explanations and would be happy to change my mind!

Something that most certainly did *not* look cool was Luigi's feet. Luigi, the third well-known character and mendicant pilgrim I encountered on the Camino, obviously believed the German adage, *Einmal ist keinmal* – what happens only once has not happened at all. He was the 'ultimate pilgrim', walking the 'ultimate pilgrim route' – a pilgrimage between the three most holy pilgrimage cities of Jerusalem, Rome and Santiago de Compostela. The only people who knew anything about him were a couple of *hospitaleros* I chatted to. He obviously did not encourage conversation with fellow-pilgrims; he walked so fast that no one could have kept up with him, or could even have joined him for a part of the way had he agreed to it. The result was that no one knew exactly how many times he'd walked this route, but, judging by the speed at which I saw him walk, as well as by the number of photographs of him that were scattered around the Camino on *refugio* walls, and references to him in the comments books in various places along the way, he must have completed this marathon pilgrimage many times. Luigi did not give the impression that he was carrying anything other than his backpack and a warm, serene smile. There seemed to be no big problems that brought a frown to his face, no nagging hang-ups or rattling skeletons from his past to put lead in his shoes. Did I say shoes? The fact of the matter was that Luigi wasn't wearing shoes. In the extreme cold of February, through areas where the mud was frozen, where the snow still lay in a thick icy layer, where the sharp stones sometimes made thick rubber soles feel as thin as paper, where the freezing Galician rain seeped into the sturdiest of boots and disproved every claim made by water-proofing agents, Luigi was walking in a simple pair of open leather sandals.

When I saw him, recognising him from afar by the thick black moustache he sported and his trademark bushwalker hat, I stopped and waited for him to get close enough so I could take a photograph of this legendary man. I hardly had time to get my camera out. By the time I found him in my sights, his soft gentle smile already filled the whole screen. The next moment he was past me, and fast disappearing into the distance – but not before I saw his feet. You would have expected his feet to have become hardened by the exposure to the elements and the daily abuse they suffered, but, whether he was perhaps walking in a new pair of sandals or because of some other explanation, the back of his ankles and heels looked like raw meat. There was actual fresh blood running down the back of his feet, leaving little droplets, like fallen rubies, glistening in the powdery dust behind him. I was aghast. What possessed a man to do this to himself? Or was I looking at someone who had become completely impervious to pain? Did his total commitment to his quest produce so many endorphins that his brain had become capable of blocking all messages of pain? Or was this what being a true pilgrim was about?

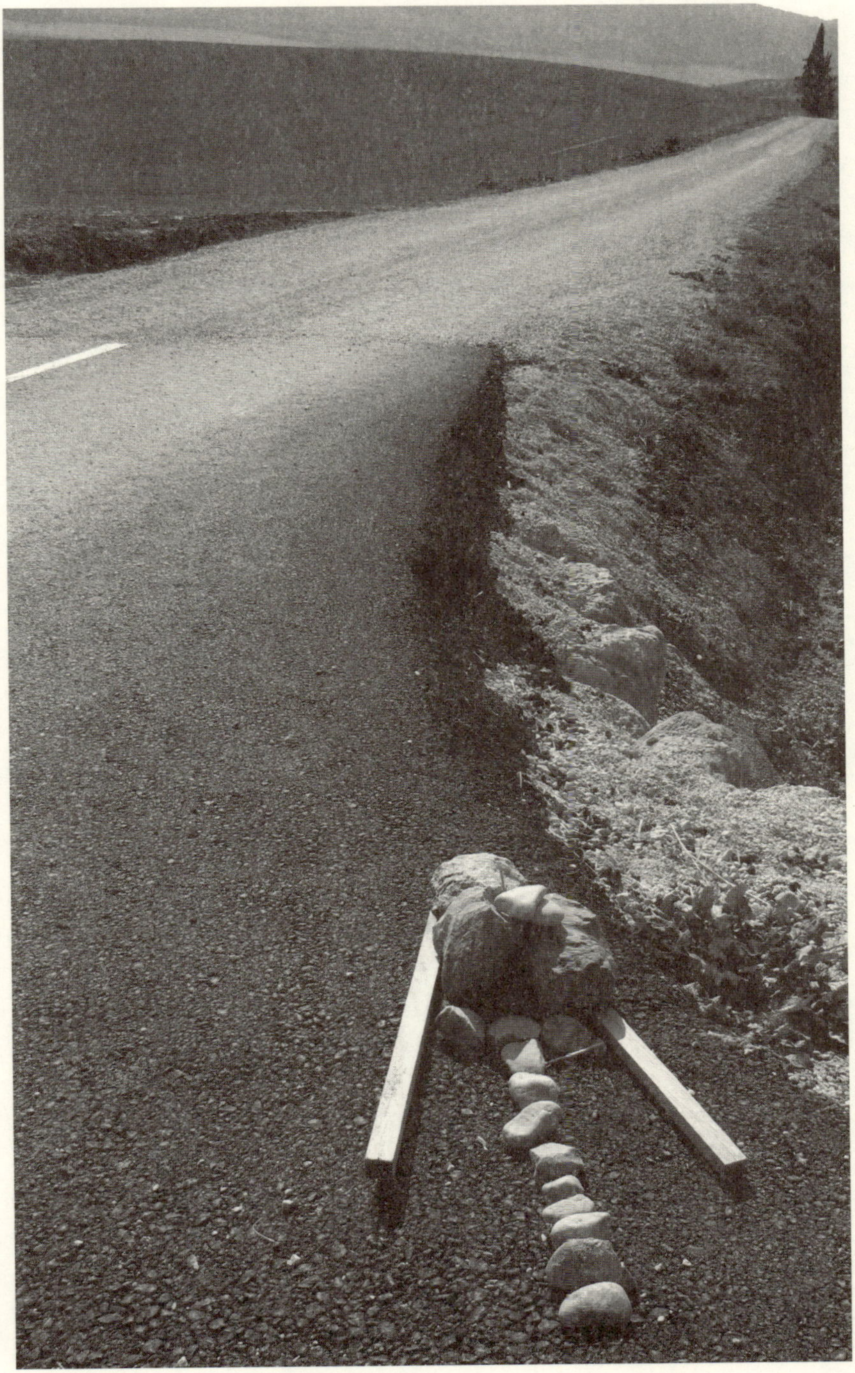

11

When life puts stones in your way, pick them up and build a bridge

Right from the moment I stepped off the road at Roncesvalles and onto the pilgrims' pathway, I started asking myself the question: How is it that no one ever said anything about the stones you have to walk on? Every pathway is covered in stones – mostly round, the size of an egg up to the size of a cricket ball, every colour on nature's palette, some smooth and polished and some rough and unhewn – layer upon layer, kilometre after kilometre, day after day, week after week, millions, trillions, gazillions of stones.

When we think of a multitude, we think of the stars in the firmament, we think of the grains of sand on the beach; we should also be thinking of the stones on the Camino. For every star in the Milky Way there's a stone on the pathway of the Camino Frances; each a reflected soul mate, an echo of the cosmos.

There is something about stones. They inspire poetry and prose. They inspire songs. In Iceland they are treated with reverence as it is believed that the 'stone people' live under them. In England walkers carry stones from Carlisle to New Castle – and back again – constantly shifting the balance of the island. In the Easter Islands they are carved spirits that stare out over the oceans, and in the Sahara camels have evolved over centuries in order to be able to walk over them. We know that when they roll they gather no moss and when you lift them you'd better be prepared for the scorpions underneath; we know about he who throws the first stone, that sticks and stones can break bones, and about people who live in glass houses… Stones form part of our idiom; our foundations are built on them.

The Camino has its own treasure trove of myths and legends about stones and much has been written about their symbolism. Since time immemorial, it seems, pilgrims have felt the need to relate to them in some way; the explanation for this *has* to be the fact that there are so many of them – and they procreate as we speak, believe me! You cannot ignore them. Every time you put your foot down on the ground, you put it on top of a stone; your foot has to adjust to the size and the shape of the stone and has to find its balance. Every time you put your foot down on the ground, the muscles in the rest of your body have to adjust to the instability of the foothold as well. The stones are slippery when wet and can be treacherous on a steep climb but they also provide dry crossings over streams and waterlogged low-lying areas. They are beautiful in their variety of shape and colour, and they're tortuous on exhausted knees and wonky hip joints. They are useful when there's a lot of mud and they are a curse when you carefully make your way down a steep slope. They hide under fallen leaves and try to trip you up. They are reincarnated in cobblestone road surfaces in towns and in the intricately stunning floors of the old refuges – where you are obliged to remove your shoes.

As you walk the Way, you find that not only do you walk over the stones, but every ten metres or so someone before you has placed a stone on a wall, or on the side of the pathway, or at the foot of every cross to remember a fallen pilgrim; and the person who followed added another stone; the one after, another, and so on. There are hearts drawn in stones. There are stone arrows pointing the way – large arrows that must have taken many hours to build, and small arrows that someone with a little energy to spare quickly put together. There are countless little cairns that have sprouted up along the entire pathway and which add their own particular charm and mystery to the Camino legend. Why is this cairn here, you wonder? What was the pilgrim who put down the first stone thinking of when he did so? What thought is held in each one of those stones? Sometimes the cairns are large and tall and the stones are precariously balancing one on top of the other and you wonder how the last passing pilgrim had reached the top. Sometimes you can see that an artistic pilgrim has spent some time arranging the stones according to shape and colour to form a beautiful little constructed sculpture. On one occasion there was a small installation where three large flat stones had been placed like menhirs – two upright, with one across the top to form a platform on which the wannabe-Celtic-druid-pilgrim-artist had added a variety of differently coloured and textured stones in a beautiful display.

The most famous, and by far the largest cairn on the Camino is at

Cruz de Ferro, on Monte Irago, the highest point on the Camino Frances. No one is sure when this cross was planted here or why. It could simply have been to mark the highest spot on the pilgrimage (1 535 metres), or it could have been a boundary post erected in 1103 by King Alfonso VI or, as some claim, it was originally a Roman altar dedicated to one of the Roman gods and their patron of travellers, Merkur. Whatever the reason, since the iron cross was erected on top of the forty-metre-tall oak pole, pilgrims have brought stones to lay at the base of the cross. The Cruz de Ferro prayer is (according to Cordula Rabe's *Way of St James from the Pyrenees to Santiago in 41 stages*): 'Lord, may this stone, a symbol of my efforts on the pilgrimage, that I lay at the foot of the cross of the Saviour, weigh the balance in favour of my good deeds some day when the deeds of my life are judged. Amen.' Today the pile of stones is about twenty metres high and pilgrims still climb to the top to lay their own stones at the foot of the pole. These are stones that pilgrims carry with them as a symbol of their burden of sin (as if the stones *under* their feet and the stones *in* their shoes were not already enough penitence). Pilgrims are supposed to bring the stone from their home and carry it with them all the way, and Cruz de Ferro, being on the highest point of the Camino, probably looked like as good a place as any to deposit them. And so, over hundreds of years the huge hill of stones evolved. Consequently, I asked myself, could you assume that many of the stones on the Camino route were from all over Europe – stones that pilgrims had brought with them and then dropped along the way? Perhaps they were the stones that didn't quite make it to the foot of Ferro de Cruz? Perhaps it was a conspiracy among the pilgrims of ten centuries ago to make life difficult for pilgrims who were going to come after them! Whatever their reasoning, it was just as well that the pilgrims left their stones at the Cruz de Ferro and didn't take them all the way to Santiago de Compostela, for if they had, the holy city would by now have been buried under pilgrim sins and pilgrim stones!

Be that as it may, in recent years a new myth has been propagated: the stones that pilgrims carry with them from home to the Camino and which they deposit at the foot of the cross on Monte Irago, are supposed to symbolise not their sins, but the sorrow in their lives. This altered symbolism could be ascribed to the modern approach to religion and to sin, two concepts that have largely lost their significance and importance in our modern day and age. In a world obsessed with political correctness, where anything is permitted because everything has been pardoned in advance, 'sin' has become an archaic concept. On the other hand, 'sorrow' is very much an accepted – and an expected – emotion to have. Members of the 'me-generation' don't care so much about what wrongs they have done, but they do very much care about the wrongs that have been done to them.

So, even if the meaning of the stones that pilgrims carry and place at the foot of the cross has changed over the centuries, the Cruz de Ferro has long been regarded as one of the most special places – *the* highlight of the Camino. Sadly, to me it was *the* biggest disappointment.

So much has been made of the stone-carrying tradition. I, too, carried a stone – one that I'd been carrying with me for many years – not as a symbol of my sins, but as a receptacle of a life that can never be recaptured or re-lived, of sacred memories and of precious moments, of tears and hurt and confusion and pain, of loved ones who have gone and of the legacy they've left behind, of joy and laughter and so much, so very much love. It held the oh-so-delicate curve of my first-born's little rosy cheek against my breast. It held the look in my father's eyes when he lifted my wedding veil. It held the smell of African dust and the feel of African soil slipping through my fingers, leaving its red richness clinging lovingly behind. It held the lies and deception of a lover whose professed adoration was a self-deluded sham, the genuine emotion being way beyond his grasp.

And it held the dream of a world without pain. Somewhere, some time long, long ago, I walked along a lonely beach with the waves chasing to erase my footprints behind me, with the clouds streaking the skies in pinks and purples and yellows and with the sun sitting majestically on the horizon, reluctant to pull the covers up and go to sleep; and I picked up this stone. It had come from the sea, had been smashed against the sand, tossed in the waves, carried along the currents, and finally it was home; it nestled snugly in the palm of my hand as if designed for it, a perfect fit. And I had assigned to it – for safekeeping, for reference, for constant reminding – everything that was me. This was the stone I carried with me on my own Camino.

But, when I reached the Cruz de Ferro, it was not this stone that I planned to place at the foot of the cross. This stone was no load at all; this stone still had a purpose to fulfil. The three stones I'd planned to place there were: a stone I'd brought from France that I'd picked up the day I learned about Terrie's cancer. (At the time, I had no notion of walking the Camino any time soon and hadn't heard of the story of the sorrow-bearing stones. So call it destiny if you wish, but that day I picked up the stone and put it in my pocket as a reminder of the burden my friend had to carry.) The second stone was one I'd picked up along the way for the sorrow that Thorsten was carrying, and the third was for the sorrow that Akira had in his life. Neither of them had reached the cross on this pilgrimage and I felt it a small act of friendship to carry and offer the stones on their behalf.

I am reluctant to record my impressions of the Cruz de Ferro, for no doubt many pilgrims after me will go there with their stones and do as the guide books tell them; place the stones at the foot of the cross and leave their sorrow behind. It may be a healing experience for many people in the future, as it has been in the past. It may relieve all that pain and sorrow that bear down on pilgrims' lives. It may lift the weight off their hearts. The simple action of placing a stone at the foot of that cross may change their lives. But for me it was not so.

The day I reached the Cruz de Ferro was the day that I was walking in the heart of the hurricane that had hit northern Spain. The winds were blowing gale force, the sleet and ice-rain was cutting my face and the temperature was below zero. When I arrived at the cross, two young Spaniards I'd met in Molinaseca, Paco and Tonio, were already there and taking photographs of each other fighting the wind to climb to the top of the hill of stones. They greeted me as I arrived and offered to help me up to the top, to the foot of the cross. 'But,' cautioned Paco, the young architect from Madrid, 'if you were expecting a special moment here at the Cruz, I think that maybe you should not go to the top.'

'Why?' I asked. We had to shout at the tops of our voices to make ourselves heard and I was also fighting my own private battle with my poncho, which had been shredded into a thousand ribbons by the wind and was flapping around me like a feather duster. 'The whole idea is to take the stones up there and place them at the foot of the cross. Just because the wind is going to make it difficult, doesn't mean I must give up before I've even tried.'

'It's not the wind – I can help you go up, because it is really difficult. You'll see. You can get seriously hurt going up there. But it is what you'll find when you go up that makes me warn you.'

It was too hard to have a conversation under those extreme conditions, so I just thanked Paco and indicated that if he could watch over my backpack, I was going to do the pilgrim-thing and go to the top of the hill with my three stones. I wanted to leave them at the foot of the cross, for all time, and on behalf of my three friends.

It was a mistake. As I climbed higher and higher up the hill, with great difficulty, I saw why Paco had tried to dissuade me from going up there. If the idea was to leave behind your sins and your sorrows in the symbolic shape of a stone, the pile of stones would have been awesome… hundreds of thousands of stones put there over hundreds of years by hundreds of thousands of pilgrims – an impressive pile of stones. But, not all pilgrims are tough enough to carry stones with them. And those who didn't want to carry heavy stones in their pockets, but who still wanted to do the 'pilgrim-thing' and leave their 'sins' behind, did so in another way. Any object that they felt symbolised their sins or their sorrows – perhaps even their weaknesses, addictions, bad habits or taboos – they left behind at the foot of the Cruz de Ferro. There, scattered among the thousands of stones were countless packets of cigarettes, cigarette lighters, used syringes, broken bottle-top hash pipes, condoms of every variety, stones with names scratched on them, an envelope with a handwritten letter inside (who had written it, what did it say and why was it discarded?), a cast that had been cut off a fractured arm – signed and decorated, several women's bras, chewing gum, a fast-food outlet loyalty card, pencils, inner soles of shoes, scarves, bits of ribbon, crumpled-up chocolate bar wrappers, dried flowers, a tube of sunscreen. My mind boggled at the possible rationale behind some of the offerings. If it weren't so disgusting, it could have been funny. I stood at the top of that pile, holding on for dear life to the wooden pole to stop the wind from blowing me over. I looked around me at the debris, the flotsam of a million souls, and I asked myself: if symbolism was to be found in everything we do and in everything around us, what did this mess symbolise? What was the deeper meaning of this hill of rubbish that was the sum of the sacrifices and the offerings of countless pilgrims, placed at the foot of the most sacred of religious symbols?

I put the Cruz de Ferro behind me and continued on my journey, my stones still heavy in my pocket.

Many days later, on a long straight stretch over a particularly stony terrain that seemed to stretch past the horizon, there was yet another ploughed field of stones. How these fields were in fact ploughed I never managed to establish, for no conventional shear would have lasted more than one minute; a stone cutting machine would have been more suited for the job. Why they were ploughed was another mystery – except occasionally I did see gnarled grape vines growing out of these fields of stone, their big fat, chocolate brown limbs shiny and contorted and seeming to simulate a thousand and one Nubian belly dancers performing in perfect synchrony.

There was no one within sight; no other living creature anywhere near, not even the little robin that had accompanied me earlier that day. The sky was a faded duck-egg blue; a few tufts of white fluff the only remains of the contrails of a jumbo jet overhead. There was a stillness over the landscape; a hushed silence that filled the space. I stopped and breathed in the beauty, filling my soul to bursting with the immense serenity of the moment. 'This is the place for my stones,' I thought. This was a fitting place to leave the burdens and the sorrows of my friends. A vast, endless field of stones. My three stones among these millions would be lost forever; gone, untraceable, irretrievable. 'This is the place to leave behind the pain and the hurt and the grief,' I said out loud. I took the stones from my trouser pocket and for a moment it felt strange to have the familiar weight lifted off me; for a while I could still feel their pressing hardness against my thigh. I took Terrie's burden of cancer and, using every bit of strength that I had in my body, threw it as far as I possibly could. It cut an arc through the sky, and after what seemed like minutes, came down so far away in this huge field that I could scarcely make out the sound as it landed, just a soft little tinkling sound of stone against stone. I did the same with the other stones; I threw them so far into this field that I know they are gone forever. They are gone for all time...

※

As reluctant as I was to spoil anyone else's experience of the Cruz de Ferro, just so eager am I to share the spirit-lifting experience of reaching the top of the hill between Atapuerca and the town of Burgos.

After leaving Atapuerca, with its remnants of prehistoric man, there's a steady climb for several kilometres over particularly stony ground. When you near the top of the hill you simply have to stop for a moment — for there in front of you, slightly to your left on the side of the pathway, is a very tall cross, etched against the open sky. On your right, higher up in the distance, there's a straight line of windmills against the horizon that seem to be standing with their feet in the clouds. The cross and the windmills — both, in their own way, symbols of hope and salvation — on opposite sides of this beautiful scene, and on opposing ends of the spectrum of spiritual and physical need.

When you continue up the hill, suddenly, without warning, a vast plateau opens in front of you. If you're lucky, there's no one else around – that is, no other actual person – and you stand completely alone, in silence and solitude, to fully appreciate this amazing scene. For in the middle of this wide-open plateau on top of the world is a stone spiral; a spiral made of a single continuous line of stones, one against the other, that pilgrims have placed there over time. The spiral covers an enormous area. When I walked from the centre, stepping out the distance, I calculated that the total length of the spiral must be more than a kilometre. And if you consider that the stones are small, the biggest no larger than the size of an orange, you can only marvel at the number of stones there must be, and consequently the incalculable number of pilgrims who have passed through here and added their stones to the spiral. I've never seen any of the huge geoglyphs on the Nazca plains in Peru, nor those in Malta, or Chile or Bolivia, but I could well imagine that this stone spiral on the Camino de Santiago de Compostela was well on its way to becoming something similar to those enigmatic phenomena. From the air, I'm sure it would have shown up as an impressive piece of work already, were the stones not all white and on a white dusty background.

But it was not the physical aspect of the spiral that made the biggest impression on me. It was the atmosphere of the place, the strong presence that I felt. I stood in the centre of that stone spiral and I was aware of the million pilgrims who'd gone before me – surrounding me, embracing me in their lingering presence, wrapping me in their protective warmth, enveloping my spirit in the spirit of the Camino. I felt as if I was standing on holy ground. And when I added my own stone at the end of the line – the very last stone in the spiral, until such time as the next pilgrim passed this way – I felt as if I was making my own contribution to a most hallowed place.

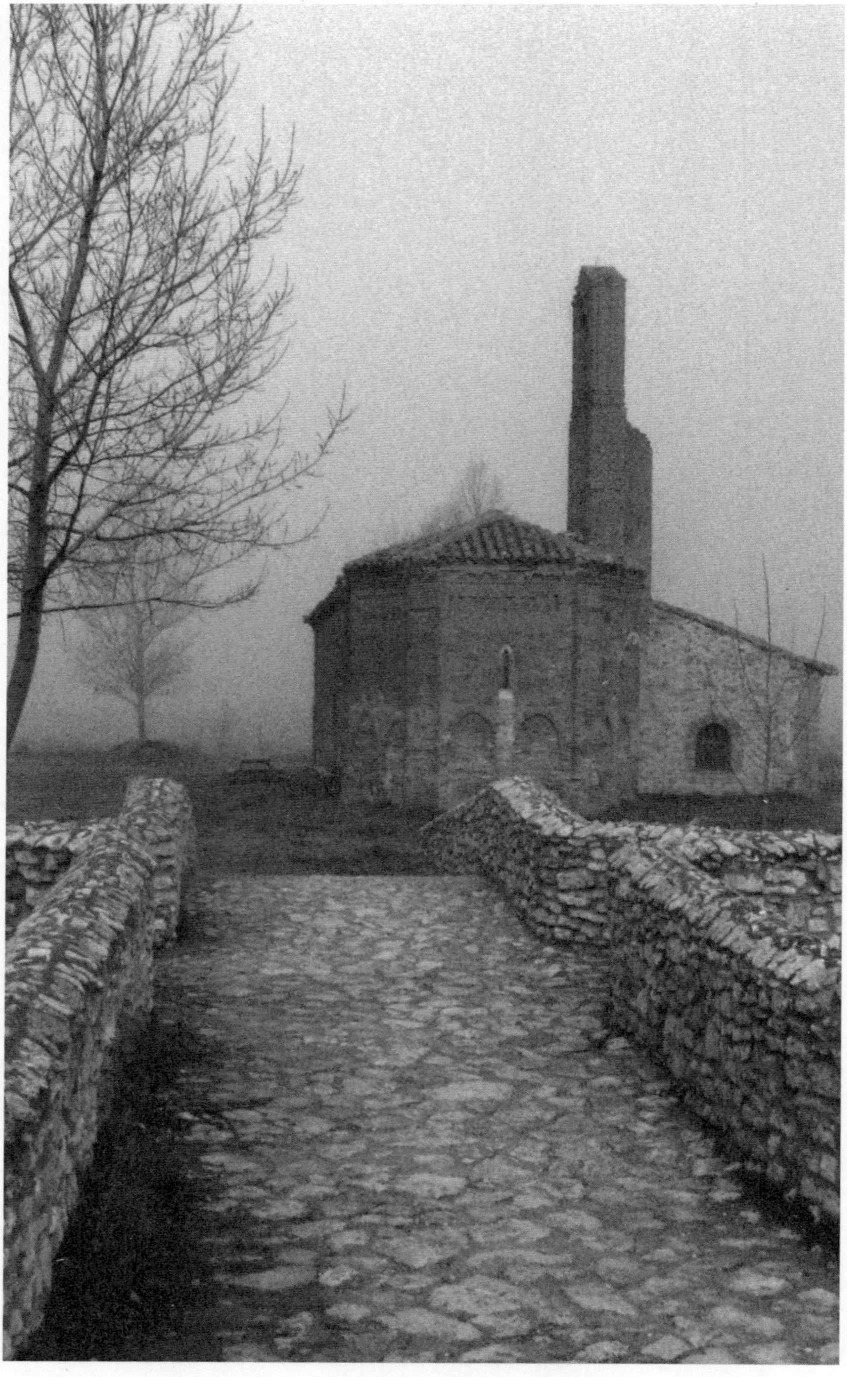

12
Somewhere somebody knows your name

Do not follow in the footsteps of the old masters, but seek what they sought. Achieve enlightenment, then return to this world of ordinary humanity.

– Basho

for Thorsten and Akira

One day I was walking through a pine forest on a plateau at the top of the Oca mountain range. Although not a very high range, only about 1 160 metres, the climb from Belorado, where I'd spent the previous night, had been steep and unrelenting, lasting more than five hours. The last stop before the final climb was Villafranca Montes de Oca, where I'd gone into the *refugio* for a little rest. This was, according to the guidebooks, where pilgrims used to 'recover their energies for the long and dangerous crossing of the Oca mountains, in the woods of which robbers and bandits did their foul work.'

There was no one at the *refugio*, but a hand-written note on the door told me that I was welcome to enter, make myself a cup of something warm and, if I so wished, enjoy a re-energising nap. The invitation was too good to pass up. To tell the truth, my right leg, which had been very brave and uncomplaining all day, despite the severely painful tendonitis that had it in its grip, took on a life all of its own and took the first step over the threshold. The rest of me simply had to follow.

Once upstairs I relieved myself of my backpack and took out, from its safe and dry hiding place, a precious little cache of Japanese green tea leaves. I searched in the cupboards and on the shelves and finally discovered, tucked in behind a couple of cups without handles and cracked glasses, an old chipped ceramic bowl that was perfect for my green tea. While I waited for the water to boil on the rusty but functional hot plate in this very basic 'kitchen', I paged through the *refugio* register book. I recognised a few names of people who'd stopped there recently – some to stay for a night, some only to refresh themselves as I was doing. It was always interesting to see who'd gone before me and it was amazing how encouraged I felt to see the names of those I'd met, spoken to, and with whom I'd shared a meal or a dormitory. I thought, 'If they could do it, so can I' – not in a competitive way, but more to urge me on, as in, 'They're ahead, and I want to catch up and see them again!'

Right at the bottom of the last used page was a name I did not recognise. Written in big confident letters, was '*Buen Camino, peregrina!* – Guillermo.' I looked at my watch and saw that we must have missed each other by a hair's breadth – he'd been there no longer than an hour before. I had not met a 'Guillermo' or seen this name in a *refugio* register book, which could mean that he'd only started his Camino recently. But I had also definitely not seen anyone ahead of me that day. That could have been because there were no long straight stretches on this particular day's walk, otherwise, how could I possibly have missed him? And he had written '*peregrina*', almost as if he'd guessed that the person to arrive after him would be a woman.

Anyway, I poured the boiling water on the green tea leaves in the bowl and, while waiting for it to draw, I went into the dormitory and lay down on one of the beds for a twenty-minute rest. When I finally left the *refugio* about an hour later and set off on the Way again, I felt revived, renewed and ready for whatever danger, bandit or robber the woods on Mount Oca had waiting for me.

The woods, or more specifically the pine forests on the mountain, seemed to go on forever, kilometre after kilometre, hour after hour. Yet I didn't want it to end. Not only was the walk soft underfoot, the years of pine-needles forming a thick carpet that cushioned every step, but the air was heavy with the perfume of the forest. It must have rained the night before because there were puddles of water here and there and at times, when the sun shone through the thick canopy of the trees, the water drops lingering on the tips of the needles sparkled like a million crystal prisms.

Just as I reached the summit of the mountain, the pathway through the trees opened up onto a large clearing where it seemed that bulldozers had been preparing the area for something to be built. Perhaps a road? But no:

It started nowhere and went nowhere, so it couldn't be a road. It was also far too wide, almost as wide as it was long. The red soil was churned up in a wide-open ugly gash, like a wound across the back of the mountain and it suddenly felt very strange to be so exposed after having walked among the dense trees for so long. Oddly enough I hadn't felt even a tinge of fear while walking through the dense forest. If there were bandits and robbers along the way, I never saw them, let alone sensed them. However, the moment I stepped into this huge man-made gaping space on top of the mountain, I felt threatened. Generally, my vivid imagination was put to good and positive use and I didn't dabble in the pursuit of imaginary threats, but here I felt the presence of something evil. Demons, real or imaginary, seemed to be lurking among the dark trees fringing this open space. It was a feeling that had no foundation; that made no logical sense; I could not explain it, but neither could I control it.

Emotions on the Camino were like that. Everyone I spoke to had had a similar kind of experience on at least one occasion. Whether it was the tiredness, the actual state of exhaustion that caused me to feel more vulnerable and less able to resist whatever came my way, or whether it was being completely out of my comfort zone, I couldn't tell. I was ready for anything ninety-nine per cent of the time and, even if this was a façade, it didn't matter; it worked. What I could tell you, however, was that feigning confidence is something that comes with practise. Think confident, tell yourself you're confident, and that's the way you will seem. Do this long enough and often enough, and the confidence will begin to come naturally. It's as simple as that. The same for courage and inner strength; the world can be fooled quite effortlessly into believing that you're strong and courageous, and consequently you yourself will believe – will *know* – that you have those attributes.

This theory was nothing new and it was something that I'd coached people in. I remembered years before spending a week with a group of young girls of about fifteen or sixteen years of age, teaching them about self-esteem; finding it and maintaining it. For many this would have seemed insignificant, but for these girls it could possibly have been a life-saving skill. They were from a small mining community where male chauvinism in its very worst form was the norm, where wife battering, child abuse and incest were no strangers and where girls were expected to stay – as the saying went – barefoot and pregnant in the kitchen. One of the exercises we did that week was to look at ourselves in a mirror and say out loud:

'You are special. You are strong. Your life is yours and you can decide what you want to do with your life.' It was only much later that the precious moment came when they managed to turn the 'you' into 'I' – the moment when they looked at themselves in the mirror and actually related to the person they saw, recognised themselves in the mirror and believed their own voices and their own words.

Yes, ninety-nine per cent of the time you were ready for anything on the Camino, but then came that single moment, that one experience, when the alien circumstances of the pilgrimage inevitably brought you face-to-face with whatever weakness there was in your make-up – no matter how tiny, how insignificant in the greater scheme of your life. When it happened to me, there, on top of Montes de Oca, it caught me completely by surprise. My breathing had sped up to an almost-hyperventilation. My heart was thumping so loud in my chest that it hurt. I felt that slight nausea of dread creeping up into my throat. I stopped in my tracks.

'Pull yourself together...' I told myself. 'There's nothing out there. No one.'

'No?' said the malicious little inner voice. 'And who, then, is casting that shadow behind you?'

As I stood there in that wide-open space though, it was my friend Terrie's face that sprang up in front of me. She was the one whose text messages all the way from Australia woke me up every morning out of a deep sleep and gave me a couple of words of encouragement, urging me on, expressing admiration and generously offering praise. Those text messages came to mean more than the world to me and it was almost a physical little push to get going and to continue on the pilgrimage. But standing there, I suddenly realised that if I, confident and strong, could have this paralysing fear grip me – this fear that came out of nowhere and caught me so on the left foot, then how hard must it be for her in her battle against cancer. Everyone was always marvelling at how strong and courageous and positive Terrie was – for that was all everyone ever saw when they looked at her. But surely she must have had her moments of stepping into the clearing – stepping into that wide-open space where she was utterly vulnerable and exposed? How did Terrie manage those moments? How did she get through them and continue? How did she subdue her fear, for fear there must have been; fear of the test results, fear of the new growth of tumours, fear of the cancer spreading into more organs, fear of the existing metastases, fear of the pain, fear of death. Oh!

Terrie, my dearest friend, how I wished I could be there with you and let you know that you were not alone. That you would never be alone.

I took a deep breath, then another, and breathing out the second time, mentally pushed down this turbulence inside me, down into the core of me, forcing it to stay. I *can* face myself. Of course I can face myself as well as all the demons and dark spots and scary bits that I give shelter to. If a large open space was what was needed for me to confront that which I usually kept well suppressed and hidden, then so be it. I was strong. I *was* strong…

And then I noticed something I hadn't seen before. Just ahead of me was the start of two parallel lines of clusters of dry sticks — branches broken off of the dead bushes that had been dug up and moved to the edge of the clearing. These had been carefully placed down the middle of the clearing, in two long lines, stretching for probably about twenty or thirty metres, forming a perfect little pathway across the red soil.

I did not hesitate; I took the pathway. I walked between the two lines of dead branches, immediately focused on continuing my journey, all fear pushed aside, all dread and demons left behind me. I even smiled as I felt the confidence growing inside me again, my back straightening and my chest filling out. It was an amazing experience. Someone — another pilgrim perhaps, who had gone here before me and who must have felt the same fear, the same vulnerability, the same confrontation with his demons, had taken the time and the tremendous effort to gather the dried sticks and to define a new pathway that would feel safe and protected, that gave direction and comfort. How to describe the feeling this gave me? From feeling totally lost and insignificant and exposed one moment, I now felt the presence of a friend, a protector, of someone willing to lead the way for me and show me the safe route.

And then came another surprise. Not far before the end of the clearing, where again you were plunged back into the forest and the comfort zone of the pilgrims' trodden pathway, the two stick lines came to an end. And there, across the wide clearing, in letters two metres high and one metre wide, my name was spelt out in stones. 'Wilna' it said. Big round red stones, ranging from the size of oranges to the size of watermelons, collected fifty metres away on the edge of the clearing where the churned-up soil had been dumped, carried back to the middle and placed on the ground — to spell my name.

Pilgrims through the centuries had developed countless stories of Saint

James – or Sant Iago, revealing himself to them to help them in their hour of need. Sometimes he came to a pilgrim's rescue in the shape of another pilgrim, sometimes he simply left a sign of some sort, showing the pilgrim the way out of his danger or trouble.

And once he came to the top of a mountain and made a pathway with sticks and spelled my name across the Way in stones and so led me out of a dark place, back into the light.

Yes – how to describe the feeling this gave me? Best not even to try.

Because of the rest I'd had in the *refugio* earlier and the time I spent on top of the mountain, first in panic and then in wonderment (and of course taking photographs), the time had marched on and I realised I'd have to walk a little faster to get to the next village before dark. But, first there was to be one more stop.

Just before the sharp descent down the mountain, on the side of the pathway, was a memorial for Republican soldiers who had been shot there in 1936, during the Spanish Civil War. The memorial was not exceptional – until I read the inscription carved on the side:

It was not their death that was unnecessary.
It was their shooting.

I felt such a strong affinity with these soldiers – soldiers whom I'd never met, whose names I did not even know, who fought in a civil war that I had read about and sometimes thought about, but which had no specific meaning for me other than the horror of the mere thought of a civil war. I wondered whether their presence and their death had had an effect on what I'd felt in the clearing. And I wished that they'd had an angel or a saint write their names in stones to show them the way to their final resting place.

I had planned to spend that night in San Juan de Ortega where there was a *refugio,* named after the man who built it way back in the 11th century. Historically, San Juan de Ortega, together with Santo Domingo, was the second-most important patron of the Camino. He had built roads and bridges on the Way, as well as the *Iglesia de San Nicolas*, with this *refugio* attached, for the benefit of pilgrims. I'd hoped to stop at this refuge, not because it housed the tomb of San Juan, nor because a visit to this church was the last hope of childless women (I was quite content with my three, thank you), but because I wanted to see the spot where the *Milagro de la Luz*, or the Miracle of Light takes place on the equinox, when the sun falls on a specific place on the altar, lighting up the depiction of the Annunciation. However, the doors were firmly shut and locked and no amount of ringing the bell managed to rouse anybody. I was not impressed.

During the winter months many of the refuges were closed. This was quite understandable as there were so few pilgrims it would hardly have been worth keeping the refuges open and staffed. I didn't believe that the cost of heating and hot water would have been the deciding factor for them staying open despite the small number of pilgrims; quite a few of the refuges that were open during the winter months didn't bother too much about such luxuries and were quite often positively Dickensian and freezing cold. On the other hand, when you considered what a meagre three or five or, at the most, seven euros could buy, finding a hot shower and a warm comfortable bed waiting for you at the end of a long day's walk for that price was a miracle. How the refuges survived was a mystery to me. When I raised the question, I was reminded that during summer there were tens of thousands of pilgrims who walked the Camino and the refuges would all be full to the rafters every single night and thus earn enough to see them through winter. But, as such a concept was impossible to envisage during the month of February when there were hardly fifty pilgrims on the entire 800-kilometre route, the mystery remained for the time being.

So why was I not impressed to find the doors closed? Because the guidebooks had all said that they'd be open. And, when the guidebooks misled pilgrims with erroneous information, pilgrims became very grumpy. They relied on those guidebooks to indicate where the facilities and services were and, when planning a day's walk, it was important to calculate where you were going to sleep the following night. It was no good continuing past open refuges only to find yourself, at sunset, caught out by the dark and with another two or three hours' walk to get to the next open refuge. You had to remember that the pathways mostly crossed remote countryside – across fields and plains, through forests and alongside rivers or over mountains – and you seldom came close to any source of light. To walk after sunset was simply irresponsible and looking for trouble;

and of course, in the winter months, the days were shorter by several hours than in summer.

※

At this little crossroads in my story it's probably a good moment to stop for a sip of water and to pay homage to the writers of Camino guidebooks. I mentioned that pilgrims became grumpy when they were wrong with their information, but in fact, pilgrims are in awe of their respective guidebooks. I heard a couple of pilgrims even refer to them as their 'bibles'. Almost everyone had a different book – or should I say, each nationality seemed to have their favourite; often the German pilgrims had the same one, the Swedish had theirs, the Italians theirs, the Spanish theirs, and so on. As for the English speakers, or any nationality that did not have guidebooks written or translated into their own language, the books varied as much as did the owners. The one thing they all had in common though, was the astounding amount of detailed information they contained – especially when you considered how vitally important that information was to the pilgrim.

Whenever the subject came up, we would wonder at the patience and effort of the authors. Walking the Camino was demanding. You had to fight simply to survive each day. But then, making notes every step of the way, measuring the distance and time it took to the next turn-off, checking the opening times of churches, looking for landmarks to help pilgrims find the correct route, verifying the telephone numbers and prices of the refuges – not only of the ones they'd stayed in but of all the others in every village and town… We stood in awe (and appreciation) at the people who'd done this for the pilgrims who came after them. And we all agreed that the Pope should be advised that all authors of guidebooks should be canonised. (Except of course the ones who told you that a *refugio* was open in February when it was not!)

We talked about this quite often, looking at each other's guidebooks and comparing information and presentation. What was fascinating was how common it was for the guidebook to dictate how long your pilgrimage was going to take. For instance, some people aimed on finishing their walk in thirty days, because that was what their guidebook indicated – giving each day's distance to be accomplished and suggesting the refuges for the end of the day. My guidebook recommended a forty-day walk and therefore my suggested refuges could be in villages that hardly got a mention in someone else's guidebook.

The content also differed, depending on the personal interests of the authors or their reasons for undertaking the pilgrimage. One guidebook might describe in great detail the many churches, little chapels, monasteries and religious significance of the Camino, while another guidebook may hardly mention these but describe in mouth-watering detail the different types of food, traditional dishes and recipes of the various areas through which you walk. My guidebook had no mention of taxi and bus services, for example, and I didn't even know they existed until I was well on my way. But another book I saw listed, under the name of each village, the telephone numbers for these services and even included a little map showing where the stops were.

And then there was the Japanese guidebook I saw in the refuge in Cezur Menor! A Japanese pilgrim had apparently left it for the *hospitalero* as a gift – and as she happened to be one of those angels I met on the way – with her knowledge of ice foot baths with salt and vinegar (for me) and painlessly fixing blisters under toenails (for Brigitte) – I could easily understand why he'd offered her this beautiful gift. It was written in Japanese, in beautiful vertical lines of kanji, starting from the back, as Japanese books do, describing the route in great detail (at least that's what Akira told me the writing said). But what made it exceptional was that down the side of each page was a hand-drawn pictorial map of the route – a map such as a child might draw, with realistic looking trees and little houses, rivers and streams of water, here a horse and there a dog. He even had the frequent crosses or memorials for pilgrims who'd died on the way, including the name and date of death as marked on the cross. As you turned the pages, the drawn route continued from one page to the next, from the first to the very last page, and anyone picking up the book would have been able to follow the entire route without ever getting lost, it was that clearly depicted. It was a work of art, and I just so wished I'd written down the information I needed to search for and find the book. I'll have to walk the Camino again and get it next time...

But now, let's finish the day's journey: The next village was Agés and, since the same guidebook that had misled me about the *refugio* in San Juan de

Ortega told me that it was only forty-five minutes' walk away (and since I already knew that the author's forty-five minutes was generally my ninety minutes) I realised I wasn't going to beat the sun to the horizon.

Apart from it being impractical, difficult and dangerous to walk in the darkness, if there was one thing that quickly discouraged a pilgrim, it was the sight of the setting sun, no matter how spectacular. Funny how it didn't worry me in the least walking in the pitch darkness before sunrise in the morning, even when the mist was so thick you could cut it with a knife. But when I reached the end of the day and the sun started setting in the west, I wanted to be safely ensconced in a *refugio*. Furthermore, when you had prepared yourself to walk a certain number of kilometres, be it ten or twenty or fifty, your body seemed to programme that number into its system. Once you reached that number, your whole system came to a grinding halt. 'So far and no further, thank you very much!' your body seemed to say. This was not a conscious thing; subconsciously your body seemed to know when it had reached the planned distance – and once there it simply did not want to continue. San Juan de Ortega had been my destination for the day and my body let me know loud and clear that it was not prepared to go one step more. But the doors were closed and I had no choice; I had to continue.

I emptied my mind of any negative thoughts about sunsets and darkness, tiredness and misleading guidebooks, and filled the space with names written in stones on mountaintops, the smell of pine forests, the bravery and commitment of young soldiers, a mysterious man called Guillermo and the anticipation of meeting fellow-pilgrims around a warm meal and sharing with them my day's experiences.

It never ceased to amaze me how positive and pleasant thoughts fuelled the engine. There was a renewed spring in my step and energy in my movement and I revelled in the winding pathway continuing through more pine forests and then opening out onto an open hilltop where two ancient, gnarled oak trees stood guard over a beautiful shape on the ground, made with stones. It was a single line of small round pebbles with an arrow head at one end, pointing in the direction from which I'd just come, the body running through the middle of the two trees and the other end turning round and round in a spiral; the special arrow for pilgrims returning home. I'd occasionally seen small, blue spiral-arrow signs along the Way, but this was the first time I'd seen it done in stones. It was beautiful. I stopped for a moment to admire this lovely sign, when

I realised that the light was suddenly fading very fast. Looking up, I saw the sun, bright red and glowing, bidding a last farewell before tumbling below the horizon. I wasted no more time, but sent a silent message to all returning pilgrims that may come that way, wishing them a *Buen Camino*, and headed down the hill towards the twinkling lights of Agés, beckoning from the valley below.

The next thing, halfway down the hill, with no warning whatsoever, I was flat on my back. Like an upturned tortoise, I lay there looking up at the stars in the already black sky, my backpack forming an uncomfortable hump under my back. My legs had simply given way. I hadn't been aware of slipping or stumbling; one moment I was upright and the next I was on my back! I just burst out laughing. The sight of me balancing on my backpack in the middle of a stony pathway going down a hill must have been quite comical, and with everything that had happened that day, I could somehow see nothing but the funny side of this strange situation. And, if I laughed at the sight I must have been, I was nearly hysterical with the almost impossible challenge of getting into a position to stand up again. Exactly like a tortoise on its back – no matter which way I turned, the backpack made it impossible for me to move into a position where I could get a foothold and turn myself over. Suffice it to say that I was grateful there was no Candid Camera close by!

And then I got to the *refugio* in Agés and the whole day made sense. I'd never been one to believe that everything happened for a purpose. That was, to my way of thinking, an all too facile explanation of the way our choices turn out. But on this night I could not have argued against the notion. For there, as I walked into the *refugio* – 'Agés; 971 m, pop.48; El Pajar de Agés, Maria Isabel (proprietor); washing machine, internet, cheap meals, All day, All year' – I was welcomed by a riot of laughter and noise and children running around (Maria Isabel's grandchildren) and dogs wagging their tails. And best of all, the most wonderful sight imaginable: there was Kamil sitting at the internet in one corner, looking up with a big, welcoming smile. Over there was Thorsten, pouring a gin and tonic in readiness for me; Akira was coming into the room from the back with an ice pack that he'd prepared for my feet for when I arrived. And at the bar, drinking a beer and looking around to greet me with another big smile, a lovely young man in cyclists' clothing, who called out as I stepped into the room: 'She has arrived!'

He came over to me and helped me take off my backpack. 'You must be Wilna. I am Guillermo. Come, we were waiting for you before sitting down to the delicious dinner Maria Isabel has prepared for us!'

Was it possible that anyone had ever had such a warm, such a generous welcome anywhere?

'How did you know I would be coming here tonight? And how did you know I would be arriving right now?' They all seemed to have known at exactly which second I'd be walking through the door. For a moment I even had the fleeting thought that they might have seen me looking ridiculous on the side of the hill. 'And hey! You guys said the other day that you were going to sleep in Atapuerca! That's the next stop. What are you doing here?'

'Well', replied Thorsten, pulling the chair out for me and sliding the gin and tonic in front of me. 'You can call it Camino Magic, but it was simple, really. It is of course how Camino communication travels down the Camino pathway. We knew you'd left Belorado this morning and we knew you wanted to stop in San Juan. When we walked past the *refugio* we saw it was closed and it was already late so we were worried about you walking so far and walking in the dark on your own. But we knew you were strong and you would get to Agés, for sure. So we decided to wait for you here to make sure you were okay.'

Akira had both my feet up on a chair and was applying ice packs to them, and Kamil had come over from the computer to sit with us. 'It is good to see you – I was worrying so much that I will not see you again. I was walking alone for a few days now and I don't like that so I was very happy when I come here tonight and I find Thorsten and Akira. And now you are here too and we are all together again!'

I was deeply touched by the thoughtfulness of 'my boys' and, for once, at a complete loss for words. I had to fight to keep the tears at bay.

'You are my angels – my little Camino family! I don't know how to thank you.' Without having to say anything more, I simply put my arms out and the three of them came to me for a wonderful warm group hug.

'Can we go eat now? I am starving!' Guillermo stood there, obviously a little uncomfortable with all this show of emotion and not quite sure how to react.

'Yes, me too. Let's go! And I have so much to tell you about! It has been the most amazing day!'

'Oh Wilna, you say that every day!' laughed Akira. 'But come, I bring the ice pack so you can put your feet on it while we eat.'

And over Maria Isabel's superb pilgrims' menu of vegetable soup, a huge dish of pasta with a stew rich in meat and tomatoes, carrots and broad beans, followed by a salad and then a hot creamy bread pudding full of plump, juicy raisins for dessert – all for the grand sum of six euros – we talked and talked, late into the night. I told them about the few days since I'd seen them; they told me about theirs. I heard all about Guillermo, from Barcelona, and how he took one week's leave a year and cycled a section of the Camino, starting each time at the spot where he'd stopped the previous year. He spoke only Spanish – but it was the beautiful, clear Spanish spoken in Catelonia, which we all somehow managed to understand. Or perhaps our understanding had something to do with the fact that his whole face was so animated with his enthusiasm and love for life, and his passion for the Camino shone so brilliantly from his dark eyes.

When I told them about my experience on top of the mountain where I'd found the pathway made of sticks and my name written in stones, I caught the look that passed between Thorsten and Akira. I suddenly realised what I must have known all along; that they were the ones who'd left it there for me.

'It must have taken you hours to do!' I exclaimed. 'If only you knew how much it meant to me – it was exactly what I needed, exactly there and exactly then, to give me courage to go on. It was as if you'd *known* that… How *did* you know?'

The two of them just smiled. Then Thorsten spoke softly. 'We admire you so much for walking alone. But we know that sometimes it must be very hard for you, for sure. Up on the mountain today it was hard even for us…'

'…So we wanted to leave something for you to help you,' Akira finished the sentence.

'It did more than that, my friends. It did much more than that…'

In the weeks that followed, every time I met fellow-pilgrims who'd been on the Camino behind me, I asked if they'd seen my name written in that huge clearing in the forest on top of Montes de Oca. No one could remember that they'd seen anything of the sort. And I wondered how it was possible that they could *not* have seen it when they would have had to walk right across it. Then, some time later, someone mentioned that when he'd crossed Montes de Oca the day after I did, there, in the clearing, was a whole bunch of boys on motor bikes – youngsters racing, ramping and having fun, far away from the disapproving eyes of their elders. No doubt they must have scattered the stones and made my name disappear. And that was fine, for when it was needed, the right person had discovered it.

Writing the name of a fellow-pilgrim in stones was probably the most wonderful gift you could give someone. It was a subtle acknowledgement, on the pilgrim pathway, of another's inner journey. A reminder that, although this journey has to be made in solitude, you need never feel alone; there are still people around you who know your name. It was recognition. It was a gift of friendship.

I often wondered if other pilgrims had such good fortune as I had in the people that I met on my pilgrimage. Or was I just extremely blessed? There were so few people on the Way and yet everyone I met was someone exceptional.

One day, as I came over a rise of a particularly arid and stony hill, my breath was nearly taken away by the sight down the other side. Before me lay a vast expanse of wide, open space. It stretched for kilometre upon kilometre, the dusty pathway ahead looking like a white ribbon that had carelessly been dropped on the landscape, cutting a swathe across the earth, its one end pinned down under my own two feet. There were some ploughed fields and others were covered in an almost transparent gauze of green. A slight late afternoon haze softened the lines and blurred the horizon; the light blue sky looked as if it bled into the landscape, the landscape bleeding into the sky. Not another soul in sight for as far as the human eye could see. I was standing on top of the world in perfect solitude.

You often read how, at a moment like this, a person feels so infinitely tiny and insignificant. People feel humbled by the immensity of the earth, by the magnificence of creation; they realise how terribly small they are in the universe. I had none of those feelings. I was one with this landscape. It was me and I was it; we were of the same molecules, the same matter, the same energy. I was part of this universe and the universe was part of me. It was empowering beyond words.

In this magic moment I noticed, a little way down the hill, a young tree – no more than a sapling, no more than my own height, standing precariously but bravely rooted in the stony ground on the side of this vast landscape. Coming closer to the little tree, I saw that it was some kind of fruit tree – but as it had no leaves on yet, I couldn't tell what kind. It was easy to imagine though, how a pilgrim had walked down this hill, stopped to admire the beauty spread out before him, eaten a peach or an apricot, or perhaps a handful of cherries, spat out the pip, wiped his mouth and continued on his way. At the right moment, the pip had drunk in a few drops of rain, gathered enough energy together to germinate, found a small pocket of soil among all the stones to get a grip with his roots and grow into this brave little sapling. And who knows; maybe one day another pilgrim will stop right here, under the shade of this tree, pick a fruit, and stop to enjoy the beautiful landscape below him.

But for now, the sapling had another purpose. Each time I'd visited Japan, I always found a few quiet moments to spend in one of the many temples. One of the traditions I came to love there was the use of prayer trees; a prayer is written on a small, narrow strip of white paper and then tied to a twig or a branch of a living tree. I loved how a prayer is written on paper – which itself comes from the tree, and is then attached to another tree which is alive, part of nature, and which can then keep the prayer or the wish infused with its own energy. So, when I greeted this lone young sapling on the side of that beautiful hill that day, I recognised in him the ideal bearer of prayers.

I took off my backpack and pulled out one of my notebooks in which I kept my journal. Don't ask me why, but I'd forgotten, at the bottom of my backpack, a handful of coloured pencils. I seemed to remember thinking, when I threw them in the backpack, that I may need them for my sketches, but up to this day I hadn't retrieved them. They were perfect for this task. I carefully folded seams and tore long, narrow strips of paper from my notebook. Then I wrote a carefully chosen quote or a thought or a wish on each strip with a different coloured pencil. On the back of each strip, I wrote the name of one of my fellow-pilgrims on the Camino for whom the words had been chosen, one of the nine people who'd helped to make my own pilgrimage so special and unique. Thorsten. Akira-san. Kamil. Brigitte. Lisl. Golda. Gabi. Ernst. Peter. If I had found that little tree a few weeks later, there would have been many more names – the tree would have been festooned with colourful prayers and wishes blowing in the breeze for Marcus, for David and Marilyn, for Herve and Paco and Tonio, for Klaus, Mike from Brazil and Mauro from Italy, and Alphonzo and Jiocasta from Madrid, for Rene and Denis and Caresse, for Julia and Kim and Annie and Christl, for David and James and Petr – but those good people I was yet to meet and their prayers would have to wait for another time.

I tied each of the strips to the little tree, careful not to damage the tree and careful to make sure that the knots would hold. I stood back and looked. It looked stunning. The little tree was blossoming with good wishes and prayers, the delicate white strips fluttering joyously in the breeze, the brightly coloured names looking festive; the young sapling had transformed into a beautiful prayer tree that looked proud and important. This was not a name spelled out in stones across the pathway, but it was my way of acknowledging the important role fellow-pilgrims play when they touch one another's lives.

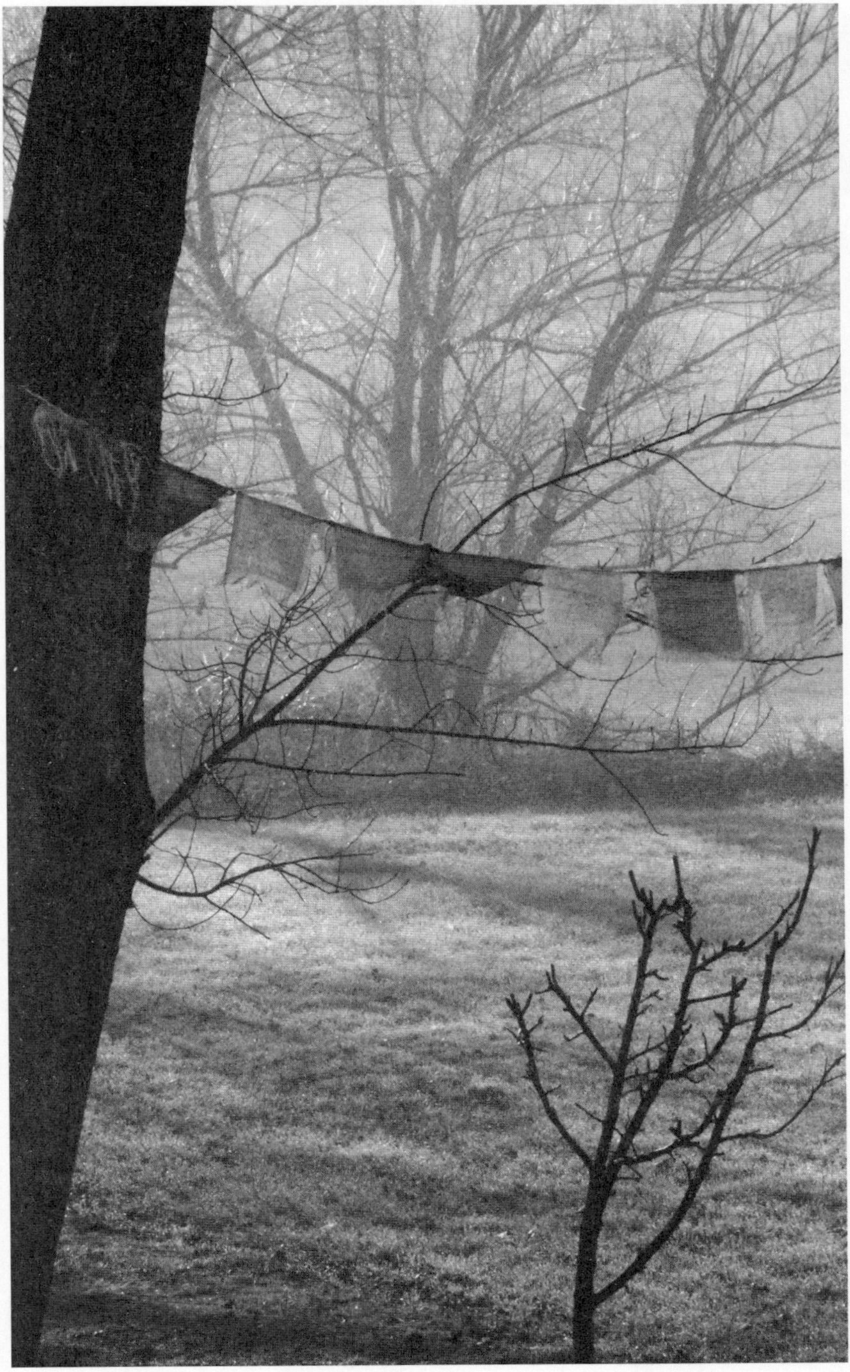

13

What goes around, comes around…

Sticks in a bundle are unbreakable. Sticks alone can be broken by a child.
— African proverb

During the night in Santo Domingo de la Calzada, a thick mist came down to shroud the town, enveloping the buildings and the trees in a white cashmere blanket. It was dense, yet light and feathery, the slightest movement causing wisps and swirls on its surface. Each lamp post wore a glowing golden halo and at its feet was a circle of glistening wet cobblestones. They looked like rows of angels and saints lining the streets. It was a night to be indoors, sit around a log fire, and tell stories…

Most towns and villages along the pilgrimage route have their own legends. It may be a story about a little church with a spectacularly carved and gilded rococo altarpiece, or the remnants of an ancient Roman road from when the Camino was still a trading route. There may be a beautifully preserved pilgrims' cross in the centre square with a particular history, or the ruins of an 11th-century pilgrims' hospital. Almost every second church along the way, small or large, has some historical person buried in its crypt or under its flagstones – somebody who'd passed through one day and had passed away the next. There are stories of miracles and of events that occurred when kings and queens, popes and paupers walked the pilgrimage a long time ago. There are relics in caskets and vials, bits and pieces of religious and holy importance.

Some of these stories date back centuries. Often the timing has become a little confused, such as in the many legends of Saint James, who led the battles against the Moors. He was said to have saved Spain from the

Moorish Jihad in Spain, which lasted from 711 to 1492, having come into the Reconquista in the legendary Battle of Clavijo in the year 844. So great was his valour, it is said, that he became known as Matamoros – the Moor Slayer, and to this day he can be seen in various places, immortalised in stone, seated valiantly on his rearing white steed, with a hapless Moor under its hooves. Few people question whether there was, in fact, an actual Battle of Clavijo, or that Sant Iago, the brother of Jesus Christ, must have been well over 800 years old to have fought in this battle.

Many of the Camino stories exist in folklore in other countries and cultures and even in other religions as well, and are not unique to the Camino. Most of them, no doubt, were probably no more than the urban legends of their time; urban legends of a Camino kind, that had been created and then developed over time by the pilgrims themselves.

The story of Santo Domingo de la Calzada concerns one white cock (alive) and one white hen (equally alive), both comfortably housed in the cathedral in an elaborately carved hutch opposite the tomb of Santo Domingo himself. The inscription on the hutch reads: *Santo Domingo de la Calzada, donde cantó la gallina después de asada* (Santo Domingo de la Calzada, where the hen clucks after being roasted).

Apparently, or so the most popular story has been passed down through the centuries, a certain young pilgrim of no more than eighteen years of age, who went by the name of Hugonell, passed through Santo Domigo de la Calzada with his parents. It was only the 10th century, (some say the 13th, others the 14th, but we know it was a long, long time ago) and already young girls were on the lookout for talent among the pilgrims, as indeed they are to this day. So it was then that the daughter of the innkeeper fell head over heels in love with our young hero, Hugonell. Alas! He was a good-looking young man, but he was also a serious young man and his attention was focused on the pilgrimage and the redemption of his sins; he refused the advances of the young girl. The scorned girl was furious and the rejection brought out the worst in her. She hid a silver cup among Hugonell's belongings and reported him to the authorities, who tried him for theft and hanged him.

One version of the story tells us that Sant Iago himself came and stood under the gallows, bore the hanged boy's weight and so kept him alive. Others say that it was Santo Domingo who did this, but everyone agrees that, when the parents came to the gallows, they found that their son was still alive. They immediately rushed off to Santiago de Compostela to inform the chief judge and obtain a pardon. Arriving in Santiago, they found the important man sitting down to eat. In front of him were two roast chickens; a rooster and a hen.

'Lord, pity us!' the parents cried. 'Our son was innocent of this crime. Nevertheless, he has been hanged on the gallows, but he is still alive! Sant Iago has performed a miracle and he is holding our son on his shoulders right now. We beg you to pardon him so we may cut him down from the gallows and he may continue his pilgrimage.'

'Alive?' the judge called out. 'Alive? What a ridiculous notion. Your son is as alive as these two roast chickens that I am about to eat! Indeed, I will believe that he is alive, if they were alive!'

With that, the roasted rooster and the roasted hen on the platter did come alive, jumped upright and started crowing and clucking. Of course, (it was a miracle after all) young Hugonell was pardoned and allowed to continue on his pilgrimage.

To this day, the so-called descendants of that first rooster and hen can be seen where they are kept in the specially made hutch in the church of Santo Domingo. Pilgrims prize the white feathers of these birds to put onto their hats and some believe that, if the chickens take crumbs from the end of their walking sticks, they will be assured a safe arrival in Santiago de Compostela.

According to a few guidebooks there is also a wayside shrine – a *hornacina* – which was built in 1445 and which holds a piece of the gallows on which Hugonell was hanged. It is said that in the 15th century, a German pilgrim, Hermann Künig, claimed that he'd actually seen the room where the miracle of the poultry resurrection had taken place. Many pilgrims, through the centuries, have claimed that the shirt of Hugonell was kept safe by the church of Santo Domingo and that the gallows itself was conserved there as well. If that is so, these relics are no longer there.

The morning that I woke up in Santo Domingo de la Calzada, the first thing I saw through the window was that it was still dark outside, the mist blanket of the previous night draped loosely over the rooftops and snuggling up to the window pane, but all around me was a cacophony of sound. People were shouting at each other and music was blaring; a disembodied lit torch was being swung around wildly, its beam bouncing off angry faces, waving arms and people still in their beds. A rooster, that sounded as if he was right there in the room with us, was cock-a-doodle-doo-ing as if his life depended on it. It was a scene out of a Fellini film.

I sat up and looked at my watch to see the time. Six-oh-five. I would have been woken a few minutes later – either by the vibration of my mobile phone alarm, set for six fifteen, or by the short 'blip' that told me there was a good-morning and good luck text message from Terrie. This was the first time that I'd seen such mayhem in a dormitory. I got up and switched on the light – something that was usually never done in the early mornings – in case one of the pilgrims needed to rest a little longer, but I guessed that, by this time, everyone had to be awake.

'What is the problem?' I asked no one in particular. 'And where is that rooster that's crowing? It sounds like he's in the room!' No one seemed to notice or hear me. They were embroiled in a different matter.

'Uli, all I'm saying is that you went to fetch all our laundry last night and now half my clothes have disappeared!'

'Stop accusing me of something I did not do! I did nothing wrong! You can look through my backpack and see for yourself, I only have my own stuff!'

It was almost a re-enactment of the event that had occurred here centuries before. Only this time it was not about a mere stolen silver cup; it was about something much more important; a pilgrim's missing underwear.

In the middle of the dormitory was a huge pile of pilgrims' clothes. There were six other pilgrims who'd spent the night at this *refugio* of the Confraternity of Sant Iago. Early the previous evening, one of them had come running in to inform everyone of the good news: there was a laundromat across the street – a rare luxury on the Camino! In a scrabble of excitement, everyone went to the dorm, upended their backpacks and came out with bundles of dirty washing, spilling socks and underwear and bits and pieces in their wake. The whole lot was carried down the stairs, across the road and, in an attempt to try to save a few euros, they all threw their washing into the cavernous jaws of the single, enormous, industrial washing machine. Not a good idea. Everything that went in, and everything that came out an hour later, looked the same. Everyone who goes out to buy clothes for the winter Camino buys thermal underwear – usually in black – or black – or, if you were a little adventurous, in black. What was always going to happen in this situation was perfectly predictable; there was a complete mix-up of socks and underwear and everything else in the mangled pile in the middle of the floor!

I decided to stay out of the fray that was about to ensue, and to go and find the source of the blaring radio, (which no one else seemed to have noticed either) and that infernally infuriating rooster that was still crowing at the top of his voice. Only, at this stage, it sounded as if he'd acquired the additional help of a megaphone.

The radio was easy to find. It was a small portable one that stood abandoned on the table in the communal kitchen. Who had switched it on and turned the volume up full blast, was going to remain a mystery. There was a very vocal rooster that had to be found.

Following the incessant sound, I headed down the stairs and through a half-open door leading to the back courtyard. And there they were. The direct descendents of the rooster and the hen that had come back to life and saved a serious young man named Hugonell from the gallows. Ten roosters and ten hens in the same coop. It was the back-up team for the poultry couple that were the stars in the church. Every month the two on show were replaced with another couple, and the stand-ins stayed in a large chicken coop in the back courtyard of the Confraternity refuge.

Half of the roosters had discovered a hole in the diamond wire fence down the middle of the coop and had decided to join the hen party. The other half that had remained on the rooster side were not happy and were expressing their dissatisfaction vociferously, crowing at full volume and taking their frustration out on their mates. Meanwhile, on the hen side, the escapees were, let's just say, very busy ensuring the continuation of the family tree of the miracle-working chickens.

'Come on, guys!' I laughed. Perhaps they only understood Spanish, but I felt it my duty to at least sort out *this* mayhem, since I'd left the mayhem up in the dormitory to sort itself out. 'You really have a very important role to play in the history of the Camino. You're the backup team, and we all know that no one can achieve anything without a backup team.' These chickens may have had ancestral miracle worker blood in their veins, but, like everyone else on that day, they obviously were not going to pay attention to me.

We live in an era where so much is written about teams and the importance of teamwork. Sports organisations, as well as corporations and institutions, pay consultants handsomely to take their teams or employees out for a day, a week or longer to put them through their paces. The team builders work with those 'thousand fibres' that Herman Melville spoke about, 'that connect us with our fellow men'. I have, on many occasions, taken groups of people through these team-building exercises myself and shown them how much more they can achieve when they pool their individual resources and work together as a team. It's a wonderfully revealing and enlightening process, discovering just how much stronger we are when we form a team. Mostly we prefer to believe that we work better on our own; we get more done, we do it the way we want it done, we do it much better, much quicker, much easier than having to be accountable to others. And mostly we'd be right, because unfortunately, we're not always in a position to handpick our teammates. Even if we were, few of us can judge people accurately enough to choose wisely and correctly. Yet, the moment we're lucky enough to be in an almost perfectly compatible team, and we discover the many and diverse benefits of working alongside others, it doesn't take much to get even the most hardened loners to be converted into effective team workers.

But, a pilgrimage, I believe, is not meant to be a team effort in the conventional sense of the term. Not only is a pilgrimage a highly personal and spiritual experience, but the pilgrimage itself already demands so much from you, already exerts so much pressure on your perseverance and resolve, that I do not believe you have the energy or the resources to carry a team member. You have to be completely focused on the task at hand in order to survive, physically as well as mentally. A pilgrimage *is* a matter of survival of the fittest. You have just so much energy, just so much resolve, and if a teammate needs help, the added responsibility could become a burden to you. You're bound to let your teammate as well as yourself down. Earlier I mentioned the remarkable spirit among pilgrims, the acts of random kindness, the unselfish and selfless behaviour of pilgrims towards each other. But it is exactly the fact that these acts are unsolicited, and consequently unexpected, that makes them so special. When you walk alone, there are no expectations from anyone, except those you place on yourself. There are no demands made on you from anyone other than yourself. You don't *have* to give to others of your time and your energy and your generosity. When you do choose to help another pilgrim by sharing your own resources, the rewards are bountiful. When you do receive assistance from someone else, the pleasure brings an injection of renewed faith in your fellow man. But this spontaneous benevolence is the phenomenon of the Camino and not a prescribed behavioural rule laid down for all pilgrims.

Many people were surprised that I would choose to walk alone. I was surprised that they thought you could walk the pilgrimage with a partner, a spouse, or a friend, even though the generally accepted view is that it's something people do together.

Since I moved to France, and because I live on the edge of one of the routes of the Camino, I'd had many opportunities to listen to people giving talks about their Camino experience. There was one piece of advice that almost all agreed on. 'When you walk the pilgrimage for religious or spiritual reasons, rather walk alone than with a partner, a spouse or even your best friend. No two people experience anything in the same way. No two people walk at the same pace – not over such a long distance. No two people can have the same levels of energy, the same levels of courage and perseverance – not at the same time and over a period of thirty or forty days.'

'What almost drove a permanent wedge between my wife Lucille and I, after forty-four years of a good marriage, was our difference in attitude,' explained Paul, one veteran pilgrim I spoke to. 'I thought we knew and understood each other better than anyone; that we were sensitive to each other's nuances of mood and state of mind.' But, faced with the continuous and relentless challenges of the pilgrimage, aspects of our character that even we may never have been aware of, are brought to the fore. As Paul's resolve to finish the pilgrimage increased, so Lucille's waned. The more he became aware of the importance of being positive all the time, the more Lucille mentioned the possibility of not finishing, of taking a bus, of coming back the next year to do the rest. Eventually Paul asked Lucille to go home and allow him to finish the Camino by himself. Fortunately their relationship had a strong enough foundation for them to do this and still be together.

Another pilgrim, Richard, a friend of a friend who came to my home to share a glass of wine and some of his impressions of walking the Camino one late summer afternoon, had had a completely different experience.

'It was sheer hell. The hardest thing I have ever done. I never imagined that you could be so utterly lonely as I was on the Camino.'

Richard had lost his wife to cancer six months before and, being a deeply religious man, had walked the Camino in the hope of finding understanding, acceptance and spiritual solace. He'd planned to walk alone, but not quite as alone as he ended up doing. An exceptionally tall man, Richard's stride was the length of at least two large steps of an average man's. As he'd walked a huge distance, from the Porte de St Jacques in Paris, all the way to Santiago de Compostela, and had done so early in the summer when there was already a large number of people on the pilgrimage, he normally would have had quite some company along the way, but it didn't happen.

The result was that he completed the entire 1 800 kilometres without anyone coming to walk alongside him, and he never met the same person twice in any of the refuges at night. He never had anyone with whom to share the moments of joy or the anguish and the pain. He never had anyone to ask him if he needed to talk or offer to listen, or someone with whom to sit in silence. At least, not until the very last week when he deliberately slowed down and so befriended another pilgrim, a Muslim man who happened to be walking the Camino for the exact same reasons as Richard was. The two of them finished the last hundred kilometres together, rejoicing in the companionship, the conversation, the cross-cultural discovery and the mutual understanding of each other's sorrow and grief.

'The best moment for me, a Catholic in bone and marrow, was to stand at the desk in the Camino office in Santiago and receive the *compostela* certificate for a religious pilgrimage alongside my bearded Muslim friend who was receiving the same. That was my Camino miracle...'

At the end of the day, most people will seek a companion on the Way. It is, after all, human nature to want to have someone by your side. We humans seem to fear solitude more than anything else. And no matter what people with experience will advise, most pilgrims still prefer to walk with someone else. Personally, I believe that if you do that – other than for the odd couple of days or for a few hours here and there, when it is wonderful to share your experience with a kindred spirit – you take away from the experience of self-discovery, of self-confrontation, of getting to know yourself; of making friends with your shadow.

You would do well to remember, though, that you can only rely on yourself to get through every day. When you're on the side of the mountain and your lungs are on fire, both your legs are cramped up, the wind is blowing gale force, the ice-rain is slamming onto your face, slashing your skin, piercing your eyes; when the icy cold water is seeping in under your collar, your ears ache so much from the cold you fear losing your hearing; when the cloying mud is building up on your shoe soles and dragging your feet down with every step; when the stones you walk across are slippery and cause you to stumble and fall and crash down on your knees or your hip or your elbow, covering you with mud and bruises and leaving you drenched and cold to the marrow; when all of this is coming down on you like the woes of Job, you, and only you, can get through it. Only *your* strength and *your* energy and your spirit can get you to the top of that mountain, down the other side and to the next warm, dry, welcoming log fire somewhere in a refuge along the way. You don't want to have the added burden of keeping your teammate's spirits up. You don't want to have to use your ration of energy and positive power to encourage and cajole your teammate to keep going. And you don't want to lose that unique moment when you realise that this is *your* Camino, these are *your* trials and *your* tribulations, these challenges are yours and yours alone to face and to conquer. And when you have succeeded – for succeed you will – the sense of achievement, of having found your own indomitable spirit without anyone else having to push or to pull or support you, that incredible sense of having discovered a strength within yourself you never knew existed, *that* sense will also be yours and yours alone. In so many ways, a pilgrimage is like a cancer sufferer fighting the disease; it is about the individual's spirit, about you and your creator. It is not about anyone else and most certainly not about group dynamics.

By making the pilgrimage a buddy exercise or a team effort, your pilgrimage becomes a 'walk'. The list of what you could call the experience is almost endless: a hike across beautiful countryside, an interesting way to pass a few weeks in summer, a lovely way to spend time with a loved one or a friend, that item on your 'Things I want to do before I turn fifty list' or on your 'Bucket List' that you can finally tick off with pride. But, you may never know what you've missed…

However – don't get me wrong. I did say '…a pilgrimage, I believe, is not meant to be a team effort in the *conventional* sense of the term,' and I believe that implicitly. A pilgrim can only make a pilgrimage alone. That is true. But – just as the two chickens in the church in Santo Domingo de Calzada could not possible stay cooped up in a hutch in a church all their lives, and needed a backup team to make their 'miracle working performance' possible, just so the pilgrimage cannot be made without the Camino backup team. And what a backup team that is!

What would we pilgrims have done without the books that guided us on our pilgrimage with the necessary information, the history, the logistics of the Camino? How many pilgrims would finish their pilgrimage without the care and kindness of the doctors and dentists and the friendly assistants in the pharmacies along the way? What would you do without the amazing expertise and craftsmanship of the *zabatero* – the cobbler who will deconstruct and reconstruct a pilgrim's fallen-apart shoe for the princely sum of four euros, so that you can continue on your way? How would pilgrims manage the pathways if they were not kept tidy and cleared and planted and pruned and tended, and how would they find their way if someone did not make sure that there were visible little yellow arrows painted all along the pathways? How would pilgrims eat if, in every little hamlet and village where there were no shops and only a little white van that came through once a week with groceries and water, there was not at least one little old lady who had a larder full of nourishing food that she was willing to sell cheaply to the clever pilgrims who managed to find her door? Where would pilgrims be if there weren't the occasional old bent man standing at the exit of a town, pointing the way to Santiago de Compostela with an encouraging *Buen Camino* to see you on your way?

And what would we do without those *hospitaleros* – those saints and angels in the backup teams of Juan, Filippe, Carlos, Michelangelo, Gustav, Isabel, and yes, Janine. There are many pilgrims who feel that the walk itself is already enough hardship to endure to buy them some leniency in Purgatory. Spending nights in a dormitory full of smelly, snoring strangers, on foam mattresses in bunk beds, sharing cold showers and being subjected to strict lights-off and silence rules, is unnecessary added torture that they can do without. Yet, anyone who decides to stay in a more comfortable *posada* or little hotel along the way, misses out on meeting some of the most amazing people in the world; the *hospitaleros* of the Camino – the inn keepers, the caretakers, the counsellors and advisors, the elders, the veterans, the wrappers of parcels and providers of comfort, the patron saints of the pilgrimage – those people who manage the *refugios*.

'The first time I did the Camino, I did it in thirteen days!' Freda was busy hanging a few bits of washing on a makeshift line strung across the little patch of a garden behind the *refugio* in Hospital de Órbigo.

'Thirteen days?' I gasped. Then I quickly guessed why. 'You cycled?'

'Yes, of course! But even so, thirteen days was quick; far, far too quick. I didn't see anything on the way.'

Freda was another of the few female *hospitaleros* that I came across. An attractive Belgian, probably in her forties, with sun-bleached hair cropped very short, piercing blue eyes that sparkled with the joy of living, and a tanned complexion that had been exposed to far too much sun and weather. Her warm smile creased up her entire face, and it was that smile that welcomed Akira and me when we walked into the beautiful courtyard of the *refugio* where she was in charge.

She continued her story in her excellent English, softened with the lovely nuances and lilts of her Belgian accent. 'So the next year I came to the Camino again, but this time I walked. It was so much better! I could stop and look and enjoy!'

'Oh, I can well believe that. Every time I've seen a cyclist – and that has not been too often – he whizzes past and is gone before I've even had a chance to wish him *Buen Camino*. I think their Camino must be something else all together, but it surely cannot be a pilgrimage. A physical challenge yes, or proving something to yourself, or the sheer pleasure of riding a bicycle across impossible terrain perhaps…'

Freda picked up the empty washing basket and beckoned me to follow her back into the refuge. 'The washing will probably freeze again on the line tonight, but if I hang it up in my room, it will do so as well,' she laughed. 'I don't think I've ever been as cold as I am in this place!'

'Don't you have heating in your room?' I was aghast. Being a pilgrim, sleeping in a sleeping bag and not always having heating in the dormitories was part of the pilgrimage, but living in what is your permanent home and having no heating during these sub-zero days and nights had to be a nightmare. 'Why are you not provided with heating?'

'No heating, no hot water. No money!' Freda bent down in front of the wood stove in the kitchen, opened the door and tossed in another small log from the neat little pile stacked against the wall. 'The church provides everything here and of course the pilgrim comes first. The priest and the two old monks who are still here don't have heating in their quarters, so why should the *hospitalero*? The fact that I'm a woman makes no difference. It was my choice to do the job. And anyway, you will see later there are brand new showers for the pilgrims, with hot water – over there in the corner of the courtyard – so when I get too cold in the night,

I sneak downstairs and stand under the hot shower for a few minutes to thaw out!' She smiled and pulled the register down from a shelf above the scrubbed table.

I handed her my *credenciales* to take my information and put in the stamp – a beautiful, large picture depicting the famous thirteenth century twenty-arch bridge of Órbigo. 'That will be five euros for each of you, please.'

'Akira will bring you his *credenciales* and money soon – he's just studying the map while there is still light, to see what time he'll have to get up in the morning to get to Astorga for the ten o'clock bus to Madrid. The poor man – he's heartbroken that he has to cut his Camino short, but he needs to get back to work in Japan.'

I passed over my five euros. 'I must say, every night I pay the fee for the *refugio*, I'm amazed that it is so little. The accommodation isn't exactly five star, but still – three or four or even nine euros per person can hardly cover the electricity and water, let alone the upkeep of the place.'

'No, it goes nowhere near covering the cost in winter, but the authorities rely on the large numbers of pilgrims in the summer to carry the cost. The Camino looks very, very different in the summer, I can assure you!'

'But what made you come and be a *hospitalero*, and why Órbigo ?' I was still horrified at the thought of Freda having to work in a place where no heating or hot water was provided.

'Well, what made *you* stop in Órbigo ?' she turned the question around.

I laughed. Akira and I had looked at our two different guidebooks the night before to see where the best place was to go for his last night on the Camino. By agreement we had walked together from time to time over the previous couple of days and stayed in the same refuges, in order to spend some time together before he had to return to Japan.

We had not planned to do so, but as Camino luck would have it, two days before, on the Sunday, I'd caught up with him and Thorsten in León, one of the largest cities on the Camino, a magnificent city steeped in history and folklore. They'd arrived there on the Friday, hoping to find a dentist for Thorsten, who was in agony with toothache. However, everything was closed when they arrived and Thorsten would have to wait (and suffer) until the Monday to see a dentist. The refuge in León – one of the largest I'd come across, with at least a hundred beds – was right in the centre of the old cobblestone city, close to the beautiful cathedral, and was run by monks from the Benedictine order.

When I arrived on the outskirts of León, no amount of breathing out or releasing of neurotransmitters could suppress the pain in my feet. To add to an already very difficult day, when I could see the cathedral spires in the distance and almost taste the pleasure of the relief of rest, my worst nightmare suddenly loomed large and ugly ahead of me: a foot bridge across a major twelve-lane national highway. Some people fear flying. Some people fear heights. For some even the thought of being confined in a small space is enough to make them hyperventilate and break out in a sweat. I can handle most anything – except for footbridges across busy roads. I have no idea why this should be, but I do know that normally I'd rather walk an extra ten kilometres than walk over traffic screaming in both directions at high speeds.

Anyone who has seen this bridge would probably wonder to themselves, 'What the heck! You can't be serious! It's a large, wide, solid, timber bridge!' But that is the way with nightmares, isn't it? Silly and illogical – but real.

However, I'd already completed my own personal fire-walk and I knew that I could do anything, so I lined myself up with the centre of the bridge, took a deep breath in an attempt to push the feeling of nausea deep down into the pit of my stomach, b-r-ea-th-ed out and, looking straight ahead, started walking. At that moment, I was startled by sounds behind me. I looked around and there was Herve, a big, burley tattooed young Spanish plumber, whom I'd had the pleasure of meeting a few times before, coming towards me at his steady pace. He'd started his Camino on the Northern Route along the coastline of Spain, and when the coastline was hit by the hurricane (which I'd walked through when crossing the Irago mountains) and it made the going almost impossible, he had cut down through the mountains and joined the Camino Frances. Herve had teamed up with a young German, Johannes, and the two of them were walking side by side, in companionable silence.

'¡Hola, peregrina!' they both called out as they approached. 'Come, walk with us into the Kingdom of León!'

I did not hesitate for a moment. Focusing only on the intricate and colourful tattoos on the Herve's bare calves (he was wearing long shorts and short socks, leaving the masterpieces on his legs exposed to both admiring tattoo connoisseurs and amateurs alike), I forged ahead, barely aware of the hollow echo of my feet on the timber slats and rushing sounds of speeding traffic below my feet. My guiding angel had fiery, winged dragons, beautiful bare-breasted damsels, floating butterflies and sprites, roses and lilies, clouds and skulls and elves — an entire travelling fairytale circus flying over his bulging calf muscles.

Johannes glanced over his shoulder from time to time to make sure I was still following, but Herve was walking with a purpose: a hot shower and a cold beer, and not necessarily in that order. I had a purpose too — to keep up with them — and all pain, all fear, and all fear of pain was, for the moment, sufficiently suppressed to make it possible.

León is one of the largest cities on the Camino, sprawled out over a vast area, with the old city, the cathedral, and consequently the main refuges, right in the centre of it. It has a long and colourful history that stretches back to Roman times and, through the centuries, it resisted attacks from the Visigoths, was the last refuge of Spanish independence during the Muslim invasions, and later became one of the most important Christian cities of Iberia. As with all the bigger towns and the three largest cities on the Camino, the walk to the centre is not a pleasant one. If the map says 'León 5km', you know that this is to the outer edge of the city, and from that point there could be anything up to fifteen kilometres to walk before you reach the centre of the city where the refuge is. Apart from the extra distance, these sections are usually through the industrial areas, often with no sidewalks, over badly cracked and uneven surfaces, noise, traffic, smells, nowhere to stop for a while and definitely nothing to hide behind when you desperately need a toilet! It is always wise to plan a much shorter walk on the days that you have to enter a town or city.

'Phew!' Freda's exclamation interrupted my story. 'You remind me what it was like to walk those bits into and out of the cities! It is horrible! And I know the refuge in León. It's really a lovely refuge, but the rules! You feel like a school child in a convent, all over again!'

'You're right! Vespers at seven o'clock, Vespers again at nine-thirty, lights out and total silence at ten, matins and breakfast at six-thirty. But I have to admit that the separation of men and women in the dormitories was absolute bliss! I can't remember when last I had such a peaceful night!'

Freda laughed. 'That is true! But not many of the youngsters like that rule. No drink, drugs or sex in León…'

'Yes, when I arrived at the refuge, there were three taxis lined up outside the doors and all the twenty-somethings were loading their backpacks to move to the refuge on the other side of the city. They said it was because they wanted to stay an extra day to do sight-seeing though.'

'Sight-seeing is what they call it, eh?' Freda winked. 'I suspect it is because of the strictness of the León refuge that you have the total opposite in the next stop in Villar de Mazarife. That is a real nest for sex and sin, I'm told.'

I laughed. 'You better believe it, Freda! Akira and I stayed there last night and we were the only ones there. We spent the entire evening looking at the drawings and paintings on the walls. Some of them were quite something!'

'But then, Hospital de Órbigo?' Freda brought us back to the original question.

'Well, apart from the fact that this was a good place from where Akira could get to Astorga in time for his bus tomorrow morning, all the guidebooks recommend it as a stop because of the lovely medieval story of the bridge and then, of course, because of this *refugio*. It really is beautiful.'

This *refugio* in Hospital de Órbigo, where Freda presided, is reputed to be the oldest still-functioning refuge on the Camino, and, with its cobblestoned courtyard overlooked by the balconies of the first floor, is undoubtedly one of the most beautiful. The arrangement of fresh fruit in a basket on the table, an interesting book lying ready to be picked up and paged through, an easel with a folder containing her photographs and inspirational thoughts… these were all little touches that showed there was a woman's hand behind the lovely visual aspect of the refuge. As the name of the town implies, Hospital de Órbigo was one of the many towns along the Way that came into existence as a result of the Camino. It started back in the 13th century when the church built this refuge to serve as a hospital for the pilgrims who came through the area. The church itself was added afterwards, as was the accommodation for all the people who served the church and the hospital, and that's how the town was born.

'And *that* is exactly why I came here, stopped and decided to stay,' she concluded.

By this time, Akira had come to join the conversation. As there would be a grocery store in Órbigo where I could buy fresh provisions the next day, and as Akira was leaving the following morning early, we had unpacked the little sausage and cheese we had left in our backpacks and placed it on the table in the corner of the courtyard, alongside my last tin of sardines and a piece of baguette, cut in slices. I'd invited Freda to share our pre-dinner snack with us, but she declined. Instead, she brought a bottle of red wine and three glasses and came to sit with us and continue her story.

'Although I had already "done" the Camino before, albeit on a bicycle and in double-quick time, I had to complete it again on foot before they would give me the job. You know that all *hospitaleros* of the official refuges, of the church and the state, must have walked the Camino themselves before they can be appointed? But that was not a problem, because I walked the Camino three more times before I decided that this was where I wanted to be. I went back to Belgium and decided one day to apply for this job. I was very lucky that the church was looking for a *hospitalero* for this refuge just at the time I applied. So, I resigned from my old job, sold most of my things, organised my life and came down here.'

After her 'Speedy Gonzalez' Camino, Freda came back to the Camino a second and a third time, both times to walk it and experience more than just the countryside flying past, and that was when she felt that sense of gratitude that so many pilgrims feel. She wanted to put something back into the Camino. As happens with so many pilgrims, she wanted to give something of herself to help ensure the future of the Way, to help make it as special for other pilgrims as it had been made for her. And it was when she stayed at the refuge in Hospital de Órbigo that she fell in love completely and decided she wanted to be *hospitalero*. When she explained that she did what most *hospitaleros* do, namely stay on the job for several weeks several times a year – and not full time and year-round, as I had assumed, I understood a little better why she could cope with the uncomfortable and Spartan living conditions. Freda went back to Belgium to care for her ageing mother when she was not working in Órbigo. Most other *hospitaleros* I spoke to used the time that they were not working to walk the Camino.

Hospital de Órbigo itself is beautiful. Approaching the town, the pilgrim is greeted by a wonderful sight. Over the river Órbigo, quite a large river, is a bridge that looks like something out of a fairytale. In fact, it is a living fairytale, because this is where knights still brandish their swords and mount their steeds in the *Passo honroso*, the jousting tournaments that still take place every year, just as they did in the Middle Ages when some young knight felt compelled to fight valiantly to stop anyone coming into the village where the love of his life resided. The Órbigo River is very famous in all of Spain for its delicious trout that, as the official

Órbigo tourist brochure tells us, can be enjoyed 'fried, pickled, smoky, in salmagundi, honored, etc'. Quite what 'honored' trout tastes like, I never did find out, but I did regret not having my smuggler's trout rod tucked in my backpack because I saw the fattest, shiniest, laziest, most delicious-looking trout – ready for the catching – as far as I walked along the river. According to the same brochure, obviously written by a person whose English was not perfect but who was well skilled in the art of political correctness:

> The Órbigo is river without origin source, neither mother that baptizes him/her. Their birth is double, that of the Moon and that of the Omaña. When both rivers join their flows, the resultant takes the name of Órbigo, *hidrónimo* of root prehistoric **orbi-cua**, fork of rivers. It is river with history and legend. They say that their waters lowered colored of blood during several days in the year 456, when the battle between the Goths of Teodorico and the suevos of Requiario. It is also spoken of fights in the times of the Reconquest. The Bridge also gave fame to the river and the river gave its name to the Bridge like last name. Their appearance is medieval, but he/she is considered like one of the oldest of the county Leónesa. For their long and tortuous roadway, they passed thousands and pilgrims' of all kind thousands, from the *pedigüeños* and scamps until the kings and the saints. To the left part of the Road, he/she was formed a small town, presided over by Santa María's church, with their reed-mace, their nest and their stork, permanent neighbor that gives up the emigration. To this neighborhood he/she was called **Bridge**.

What an utterly delightful way in which to have your town's history written!

After sharing a glass of wine with Freda and chatting some more about her interesting experiences in the course of her duties as *hospitalero*, Akira and I left to go and treat ourselves to his final pilgrims' menu meal. We wandered through the narrow streets of the town and came across a smoke-filled, warm restaurant where a large log fire was burning in the hearth and delicious smells emanated from the kitchen. We ordered the pilgrims' menu, and for seven euros we each received a large mixed salad with potatoes, lettuce and onions. This was followed by the famous 'trouts soups'; a big terracotta bowl filled with a tomato and onion soup in which at least six thick slices of fresh home-baked bread, crust and all, had been dunked to allow it to soak up all the liquid of the soup. On top of this was placed a whole, freshly cooked, filleted trout. It was magnificent! Akira and I both decided it had to be the best food we'd ever eaten. I laughed at our enthusiasm.

'The king must have been hungry,' I said. Akira looked at me blankly. 'The king?'

'Yes, you see, my mother was the best cook in the world, and every time we complemented her on her delicious meals, she always responded with "The king must have been hungry." Do you want to hear the story of the king?'

We poured more wine into our glasses from the earthenware pitcher, turned our chairs towards the glowing fire, and I told him my mother's story.

'A long, long time ago there was a king who loved to go hunting with his knights – the same knights who came to Órbigo to joust and show off in front of the beautiful ladies. They used to hunt in the forests, and because the forests were so big and dark and dense, it was important for them always to stay together. But one day the king was going after a particularly large stag and in his enthusiasm to get the stag, he went too far into the dark forest. Something must have startled his horse, because it bolted and reared, threw the king off and ran away. His clothes were torn from the fall, he was dirty, cold, tired, hungry, lost and alone. After wandering around for a very long time, he came across a little cottage in the forest where an old man welcomed him in.

'"Make yourself at home," he said to the king, who, of course, he hadn't recognised. "I do not have much, but what I have, I will share with you. Then you may sleep here on the straw in front of the fire and tomorrow morning I shall show you where to go to get out of the forest."

'The king was very grateful to sit in front of the warm fire and rest his weary legs. There was a large iron pot hanging over the fire from which the most wonderful smells came.'

'Just like the smells that came from this kitchen tonight!' Akira interrupted.

'Exactly!' I continued. 'He could smell tomatoes and onions and garlic and fish and freshly baked bread – in fact, I think this old man must have come from Órbigo!'

Akira was leaning forward in his chair, the red glow from the flames in the fireplace playing light and shadow games on his bearded face, his eyes sparkling as his theatrical imagination painted vivid pictures in his mind of the dishevelled king sitting in front of a similar fire, smelling the same smells we had just been enjoying.

'Anyway, the old man shared his meal with the king that night – a simple stew, rich in flavour, served in a plain wooden bowl, and the king used bread crusts to wipe the bowl completely clean. Licking his lips, he leaned back and complemented the old man on the meal.

'"That is the best meal I have ever tasted," he said. "Thank you!"

'The next morning the old man accompanied the king to the edge of the forest and showed him the direction to take to get back to the town. When the king arrived back at the castle, everyone was in a spin for they had thought they would never see the king again and that they would, at best, be banished from the kingdom for having lost their king during the hunting expedition. But the king was not angry at all. On the contrary, he was in a happy and jovial mood. He told everyone about the wonderful hospitality he had received from the old man in the forest and about the superb meal he had eaten. "I have never, ever tasted food like that! Not the most elaborate and expensive banquets we have ever tasted so good! I want every knight in my court to get on his horse and go out to look for the old man in the forest. I want him to be brought back to the castle and to take on the duties as head chef in my kitchens!"'

Akira laughed at my melodramatic gestures and voice as I warmed to the story I was telling and adopted the voice of a king issuing important orders. His theatrical side was revelling in the story-telling, and being in a place where, no doubt, very similar scenes must have played themselves off hundreds of years before, he was in his element.

'So, all the knights rode off into the forest and searched and searched for the old man. As the days passed, the knights came back with dozens and dozens of old men that they had found, and each old man was promised the best job, for life, as the king's head cook, if he could prepare the same meal the king had eaten that night in the forest. They cooked up a storm in the castle's kitchens. There was a hubbub going on as never seen before. They all tried their best recipes, they used secrets passed down to them through generations and generations, special herbs and spices, ingredients that only they knew how to grow. They brought special wood with which to make their cooking fires, they wore their lucky aprons and sang their magic songs as they worked, but every plate taken up to the king's parlour was tasted, and then swept aside.

'"No! that is not right! It looks the same. It even almost smells the same, but the taste was completely different!" the king cried, and yet another hopeful cook was sent packing.

'Then, one day…' and I paused for effect, loving Akira's expectant face looking up at me, '…then, one day yet another old man was brought into the king's parlour. He was carrying a plain wooden bowl of delicious smelling stew. The king sat up. His face lit up. His eyes started sparkling. He recognised the smells: tomatoes, onions, garlic, freshly baked crusty bread and fresh river trout… "Ah!" he said. "At last! I think we have found the old man who saved my life that night I was lost and who cooked me the best meal I have ever tasted!"

'The old man put the wooden bowl in front of the king and stood back, waiting for the king to start eating.

'The king took one mouthful, chewed a little, and then, with a thunderous noise, spat out the food. "ARGH!" he shouted. "That is not the dish I ate! Oh woe is me! I shall never find that old man from the forest!"

'The old man stood his ground. He was not perturbed by the king's reaction at all and stayed calm. "You do not recognise me, sire, just as I am ashamed to say I did not recognise you the night you knocked at my door. But I am indeed the man who welcomed you into my humble home, offered you a place at my fire and a share of my modest meal."

'"How can you be that man?" the king implored. "If you are that same old man, why did you not prepare for me the same meal you prepared that night in your cottage? Surely you must know the rich rewards I have offered?"

'"I have prepared the same meal, sire. Exactly the same meal as I offered you that night in the forest."

'"But why does it then not taste the same?" the king wailed.

'"Because, sire, and forgive me my impertinence, but the meal today did not taste the same simply because you are not hungry, sire. That night in the forest, the king was hungry!"'

Akira leaned back in his chair and burst out laughing, slapping his leg in merriment. 'For sure!' he called out, obviously having picked up Thorsten's favourite saying during their three weeks together on the Way. 'For sure! When the king was hungry, the food tasted very good!'

'And that, my friend-san, is why pilgrims' menus on the Camino taste like the food of the gods!'

The next morning, just before five o'clock, I was awakened by a quiet stirring. It was Akira quietly taking his things outside the room where he could get dressed and pack his backpack without waking me. I gave him a little time to do his stretches and get dressed before getting up and going outside to say my goodbyes. I was very sad to see him go, knowing that I was not likely to hear from him too often; if he hardly spoke any English, he wrote even less, and I knew that our friendship was one of those unique Camino friendships where you feel utterly blessed and privileged to have had your path through life cross with that of such a special person.

Outside, Akira had already packed, and his bag and his pilgrim's stick were standing at the refuge entrance, ready to go. It was still very dark, with bright stars studding the night sky and the cold, pre-dawn air was crisp with the snow and ice off the mountains on the northern horizon. He was sitting at the table, his miner's lamp shining a yellow spotlight on a piece of paper in front of him. He was writing a little note, concentrating on each letter as he searched his mind for the words he needed.

'Akira-san,' I whispered. He looked up and I could make out a moist shininess in his eyes, as I am sure he could detect in my own.

'Ah, Wilna-san. I wake you. I am sorry.'

'It is fine. Not a problem. I wanted to be here to say goodbye. And also, I insist on walking with you for a little way.'

'No! you must rest your feet. I will be okay.' We both knew that for him to walk out into the darkness was going to be extremely hard, but he had no choice. To squeeze in a last special night on the Camino, he had stayed in Órbigo instead of Astorga from where buses leave for Madrid. This meant that he was going to have to walk hard and fast to cover the eighteen kilometres to get to Astorga in time for the ten o'clock train to Madrid, where he was catching a plane back to Tokyo that same day.

'I insist, Akira-san, just for a little way…'

Akira did not argue any more, but quietly put his backpack on, pulled on his gloves, put on his woollen cap and checked the light of his torch. He then took his stick and walked towards the door. One last time he turned around, gave a little bow of thanks to the refuge, and walked out onto the street. I closed the door as quietly as I could, making sure that it was still unlocked so that I could get in when I came back, and joined Akira in the dark, quiet street. We walked in silence, side by side, until we reached the end of the street and the end of the town, where the Camino pathway was shown, in the light of Akira's headlamp, to go off over an open field.

He stopped and turned towards me. He opened his arms wide and I stepped into them, leaning against his chest. 'I wish you that the king will always be hungry, Wilna-san, so everything you do always be the best of your life.' He let go and, as he turned away and started walking, whispered under his breath; '*Buen Camino*, good friend. We will meet again, for sure.' The next thing he had disappeared into the darkness. It was as if he had never been there.

'*Buen Camino!*' I whispered after him. '*Buen Camino*, dearest friend.'

When I returned to the refuge, I found that he'd left something on the table in the courtyard. There, holding down a little scrap of paper, was a small plastic bag of flour – for the white sauce base he used for his delicious cauliflower and potato soup, or to lightly dust the fish before frying it in a pan; another small bag containing a handful of his superb, top-quality green tea, a little tube with some of the cream he had rubbed on my feet, a thin roll of the tape he had used to bind my feet, and, most precious of all, his lovely striped woollen scarf which he never went without. A cornucopia of useful and generous gifts, each a little of the special magic that Akira had brought to the Camino. I took the scrap of paper with me back to my bunk, took off my jacket and my shoes, crawled back into my sleeping bag and in the light of my torch, read what he had written.

'Thank you make my Camino very special. You and Thorsten my Camino family walk together in Santiago. I be there with you,' it said, and underneath was written his e-mail address.

With both the members of my own little Camino family – my own personal little back-up team suddenly gone, I felt a bit like a deserted orphan. But, I was grateful for the many good memories, the smiles and the laughter, the thought-provoking conversations and the tremendous support I'd had from the two of them. Even though they were now both gone, I could still imagine them somewhere ahead of me or behind me, and everything I experienced or heard or saw after that day, I sent out to them on those thousand fibres that connect us with our fellow men, across the space above us that we all share.

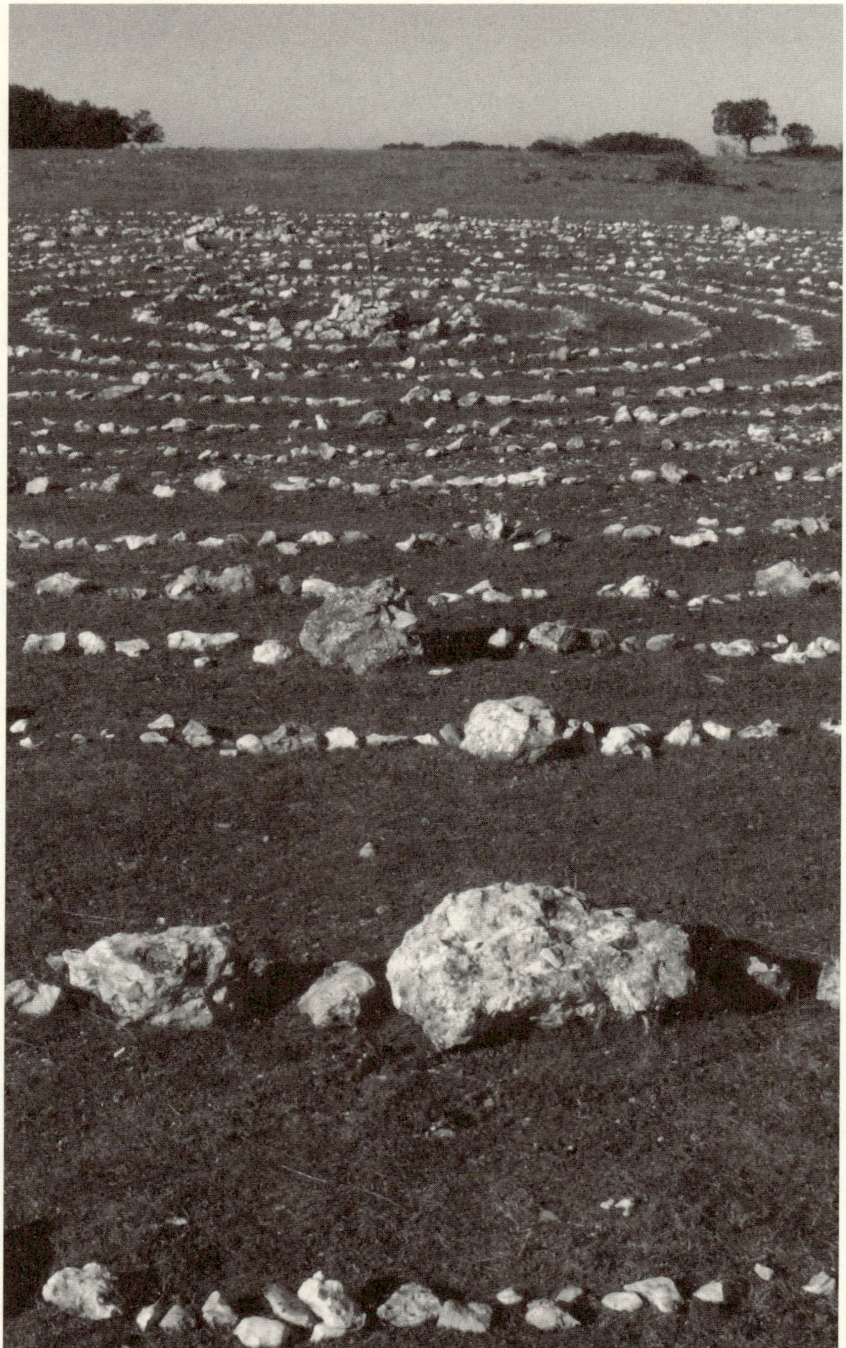

14

Not every person you meet is a fellow-traveller, and not all fellow-travellers are fellow-pilgrims

The real voyage of discovery consists not in seeking new landscapes but in having new eyes.

— Marcel Proust

I believed there were still a few bears in the mountains of northern Spain. I never saw one on my walk, but when I took off my boots at the heavy double doors of the *refugio* in Domingo de la Calzada, gingerly crossed the entrance hall that was paved with a superb star design in small, smooth river pebbles – not laid flat with their smooth sides up but standing up on their sides – limped up the stairs to the first floor and followed my nose down the passage to where a delicious smell of food was coming out of the kitchen, I was met, and completely enveloped by, what could have passed for a bear.

Hermano, (I never knew whether that was his name or whether he was simply called 'Brother' by everyone because he was a monk) was indeed a bear of a man; large and imposing, with a big bushy salt-and-pepper beard, dressed in a woolly jumper that had seen many a winter and corduroy trousers that were tied around his waist with a length of soft rope. He looked gentle, his eyes warm and welcoming; his smile so generous you felt like you had come home. All this soft cuddliness was juxtaposed with the music he had playing in the background: Mozart at his genial best – angular, mathematical, precise and pure. If my first impression of this man was an instant 'Yes!', then his passion for Mozart clinched the deal.

Hermano accompanied me to the dormitory to claim my bed. This dormitory was a sight for sore eyes. A long narrow room under the ancient black oak rafters on the top floor, there were bright red-and-green tartan bed spreads on the single beds and a floor that was so shiny under the last rays of sunshine streaming in through the dormer windows that you could see your own reflection in it. I put my backpack on the bed of my choice, close to a window as well as a lovely warm heater, then took out my soap, towel and clean set of underwear and went to the bathroom to enjoy a hot shower and wash the clothes I'd been wearing that day. After draping my washing over the heater next to my bed and feeling much refreshed, I went to rejoin Hermano in the kitchen.

'Take a seat. We are making a *Caldo Gallego* stew tonight. I think you will like it.'

The famous *Caldo Gallego!* This stew is a common dish here and is named after the province of Galicia. However, because it's a dish that is designed to fight humidity and cold, for which this province is notorious, and because it traditionally consists of cabbage, potatoes, beans and, depending on the cook's purse, ham, chorizo, spare ribs – in fact, anything that comes to hand – it is also the dish that pilgrims get to know and love well.

Hermano was one of few *hospitaleros* who prepared an evening meal for passing pilgrims. When it happened, it was like a gift from the gods. Nothing was more luxurious for a weary pilgrim than arriving at a refuge where the aromas of a hot wholesome meal wafted through the refuge to the front door. Sometimes the *hospitaleros* asked for a small donation towards the meal, sometimes they specified three or four or five euros, and sometimes, when the *refugio* was in a town where there was a grocery shop, they did what Hermano did; he had on the table a number of post-it notes with an ingredient written on each one. As the pilgrims arrived, and if they chose to eat the communal meal rather than make something for themselves, they could choose one of the notes and go out to buy that ingredient. A few potatoes. A few tomatoes. A chorizo sausage. A loaf of crispy bread. A kilo of broad beans. A packet of chickpeas. A bottle of wine. Whatever arrived went into the big pot bubbling away and doing its magic on the stove. And so the *Caldo Gallego* took on a personality of its own, depending on the group of pilgrims in the refuge that particular night.

Hermano pushed a pile of potatoes in front of me and a sharp knife and returned to cutting the broad beans he had in front of him. There we were, Hermano and I, almost as if we'd known each other all our lives, sitting across from one another at the refectory table, preparing vegetables for the delicious stew that he was preparing for the evening meal.

'I like this time of the day best,' he said. 'I come to the kitchen and start preparing a meal for the evening. I don't know how many pilgrims will come tonight or even if any will come. But I like to have a good smell of good food to wait for them when they arrive. I think when I make good smells in my kitchen I will have good pilgrims in my *refugio* every night.'

I laughed. 'It worked for me! There is nothing better than walking into a *refugio* where someone has already started cooking!'

'I know. When I walked the Camino, I followed my nose all the way.' His eyes creased shut and his large round belly shook as he laughed at the thought of all that good food waiting for him in *refugio* kitchens.

'Unfortunately not all *hospitaleros* have your philosophy. I have only come across one other *hospitalero* who cooked for pilgrims.'

'Ah! It is sad but it may be because not all travellers are pilgrims.' Hermano got up, scooped up the cut broad beans in his large hands, walked over to the stove and added them to the chicken stock, sliced chorizo sausages, the chopped tomatoes and onions already boiling in the casserole. He then came over, took the bowl with the peeled potatoes and added them to the casserole as well.

'It is interesting that you say that. I was just thinking over the last few days that the one thing I find very different from what I expected – although, I have to say – *every*thing is different from what I expected – but the one thing that struck me this week was that not all my fellow travellers are fellow-pilgrims.'

Hermano slid into the bench again, his stomach straining against the table.

Looking at the surface of the table, it was like being back at our family kitchen table, its surface marked and scarred by many years of use. Years before, my daughter Nici had written an essay for an English class. The title of the essay was 'A family portrait' and she used the surface of our old kitchen table as a metaphor for the portrait. Each mark, each scar was described – when and by whom the scar had been made and what the circumstances were around that happening. That gash over there was made when Pierre was building his remote-control racing car and the modelling knife slipped, almost taking a couple of fingers with it; these rings were from the night we all sat around the table drinking endless cups of hot chocolate, waiting to hear if Marc had been chosen for the South African schools water polo team. Over there was a stain from when I was creating a marzipan fish pond, complete with fish and frogs and water lilies, as a fifth birthday cake for Nici and the bottle of green food colouring was bumped over. And so she related something about each member of the family and the event in each one of their lives that was significant. No doubt, on this table too, each scar told a story of one or another pilgrim who had passed through this *refugio* and had sat there, surrounded by other pilgrims, recounting the events of their day on the Camino. No doubt some of the scars had tasted the salt of tears, had been deepened by anger, had been made in frustration. The dark rings would have told of endless hot mugs on freezing cold winter mornings; the burns would have told of dishes put down too hot but in haste to feed hungry pilgrims at the end of a long, weary day's walking. The beautifully grained oak wood had been polished to a rich sheen by countless arms resting on it as, at the end of a good nourishing meal, the plates pushed to one side, pilgrims had leant over the table and discussed their reasons for making the pilgrimage and their experiences along the way. I felt strangely moved by that table. It was almost as if I could feel the presence around me of the many pilgrims who had sat there where I now sat, in comfortable silence, opposite the *hospitalero,* peeling potatoes for the evening meal. And, once again, I felt so incredibly privileged to be part of that band of people who had walked the Camino de Santiago – the Way of St James – Le Chemin de St Jacques.

'Then you are not walking to get to Santiago de Compostela.'

The words brought me out of my reverie. His statement was just that. Not a question; not even a rhetorical question, but a statement of fact.

I thought about what he'd said. 'No...' I hesitated slightly. Then I realised that what he was saying was something that had been lingering in the back of my mind, not quite formulated into proper thoughts; little seeds that were waiting for the sunlight to germinate and grow. Hermano was providing the sunlight and forcing me to bring those seeds right to the front for me to acknowledge.

'No. This is not about reaching the destination, is it? And that is what makes some fellow-travellers fellow-pilgrims and others not.' The words I used to express my thoughts may have been awkward, but suddenly those thoughts were crystal clear. 'The pilgrimage is about walking the Camino – walking the Way, *not* about reaching the end. Each moment, each revelation, each day, each encounter, each experience could be regarded as a destination in itself.'

Hermano's nodding head was enough encouragement to continue.

'For years I have been teaching people to live in the here and now – to be whole-heartedly "present" at all times. It is not so easy, but I have often seen people who are not present – who cling to things that were in their past or spend all their time wondering and worrying about things that may or may not happen in the future – and as a result they miss everything that is around them. How often opportunities present themselves to us, but we miss them completely because we're too busy thinking about past problems or future possibilities.'

'Yes – I see that all the time with the pilgrims who come through the refuge. They also wait for life's circumstances to be right before they begin whatever it is they plan to do, but in the meantime, the people who succeed in this world are the ones who get up and look for the circumstances they want, which are usually right there under our noses but, if they can't find those circumstances, then they make them.'

It was something that I'd always felt strongly about and that really became an urgent issue for me when we moved from South Africa to Great Britain. Among the expatriates that I met, this phenomenon was more often than not the cause of huge unhappiness and inability to settle in a new environment. People were so busy yearning back to what they'd left behind that they never noticed the tremendous – different, but tremendous – opportunities not only available to them, but well within their reach.

'…There were days when I phoned fellow expats to invite them for a drink outside in the garden to enjoy the magnificent Indian summer weather – you know, those long light balmy evenings that make September and October such special months. But before I could tell them why I was calling, I had to sit there and listen to a ten-minute diatribe about how bad the weather was in the UK and how they couldn't wait to get back to South Africa for the Christmas holidays, the sunshine and the outdoor life.'

Hermano laughed. 'I know exactly what you're saying. And now you have found the same thing with your fellow-travellers?'

'Yes! I meet people along the way who are so adamant about reaching Santiago within a certain given time that they're completely missing the amazing things that they are walking past! There are also those who have such fixed ideas about what they wanted from the pilgrimage – they hoped for a revelation of some kind, a religious epiphany, a solution to problems they had – but these preconceptions were so strong and they were so busy looking for what they were seeking, that they weren't present in the moment and they never saw the many things around them. The revelations are there. The epiphanies are there, but because they don't look the way, or present themselves in the way as expected, they are not recognised as such.'

Hermano reached back and picked up a half-full bottle of red wine from the windowsill. I looked around for glasses and noticed them on a shelf above the sink. As I got up to fetch a couple, thinking how quickly you could feel completely at home and comfortable in a place you'd never been and with a person you'd never met, I put the glasses on the table between us and Hermano poured the wine. It was a lovely Rioja, just the right temperature, slightly chilled from having been on the windowsill, but above the radiator. Rioja was a wine I had always enjoyed as a treat, but here in northern Spain it was 'just the local wine.'

(I say 'lovely' when describing the wine, but it could have been anything. Pilgrims tend to be Philistines when it comes to wine. No one turned up their noses at any wine that was on offer; on the Camino, wine was a necessity, and no longer a luxury. Many of us even carried a small plastic water bottle filled with red wine in the side of our backpacks – as pilgrims did through the centuries; a sip of red wine could make all the difference when the going got very tough, so the added weight, however small, was not a sacrifice.)

'That is what separates the *peregrinos* from the *tourigrinos*,' Hermano continued. Holding the glass against the light and admiring the rich garnet colour of the Rioja.

'*Tourigrinos*? Ah yes! Of course! What a good name for them!'

That *was* a good name for the many who walked the Camino, but not necessarily as pilgrims. Apparently, according to statistics (if they're reliable) less than ten per cent of the people who start the pilgrimage in Roncesvalles, the first major Camino town on the Spanish side of the Pyrenees, walked the entire pilgrimage to Santiago de Compostela. Less than ten per cent! I understood that it wasn't these that Hermano referred to as *tourigrinos* – tourist walkers – rather than *peregrinos* – pilgrims. Although, often, time constraints and leave allocation dictated that a person could only walk a week at a time, and they came back year after year until the entire pilgrimage was done. Sometimes physical constraints or injuries dictated how far and how long you could walk and whether you could carry your own pack all the way or sent it ahead with the vehicles used for that purpose.

'Bah! If you only walk to get to the destination, then take a bus. It is much easier, much quicker, much kinder to the body.'

'You are harsh on them, Hermano,' I found myself defending my fellow-*travellers*. 'They may not be fellow-pilgrims, but each to his own, surely? And anyway; if they took a bus, they would need to have someone standing on each side of their legs with a sledgehammer that has the same weight as themselves plus their backpacks, hitting the soles of their feet with the hammers, every foot every second. Because that is what it is like to walk the Camino.'

Hermano's laugh quickly made his frown disappear. 'Perhaps I am harsh, but you are too kind. Most people take the bus for all the hard stretches anyway, and their backpacks arrive at the *refugios* in cars long before they do... But, you are right, of course. Each to his own. Everyone walks the Camino for his own reasons and in his own way.'

I laughed. 'It is a bit like they say about friends and family, isn't it? You can choose your friends, but you can't choose your family. No one can choose the people they will meet on the Camino; be it this pilgrimage or the journey through life.'

'No, you are right. We can only choose the ones we want to make our friends. But that is not the problem that concerns me, though. The problem is a practical one. There is a lot of debate about the future of the Camino. There are too many people on the Way. In the summer there are thousands and thousands. It is not like you are now experiencing the Camino at all. Look at the time – it is six o'clock and you are still the only one here at the *refugio*, but in summer you have to walk very fast and wait outside the *refugio* door from early in the afternoon to get a place there that night. Otherwise you must continue to walk until you get a place where there is still a bed, or else sleep on the church floor. And look at the mess along the way. Too many people cause too much pollution. Who must keep the paths clean and tidy?'

It was true; even with so few people on the Way, there were always those who left their rubbish behind them. Thorsten, Akira and I carried plastic bags with us and picked up some of the rubbish as we walked every day. There were others who did the same, but I could imagine that during the rush of summer, those few would make no noticeable difference.

As if on cue, we heard footsteps coming up the stairs and in the next moment the kitchen was bustling with dusty, tired travellers. Hermano got up, checked the stew as he passed the stove and went off to show everyone where the dorm was and the showers. Then, putting his head around the door, he came to tell me to come downstairs so he could write me up in the register and stamp my *credenciales*. The stew was bubbling away in the old, battered casserole on the gas flame and the *refugio* was filled with the wonderful aroma of the food, and the lively sound of a bunch of pilgrims who'd reached their day's destination. Were these fellow-travellers or were they fellow-pilgrims? *Peregrinos* or *tourigrinos*? – I still had to find out, but for the time being, I realised that whichever they were, this was the time of day that helped to make the Camino such a special experience; a *refugio* full of interesting people, all having walked a distance that day, all having sore feet and stories to tell, all anticipating a mouth-watering meal around a solid oak table, a glass of wine and a fascinating discussion right up to the nine-thirty curfew. Where else would you find this precious gift; a monk who welcomed you with an enveloping bear-hug and cooked five-star meals, an ancient, medieval building with pebble floors and tartan bedspreads, filled to the rafters by a group of individuals who all shared a common goal, who were all related in some definite way that differentiated them from anyone else?

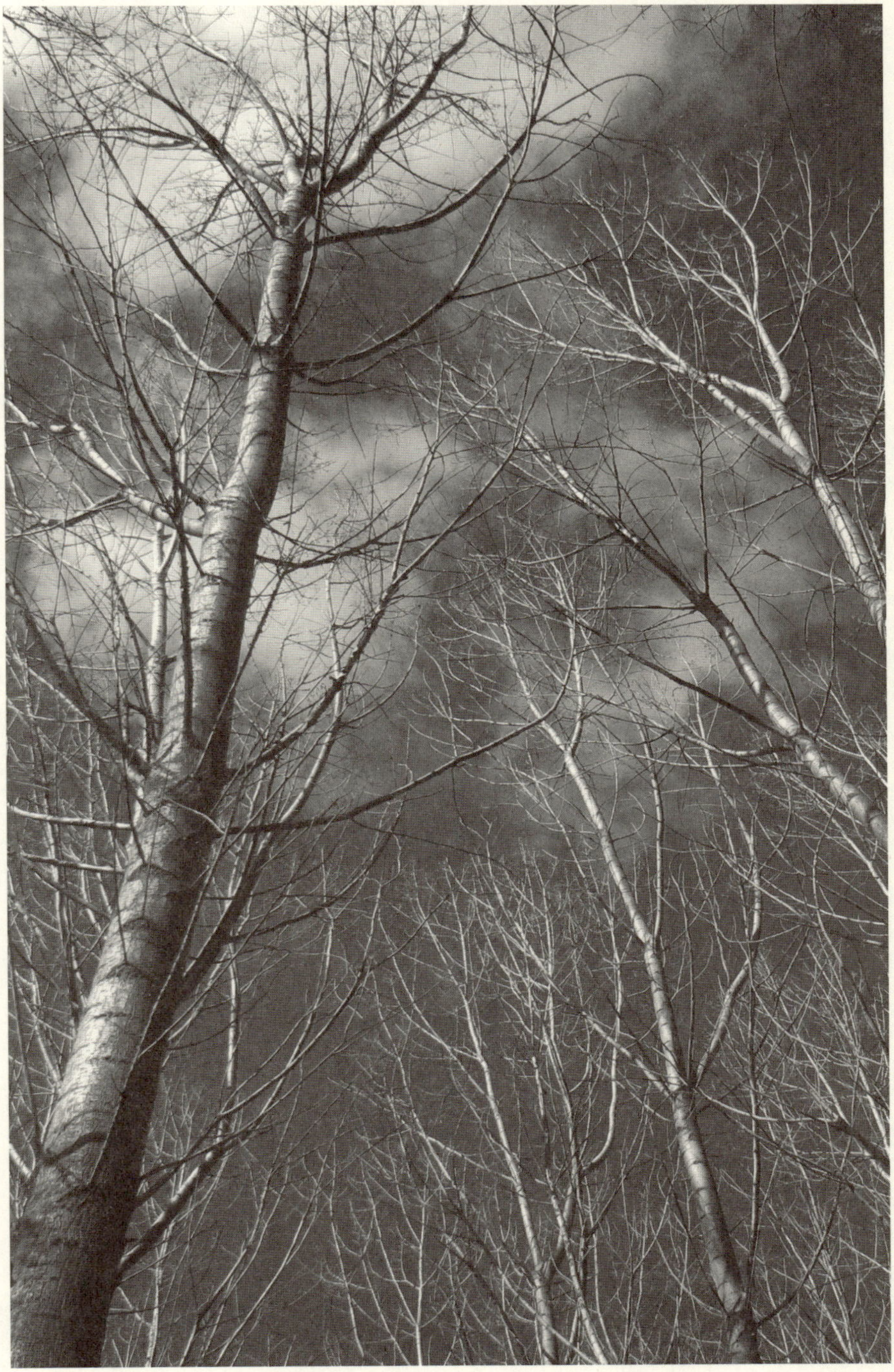

15

Recognise your angels, for sometimes they may come past you but once (and remember, not all angels have wings)

From the time we first tamed fire, we gathered 'round to tell each other stories.
– Mary Southard

Journal entry:
I met a fellow pilgrim today. I do not know who she was or when she had walked the Camino, but she was beautiful.

The last stretch of about eighteen kilometres unfolded along a relatively straight, almost flat path (flat but very stony – everywhere was so very stony – impossibly and agonisingly stony). It crossed a landscape so huge and so beautiful that it took my breath away. The sky, which had been pouring buckets on me the last few days, was alive with blue, grey, white and charcoal clouds in magnificent formations. Every now and then a bright spotlight of sun broke through the clouds and turned the green fields and red clay soil and almost-black trees that dotted the horizon into such vivid and intense colours that you had to stop and look, and look again.

That particular section I was walking across was called the *Meseta* – a seemingly never-ending plateau that was, because of its flatness, described in the guidebooks as 'a boring and a soul-destroying stretch'.

Boring? I stopped for a moment to get my guidebook out of my trouser-leg pocket. I wanted to confirm that the book actually warned the pilgrim against boredom. With some difficulty I opened the little book and pried the pages apart, as they had become stuck together after getting thoroughly soaked in the rain of the previous days.

And yes, there it was. I had remembered correctly. 'The Via Aquitana is a long arid plane of eighteen kilometres where you are not likely to see another person. No place to eat or get water until you get to Caldazilla de la Cueza. Make sure you take water and food. The endless wide-open spaces can provide some of the most powerful experiences along the path, or be utterly disheartening and boring – depending on your state of mind. If you don't like being alone, find someone to walk with you…' it said, clearly printed in black on white. I shook my head at the thought – and wondered at the fickleness of mankind…

Perhaps it was the lack of human life along the way that would have worried some people. There were no farmhouses, no little clusters of adobe huts or hamlets and definitely no villages – not even empty ones. The fields seemed to be well tended, but there was no sign of farm workers or tractors or human life of any description. For hours the only sign that I was not alone in this vast universe was the occasional hare, chased up out of the grass alongside the pathway and white-tailing his escape over the ploughed fields, or a small black beetle waddling across my shadow, or the contrails of jumbo jets criss-crossing the sky.

Bored? No – for me the soothing monotony of the flatness of the landscape provided the time to realise what an incredible privilege it was to be walking this pilgrimage. I suddenly realised, too, the enormity of the gift of the Camino; to have this luxury of time, of solitude, silence, serenity and endless, endless space! It was a space where I was able to breathe and to live the moment. How could anyone possibly be bored when they were given such an opportunity – to contemplate their life, to empty their minds of cobwebs and the birds-nests of tangled emotions and snarled perceptions. It was simply the most cathartic experience, this unravelling of the mess of complicated and contrived issues that clutter your brain, leaving a wide-open space to let in the present – the here and now. It was an amazing experience, an epiphany; a moment of coming up close and personal with the creation, of which I felt such an integral part.

I loved it. I loved the solitude. I loved walking hour after hour, kilometre after kilometre across the flat earth, my soft footfalls on the path echoing the rhythm of my heartbeat. There was something so soothing about being part of that glorious landscape, feeling the energy of the earth seeping in through my soles, my body absorbing the strength and vitality of nature, drinking in the clear, clean air. I revelled in the clouds dramatically swirling above in the otherwise azure-blue dome of the sky. I marvelled at the slight soft breeze touching the tips of the grasses in the fields, as if urging them on in their joyous dancing and sensuous movement. I laughed out loud as little dust devils darted mischievously across the fields, this way and that, indecisive as to which direction to take, chasing up clouds of red dust and teasing the poppies and wild flowers to join in the fun. It was a continuing and exhilarating conversation between nature and me; a meeting of minds; a rendezvous with my creator. I was feeling so intensely close to the earth; I felt part of it – not *on* it, not *with* it, but feeling that it *was* me and I *was* it.

From somewhere in my memory came the words of a Navajo prayer that I had once read, and I suddenly understood, for the first time, what their meaning was:

As I walk, as I walk
The universe is walking with me
In beauty it walks before me
In beauty it walks behind me
In beauty it walks below me
In beauty it walks above me
Beauty is on every side
As I walk, I walk with Beauty

During the previous few days when it had been raining non-stop, I'd had to keep moving and somehow forgot to stop and eat. This quickly resulted in my body starting to complain and becoming sluggish as it ran out of fuel, but the thought of sitting down on the muddy ground, of taking off a backpack, out from under an awkward poncho and getting everything soaking wet, and of trying to eat a piece of bread that was soggy with rain, was enough to urge me to keep going, regardless of the empty stomach and the sore feet.

However, with the absence of rain that day it was pure bliss to be able to stop and sit down on the side of the pathway, take off my backpack for a little while and enjoy my surroundings. I took the opportunity to lay out my scarf on the ground and arrange on it a feast of dried sausage, half a baguette which I had left over from the day before, a piece of hard cheese and two lemons that I'd picked from a tree along the way. And that was when she came to me; the spirit of a *peregrina*.

She came from nowhere. She literally came from *nowhere*. One moment

I was alone and the next she was there with me. I was sitting there on the ground, enjoying the splendour of this incredible empty countryside, the silence and the solitude, when I looked up and there she was, an exquisite little cat standing no more than a metre away from me, staring at me with her big eyes. She was gorgeous; a petite and delicate creature that immediately captivated and touched my heart. The fur around her neck and on her legs was the purest white, soft and velvety and she was decorated with swirls of light and darker russet tiger stripes down her back and sides; not randomly, but in absolutely perfect symmetry, exactly the same on both sides. Her face radiating out from the perfect little pink nose and the longest white whiskers, was outlined with a *kabuki* mask; the most captivating large yellow eyes framed by diamond-shaped linear designs in a pinkish-brown. On each cheek was another diamond in the same russet colours as the four lines on her forehead. The background of this beautiful little mask was snow white, softly merging into a pinkish-beige frame and two shell-pink, almost transparent ears.

The moment our eyes connected, she started 'talking' to me – as if she was announcing herself, and, all the while that she spent with me, she never stopped this happy conversation. In soft, soothing little meows, it was a whole long story she told me as she came to sit on my outstretched legs to be stroked and cuddled. Every now and then she would hop off and go and chase after an insect in the grass or toss a small pebble into the air with her front paw, then jump straight up to try to catch it again. Next she would come back on my lap, purring and nudging my hand with her head, asking for more cuddles, and, when she had my full attention, she would continue her conversation.

I had no idea where she came from. Before sitting down, I'd walked for more than three hours without seeing any form of human life. I knew that the next village (pop. 27) was at least another two hours away. And yet, here was this perfect little creature – not wild and scruffy – not even a stray dry leaf or grass stem on her, but spotless, looking like a well-fed, well-groomed and much-loved domestic pet; no longer a kitten, but not quite an adult cat either. It was an enigma. I offered her some of my cheese but she wasn't interested. What about a small piece of the sausage? I asked. Without even looking at the offered morsel, not even sniffing at it, she just looked straight into my eyes and continued with her 'chatting', almost as if to say 'let's not waste time with silly food. I am here to talk to you!'

When it was time to get up and put the remains of my food away and return the pack to my back, I was worried that she would follow me and not sure what I would do if she did. With not another soul in sight for possibly another day, I couldn't believe that she would not want to follow me, but I knew that it would be impractical and unwise to have her accompany me. By the same token, I was distraught at the idea of leaving her there. Who would look after her, where would she get water, what shelter was there for her there? It seemed a little silly to be asking those questions though. This was no normal little cat – I knew – and yet, almost furtively I checked the screen of my camera once again to assure myself that there really were pictures of her on it. I was finally ready to leave and continue on my way. Still happily chatting away, she came and stroked herself against my legs and rubbed her head against my boot for one last time. Then she looked up at me and held the gaze for a full minute, turned around and sat down on the side of the path, where she stayed, watching me until we could no longer see each other.

I had no doubt that she was the spirit of another *peregrina* of another time...

The mornings were mostly very misty. At that time of the year, early February, it was only around eight o'clock that the sun started to make its presence known in the east and then another hour or two before it started to burn off the mist. As I liked to set off from the *refugio* early in the mornings, I often walked in thick mist for a couple of hours. There were days when the mist whirled and swirled across the landscape, causing the geographical features to play hide and seek – now you see them, now you don't – a glimpse of a clump of trees here, an interestingly shaped cairn of stones over there. Other times there was no breeze at all, not even a soft breath of air, and the mist would lie thick and dense and still, clinging and cloying and you would almost feel it dragging you down as you pushed your way through the heaviness of it.

Often the path was hardly visible and losing my way was always a worry; starting a day's walk and getting lost in the dark and the mist could result in many more kilometres than intended. At times I had to stop, switch on my small but very effective LED torch and find a landmark to guide me. The bright yellow Camino signs – the scallop shells or the arrows painted on walls, rocks, trees, fence poles, were mostly easily visible – but only if you could find them. There were times, even in broad daylight that you had to look really hard to locate the next sign, so peering through the thick curtain of mist an hour before sunrise could be a tricky exercise. When the mist enveloped me like that, I was only too aware of the importance of marking my bearings. The simple exercise of looking for a sign could mean turning round and round on one spot and then going off at a tangent, and anyone who has ever had the experience would know how disorienting mist can be; it does not take much to have you continuing on your way, but in the wrong direction.

The mist had an added effect – it felt as if it was pressing down on my eardrums, dampening any sound that came from further away, but seeming to enhance, to intensify, sounds close by. A strange sensation indeed. Sometimes I was aware that I must be passing a farmyard in the process of waking up and getting ready for the day's work: the dogs yapping in excited greetings for their master, the farmer's wife calling the chooks to be fed, the rooster reaffirming his dominance over the yard, the bellowing of the cow, impatient to be relieved of her uncomfortably heavy udder; a busy noisy happy scene, but I did not know its provenance as I couldn't see this farmyard. I did not even know how near or far it was from the pathway. Sometimes there were no sounds around me, but I could hear the sound of my feet on the loose stones in the path, each footfall seeming loud and heavy, crashing down and resonating as the stones were disturbed and tumbled over each other, mini-rockfalls underfoot with each step of the way.

It was in such thick mist one morning that I met Sant Iago again. I had come to a spot where the pilgrims' path crossed a major road. I'd been prepared for this, having studied the map before I left the *refugio* a few hours before. I knew that when I came to this crossing I had to turn left, follow the tarred road for about twenty metres, then cross over and rejoin the pathway. The guidebook said there were clear signs to follow.

However, as I came to the main road, the mist was still so thick that it was only when I stepped on the tarmac that I realised I had reached it. I was on the point of turning left to walk alongside the main road, intending to count off the twenty metres, when I noticed a bright yellow arrow painted on the tar. The arrow pointed straight across the road. I looked left and right for another sign, but there was none, only this one arrow confidently pointing straight ahead. So, I followed the instruction and crossed the road and found that the pathway continued on the other side.

The guidebook must be wrong, I thought, for the yellow arrows would not lie. Once across, the pathway dropped down from the road and, from what I could see through the mist, was lined with a guard of honour of tall shimmering poplar trees. I could not see any more yellow arrows or scallop shells anywhere, but put this down to the thick mist, and I was not worried because I knew there was a small monastery a few kilometres on and that would confirm that I was on the right route.

Suddenly, as if from underwater, came a sound through the mist. I stopped, and listened. It seemed to come from behind me, but the mist had closed like a thick grey velvet curtain between me and the road. Again I heard the sound and this time I could hear that it was a man's voice and he was shouting '*Peregrina! Peregrina!*'

Something made me respond. I did what no pilgrim ever willingly does; I retraced my steps and started walking back the way I'd come. I did not know where the voice came from for I could still see nothing but a white wall of mist around me, but I was sure that what I had heard was someone calling me.

When I finally got back to the edge of the main road I stopped, and, peering this way then that through the swirling mist, I waited. Then, to my left, about ten or twenty metres away, the mist seemed to lift for a moment over the main road, and there, walking towards me, along the other side of the road, was a man. I still see him in front of me. He was a tall dark-haired man, dressed from head to toe in black – a black open-necked cotton shirt, black lightweight trousers and black leather shoes – walking as if, for all the world, he was on a Sunday afternoon stroll. Still I waited. I did not question at the time why this man would be walking along a main country road at seven-thirty in the morning, in freezing temperatures but dressed in smart, black summer clothing, or, more importantly, how he could have seen me through the mist from so far away and why he would be calling me? I also did not question my own reaction; why I was responding to a total stranger in very strange circumstances; a stranger who was dressed strangely and who was acting strangely? If I had questioned myself, the next question would have been: 'Why is he not stopping? Why is he continuing walking, looking not at me but straight ahead; and why is he not saying anything to me, but pointing down the main road, to my right?'

The fact was that I did not ask any questions, for somehow I just accepted that this was no ordinary man. This was probably one of those moments on the Camino when you simply had to have faith and follow blindly, and, albeit contrary to my normal, 'non-pilgrim' character, I did exactly that. I turned right and walked down the road in the direction where the man in black had already disappeared in the mist that had folded in on itself behind him. And twenty metres further, there on my right, was the scallop shell on a wooden post, pointing to the Camino pathway.

Later, when the mist had lifted and I'd stopped for a drink of water and a bit to eat, I opened my guidebook and looked at the map; if Sant Iago – or the black angel in the mist – had not called me and set me on the right road, I would have unwittingly gone off in the wrong direction, and who knows, I might have been swallowed by the mist completely and never seen again…

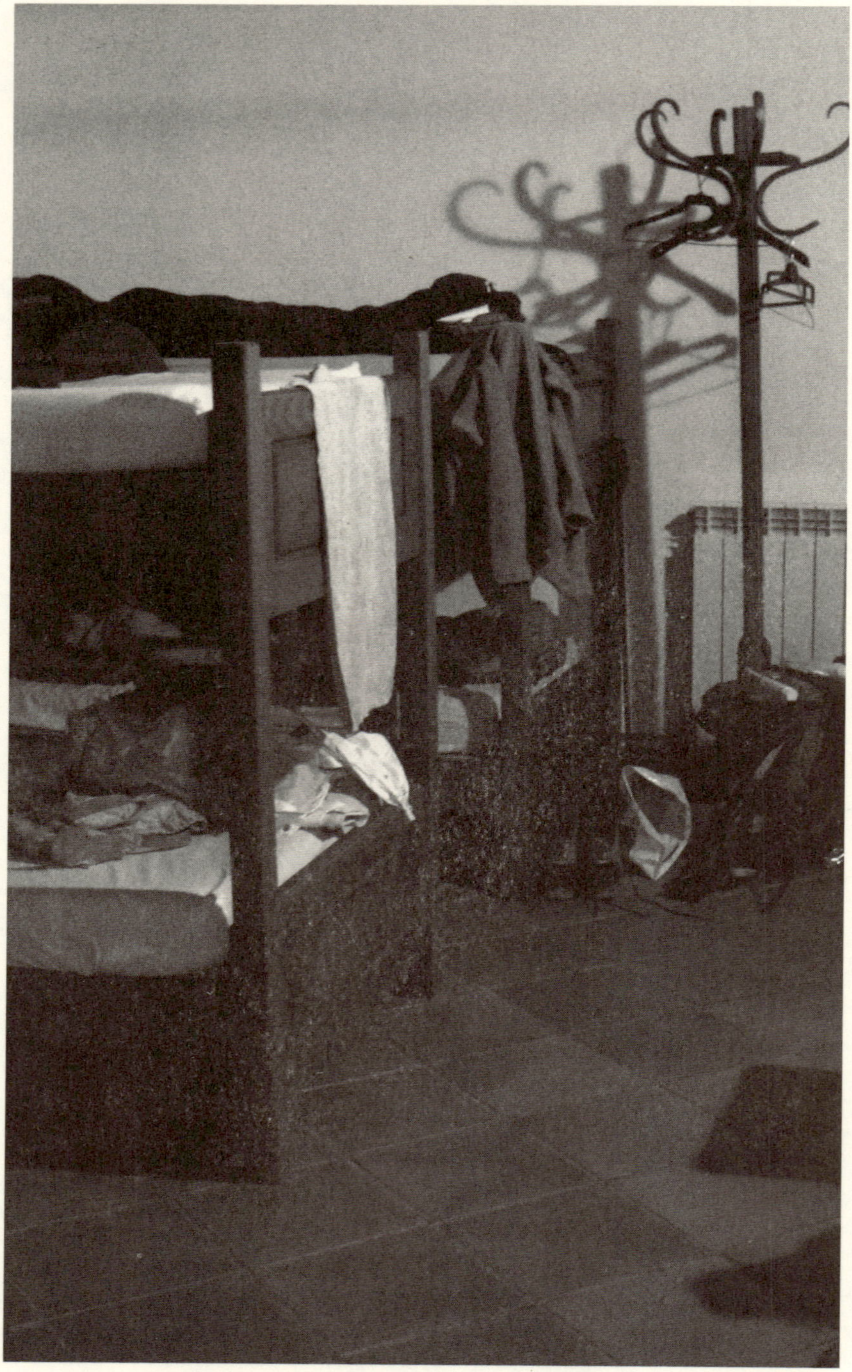

16

The Camino changes people and the people change the Camino

A l'aurore, armés d'une ardente patience, nous entrerons aux splendides Villes. (In the dawn, armed with a burning patience, we shall enter the splendid Cities.)

– Arthur Rimbaud

'Fly-y-y-y-y-y me to the moon and let me play-y-y-y-y-y amongst the stars…'

Off-key and out of tune, but coming with the full support of diaphragms of steel and twenty-nine pairs of healthy lungs full of air, Sinatra's song was bellowed out into the atmosphere already heavily laden with the fetid smell of sweaty male bodies, damp woollen socks, discarded trainers that had been worn just that little too long and the unwashed underwear of twenty-nine young, masculine, testosterone-pumping Spanish cyclists.

I found myself in the middle of a Camino nightmare. The only woman in a dormitory for thirty, every bunk bed – including the top bed of my bunk occupied by one of the large group of twenty-something cyclists, the bathrooms an open-plan shower room with no privacy, and Frank Sinatra music obviously the order of the day. The refuge in Melide was one of the largest I'd stayed in. My dormitory was only one of about ten copies of this one and each was filled to the rafters with young, bursting-with-energy Spanish youths who were doing the last one hundred kilometres of the Camino.

Standing on the edge of the town where the streets were lined with camellia trees that hung heavy with the colour and fragrance of the flower of Galicia, Melide was different to anything I had experienced before. I was lucky to get a bed in this town, and that was something that had never happened to me before. I was shown to my bed and had no choice of a bed by the window or a bed next to the heater or a bed near the door. The bed I was assigned was the only one left in the entire refuge. The place was alive with people. They were sitting on the stairs. They were milling about in the huge kitchen, sitting in groups at tables, eating or drinking or just talking. There were pilgrims outside on the veranda talking on cellphones. There was a queue lined up outside a door with a sign that said 'internet' in green neon letters. There were groups of youngsters walking back from a grocery store with brown paper bags spilling beers and sausages and packets of pasta. There were young men doing t'ai chi on the handkerchief-sized lawn behind the building and girls sitting in the lotus position meditating on the little wall outside the front door.

It was colourful, noisy, busy and bustling; it was exhilarating, exciting and enervating; and it was beautiful. But it did not make the dormitory any less smelly or stuffy or the bathroom any less public, and it did not make the off-key and out of tune Sinatra's pleas to be flown to the moon any easier on the ear.

Nevertheless, it did make me smile, it did make me ponder the incalculable and almost unbearable lightness of being and it did cause me to wonder at the immense journey I had made to reach this specific point in my wonderful life.

You only need to complete the last one hundred kilometres of the Camino to get the *compostela* – the certificate that attests to the fact that you have walked the Camino de Santiago de Compostela.

Like a spider web, many different routes of the Camino converge in the city of Santiago de Compostela; marked and sign-posted routes from Paris, from Vézelay and Le Puy-en-Velay, from Arles, Portugal, from Seville, Valencia and from the United Kingdom, and from the north coast of Spain. During the warm summer months when over a hundred thousand people are on the Camino, it would probably not be as noticeable as it was during these cold winter months when, for the first half of the 800 kilometres, there were no more than a total of twenty or thirty of us on the entire pathway, but the further we went along the Way, the more pilgrims we encountered, and then, suddenly, when we reached Sarria on the hundred-kilometre mark from Santiago de Compostela, as if out of the blue, there were hundreds of them! Suddenly they are everywhere! It takes roughly a week to walk a hundred kilometres, and exactly one week before Easter Sunday, Sarria becomes the busiest town in all of Spain. There was a festive mood as people arrived from all over the world to start their one hundred-kilometre pilgrimage and arrive in Santiago de Compostela in time for the Easter celebrations.

What a strange new experience indeed. Where did they all come from? Suddenly, at that one hundred kilometre-from-Santiago de Compostela-mark, pilgrims seemed to appear from behind every bush. Like water seeping through a crumbling dam wall, they streamed in from every direction. Buses disgorged their loads, they spilled out of parked cars, they teemed like a colony of angry ants. They walked, they cycled, they ambled, they sang, they talked, they played their music, they talked on their phones, they filled little restaurants that miraculously started appearing along the way, they queued up outside refuge doors, they lined up for *sellas* at every little bar, church or grocery stall.

Suddenly on the pathway there were people behind you, in front of you, all around you! They were a different kind of people; people who simply wanted to get to Santiago and for whom the journey itself was of no great significance. They were people who wanted the certificate to prove 'they had done it', who wanted to experience the holy week on the Camino, who wanted to be in Santiago for Easter, who wanted to spend a week with friends doing something fun, who wanted to practise their singing, who wanted to see this beautiful part of Spain, who had only one week of holiday in the year and who had chosen this part of the Camino for that week. Everywhere you looked, there they were. In the middle of nowhere, people parked their cars next to the road, came onto the pathway and started walking westwards. There were people who looked as if they were on a Sunday afternoon stroll – and perhaps they were! There were young women dressed out of a fashion magazine; colour co-ordinated, the latest and smartest and chic-est tracksuits and hiking gear, with their hair done for the occasion. There were people with posh picnic baskets that had been sent ahead by car, people who slept in hotels and who ate in restaurants.

The five of us who'd started our Camino on the tenth of February on the other side of the Pyrenees, and those who joined the route on the way – mainly from Pamplona, Burgos and Astorga – still added up to no more than a few dozen. That was the joy of walking the pilgrimage in winter; for roughly five weeks, we'd felt as if we had the entire Camino, an entire 800-kilometre footpath all to ourselves. Then the hordes arrived and, when we reached Santiago de Compostela, it was quite strange to see hundreds of pilgrims we'd never laid eyes on before.

The night before I reached the holy city, I stayed at Monte de Gozo, a town about five kilometres from Santiago de Compostela. On the hill behind the refuge – a large modern complex of row upon row of dormitories which were absolutely fit-for-purpose but absolutely impersonal too – was an impressive life-size sculpture of pilgrims arriving at this spot, giving a huge sigh of utmost pleasure (*gozo* means utmost pleasure in Spanish) and excitedly pointing out their first sight of the spires of the cathedral. The legend is told that the first in a group of pilgrims to spot the spires is called the 'king of the pilgrims' and thus originated all the surnames today that have any derivation of the word 'king'; these include King, Roy or Leroi in French, Rey in Spanish. I was on my own when I arrived and cannot really claim that I saw the spires 'first', but when I stood there on that hill where millions of pilgrims had stood before me and I saw those majestic spires against the backdrop of a hazy fading of the day's light, I most certainly felt like royalty – important, special and privileged. It was a magic moment.

I had time before darkness fell to walk the last five kilometres and enter the city, but I made the choice not to do so. In fact, for the whole preceding week I found myself putting on the brakes; I was walking slower, covering smaller distances between refuges, lingering a little longer over food stops. I even stopped one day to have lunch at a little restaurant and spent two hours over a big glass of red wine and a plate of *pulpo gallego*, a dish for which this part of Galicia is famous. It consists of an octopus which is cooked whole and then beaten to soften it, seasoned with salt, paprika and oil, and finally cut into bite-size pieces, preserved in its original shape and served on a plate. It is delicious.

I also took time to simply enjoy the beautiful Galician countryside. The first signs of spring had well established themselves in this wet and rainy, secretive province and the lush green landscape was covered with stunningly beautiful dry stone walls demarcating the fields of emerald-green pastures, flamboyant splashes of lavender, pink and yellow heather and gorse, and every here and there, a eucalyptus forest that made you feel as if you were walking into a massive cathedral, with the heady aroma of the trees filling the air like incense during a high mass of another time, another place. When I finally walked up the hill into Monte de Gozo, it was with a definite reluctance. I did not want the journey to end. I did not want the pilgrimage to be over. I did not want to go back to 'real life' and the 'real world', to responsibilities, disappointments, worries, decisions, materialism, the dependence on money and possessions, and to where conformism and compromise were tantamount to survival.

However, when I woke up the following morning at four-thirty and, as quiet as a mouse, got up, dressed and packed my backpack, it was with an enormous sense of excitement and anticipation. I was about to stand in the square in front of the cathedral of Santiago de Compostela and see the sun rise from behind its glorious spires.

There is much made of the pilgrim's arrival in Santiago de Compostela. If there are a thousand score myths and legends on the Camino, they multiply a hundred-fold in this holy city. The stories of old are adapted and adjusted and customised to suit the evolving modern-day pilgrim, and are kept alive with love and devotion and a jealous sense of ownership.

'Have you banged your head with Master Mateo?' is often the first question asked when you meet a familiar face. 'Did you see the way the perspiration and body oils and pressure of the millions of pilgrims' hands have hollowed out the marble where you lean when you bend down to bang his head?' One of the many customs that pilgrims have cultivated over the centuries is to bend down and bang their heads against that of the self-portrait bust of Mateo – or *Santo dos Croques*, Saint Headbanger, as he is also lovingly referred to, the architect of the cathedral – in order that some of his wisdom may enter their heads. (Is there something ironically paradoxical about that last sentence, or is it just me?) Because you have to bend right down to put your head against Mateo's, it is necessary to balance yourself against something, and the natural reaction is to put your hand against the pillar. Today some pilgrims have added this as yet another rite to the already long list of 'Things the pilgrim must do when he reaches Santiago', namely to put your hand in the exact spot of your countless predecessors.

Then there is the silver ark in the crypt underneath the altar; a beautifully simple casket that supposedly holds the relics of Saint James or Sant Iago. Away from the hubbub and excitement of the maddening crowds and the noise in the square in front of the cathedral and even in the cathedral itself, it is a sweet relief to go down into the crypt for a quiet moment of contemplation. I'm not sure what exactly is in that casket or whether the bones of Saint James are in fact enshrined there – if indeed the casket does contain bones – but going down into the crypt and spending a little while gazing upon this lovely silver coffer provided a magical spell of peace and serenity. I found myself completely alone for those few moments; alone with the saint of the Camino, with the spirits, the angels and the memories of the Camino…

Next, I went round to the back of the altarpiece to walk up the narrow staircase behind the altar, across the little passageway to the middle where hugging Saint James marks the official end of the pilgrimage. He did not welcome me with open arms, nor was there any warmth in the hug. In fact, he had his back turned to me – a larger-than-life, gold and bejewelled statue, sitting there, looking out over the cathedral, silently watching the hundreds of thousands of pilgrims as they stagger into the entrance, hobble down the centre aisle and make their way to the little passage behind him from where they can put their arms around him and give him a hug. I was disappointed. Not sure what I'd expected, I was still not impressed with the experience. Hugging a fellow-pilgrim, equally tired and sore and exhilarated at having successfully completed a super-human, enormous effort, was far more satisfying. But I put my arms around Sant Iago anyway, and gave that crusty old cold statue an extra little hug to thank him for sending the angels and the saints onto my pathway – and for even appearing himself from time to time on my long journey. I then walked out of the cathedral in search of the pilgrims' office to get my *credenciales* stamped for a last time and collect my *compostela*, the beautiful, Latin-inscribed certificate that named me a successful pilgrim!

And it was then that the last 'miracle' of my pilgrimage happened!

Still pondering the effect of watching the sun rise over the spires of the cathedral earlier that morning; standing so completely alone in the vast Plaza del Obradorio (one of the most moving moments in my life); and then the cold, impersonal welcome of Sant Iago (such a disappointing comedown), I made my way up the hill on the side of the cathedral – my feet two burning, agonising stones as I limped painfully along, 'Nici', my little bell, marking out the pace and urging me on: *ting-TING, ting-TING, ting-TING, Come on mom, you can do it!*

Suddenly I heard someone shouting. The voice was loud and bounced off the stone walls of the narrow street. I peered ahead to see where the call had come from, but the sun was now directly in my eyes and I couldn't see anyone or anything. Again the voice called – it sounded almost like someone was shouting my name, but as I knew this was impossible I put that notion out of my head. 'You are hallucinating, Wilna,' I told myself and continued my ting-TING-ing up the hill.

And again the voice called, louder and more urgently now. Again I stopped and looked around me, but there was no one. I was the only person up and about at this early hour.

'Wilna! Up here! Look up! I am here!'

I stopped and looked up. The cathedral walls loomed high and dark above me. I turned around and looked up on the other side, and there, hanging out from a small window on the fourth floor, was the familiar and wonderful sight of Brigitte, her hair a wild blonde halo around her beautiful smiling face.

I nearly fell on my back. In what seemed like seconds, she was downstairs and standing in front of me, still in her pyjamas – or rather, in her thermal underwear that served as pyjamas, bare feet, freezing hands and nose, and this time the hug was reciprocated – warm, welcoming and wonderful!

A few minutes later she had dragged me up the four flights of stairs and I found myself inside her and Lisl's room, clothes and backpacks and socks and water bottles and a box with a half-eaten pizza and pilgrims' sticks and hiking boots scattered in a joyful jumble of pilgrim-ness.

'I heard Nici!' Brigitte bubbled. 'I heard that *ting-TING, ting-TING*! And I woke Lisl and said to her, 'Listen! It can only be Wilna! It is Wilna's daughter telling her, *You can do it! You can do it!*'

'And I wasn't happy being woken so early,' Lisl groaned. They'd had a late night, celebrating with fellow-pilgrims who had been arriving from different directions. 'We had a bit too much red wine last night. But, welcome to Santiago, Wilna. I am happy for you…' and with that she pulled the covers back over her head and went back to sleep.

'I *knew* it had to be you when I heard the bell! It was so funny. That bell was with me every day on the Camino, you know. I heard it every time we went up a mountain and every time we thought we couldn't continue. That bell told me every day, "*You can do it, Brigitte! You **can** do it!*" Your daughter pushed me all the way!'

Brigitte sat on her bed with her knees pulled up to her chest, her blistered toes still individually bandaged, exactly as they were the last time

I'd seen them weeks before. She told me about how they had continued on to Finisterre and how that was the highlight of the Camino for her. 'Standing on that rock at Muxia was just wonderful,' she told me. 'You have to go there! I burned my trousers and then we spent a long time there, just sitting on the rock and looking out to the sun setting on the horizon. It was so beautiful.'

Brigitte was talking about the pilgrims' custom of burning something from their 'old life' when they reached the 'end of the earth' – yet another pilgrims' rite that has been adjusted and adapted over the years. 'But it was quite ridiculous to see some of the pilgrims burning their thousand euro boots or their expensive jackets. And then they turn around and find they can't walk back to Santiago without the stuff they've burned. It was just plain stupid.'

'Well, I'm sure you won't miss that ugly pair of trousers!' I teased.

Brigitte laughed. 'No, I won't miss them one bit! So, tell me, who have you seen? When last did you see Thorsten and Akira? I never saw them for weeks!'

Soon we were swapping news about fellow-pilgrims and I filled her in about Thorsten's emergency that forced him to go home and Akira who had to leave after three weeks. 'And I had a text from Kamil three days ago telling me he will meet me in Santiago! Isn't that amazing? If you think that first night we fixed him up in Puente de la Reina…'

'I have seen him! He looks fabulous! You will not recognise him! We are meeting him for breakfast at nine o'clock, so you must join us. He will be so pleased to see you!'

We agreed on the place and time to meet, said our goodbyes with more hugs and I made my way back down the narrow, creaky staircase to go and find the pilgrims' office and get my certificate. I was already looking forward to seeing Kamil again and talking a lot more with Brigitte and Lisl, to find out whether they'd achieved what they had set out to do and to hear all their stories of their Camino.

⁂

And then it was back to discover and explore the 'event', the 'happening' that is Santiago de Compostela.

Orchestrated to the finest detail, the activities around the cathedral never stop. Every second of every day, hundreds of pilgrims flood onto Plaza del

Obradorio, joyously embracing each other, laughing, crying, falling on their knees – be it in deep prayer or simply from sheer exhaustion – taking photographs, looking bewildered, looking ecstatic. Every day at noon there is a pilgrims' mass held in the cathedral. Because it was Easter when I arrived, the first mass was only held on Easter Sunday, although there were services almost every hour. The 'Ecclesiastical karaoke', as David so aptly called it, could be listened to a few times a day; the Offices beautifully sung in harmony, a cappella, in Latin, by three or four or more priests. Vespers, matins, and everything in between: a performance almost each hour of the day. Even if you're not attending a service of some sort, the church itself offers much to look at.

The elaborate carvings and sculptures framing the three doorways are a mass of writhing and convoluted figures that depict Purgatory and the Last Judgement. There are prophets and saints, kings and queens, pilgrims and animals and, watching over the scene, the twenty-four Elders of the Apocalypse serenely playing medieval musical instruments – all frozen in stone, for all time, in Romanesque drama and Gothic realism. I had to wonder at this kaleidoscope of stone sculptures. For a pilgrim who has just finished walking over a field of stones and under a canopy of stars for a thousand kilometres; who has been doing daily soul-searching and painful penitence for months and who, arriving at last at the cathedral of Santiago de Compostela – the concrete symbol of his faith, the promise of the relief of his sins, the proof that his time in Purgatory will be shortened – is confronted with a graphic depiction of what he believed he would be freed of, could not exactly be called fair.

There is a touch of humour though. On one side of the entrance is a statue of Daniel. He has such a stupid, lecherous look on his smiling face that you simply have to turn around to see what or who it is he's looking at. And there, on the opposite wall, is Esther, a pretty sweet maiden. But why, then, the ridiculous look on Daniel's face? As with most things on the Camino, this, too, has a story attached. Apparently Esther used to be exceptionally well endowed – that is, the *statue* of Esther used to have a very 'femininely ample' figure. When the church fathers noticed the look on Daniel's face and realised what the cause of his lascivious expression was, they had a stone mason spend a good few days sanding down the two guilty peaks on the form of Esther to leave her flat-chested and demure. The people of the city were furious at having had their – and Daniel's – pleasurable secret destroyed, but, having no recourse against the church, they devised another plan. They changed the shape of their local cheese; instead of a flat round shape, they took Esther's (now-sanded down) twin peaks as their model and started shaping all their cheeses in a similar fashion. To this day the delicious cheeses of Santiago make pilgrims either blush in embarrassment or smile with pleasure; and their voluptuous shapes continue to keep Daniel leering lasciviously!

For the more pious, there's the beautiful gold and ivory crucifix – displayed in the *Capilla del Relicario* (Chapel of the Reliquary) – which dates back to 874 and is reputed to contain a piece of the True Cross; or the cathedral museum, which has a rich display of precious tapestries and archaeological fragments.

But for most pilgrims, the highlight of Santiago de Compostela is the main feature of each day: at eleven o'clock the church is packed to the hilt with pilgrims and travellers and spectators, with no room for even the proverbial church mouse. The day I attended, there was a hushed excitement as everyone waited for the big moment. While I sat there, squeezed in among pilgrims, travellers and tourists, I looked around me. Every now and then one of my fellow-pilgrims and I recognised each other and smiled and waved, a warm feeling of confraternity among us. Then I had this strange feeling – as if someone was looking at me, but the look did not come from anyone in the waiting audience. I looked up above my head, at the top of the dome of the cathedral, and there, right above the altar, in the centre of the dome, was a large eye, framed by a white triangle inside a pinkish circle, looking down at me. I remember learning about the *oculus Dei* (the eye of God), which is sometimes painted in the centre of a dome if there is no opening – but this eye looked human rather than divine. It was looking straight down at me, hard, unblinking, relentless. When was it painted up there? I wondered. I hadn't read anywhere about this eye, and somehow it didn't look as if it dated back to the origins of the cathedral. The brow is thick and bushy and feathery and the eye is sort-of yellowish-brown, with very long, almost effeminate, upper and lower lashes. But what is most peculiar is the way the whole area around the eye seems to be accentuated with a kohl pen; 'smoky' would have been the term used in a make-up and cosmetics publicity article. The construction of the cathedral began in 1060 and was completed in 1211, which makes it an Early Romanesque cathedral, but, during the 16th, 17th and 18th centuries, I believe, major exterior transformations took place, which would explain the Baroque façades. The *oculus Dei* might have been painted during that time, but this would still not explain its distinctly 'modern' look. So the eye keeps on looking down at pilgrims, and remains a mystery to me. When I later researched the subject, I could still find no reference to it, other than a single photograph taken by a person with a Japanese-sounding name.

But my attention was drawn away by the entry of the procession. All the monks, the brothers, the priests, and the archbishop himself had gone across to their quarters behind the cathedral and now appeared, an hour later, dressed in the most elaborately decorative costumes I have ever seen in a Catholic church; the red Templar's cross blazing on the plush black velvet, jewels glinting under the lights of the cathedral chandeliers, rich embossed brocades and exquisite embroidery in gold thread sweeping the worn flagstones of the cathedral floor, delicate lace brushing at wrists, tassels and braids swinging to the rhythm set by the archbishop's pilgrim staff – everyone in readiness for the star attraction of the day: the swinging of the *butafumeiro*, the biggest incense burner in the world. The procession was long and drawn out – taking full advantage of the rapt audience. Relics that were usually kept under lock and key in the vaults of the cathedral were carried down every aisle in the building – from east to west, north to south, to ensure that everyone in the vast packed interior had an opportunity to admire them. There were glass cases with realistic effigies of the Madonna, of Christ Crucified, of the head of Jesus bleeding under the Crown of Thorns. There were monks in cassocks and bare feet playing replicas of the medieval music instruments that I'd seen the twenty-four carved stone Elders of the Apocalypse play while watching the wretched perish in Purgatory. The small swinging censers emitted that sweet smell of incense and left behind puffs of haze that clouded the atmosphere. The clerics all looked stern and severe and fully played their roles as the fathers of the church.

While the procession made its slow, laborious way through the cathedral, four men came in, carrying the eighty-five kilogram, solid silver *butafumeiro*, which hung from an H-frame, the two poles resting on their shoulders. They carefully placed the giant censer on the exquisite carpet on the central dais. A thick rope that was attached to a pulley system directly under the *oculis Dei* was lowered and threaded through the ring on top of the censer, the other end of the rope resembling a cat-o'-nine-tails, with nine thinner knotted ropes coming out of the central one. Each one of these was held by one of the men standing clustered in front of the altar.

As soon as the procession had done the circuit, the archbishop, dressed in his full regalia of a purple and gold cope and a splendid mitre, as well as three priests dressed in the Templars' black and red, came onto the dais and took their positions in the chairs in front of the altar. After a considerable time, the archbishop got up and went to stand at the *butafumeiro* – which almost reached chest height. With great humility and much genuflection, the four men who'd carried the censer in came forward and awaited the signal from the archbishop before lifting the lid of the censer and handing him a taper with which to light the incense. A big cloud of sweet-smelling smoke immediately started pouring out of the ornate silver *butafumeiro*, and without further delay, the nine men holding the nine ropes heaved and pulled with all their might, the giant censer flew up into the air, right up to fifty, one hundred metres, above the heads of the onlookers. Next, they eased their hold and then pulled up again, putting every bit of energy and strength they had into the effort, causing the massive silver artefact to start swinging, back and forth, back and forth along the entire length of the nave of the transept. When it flew to it highest point, one hundred and fifty metres up in the sky, you wondered how it did not hit the high vaults of the ceiling, and when it came back down to make its way to the other side, it barely missed the heads of the pilgrims below. It seemed like a death-defying stunt, and I was amazed that I'd never heard of any pilgrims being killed by the flying *butafumeiro*. No one was injured on this day either, but everyone was left with their jaws hanging open and their heads shaking; never had they witnessed anything quite as dramatically effective.

It was only later, back in the sunlight outside the cathedral, that I realised how the whole spectacle had been meticulously planned and executed for maximum effect. But, the whole spectacle had also been nothing more than just that: a spectacle. Originally, we had been told, this swinging of the giant censer had been to expel the terrible smell of the pilgrims' unwashed bodies during the pilgrims' mass. But there'd been no mass. There had not been a single word spoken, not a single blessing given, not a single prayer said. There was no pretence, even, that it formed part of a religious ceremony. The players had come on stage, extravagantly dressed for the show, but they were nothing but extras with non-speaking parts; the star of the show was the huge silver *butafumeiro*. The entire spectacle was about getting a cathedral packed with people, and nothing more. Like the 'Ecclesiastic karaoke', the swinging of the *butafumeiro* had become just another act on the theatrical programme of the Camino; just another item in the annals of Camino folklore and Camino legend.

The *show*, the *happening*, the spectacle that *is* Santiago de Compostela, spills out into the streets during the Holy Week of Easter. People come from all over the world to celebrate this joyous festival and the Spanish, in particular, are there in their huge numbers. And the city provides the spills and the thrills, the pomp and ceremony, the colour and the drama to give each and every one full value for their time and money. On the three days of the *Semana Santa* preceding Easter Sunday, fourteen of the confraternities of the city present a procession through the streets. Proudly going under their names, such as *Confraría do Cristo da Unción e Nosa Señora da Serenidade* and *Confraría do Santísimo Cristo da Misericordia Irmandade dos Estudantes,* each of these confraternities has a turn to bring out their most valuable and precious icons, relics and life-sized statuary scenes from the New Testament, and display them to the public in a solemn procession. The processions are named as well – there's the *Procesión do encontro* (the Meeting Procession), the *Viernes Santo* (Easter Friday), and *Os Caladios* (The Silent Ones). Groups of from ten to more than fifty men from the confraternity are dressed in full-length black tunics; on their heads they wear tall, pointed hoods with holes only for their eyes. These hoods can be in deep purple or bright green, yellow, red or black satin, some standing a metre tall above their heads, and all ominously reminiscent of the Ku Klux Klan, but the only similarity is in the anonymity these hoods provide; these men do not want to be recognised because the sacrifice they make to take part in these processions has to be anonymous to have real meaning. And a sacrifice it is. They carry the wooden platforms on which the centuries-old statues stand: the Madonna, tears running down her pale cheek, dressed in heavy robes of dark blue velvet and exquisitely delicate lace, and with a magnificent gold crown on her head, standing surrounded by a field of freshly picked purple irises and lilies-of-the-field; Christ stumbling under the cross, the perspiration and droplets of blood glistening on his brow; Simon of Cyrene coming from behind to help Jesus carry the heavy cross and a soldier in full armour in front urging the two to keep moving. The craftsmanship is stunning. Each is a masterpiece, and this is the only time that they're on display to the public.

The platforms weigh tons and are often carried by no more than six men. Huge posts supporting the platforms on either side are lifted onto their shoulders, and, in the other hand, as a support to stabilise them under this massive weight, they use heavy iron staffs in the shape of a cross to stamp the pace on the cold, wet, cobblestone streets. *TONC – TONC – TONC – TONC…* the iron crosses clang down on the stones, reverberating through the very bones of the onlookers. UH! – UH! – UH! … the immense effort of each man echoes the iron staffs. It's a sinister sound as the procession moves down the narrow streets of the city, and when it takes place late at night, with the streets glistening with rain and the temperature near freezing, it is not only the temperatures and inclement weather that send a chill down your spine.

One evening, while walking back to my room, I passed a television shop where, in the window, the fifty or so screens were all on the same programme – a colourful, flickering, fly-eye multi-view of the same gory, bloody scene; the carriers who'd taken part in the procession I had only just witnessed were having their wounds attended to in a room somewhere in the city. Their faces were still not visible, but their necks and shoulders showed the 'sacrifice' they'd anonymously made on that night – they were a bleeding, raw mass, the skin sometimes completely chafed away, leaving the muscles underneath exposed. The camera moved to a pair of feet – equally raw and bleeding. Next, the screens all showed a close-up of the group earlier during the procession; the camera panned down to their bare feet on the shiny, wet stones of the street, the chain around an ankle dragging behind, the cold iron cutting into the flesh. And in the background I could still hear the *TONC! – UH! – TONC! – UH! – TONC!* Whether the sound came from the multi-screens inside the shop, or was still in my head, I did not know, but the effect was as unnerving as it had been when the hooded men had walked right past me.

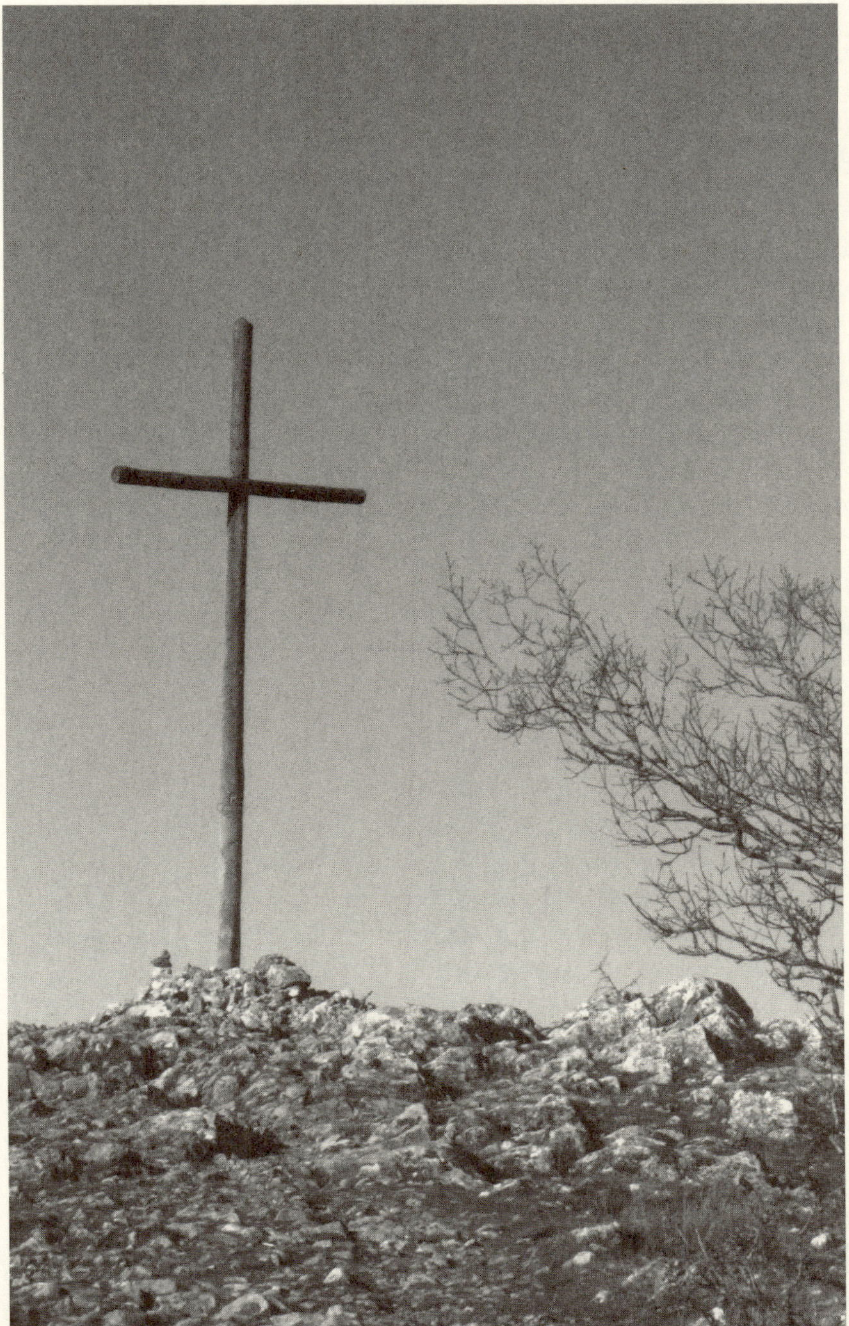

17
Dream, believe, and dare to do

Pain is temporary. It may last a minute, or an hour, or a day, or a year, but eventually it will subside and something else will take its place. If I quit however, it lasts forever.

– Lance Armstrong

Journal entry:
I walked into a glorious cathedral this morning… The entire interior was filled with light – light so splendid and luminous, and made almost tangible by the dust mites floating in the air that shimmered like a million winged diamond chips. The tall slender sapling pillars dividing the centre aisle from the side aisles and transepts looked too delicate to take the place of the solid walls that would have been necessary to hold up the soaring roof, the capitals adorned with medallions of lichen in gold and verdigris. It must have been the flying buttresses on the outer limits that bore the weight of those high vaults. Around the apse, there was a system of uniformly precisioned pillars and arches, gothically pointed in the middle, underscoring the heavenward dynamism of the whole edifice. I wandered deeper into this wondrous space and I felt that this elaborate 'architecture' had to have come from some celestial drawing board. There was a great white stone, like a high altar in what would have been the inner choir, and an ambulatory adjoining a circle of chapels. Around me the pillars were made up of a large number of huge round trunks – vines clinging with filigreed fingers to the bark – the vaults being supported by fine ribs, here decorated with capitals made up of gilded leaves and dissolving in a myriad of arches and a delicately fine tracery as they soared upwards into the open blue sky.

Nature builds its own cathedrals. More magnificent than those of man.

On the Camino the rule of thumb is that when you see the spire of a church, you are ten kilometres away from the village; when you can see the roof top of the church, you are five kilometres away and, when you can make out the bell in the bell tower, you are one kilometre away from the next refuge. Being a pilgrimage, the Camino frame of reference is often constructed around churches, religious symbolism and reminders of what a pilgrimage is about. I was not unmoved by these places, but my true pilgrimage took place in the cathedrals of nature.

In *The Face Beside the Fire* Laurens van der Post wrote: 'An explorer who had at last walked into the true unknown, found that the treasure of discovery was the realisation that true awareness needs not only the fact, but also the dream of the fact: these are the two vital ends to the journey between.' For many hundreds of years people have come to the Camino, walking into the true unknown, seeking true awareness. They come armed with the facts – the given history, the promise of redemption, the example and the stories of those who have gone before them. And they come with the dream – the expectations, the hope and the faith of the true believer. They walk over the pathway and do not feel the stones under their feet, and they walk under the field of stars, but the only stars for them are their own, which they see reflected in their fellow-pilgrims' eyes. And the greater the illusion of the 'journey between', the less likely it is that they will return to the disillusion that awaits them when they go back to the 'real' world.

At first, when I discovered how few people walked the Camino for purely religious reasons, I was – perhaps naively – surprised. I had assumed that most people on the Way would have been there because of their religion or their commitment to their faith. That faith would have been in any god of their choice – Christian, Judaic, Muslim; no import which god, but the assumption was that it would be a god. The Camino is, in many ways, like walking the fourteen Stations of the Cross during a Catholic mass on Good Friday. At every stop, every little village or town or city, and in between as well, there are churches of every size where there's usually something of great religious significance to see or do. There are beautifully carved and gilded altar-pieces – each a work of art worthy of a visit, there are special stone carvings, crypts, painted murals, and there are many places where miracles are said to have occurred and where, if you believe strongly enough, a miracle may even occur for you. Why I therefore should have expected most pilgrims to walk the pilgrimage for religious purposes was understandable. And, similarly, even if I was not walking the Camino with a religious motivation, most people who know me or knew my background, assumed that I was – probably because of the way I'd grown up.

Scientists tell us that the parietal lobe in our brain is where our spiritual centre lies. Here is where the data processing takes place and where our ability to focus, and our concentration, is determined. The parietal lobe springs into action when we pray or meditate, and the more intense these activities, the more likely that we can go into a trance or experience a sense of drifting away from reality. Most of us are not familiar with such out-of-body experiences, but all of us have a spiritual centre.

I'd grown up believing that *religion* and *faith* and the *church* were all synonymous. It was a given that you went to church – if not every Sunday, or even regularly, then at least for Christmas, Easter, christenings, weddings and funerals. It was also unthinkable that you did *not* believe in *something*. My formative years were constructed on the firm foundations of Christian principles, where you didn't really have to think about religious matters as they were all ready-prepared and in place for you to simply accept. It was all too easy. Your family, your friends, your peers, your education, your figures of authority, your entire life had at its foundation in the Christian belief.

My forefathers had had to leave their homes, their family, their friends and their lives behind, and flee their country of birth for all time, because of religious persecution. They were Protestant, but the rulers of the time were Catholic, and although both sides prayed to the same God, they couldn't accept the other's language of prayer. To this day I'm amazed that no one in my childhood circle of family and friends ever questioned a religion that forced people to sail halfway around the world to seek a new life, because if they'd stayed, their fellow-Christians would have killed them. Or, perhaps they did question it; only they never uttered the questions out loud for if they had, they too might have felt better for speaking out, but the cost would have been exile from their own community as well.

So strong were those foundations of the church that, when I decided, at the age of fifteen, to spend a year studying other religions before committing myself to confirmation in the church of my parents, my decision was accepted and even encouraged. Everyone around me knew my curious mind needed to be satisfied, but they were confident in the knowledge that I would, at the end of the year, come back into the fold. And I did – at the time. It was only much later, when I had a close encounter with the Moonies, a strong religious movement in the seventies, and I was forced to give account of the strength of my own faith; and then, still later, when I sought (and found) spiritual solace in the gentle realms of Buddhism, that I started questioning, truly questioning my commitment to the Christian religion. I became sceptical about prejudiced interpretations of the dogma, about a religion that was based on the subjective translations of fallible men, about a faith that was, in effect, the most recent or current result of two thousand years of the game of Chinese whispers. But, because I was raised to believe that you were lost without a god, and because I carried with me the baggage of my religious background – the sin and the guilt and the feeling of inadequacy and helplessness – I was too afraid to ever break away completely and declare my independence from the church of my fathers.

I do not think I'd be alone in saying that the biggest dilemma for me during these last couple of decades has been that, even once I'd broken away from the church and the formal trappings of a prescribed religion, I still had strong faith. I had faith, but no longer in the God of the Old Testament. That god, I felt was an attempt at a personification of a power, a force, an energy that had to be stronger, had to be greater, had to be more omnipotent than the other idols of the time. The writers of the history of the time described this power in the only way they knew how and according to their particular frame of reference and knowledge; as a being and as a concept that everyone could understand. It had to be a masculine figure because they lived in a patriarchal society. It had to be a god that was cruel, jealous, demanding and exacting, as they lived in such a world and understood it well. The God of Sinai and David and Abraham no longer had significance for me in my rational thought.

I had faith, but no longer in the God of New Testament either, who had been all but pushed aside to make way for the far more credible and lenient Son. This new image, still a being that can be visualised but, even more so, a figure that modern man can relate to, became an adaptation – and a world hungry for something to lean on, followed. 'Charismatic' churches, as they're called, all their off-shoots and side-kicks, a church on every corner, a crowd in every stadium, a preacher on every television channel and a numbered account in every bank. People clamouring with upturned hands for salvation, for guidance, for answers and for redemption, carrying their guilt like a badge of merit.

I had faith, but my faith was not in this fabrication of god. I had discovered that there was a distinction – an important distinction to be made between religion and faith – or spirituality. I knew that my faith was no longer in anything that any one conventional religion offered. It was rather a faith in my creator. But, until I walked the pilgrimage to Santiago de Compostela, I didn't know who or what or where this creator was.

Tenzin Gyatso, or the Dalai Lama, writes in *Ancient wisdom, modern world: Ethics for the New Millennium* about the difference between religion and faith and he describes so succinctly what I discovered during my Camino:

> Religion I take to be concerned with faith in the claims to salvation – acceptance of some form of metaphysical or supernatural reality, including perhaps an idea of heaven or nirvana. Connected with this are the religious teachings or dogma, rituals, prayer and so on.
>
> Spirituality I take to be concerned with those qualities of the human spirit – such as love and compassion, patience, tolerance, forgiveness, contentment, a sense of responsibility, a sense of harmony – which bring happiness to both self and others.
>
> While ritual and prayer, along with the questions of nirvana and salvation, are directly connected with religious faith, these inner qualities need not be, however. There is thus no reason why the individual should not develop them, even to a high degree, without recourse to any religious or metaphysical belief system. This is why I sometimes say that religion is something we can perhaps do without. What we cannot do without are these basic spiritual qualities.

He continues to write in great length about our duty and responsibility as human beings – a duty and responsibility not to an exacting god or the rituals of a church, but duty and responsibility towards our fellow-man and our habitat. There are so many other faiths, other cultures, other beliefs, and they are no less capable than yours or mine of enabling individuals to lead constructive and satisfying lives. This was displayed so clearly on the Camino. I met people who were deeply religious – of just about every religion on the planet, and I met people who'd never had any meaningful contact with one religion or another. But, what was eminently clear to me was that whether or not a person is a religious believer doesn't matter much at all. What is far, far more important is that you should be a good human being who recognises your responsibility to others as well as to the planet we inhabit.

What I found on the Camino, walking across a vast landscape hour after hour, day after day, week after week – every sense heightened by the exquisite beauty around me and by the exquisite pain in my feet, every emotion enhanced a hundred-fold by the solitude, the absence of people and the sounds and the smells of an inhabited space, every moment an intensified awareness of the relief from the constant busy-ness of life – what I found was a spiritual dimension I had never experienced before in this spiritless world of ours. Our impulsive approach to happiness, our need for a quick fix, makes us rush off to every new church group, popular charismatic preacher or A-list group of fellow-believers to try to satisfy this yearning within ourselves to belong somewhere, to have something we can call our own – and in particular, to fill a void left by a too fast, too busy, too self-centred and too-stressed lifestyle – to find 'that which seems to promise the shortest route to satisfaction'. Yet in doing so, all too frequently we deprive ourselves of the opportunity for a greater degree of fulfilment. What I found – without going out there searching for it, but in a purely serendipitous way, as so often happens when our awareness is awakened – was the realisation that I was walking with my creator, that this empty landscape was indeed filled with the wondrous miracle of creation. I became intensely aware of the fact that what I'd dreamed of, I had found: a way back to a natural and pre-scientific, pre-manmade world, of which technology and jargon and fads and peer pressure and materialism have robbed us.

I said before that there are so many other faiths, other cultures, other beliefs, and all of these are no less capable than yours or mine of enabling individuals to lead constructive and satisfying lives. I've also said how I envy those who believe so implicitly that the judgement of the world is irrelevant to them. And here, in a moment of epiphany, on the Camino pilgrimage, I found what it was that made me what I am and gave me a sense of belonging and worth: I recognised this 'greater-than-us' that gives us courage to get up each morning, to get dressed and to face the day, even when our body is riddled with cancer or racked with pain, even when it feels as if our soul is empty with despair. It is our creator that is the 'greater-than-us' that ensures the survival of the human spirit as it has done since the beginning of time and as it will do long after we are no more. It is nature that is the 'greater-than-us' that ensures the miracle of light at the beginning of every day and darkness at the end. It is the earth that is the 'greater-than-us' that feeds us, nourishes us, replenishes us. In return, it does not ask anything from us; its infinite generosity is completely unconditional. We never needed to put human form to nature, or give it human characteristics. The earth is not jealous or vengeful or demanding. Our creator does not ask for sacrifices or gifts or to be adored or venerated. It simply is, and it will always be.

On the Camino, there are many exceptional people who change the lives they touch. But there was one, in particular, who touched mine...

Ernst loomed large in the dark *refugio* dormitory. From my vantage point, just woken from a deep sleep and from the bottom bed of a double bunk, he probably looked larger than he really was. Or perhaps it was the anger and urgency and intense emotion in his loud whisper – the kind of whisper, that is still a whisper, but that would travel across the entire length of a theatre and be perfectly heard in the back rows. He was only wearing a pair of underpants and, even though it was dark, and the little light there was, was of the half-moon through the window, I could make out the huge torso, muscular arms, toned physique. His legs seemed to be exceptionally long, but again, it could have been because of my point of view or because of the fact that they were also exceptionally thin and didn't seem to belong to the muscular upper body. I did not understand everything he was saying because he was speaking in German, but no one would have needed any knowledge of the language itself to understand that what he was saying should have been PG-rated.

Ernst was standing with his back to me, cursing and swearing at Kurt, another German, who was lying sprawled out on his back on the top bed of the bunk, fast asleep, and snoring like the foghorn at Mouille Point in Cape Town.

'(expletive) Catastrophe! I cannot take it anymore! (expletive) You have to stop snoring! (expletive) Catastrophe! It is driving me insane! (expletive, expletive)'

By this time the others in the dorm were starting to stir. Drowsy pilgrims were sitting up in their sleeping bags, one or two not quite awake enough yet to have registered what was happening, but most of them laughing at Ernst's frustration, expletives and 'catastrophes'.

Ernst had joined the Camino in Pamplona and had soon teamed up with Kurt, so they must have spent quite a few nights together in the same dormitory. It seemed though that Kurt's snoring had reached its limit on this particular night – at least as far as Ernst was concerned – and, I have to admit, the snoring was a ripper. In fact, earlier in the night, I'd thought to myself that one should record the different snores and, using them as the notes, write a Camino symphony. Kurt's snore would have been more than sufficient to represent the entire percussion section – in fact he would have been the virtuoso. Not only was his volume superbly amplified, but his intricate variation in tempo, his subtle codification of the movements, his arpeggios and crashing crescendos setting off the tenor counterparts in the dormitory, provided the perfect time signature for a superb Snore Symphony.

The previous evening, Juan, a former chef and the *hospitalero* of this private refuge, had prepared a magnificent feast for us all. Around the table had been Marcus, the eighteen-year old Finnish boy who never spoke and who, we learned much later, had left home without telling his parents where he'd gone; Tashi, of indeterminate gender and age, a young watchmaker from Tokyo who was walking alone; Rene, the Czech man who was walking the other way – to his home in the Czech Republic. Thorsten and Akira, whom I had not seen for several days as they'd stopped for a day to rest Thorsten's painful knee and Akira's spot of tendonitis, had arrived; as had Ernst and Kurt. Juan was in his element with such a full refuge in the heart of winter. He was a gentle giant; a bull of a man, big, bulky, round and red, his head precariously balancing on three ample and wobbly chins, his neck nowhere to be seen. He sported a lush moustache and two bushy eyebrows. These three thick strips of hair he could wiggle in three different directions at the same time, producing a hilarious effect of hirsute gymnastics on the backdrop of his red face. He had, on the day I arrived at his refuge, acquired a small puppy, which he carried around in his hand, held close to his expansive belly. His hand was so large and the puppy so small that it took most of us a couple of hours at least before we realised that there was something there; two shiny little eyes, a tiny black nose, a delicate little rose petal tongue. Juan was one of those Camino angels who loved what he did. Every pilgrim was invited into his refuge with open arms and a big hug. It was one of those places where you immediately felt at home; warm and inviting, comfortable and clean. Through the kitchen was a large square of green lawn with a big old olive tree providing shade in the corner. This, in turn, led to the big open farmyard where all his beautiful specimens of roosters and hens and rabbits enjoyed the privilege of free range living.

While we were all enjoying the last sun rays of a blue-sky day in the back garden, chatting and smoking, comparing Camino stories, repairing gloves, tending to blisters, taping up feet and watching Juan's beautiful menagerie of rabbits and chickens – hoping that none of these Flopsys and Mopsys and Henny Pennys were going to land on our dinner table that night, Juan was busy in the kitchen cooking up a storm: there was chicken soup, followed by white beans and tripe, pork chops, fried eggs, big potatoes – halved, cooked in their skins and served with a vinegar and oil herb dressing, marinated and grilled chicken pieces, succulent pink prawns, finished off with a delicious fresh fruit salad. And of course, there was wine – a wonderfully dark rich Rioja, the local wine of the region. Juan did not charge us for this banquet but he simply put an empty cake tin on the side of the table and suggested that, if we so wished, we could make a small contribution. It was with contentment and full tummies that we had all gone to bed that night. Nothing short of a true 'catastrophe' was going to wake anyone. But then, Kurt's snoring could well be termed a true catastrophe!

'Ernst!' I sat up in bed, pulling my sleeping bag up to my chin against the freezing chill in the air. 'Ernst! You are not going to wake him up. He is sleeping like the dead.'

'This is impossible! The man sounds like a train! I can't sleep with that noise! I want to strangle him. That will make him stop! I will murder him! This is a catastrophe!' The expletives had stopped but the catastrophic nature of the drama was still in full force.

'Ernst – all you need are earplugs. Don't you have earplugs?' By this time almost everyone was awake, lying in their beds and shaking with laughter. Ernst made such a comical figure standing there, in front of Kurt's bunk, his face six inches from that of the snoring man, shouting at the top of his voice, but making not an iota of difference to the sonorous rhythm and rumble of the snore of the century.

'Earplugs?' Ernst bellowed. 'Earplugs? No! I don't have earplugs!' His breathing was laboured as he spluttered in fury. 'I will murder this man!'

'Ernst – here...' I bent down to where my backpack was leaning against the bunk and pulled out my extra pair of earplugs from the side-pocket. 'Here – I have an extra pair that you can take. They're very good. You won't hear a thing when you have them in.'

Ernst reluctantly turned away from his murderous mission and accepted the earplugs from me. 'Thank you. I think you have saved the life of a man tonight…' and with this he slunk off back to his bunk on the other side of the dormitory, inserting the earplugs as he did so.

'Ahhh, that is better. That is so much better…' and his voice trailed away as he slipped back into his sleeping bag and the dormitory came back to rest – except for Kurt's catastrophic snoring. This continued to rattle the windows and vibrate through the floor. I sighed. I was now wide awake as well and there was no way anyone could sleep with that noise. The noise filled the room, it took up every square inch of the atmosphere; it seeped into the very fabric of the sleeping bags, the mattresses, the timber of the bunk beds. It *was* a catastrophe! I put my own pair of earplugs back into my ears, zipped up my sleeping bag all the way so only my nose was still peeking out, closed my eyes and sank back into a deep sleep.

In the morning, when everyone woke up and started to emerge from their cocoons, the room was a-buzz about the 'catastrophe' of the previous night. Everyone was still laughing about Ernst's swearing and murderous intent. Kurt was sitting up on his bunk.

'Ah! I had such a good sleep! The food last night was so good, and the wine! What wonderful wine! And I must tell you – these earplugs of mine are the very best! I put them in and I sleep. Nothing, nothing will wake me!'

There was a short moment of stunned silence from us all. And then the room just exploded in laughter. Kurt had such good earplugs that he had heard nothing – not the drama that had played itself off next to his bed, not the plot to strangle him, not his own snoring. We laughed until the tears rolled, and he sat there in his bed completely flummoxed as to the source of the humour.

And then, suddenly, Thorsten held up his hand for silence. 'Listen! Listen!' he said.

We stopped laughing and listened. From the far corner of the room we heard it; a snore. Not as loud as Kurt's. Not as rhythmic or as rich in melody. But a snore that need never stand back in the greater arena of snores; deep and steady, building up to little peaks that climaxed in a short explosion of air. We listened closer. It sounded as if, at the end of each snore octave the little explosion of air actually spelled out a word: 'Catastrophe!' It was Ernst, blissfully unaware of the world around him, fast asleep and snoring like the best of them! Again the whole lot of us just collapsed with laughter, and this time, Kurt laughed with us.

Over the next few weeks I saw Ernst a number of times, either alongside the pathway where he or I was resting for a short spell or having a bit to eat, or in one of the refuges along the way when we happened to stop in the same place. Every time we saw each other we swapped a few pleasantries but, because my German is non-existent and he didn't speak very much English, we never spoke for long. He always did mention the night of the Big Snore though and thanked me over and over for the earplugs I'd donated to him. It changed his Camino, he said. He was now so much better rested because he got a good night's sleep every night. Yes, I wondered to myself, and I hope everyone who shares a dorm with you has their earplugs fixed in firmly as well! I never learned much about him, other than that I really liked him, I loved his ready smile and his warm, friendly manner, that he came from Hamburg, he grew flowers for the florist industry and he had exceptionally long legs which meant that his strides were three times the length of mine, and yet he never seemed to be ahead of me but always seemed to be more or less going at the same pace as I was. I never saw him with Kurt again – perhaps he felt guilty about almost murdering the man – but he made friends as he went and always had one, two or more people who seemed to want to be with him.

When I arrived in Santiago de Compostela, I looked round for all the people I'd met on the Way, and enquired everywhere about Ernst; but no one had seen him arrive in Santiago yet.

The second morning that I was there, I went to the Parador Los Reyes Catolicos Santiago de Compostela, apparently the oldest hotel in the world, which stands in pride of place on the Plaza del Obradorio, next to the Cathedral and the Galician President's headquarters. It is also known as the Parador 'Hostal Dos Reis Catolicos' and was built in 1499 as a Royal Hospital to give shelter to pilgrims making their way to Santiago. It is a magnificent medieval building with four cloisters of immense beauty, and a strong Arabic influence with its riad courtyards, soaring ceilings and delicate tile work. Today, scruffy, dusty, smelly pilgrims would not be allowed past the first step leading up to the grandiose entrance – and if they did, they would be firmly stopped by the liveried doormen. The hallowed portals of the Parador welcome only five-star guests with five-star wallets. However, the hotel has not quite forgotten its original purpose and, to this day, every day, the first ten pilgrims who queue up outside the underground parking garage of the hotel an hour before each of the three meals of the day, are whisked – with no time to leave a trace or a whiff behind them – through the lofty entrance, past the gilded lobby and the splendid restaurant, down a narrow spiral staircase, through the bustling kitchens, down another spiral staircase into the bowels of the earth where, in an ancient little stone room, they may enjoy a large meal free of charge.

In the queue with me on this day was Petr, a lovely man from Sweden. I had seen him only once on the pathway before – after O Cebreiro where he'd also spent the night. He looked like a relaxed, suntanned summer hiker who'd left home on a Sunday morning to be out and about to enjoy the sunshine and the outdoors; he wore shorts and a T-shirt and a bright bandanna around his shiny bald head and he sang as he walked. The morning that he passed me, he was singing 'Always on my mind' in a full baritone voice. Elvis the King would have been proud of him.

'It was so beautiful,' I told him. 'But for the rest of the way, the song turned over and over in my head and I couldn't get rid of it!'

'You should just sing it then,' he responded. 'If you sing the song out loud, it can escape and someone else can pick it up and use it! That is what I do – I give my songs to the world!'

I laughed at this lovely philosophy. 'And what else do you do?' I enquired. It turned out that he gave far more than just songs to the world. He was, among many other things, a ship builder by trade and a qualified youth counsellor by profession. After the Camino he was returning home, where he'd just obtained permission from the government to turn a ship that he was busy building into a youth centre for troubled and delinquent boys. 'The Camino has helped me a lot to prepare for this next phase of my life. I have just gone through a divorce which was not good, ('...You were always on my mind...'?) and I could not go and be a good counsellor if my own life was a mess. So now I am stronger again and I've learned so much on the pilgrimage that will help me understand and help the youngsters so much better. I think the ship will be like the Camino. It will offer similar opportunities for self-discovery and getting clarity of thinking and objectives.'

'What a wonderful idea! You know, one of the best things on the Camino has been meeting people who are such an inspiration to others. It would be impossible to go back to the "real" life and not be a changed person – a better person. The Camino is so incredibly enriching...'

'You are right,' Petr nodded his head. 'I have also met the most remarkable people. Like Ernst! Have you met Ernst?'

'Yes!' I was excited to come across someone else who knew Ernst. I quickly told him the story of the night of the Big Snore. Petr shook with laughter. 'What a wonderful snore story! I think everyone has a good snore story, but I like this one. And I can tell you, if you know Ernst, it is even funnier. He is such a big man, but he's the most gentle man I have met. Do you know the story of why he is on the Camino?'

'No, we have talked a lot, but never in great depth – because of the lack of a common language. And anyway, I don't like to ask people why they are here, unless they volunteer the information.'

'I know what you mean. I don't like to ask either, but sometimes I wished I had asked everyone for a story, because everyone has a story that is special,' Petr contemplated. 'Like Ernst's story. If you talk about inspirational, his is the most inspirational, I think.'

We had been sitting on a little wall outside the Parador's parking garage when a man dressed in a smart black suit had come to take our names and check our *credenciales*. He then told us to follow him and to stay with him and under no circumstances stop and stare once we entered the hotel. The ten of us – a sad and sorry bunch of pilgrims – then walked at a brisk pace behind the man, through the magnificent lobby and down the stairs to the kitchen. We were instructed to grab a tray and wait in line: on our trays we were given a large plate piled with a crisp fresh mixed salad, another plate with a hot, creamy, custard-y baked bread-and-butter pudding, and an empty plate on which the chef then dished huge, generous portions of grilled chicken, roast potatoes and green beans. We could also take as many freshly baked bread rolls as we wished and lashings of rich yellow butter, as well as a bottle of water and a bottle of red wine each. When everyone had their feast-on-a-tray, we all went down the second staircase into the room, just big enough for ten people and their food, where pilgrims had enjoyed a nourishing, free, cooked meal three times a day for centuries. Among the lucky ten were the delightful David and James, father and fourteen-year-old son from the States who, after having walked together for forty days seemed not only to have forged a most precious bond of understanding and love, but still to be enjoying each other's company, beautiful Julia from Sweden, and Herve – another Camino angel, my hero, he of the tattoo-ed legs, who had led me over the footbridge and into León on the day that my courage had nearly failed me.

As soon as we were all seated at the beautifully set tables with their starched white linen tablecloths and a little pot of flowers on each, Petr tucked his napkin into his collar, took a large bite of his food and finally resumed his story.

'Five years ago Ernst was in a wheelchair. Apparently there was some deformity in his back, or he had some kind of accident, but he could never walk. All his life he was in a wheelchair. Then, five or six years ago he decided that he was going to walk. Of course this was not possible because the muscles in his legs were – how you say? – atrophied. But he had decided he was going to walk and nothing would stop him. And he wanted to walk because he wanted to walk the Camino.'

'There are people who have done the pilgrimage in a wheelchair. How they do it I will never know!' This from young James – the fourteen-year-old who was having the time of his life.

'Yes! It is incredible. But I think maybe they go on the cyclists' pathways. That would be a little more possible? I don't know – but it shows you that when you want to do something you can do it, no?' Everyone was now involved in the story about Ernst.

'Anyway. Back to Ernst, because I think what he did was even more remarkable. He started to exercise his legs. He worked day after day after day. It must have been so very hard. You can imagine. The man is in his forties and he had to learn to walk. Everybody around him kept on saying that he was mad, that he could not do it. But he never gave up. And he forced himself to learn to walk and to get out of his wheelchair for good. And today, five years later, he is walking the Camino!'

I was stunned. 'It is so often the world that holds us back, isn't it? Or rather, it is we who allow the world to hold us back. It is far easier to accept the given than to prove the world wrong.' I was thinking of Terrie who'd been told that she was not supposed to live longer than six months, and that it was no use operating or giving her chemotherapy, but who had ignored the doom prophets and had made up her mind to face her cancer, fight it and conquer it.

For a few moments we both sat in silence, pondering the amazing achievement of Ernst. 'What an example. What an inspiration. And he never told anyone about this,' I was perplexed. 'He should have told everyone along the way what he was achieving. It would have helped so many people to continue when they started giving up or jumped on the bus or returned back home because of minor aches and pains.'

'But that is not what he was here for. He had to use all his energy and life force to keep himself going. I am just very grateful that he shared his story with me, because when I go back and try to help all those troubled young boys, I have a good example to teach them that when you believe in yourself, anything is possible.'

'Is he a religious man, do you know?' I asked.

'No, he said he didn't believe in all the church stuff. He said everyone around him all his life had been praying for him to get better, praying for him to manage to lead a sort of an okay life, praying for him to accept his fate. Nothing happened, of course. But he has faith stronger than I have ever seen in anyone; faith in what nature has given him. Faith in his own strength and ability. He said he had realised that he had been given everything to make it possible for him to walk the Camino, but it was only up to him – and no one else – to use those abilities and resources and make them work for him. He knew that if he just continued to sit in that wheelchair, that was where he would sit until he died. You know, I see so often people pray and pray to god to make things happen for them, but then they sit and wait for it to happen. They wait for god to make it happen. Instead of getting off their butts and doing something with all the talents and the resources they've been given. Ernst says he suddenly realised one day that there was no god that was going to appear one day and lift him out of the wheelchair and make his legs take his weight and start walking. God had already given him the means, and all he had to do was use them. But only he could do it.'

The following day I was sitting in the cathedral waiting for the start of the pilgrims' mass when I looked up and saw a tall man standing in the entrance, the light behind him making it hard to discern his features. But I recognised the silhouette; the wide torso, the long thin legs, the confident stance. I ran down the aisle as fast as my feet would allow, towards the wide, elated smile on Ernst's face. We hugged like old friends, tears of joy streaming down our cheeks; the typical meeting of two pilgrims in Santiago de Compostela.

'You are the last one of all my fellow-pilgrims to arrive, Ernst! Welcome and well done my friend! You have made it! Come, I'll take you to Sant Iago so you can give him a hug. I will show you where to go!'

Holding onto his hand, I led him down the aisle. I looked over my shoulder at Ernst. His face shone with awe and joy and tears. He gazed up at the ornate interior of the cathedral, drinking in the atmosphere and the gilded glory of the church, coming to grips with the fact that he'd finally arrived in the cathedral of Sant Iago. It was a magic moment and I felt enormously privileged to be the one to lead him towards the saint where all pilgrims' journeys officially culminate in a big hug of the gold and bejewelled effigy of Sant Iago – where he sits perched above the altar and above the crypt where his bones were allegedly lying in a silver casket.

Months later I asked Ernst if he would write down a few of his thoughts on the Camino for me. He sent me a lovely short account of his impressions, of the places and the people and the whole experience, but still did not mention his own impressive achievement. At the end he summarised: 'The Camino changes people… but people also change the Camino!'

Yes, Ernst. They most definitely do. When such humble and honest and brave people as yourself come onto the Way, you change not only the Camino, but all those whose lives you have touched. What an incredible honour to have had my pathway cross with those of people like you, people who are such a shining example to us all and such an inspiration to everyone who was privy to their amazing stories.

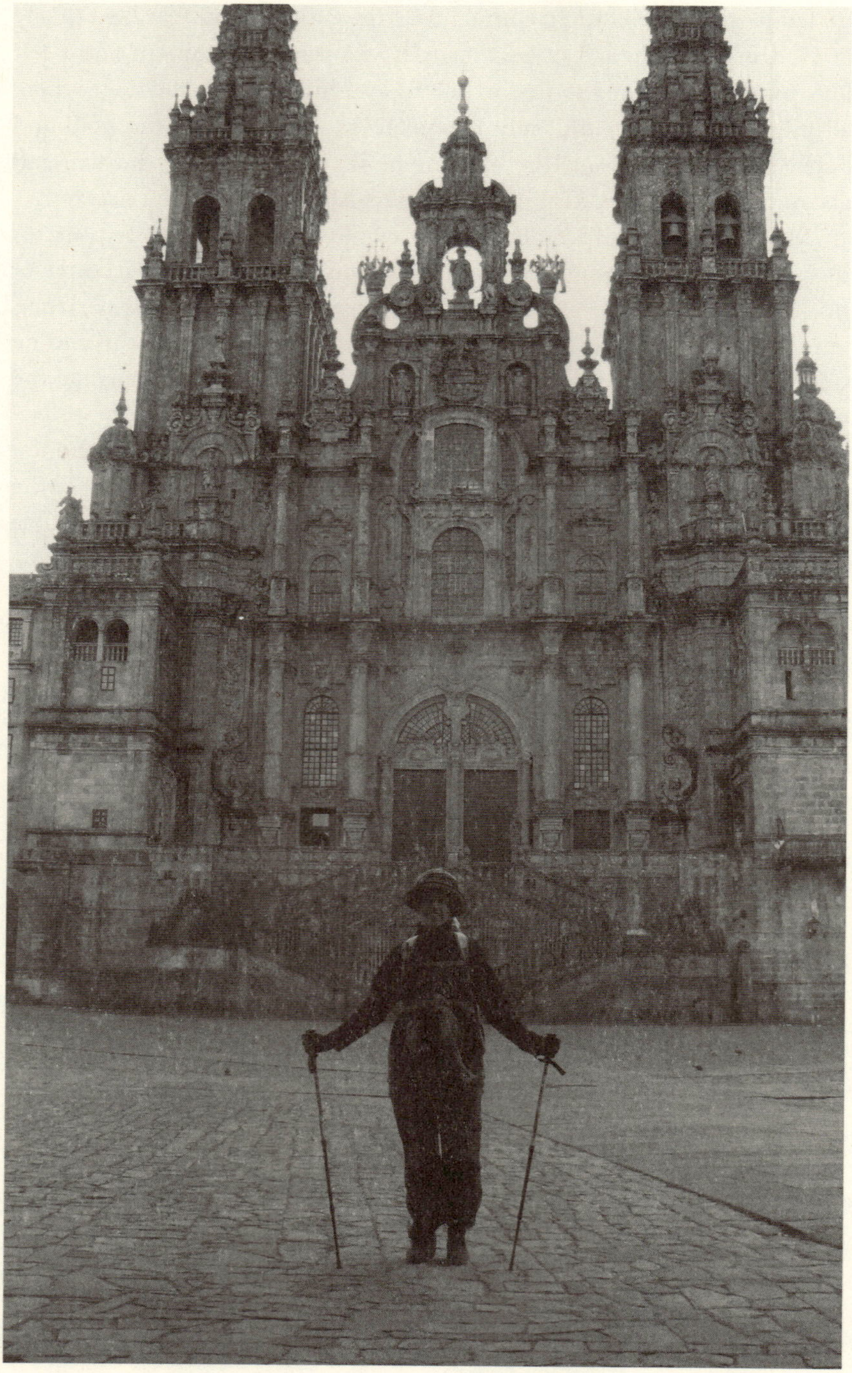

Epilogue

Things do not change. We do.
— Henry David Thoreau

The last e-mail to family and friends, 19 March 2009
Monte de Gozo, five kilometres away from Santiago de Compostela. I am almost there!

They say that everyone cries at least once on the Camino. Well, you all know what I am like! I have cried many times – mostly from joy and awe and wonder and being overwhelmed by this life-changing experience. Only once did I cry in despair – and that was when my feet were in such agony that I simply could not give one more step and then the only *refugio* that was on the way denied me entry as they were busy renovating.

I also cried a number of times in anger and quite a few times in sadness or sorrow.

As well as being quite eventful, the last two days were completely different from anything I have experienced on the Camino. It was almost as if those many, many waves that came over me and left me feeling completely overwhelmed over the last thirty-six days, turned tide and washed over me once again, but this time from the other direction and accompanied with such a strong backwash that I found it hard to stay grounded.

I have left so many things behind me on this Way under the stars and over the stones, as I have come to call the Camino.

I have carried my own stones of sorrow and burden with me and left them on the way. I have carried stones for just about everyone I love with me and left those along the way as well. I have learned things about myself that are sometimes frightening, sometimes joyful, almost always surprising.

I have found so many answers to questions that I never even knew I had.

I have made some very special friends, met some very interesting people and learned much about mankind that I never knew before. And I have finally found my faith – the answers I have sought for more than half a century were here on the Way, and I am so eternally grateful that they were waiting patiently there for me to come find them in my own time and in my own way.

I had a call from Kamil yesterday! He called from the door of the cathedral of Santiago to tell me that he has made it! Do you remember my telling of sweet rotund Kamil – the doctor from Berlin who, when I met him on his first day (he started in Pamplona) was inconsolable and in despair – his backpack was gouging holes in his back, his feet were covered in blisters and the insides of his legs were chafed so raw that they almost bled? Well – in case you never received that particular e-mail – on that night I saw the fantastic Camino spirit in action; after a good meal and much advice from fellow-pilgrims, we got his feet fixed, persuaded him to wear his pyjamas to protect his legs and removed his backpack frame to stop the broken bits sticking into his back – and yes! he walked the distance and reached Santiago! He made me promise to let him know when I am near so he can be there to welcome me in the cathedral square in the morning. Brilliant!

It will be wonderful to see who is there in the square tomorrow. At this stage I am not sure at all who is behind me and who is in front, but I am sure many of us will be meeting this weekend. I lost Mauro, the estate agent from Milan who never took his cellphone from his ear, and Alfonso and Jocasta who only walk one week every year, as well as Mike, the Brazilian restaurant owner I met a few days ago, who calls me La Principessa and has been leaving messages for me all along the way, written in the damp soil of the pathways – but I think he has gone on to Finisterre and from there down to Lisbon – as did Brigitte and Lisl. The Canadian couple, David and Marilyn, are still a few days behind I believe, and the Latvians, Petr, Ernst and Klaus should be there already. Amazing how exciting the thought can be to meet these fellow-pilgrims again. But it is a bitter-sweet anticipation, because I shall miss my two soul mates, Thorsten and Akira. Darn it, you two! You should have been here tonight, waiting for me in Monte do Gozo, so that we could walk into the square together tomorrow morning, like we said we would do, way back in Roncesvalles, on that very first night! – But I am thrilled to hear that you landed that main role in *Salieri*, Akira! I cannot quite picture you in a white powdered wig, but I am sure you will make a brilliant Mozart! And Thorsten – the news that you are now in Costa Rica teaching children and then planning to dedicate your life to taking blind people on the Camino did not surprise me at all, but it does fill my heart with immense pride – and with humility.

And Terrie – what can I say my friend! Walking into Santiago de Compostela tomorrow morning with the knowledge that you are actually winning your battle against the cancer is the greatest gift of all! Coming from 'inoperable' and 'untreatable' to 'inexplicably all clear' – well, I am not surprised the doctors are all speechless or talking about miracles – so am I! And thank you for sharing the journey with me, thank you for sharing your courage with me, thank you for inspiring me to walk my own Camino. You will be right there by my side in the morning as I watch the sun rise behind the cathedral, as you have been every step of this amazing pilgrimage!

There are so many things I realise now that I have never told you about. I still wanted to tell you about the scarf that has shrunk along the way – my 'tablecloth' is now the size of a hankie! And I wanted to tell you about the value of the Camino on your Curriculum Vitae, and about crossing the busy roads and – well – about lots and lots more, but I have three minutes left on the computer and no money in my purse and my feet are saying Rest Time! And anyway – I suspect I shall be talking about this experience for many, many years to come!

So, until the next internet café and the next time I write, from Santiago de Compostela – Stay safe and happy, *Hamba Kahle* (my South African way of saying 'Go well') and *Buen Camino* (the pilgrim's way of saying the same thing!)

Until we meet again – Wilna

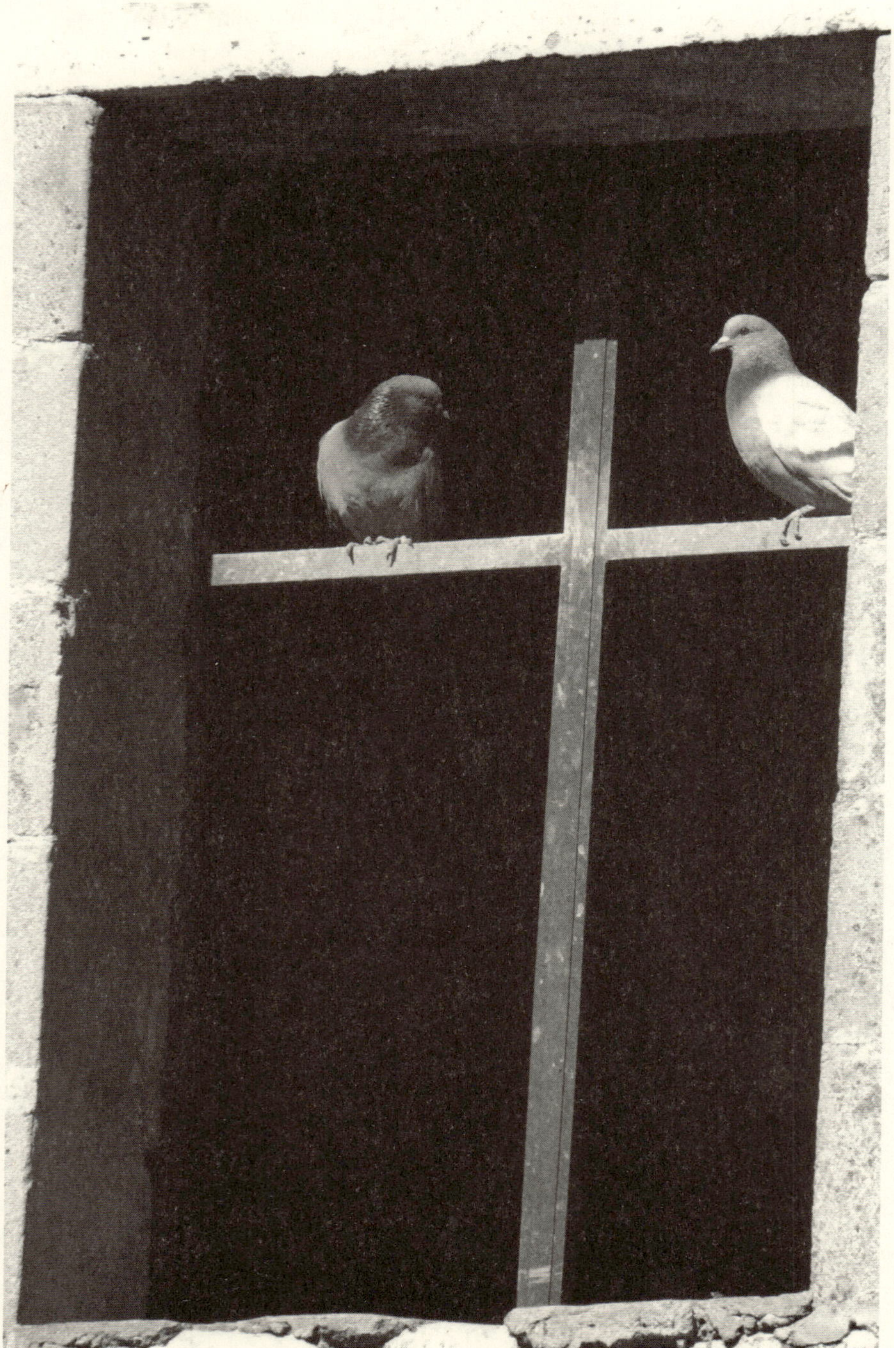

Acknowledgements

Although I walk alone, I feel no solitude.

I thank my father and mother who went before me, laying the foundations of my pathway through life.

I thank my family for never questioning my need to follow my dreams, no matter where those dreams take me, for urging me on and for catching me when I stumble.

I thank Pierre for listening, even when I do not speak, for keeping the light burning in the window, and for keeping the spirit alive.

I thank my editor Gillian Warren Brown for understanding, sharing and masterfully refining an often jumbled collection of thoughts.

I thank all my fellow-pilgrims. Out of respect for their privacy, I have changed the names of most of the characters in the book. However, I have retained the names of the *hospitaleros*, as well as those of my pilgrim friends, Terrie, Thorsten, Akira and Kamil.

And to everyone who stood beside the pathway to encourage, support and share my journey, I express my infinite gratitude.

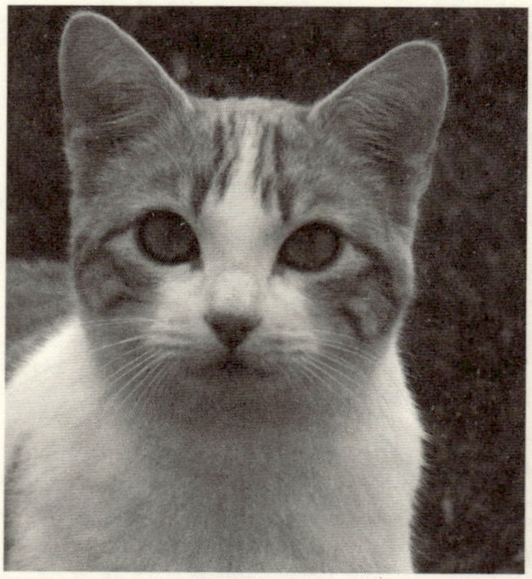
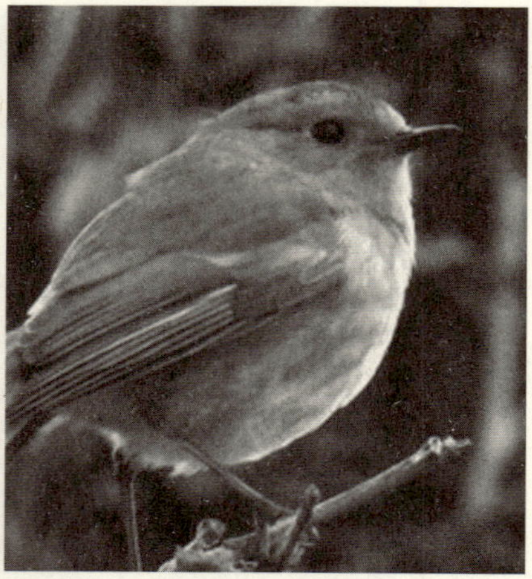
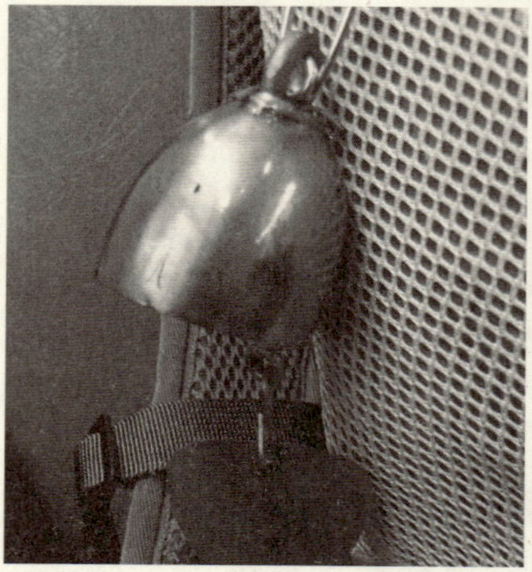
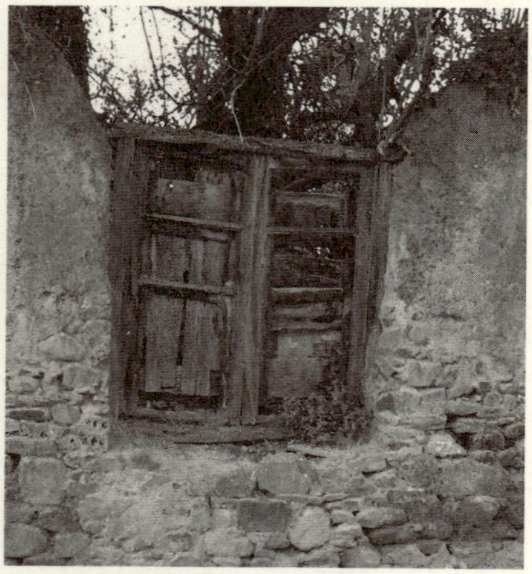
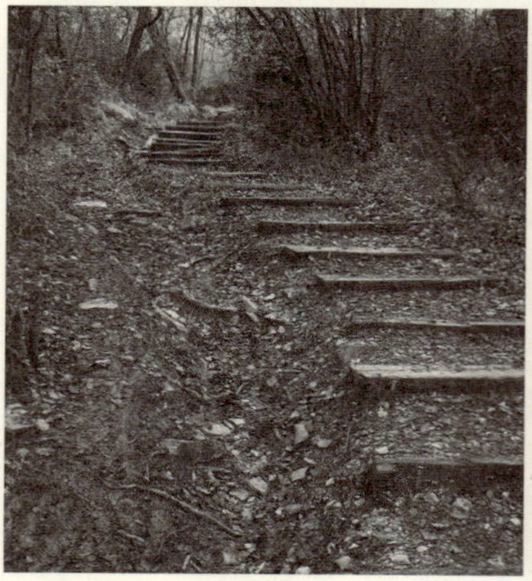
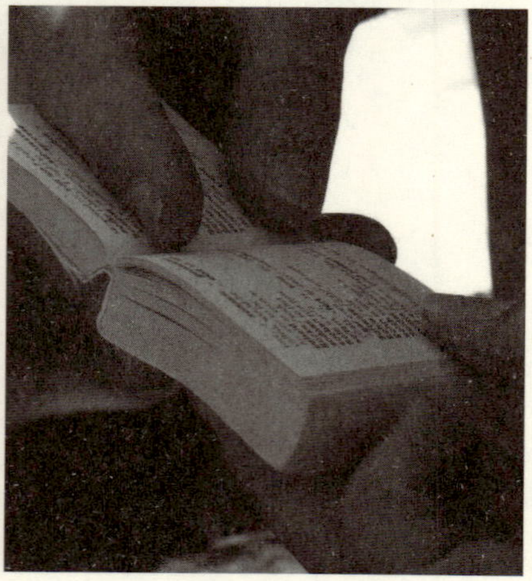

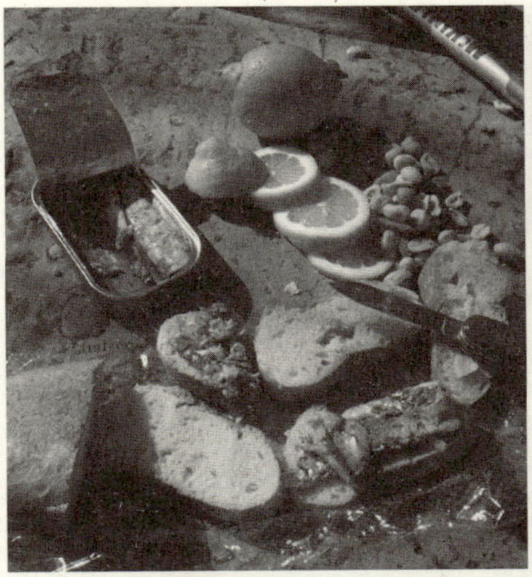

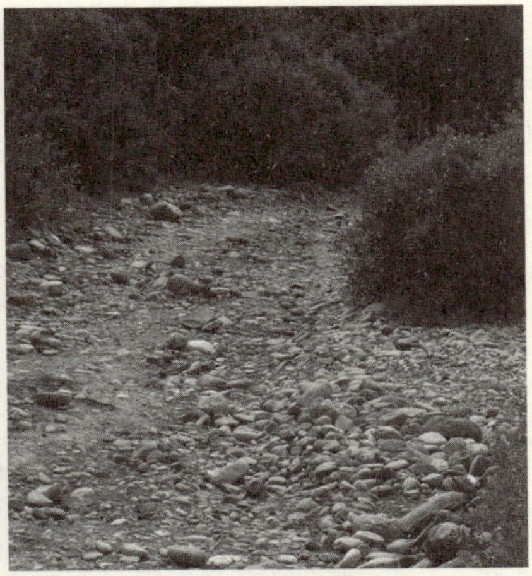

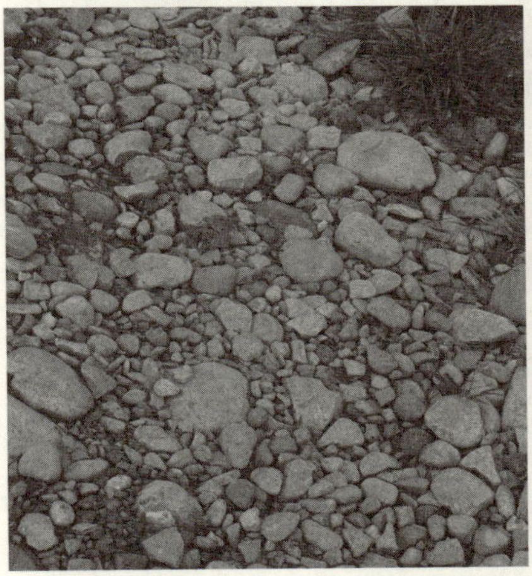

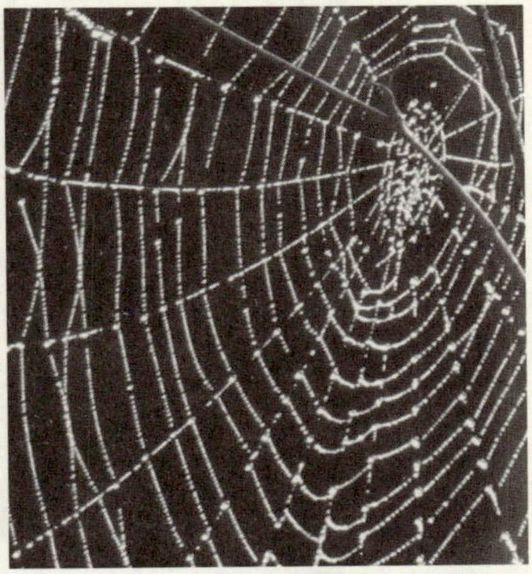

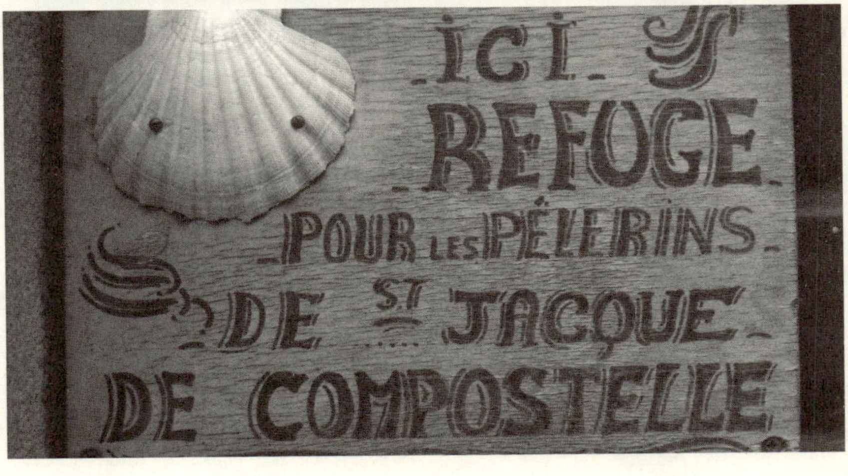
ICI
REFUGE
POUR LES PÉLERINS
DE ST JACQUE
DE COMPOSTELLE

E ← W
NAPOLEON'S WAY
HOSPITAL PEREGRINORUM SANCTI SPIRITUS
ST JEAN PIED DE PORT
RONCESVALLES
ALTO DEL PERDON
PAMPLONA
PUENTE LA REINA
SANTO DOMINGO DE LA CALZADA
CASTROJERITZ
MESETA
BURGOS
¡BUEN CAMINO!
BODEGAS IRACHE
VINO!
REFUGIO ACACIO
SANTIAGO 576 KM
ALBERGUE